ARM-BASED MICROCONTROLLER MULTITASKING PROJECTS

ARM-Based Microcontroller Multitasking Projects

Using the FreeRTOS Multitasking Kernel

DOGAN IBRAHIM

Newnes is an imprint of Elsevier
The Boulevard, Langford Lane, Kidlington, Oxford OX5 1GB, United Kingdom
50 Hampshire Street, 5th Floor, Cambridge, MA 02139, United States

Notices
Knowledge and best practice in this field are constantly changing. As new research and experience broaden our understanding, changes in research methods, professional practices, or medical treatment may become necessary.

Practitioners and researchers must always rely on their own experience and knowledge in evaluating and using any information, methods, compounds, or experiments described herein. In using such information or methods they should be mindful of their own safety and the safety of others, including parties for whom they have a professional responsibility.

To the fullest extent of the law, neither the Publisher nor the authors, contributors, or editors, assume any liability for any injury and/or damage to persons or property as a matter of products liability, negligence or otherwise, or from any use or operation of any methods, products, instructions, or ideas contained in the material herein.

Library of Congress Cataloging-in-Publication Data
A catalog record for this book is available from the Library of Congress

British Library Cataloguing-in-Publication Data
A catalogue record for this book is available from the British Library

ISBN: 978-0-12-821227-1

For information on all Newnes publications
visit our website at https://www.elsevier.com/books-and-journals

Publisher: Mara Conner
Acquisitions Editor: Tim Pitts
Editorial Project Manager: Rafael G. Trombaco
Production Project Manager: Nirmala Arumugam
Designer: Matthew Limbert

Typeset by Thomson Digital

Contents

About the author xi
Preface xiii
Acknowledgments xv

1. Microcomputer systems 1

1.1 Overview 1
1.2 Microcontroller systems 1
   1.2.1 RAM 5
   1.2.2 ROM 6
   1.2.3 PROM 6
   1.2.4 EPROM 6
   1.2.5 EEPROM 6
   1.2.6 Flash EEPROM 7
1.3 Microcontroller features 7
   1.3.1 Supply voltage 7
   1.3.2 The clock 7
   1.3.3 Timers 7
   1.3.4 Watchdog 8
   1.3.5 Reset input 8
   1.3.6 Interrupts 8
   1.3.7 Brown-out detector 8
   1.3.8 Analog-to-digital converter 9
   1.3.9 Serial input-output 9
   1.3.10 SPI and I^2C 9
   1.3.11 LCD drivers 9
   1.3.12 Analog comparator 9
   1.3.13 Real-time clock 10
   1.3.14 Sleep mode 10
   1.3.15 Power-on reset 10
   1.3.16 Low power operation 10
   1.3.17 Current sink/source
       capability 10
   1.3.18 USB interface 10
   1.3.19 CAN interface 11
   1.3.20 Ethernet interface 11
   1.3.21 Wi-Fi and/or Bluetooth
       interface 11
1.4 Microcontroller architectures 11
   1.4.1 RISC and CISC 12
1.5 Summary 12
Further readings 12

2. Architecture of arm microcontrollers 13

2.1 Overview 13
2.2 ARM microcontrollers 13
   2.2.1 Cortex-M 15
   2.2.2 Cortex-R 16
   2.2.3 Cortex-A 17
   2.2.4 Cortex-M processor comparison 17
   2.2.5 Cortex-M compatibility 18
   2.2.6 Processor performance
       measurement 18
2.3 The STM32F407VGT6 microcontroller 19
   2.3.1 Basic features of the
       STM32F407VGT6 19
   2.3.2 Internal block diagram 21
   2.3.3 The power supply 23
   2.3.4 Low power modes 23
   2.3.5 The clock circuit 23
2.4 General purpose inputs and outputs 27
2.5 Nested vectored interrupt controller
   (NVIC) 30
2.6 External interrupt controller (EXTI) 30
2.7 Timers 30
2.8 Analog-to-digital converters (ADCs) 30
2.9 Built-in temperature sensor 30
2.10 Digital-to-analog converter 31
2.11 Reset 31
2.12 Electrical characteristics 31
2.13 Summary 32
Further readings 32

3. ARM Cortex microcontroller development boards 33

3.1 Overview 33
3.2 LPC1768 33
3.3 STM32 Nucleo family 34
3.4 EasyMX Pro V7 For STM32 35
3.5 STM32F4DISCOVERY board 36
3.6 mbed application board 38
3.7 EasyMx Pro V7 for Tiva 39

3.8 MINI-M4 for STM32   40
3.9 Clicker 2 for MSP432   41
3.10 Tiva EK-TM4C123GXL LaunchPad   42
3.11 Fusion for ARM V8   43
3.12 Clicker 2 for STM32   44
3.13 Summary   44
Further readings   45

4. Clicker 2 for STM32 development board   47

4.1 Overview   47
4.2 Clicker 2 for STM32 hardware   47
    4.2.1 On-board LEDs   48
    4.2.2 On-board push-button switches   48
    4.2.3 Reset switch   49
    4.2.4 Power supply   49
    4.2.5 On-board mikroBUS sockets   50
    4.2.6 Input-output pins   51
    4.2.7 Oscillators   52
    4.2.8 Programming the on-board
          microcontroller   52
4.3 Summary   54
Further reading   54

5. Programming the ARM-based microcontrollers   55

5.1 Overview   55
5.2 IDEs supporting the ARM-based
    microcontrollers   55
    5.2.1 EWARM   56
    5.2.2 ARM Mbed   56
    5.2.3 MDK-ARM   56
    5.2.4 TrueStudio for STM32   57
    5.2.5 System Workbench for STM32 by
          AC6   57
    5.2.6 MikroC Pro for ARM   58
5.3 Summary   59
Further readings   59

6. Programming using the mikroC Pro for ARM   61

6.1 Overview   61
6.2 MikroC Pro for ARM   61
6.3 The general purpose input-output library   63
    6.3.1 GPIO_Clk_Enable   64
    6.3.2 GPIO_Clk_Disable   64

    6.3.3 GPIO_Config   64
    6.3.4 GPIO_Set_Pin_Mode   67
    6.3.5 GPIO_Digital_Input   68
    6.3.6 GPIO_Digital_Output   68
    6.3.7 GPIO_Analog_Input   68
    6.3.8 GPIO_Alternate_Function_Enable   68
6.4 Memory type specifiers   69
6.5 PORT input-output   69
6.6 Accessing individual bits   69
6.7 Bit data type   70
6.8 Interrupts and exceptions   70
    6.8.1 Exceptions   70
    6.8.2 Interrupt service routine   71
6.9 Creating a new project   72
    6.9.1 Uploading the executable code   78
6.10 Simulation   80
    6.10.1 Setting break points   83
6.11 Debugging   83
6.12 Other mikroC IDE tools   84
    6.12.1 ASCII chart   84
    6.12.2 GLCD bitmap editor   85
    6.12.3 HID terminal   85
    6.12.4 Interrupt assistant   85
    6.12.5 LCD custom character   85
    6.12.6 Seven segment editor   86
    6.12.7 UDP terminal   86
    6.12.8 USART terminal   86
    6.12.9 USB HID bootloader   88
    6.12.10 Statistics   88
    6.12.11 The library manager   88
    6.12.12 Assembly listing   89
    6.12.13 Output files   93
    6.12.14 Options window   93
6.13 Summary   95
Further readings   96

7. Introduction to multitasking   97

7.1 Overview   97
7.2 Multitasking kernel advantages   98
7.3 Need for an RTOS   98
7.4 Task scheduling algorithms   99
    7.4.1 Co-operative scheduling   99
    7.4.2 Round-robin scheduling   104
    7.4.3 Preemptive scheduling   105
    7.4.4 Scheduling algorithm goals   106
    7.4.5 Difference between preemptive and
          nonpreemptive scheduling   107
    7.4.6 Some other scheduling algorithms   107

7.5 Choosing a scheduling algorithm 108
7.6 Summary 108
Further readings 108

8. Introduction to FreeRTOS 109

8.1 Overview 109
8.2 FreeRTOS distribution 110
8.3 Installing from MikroElektronika web site 111
8.4 Developing project files 112
8.5 FreeRTOS headers files path and source files path 114
8.6 Compiler case sensitivity 114
8.7 Compiling the template program 115
8.8 Summary 116
Further readings 116

9. Using the FreeRTOS functions 117

9.1 Overview 117
9.2 FreeRTOS data types 117
9.3 FreeRTOS variable names 118
9.4 FreeRTOS function names 118
9.5 Common macro definitions 118
9.6 Task states 118
9.7 Task-related functions 120
  9.7.1 Creating a new task 121
  9.7.2 Delaying a task 122
  9.7.3 Project 1—flashing an LED every second 122
  9.7.4 Project 2—flashing two LEDs, one every second, other one every 200 ms 125
  9.7.5 Suspending a task 127
  9.7.6 Resuming a suspended task 128
  9.7.7 Project 3—suspending and resuming a task 128
  9.7.8 Deleting a task 130
  9.7.9 Project 4—flashing LEDs and deleting a task 130
  9.7.10 Getting the task handle 131
  9.7.11 Running at fixed intervals 134
  9.7.12 Tick count 134
  9.7.13 Project 5—flashing an LED using function vTaskDelayUntil() 134
  9.7.14 Task priorities 136
  9.7.15 Project 6—flashing LED and push-button switch at different priorities 136
  9.7.16 Project 7—getting/setting task priorities 137
9.8 Using an LCD 139
  9.8.1 HD44780 LCD module 141
  9.8.2 Connecting the LCD to the Clicker 2 for STM32 development board 142
  9.8.3 LCD functions 143
  9.8.4 Project 8—displaying text on the LCD 144
9.9 Task name, number of tasks, and tick count 147
9.10 Project 9—displaying a task name, number of tasks, and tick count on the LCD 148
9.11 Yield to another task of equal priority 148
9.12 Aborting delay 148
9.13 Project 10—7-segment 2-digit multiplexed LED display counter 151
9.14 Project 11—7-segment 4-digit multiplexed LED display counter 159
9.15 Project 12—7-segment 4-digit multiplexed LED display event counter 163
9.16 Project 13—traffic lights controller 167
9.17 Project 14—changing LED flashing rate 177
9.18 Project 15—sending data to a PC over USB serial link 181
9.19 Project 16—changing LED flashing rate from the PC keyboard 189
9.20 Task list 189
9.21 Project 17—displaying the task list on the PC screen 192
9.22 Task info 195
9.23 Project 19—displaying the task info on the PC screen 195
9.24 Task state 198
9.25 Project 20—displaying the task state on the PC screen 198
9.26 Task parameters 200
9.27 Summary 201
Further readings 201

10. Queue management 203

10.1 Overview–global variables 203
10.2 Why queues? 203
10.3 Creating a queue, sending and receiving data using queues 204
10.4 Project 21–changing LED flashing rate from the PC keyboard 206

10.5 Deleting a queue, name of a queue, resetting a queue   209
10.6 Project 22—using various queue functions   210
10.7 Some other queue functions   213
10.8 Project 23—ON-OFF temperature controller   214
10.9 Summary   224
Further readings   224

11. Semapores and mutexes   225

11.1 Overview   225
11.2 Creating binary semaphore and mutex   226
11.3 Creating a counting semaphore   227
11.4 Deleting a semaphore, getting the semaphore count   227
11.5 Giving and taking the semaphores   227
11.6 Project 24: sending internal and external temperature data to a PC   228
11.7 Summary   234
Further reading   234

12. Event groups   235

12.1 Overview   235
12.2 Event flags and event groups   235
12.3 Creating and deleting an event group   236
12.4 Setting, clearing, waiting For event group bits, and getting event group bits   236
12.5 Project 25—sending internal and external temperature data to a PC   238
12.6 Project 26—controlling the flashing of an LED   242
12.7 Project 27—GPS based project   246
12.8 Summary   253
Further readings   254

13. Software timers   255

13.1 Overview   255
13.2 Creating, deleting, starting, stopping, and resetting a timer   256
13.3 Change timer period, get timer period   258
13.4 Timer name and ID   259
13.5 Project 28—reaction timer   259
13.6 Project 29—generate square waveform   263
13.7 Project 30—event counter (e.g., frequency counter)   266
13.8 Summary   269
Further readings   269

14. Some example projects   271

14.1 Overview   271
14.2 Project 31: square wave generation with adjustable frequency   271
14.3 Project 32: frequency sweep waveform generator   275
14.4 Project 33: RGB light controller   279
14.5 Project 34: home alarm system with keyboard   281
14.6 Project 35: ultrasonic car parking with buzzer   292
14.7 Project 36: stepper motor project   302
14.8 Project 37: communicating with the Arduino   315
14.9 Summary   321
Further reading   321

15. The Idle task and the idle task hook   323

15.1 Overview   323
15.2 The Idle task   323
15.3 Idle task hook functions   323
15.4 Project 39: display the free processor time   324
15.5 Summary   327
Further reading   327

16. Task Notifications   329

16.1 Overview   329
16.2 xTaskNotifyGive() and ulTaskNotifyTake()   330
16.3 Project 40: start flashing an LED after receiving notification   331
16.4 xTaskNotify() and xTaskNotifyWait()   333
16.5 Project 41: flashing at different rates after receiving notifications   335
16.6 xTaskNotifyStateClear() and xTaskNotifyQuery()   338
16.7 Summary 338
Further reading   338

17. Critical sections   339

17.1 Overview   339
17.2 Project 42: critical sections – Sharing the UART   339
17.3 Suspending the scheduler   344
17.4 Project 43: suspending the scheduler   345

17.5 Summary   345
Further reading   345

18. Interrupts in Cortex-M4 based microcontrollers   347

18.1 Overview   347
18.2 Interrupts in general   347
18.3 STM32F407 interrupts   348
   18.2.1 External Interrupts   349
18.4 Project 44—External interrupt based event counter   354
18.5 Project 45—Multiple external interrupts   358
18.6 Internal interrupts (timer interrupts)   361
18.7 Project 46—Generating waveform using a timer interrupt   363
18.8 Project 47—External interrupt with timer interrupt   365
18.9 Summary   367
Further readings   369

19. USING the FreeRTOS API function calls from an ISR   371

19.1 Overview   371
19.2 The xHigherPriorityTaskWoken parameter   372
19.3 Deferred interrupt processing   372
19.4 Task related functions from ISR   373
   19.4.1 taskENTER_CRITICAL_FROM_ISR() and taskEXIT_CRITICAL_FROM_ISR()   373
   19.4.2 xTaskNotifyFromISR()   373
   19.4.3 xTaskNotifyGiveFromISR()   373
   19.4.4 xTaskResumeFromISR()   373
19.5 Project 48—Using function xTaskResumeFromISR()   374
19.6 Project 49—Deferred interrupt processing   377
19.7 Project 50—Using function xTaskNotifyFromISR()   377
19.8 Event group related functions from ISR   382
   19.8.1 xEventGroupSetBitsFromISR()   382
   19.8.2 xEventGroupClearBitsFrmISR()   382
19.9 Project 51—Using function xEventGroupSetBitsFromISR()   383
19.10 Timer related functions from ISR   386
   19.10.1 xTimerStartFromISR()   386
   19.10.2 xTimerStopFromISR()   386
   19.10.3 xTimerResetFromISR()   386

19.10.4 xTimerChangePeriod FromISR()   386
19.11 Project 52—Using functions xTimerStartFromISR() and xTimerChangePeriodFromISR()   387
19.12 Semaphore related functions from ISR   390
   19.12.1 xSemaphoreGiveFromISR()   390
   19.12.2 xSemaphoreTakeFromISR()   390
19.13 Project 53—Using functions xSemaphoreTakeFromISR() and xSemaphoreGive()   391
19.14 Queue related functions from ISR   391
   19.14.1 xQueueReceiveFromISR()   391
   19.14.2 xQueueSendFromISR()   391
19.15 Project 54—Using functions xQueueSendFromISR() and xQueueReceive()   393
19.16 Summary   396
Further reading   396

20. Car park management system   397

20.1 Overview   397
20.2 Project 55: car park control   397
Further reading   412

21. Time in different cities   413

21.1 Overview   413
21.2 Project 56: time project   413
Further reading   422

22. Mobile robot project: the Buggy   423

22.1 Overview   423
22.2 The Buggy   423
22.3 Wheel motors   427
22.4 Lights (LEDs)   431
22.5 Project 57: controlling the Buggy lights   431
22.6 Project 58: controlling the Buggy motors   432
22.7 Project 59: obstacle avoiding Buggy   438
22.8 Project 60: controlling the Buggy remotely   451
Further reading   463

Appendix A. Number systems   465

A.1 Overview   465
A.2 Decimal number system   465
A.3 Binary number system   466

A.4   Octal number system   466
A.5   Hexadecimal number system   466
A.6   Converting binary numbers into
      decimal   467
A.7   Converting decimal numbers into
      binary   468
A.8   Converting binary numbers into
      hexadecimal   469
A.9   Converting hexadecimal numbers into
      binary   469
A.10 Converting hexadecimal numbers into
      decimal   470
A.11 Converting decimal numbers into
      hexadecimal   471
A.12 Converting octal numbers into decimal   471
A.13 Converting decimal numbers into octal   472
A.14 Converting octal numbers into binary   472
A.15 Converting binary numbers into octal   473
A.16 Negative numbers   474
A.17 Adding binary numbers   475
A.18 Subtracting binary numbers   475
A.19 Multiplication of binary numbers   476
A.20 Division of binary numbers   477
A.21 Floating point numbers   477
A.22 Converting a floating point number into
      decimal   478

A.22.1 Normalizing the floating point
        numbers   479
A.22.2 Converting a decimal number into
        floating point   480
A.22.3 Multiplication and division of floating
        point numbers   481
A.22.4 Addition and subtraction of floating
        point numbers   482
A.23 BCD numbers   482

Appendix B. The program description
             language   485

B.1   Overview   485
B.2   Program development tools   485
      B.2.1 BEGIN – END   486
      B.2.2 Sequencing   486
      B.2.3 IF – THEN – ELSE – ENDIF   486
      B.2.4 DO – FOREVER – ENDDO   487
      B.2.5 DO – ENDDO   487
      B.2.6 REPEAT – UNTIL   488
      B.2.7 Subprograms   488
      B.2.8 Calling a subprogram   488
B.3   Examples   489

Index   493

About the author

Prof. Dr. Dogan Ibrahim has a BSc degree in electronic engineering, an MSc degree in automatic control engineering, and a PhD degree in digital signal processing. Dogan has worked in many industrial organizations before he returned to academic life.

Prof. Ibrahim is the author of over 80 technical books and over 200 technical articles on microcontrollers, microprocessors, and related fields. He is a Chartered electrical engineer and a Fellow of the Institution of Engineering Technology.

Preface

A microcontroller is a single-chip microprocessor system which contains data and program memory, serial and parallel I/O, timers, external and internal interrupts, all integrated into a single chip that can be purchased for as little as $2.00. About 40% of microcontroller applications are in office automation, such as PCs, laser printers, fax machines, intelligent telephones, and so forth. About one-third of microcontrollers are found in consumer electronic goods. Products like CD and DVD players, hi-fi equipment, video games, washing machines, cookers, and so on fall into this category. The communications market, automotive market, and the military share the rest of the application areas.

Microcontrollers have traditionally been programmed using the assembly language of the target processor. Although the assembly language is fast, it has the disadvantages that it is difficult to develop and maintain large projects using the assembly language. Additionally, microcontrollers from different manufacturers have different assembly language instruction sets which makes it very time consuming for the programmers to learn new assembly languages every time a different microcontroller is to be used. The assembly code developed for one type of microcontroller cannot be ported to another type of microcontroller. Nowadays microcontrollers are programmed using high-level languages, such as C, C++, Pascal, or Basic. Perhaps the biggest advantage of using a high-level language is that the developed code can easily be ported to other types of microcontrollers. Additionally, it is easier to maintain a program developed using a high-level programming language.

There are many different types of microcontrollers available from many manufacturers. Most manufacturers offer development kits (or development boards), which are invaluable tools during the early stages of project development. In this book the Clicker 2 for STM32 development board is used. This board is based on the STM32F407 type ARM Cortex-M4 processor that can operate at up to 168MHz. The highly popular mikroC Pro for ARM compiler and IDE is used for software development.

The topic of this book is FreeRTOS kernel and multitasking. Multitasking has become one of the important topics in microcontroller-based systems, namely in automation applications. As the complexity of the projects grow, more functionality is demanded from the projects and such projects require the use of several inter-related tasks running on the same processor and sharing the CPU in order to implement the required operations. As a result of this, the importance of multitasking operation in microcontroller-based applications has been growing steadily over the last several years and many complex automation projects nowadays make use of some form of a multitasking kernel. In this book the FreeRTOS multitasking kernel is used in the projects. FreeRTOS is a market leading real time multitasking kernel with millions of deployments in all market sectors. FreeRTOS is free of charge and is fully documented and supported. It is available to run on many hardware and software platforms, including the ARM processors and the mikroC Pro for ARM compiler and IDE. FreeRTOS is so popular that in 2018 it was downloaded every 175 seconds (www.freertos.org) and it came top in class in every EETimes Embedded Market Survey since 2011.

This book is project based and its main aim has been to teach the basic features and API functions of the FreeRTOS kernel. Many fully tested projects are given in the book using FreeRTOS in multitasking applications. Each project is described fully and in detail, and the complete program listings are given for each project. Readers should be able to use the projects as they are, or modify them to suit to their own needs. The following sub-headings are used while describing each project:

- Description of the project
- Aim of the project
- Background (if applicable)
- Block diagram
- Circuit diagram
- Program listing
- Suggestions for future work (if applicable)

The operation of some of the complex projects have been described using the Project Description Language (PDL), which makes it easy to understand the programs before they are developed.

Knowledge of the C-programming language will be useful to the readers. Also, familiarity with at least one microcontroller development board (preferably with an ARM processor) will be an advantage. The knowledge of assembly language programming is not required because all the projects in the book are based on using the C language.

This book is written for students, for practicing engineers, and for hobbyists interested in developing multitasking microcontroller-based real time projects using the ARM family of microcontrollers. Attempt has been made to include as many projects as possible, limited only by the size of the book.

Although the Clicker 2 for STM32 microcontroller development board and the STM32F407 type ARM processor are used in this book, readers should find it easy to use other types of development boards and other types of ARM processors.

FreeRTOS is documented and supported fully by its developers. Interested readers can obtain detailed information on FreeRTOS features and API functions from the following Internet-based sources:

Mastering the FreeRTOS Real Time Kernel: A Hands-On Tutorial Guide, by Richard Barry, web site:
https://www.freertos.org/wp-content/uploads/2018/07/161204_Mastering_the_FreeRTOS_Real_Time_Kernel-A_Hands-On_Tutorial_Guide.pdf

or

The FreeRTOS Reference Manual: API Functions and Configuration Options, web site:
https://www.freertos.org/wp-content/uploads/2018/07/FreeRTOS_Reference_Manual_V10.0.0.pdf

or

FreeRTOS web site:
www.freertos.org

Dogan Ibrahim
London, 2020

Acknowledgments

Some figures and text in this book has been taken from a variety of sources.

The FreeRTOS API function details are taken from the following documents and web sites. The author would like to thank to Mr. Richard Barry and Mr. Dirk Didascalou for giving permission to use material from the following sources in this book:

1. **Mastering the FreeRTOS Real Time Kernel: A Hands-On Tutorial Guide**, by Richard Barry, web site:
   https://www.freertos.org/wp-content/uploads/2018/07/161204_Mastering_the_FreeRTOS_Real_Time_Kernel-A_Hands-On_Tutorial_Guide.pdf

2. **The FreeRTOS Reference Manual**, web site:https://www.freertos.org/wp-content/uploads/2018/07/FreeRTOS_Reference_Manual_V10.0.0.pdf

3. https://www.freertos.org/documentation

The following figures are copyright of mikroElektronika and are taken from the mikroElektronika web site (www.mikroe.com), The author would like to thank to Mr Nebojsa Matic (CEO) for giving permission to use these figures in this book:

Figures 3.3, 3.6–3.8, 3.10, 4.1–4.9, 9.2, 9.4, 9.9, 9.12, 9.40, 9.42, 9.44, 9.45, 11.1, 12.4, 12.8, 13.1, 13.9, 14.18, 14.28, 18.8, 18.13, 18.16, 19.1, 22.1–22.6, 22.14, 22.15, 22.17, 22.18, 22.20, 22.24–22.27

The following figures and tables are copyright of STMicroelectronics and are taken from the online document "RM 0090 Reference Manual, Rev. 18, 2019" of STMicroelectronics. The author is grateful to Mr. Michael Markowitz of STMicroelectronics for giving permission to use these figures in this book:

Figures 2.1–2.3, 2.5, 2.14, 3.2, 3.4, 18.1–18.7, Tables 18.1–18.5

The following figures are the copyright of the corresponding sources and are taken with their permissions. The author would like to thank the copyright holders for giving permission to use these figures in this book:

Figure 3.1 - Pololu Robotics & Electronics, pololu.com

Figure 3.5 - From SparkFun Electronics (photos taken by Juan Peña)

Figure 3.9 – Texas Instruments (www.ti.com)

Microcomputer systems

1.1 Overview

The term microcomputer is used to describe a digital processing system that includes a minimum of a microprocessor, program memory, data memory, and input-output (I/O). Some microcomputer systems include additional components such as timers, counters, analog-to-digital converters, and so on. Thus, a microcomputer system can be anything from a large computer having hard disks, optical disks, SSD drives, printers, and plotters to a single chip embedded controller.

In this book we are going to consider only the type of microcomputers that consists of a single silicon chip. Such microcomputer systems are also called microcontrollers and they are used in many household goods such as microwave ovens, TV remote control units, cookers, hi-fi equipment, CD players, personal computers, fridges, games consoles, etc. There are a large variety of microcontrollers available in the market place, ranging from 8-bits to 32-bits or even 64-bits. In this book we shall be looking at the programming and system design using a member of the 32-bit STM32 family of microcontrollers, manufactured by the STMicroelectronics. As we shall be seeing in the next chapter, STM32 family is based on the highly popular ARM processor architecture. In this chapter we shall be looking at the features of the microcontroller systems and describe their basic building blocks.

1.2 Microcontroller systems

A microcontroller is a single-chip computer. *Micro* suggests that the device is small, and *controller* suggests that the device can be used in control applications. Another term used for microcontrollers is *embedded controller*, since most of the microcontrollers are built into (or embedded in) the devices they control.

A microprocessor differs from a microcontroller (or a microcomputer) in many ways. The main difference is that a microprocessor requires several other components for its operation, such as program memory and data memory, input-output devices, clock circuit, interrupt circuits, etc. A microcontroller, on the other hand, has all the support chips incorporated inside the same chip. All microprocessors and microcontrollers operate on a set of instructions (or the user program) stored in their program memories. A microcontroller fetches the

ARM-Based Microcontroller Multitasking Projects. http://dx.doi.org/10.1016/B978-0-12-821227-1.00001-3

instructions from its program memory one by one, decodes these instructions, and then carries out the required operations.

Microprocessors and microcontrollers have traditionally been programmed using the assembly language of the target device. Although the assembly language is fast and results in less memory usage, it has several major disadvantages. An assembly program consists of mnemonics and it is difficult to learn and maintain a program written using the assembly language. Also, microcontrollers manufactured by different firms have different assembly languages and the user is required to learn a new language every time a new microcontroller is to be used for a project. Microcontrollers can also be programmed using a high-level language, such as BASIC, PASCAL, C, etc. High-level languages offer many advantages: it is much easier to learn a high-level language than an assembler language. Also, very large and complex programs can easily be developed using a high-level language. It is much easier to maintain a program written using a high-level language. Programs written using a high-level language can easily be ported to run on different microcontrollers with simple or no modifications to the source codes. In this book we shall be learning the programming of STM32 family of microcontrollers using the popular *mikroC Pro for ARM* language and the IDE (integrated development environment), developed by *mikroElektronika* (www.mikroe.com).

In most microcontroller-based applications, a microcontroller is used for a single task, such as controlling a motor, controlling the temperature, humidity or the pressure, turning an LED ON or OFF, responding to external switches, and so on. In this book we are interested in using a microcontroller in real time as well as in multitasking applications. A real-time application differs from a normal application as it requires a very quick response from a microcontroller. For example, in a position control application it may be required to stop a motor as soon as an input condition changes. Or, in digital signal processing applications the processor is required to respond to input signal changes very quickly. In multitasking applications, there could be several interrelated tasks running on a single microcontroller such that the CPU time and the microcontroller resources are shared between these tasks. A scheduler runs in the background and it makes sure that the tasks run correctly and share the CPU as required by the application. In this book, the highly popular FreeRTOS real-time multitasking kernel is used in the projects. The book describes the operation of the FreeRTOS and gives example projects to show how the various functions supported by the FreeRTOS kernel can be used in practical applications. Many tested and working projects are given in later chapters of the book.

In general, a single chip is all that is required to have a running microcontroller system. In practical applications, however, several additional external components may be required to allow a microcomputer to be interfaced with its environment. The resulting system is then usually called a microcontroller development kit (or microcontroller development board). Microcontroller development kits simplify the tasks of developing programs greatly, since the required project is developed using the hardware kit that has already been tested by the manufacturers.

Basically, a microcontroller executes a user program which is loaded in its program memory. Under the control of this program, data is received from external devices (inputs), manipulated, and then sent to external devices (outputs). For example, in a microcontroller-based oven temperature control system, the temperature is read by the microcomputer using an external temperature sensor. The microcomputer then operates a heater or a fan to control and keep the temperature at the required set value. Fig. 1.1 shows the block diagram of our simple oven temperature control system.

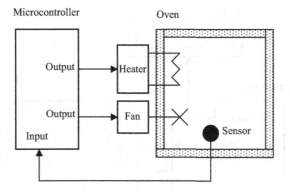

FIGURE 1.1   **Microcontroller-based oven temperature control system.**

The system shown in Fig. 1.1 is a very simplified temperature control system where the microcontroller software runs in an endless loop and its only task is to control the temperature of the oven. In such a simple system the set point temperature is usually preset in the software and cannot be changed while the program is running. This is an example of a system having only one task. In a more sophisticated system we may have a keypad to set the temperature externally while the program is running, and additionally an LCD to display the current temperature and the set point temperature. Fig. 1.2 shows the block diagram of such

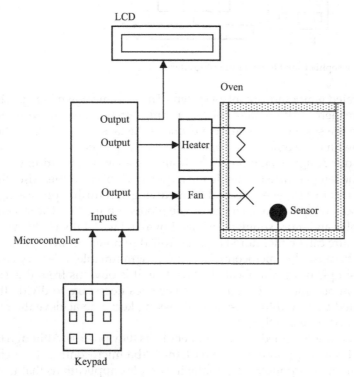

FIGURE 1.2   **Temperature control system with a keypad and LCD.**

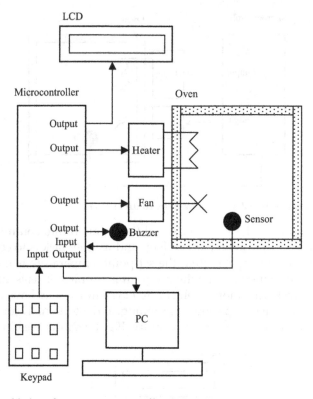

FIGURE 1.3   **More sophisticated temperature controller.**

a more sophisticated temperature control system. The system shown in Fig. 1.2 is a multitasking system where there are more than one task running on the same microcontroller and sharing the CPU and the system resources. Here, one of the tasks is controlling the temperature, while at the same time the other task responds to the keypad entries.

We can make our design even more sophisticated (see Fig. 1.3) by adding an audible alarm to inform us if the temperature is outside the required set point value. Also, the temperature readings can be sent to a PC every second for archiving and further processing. For example, a graph of the daily temperature changes can be plotted on the PC. The system can be made even more complex and more sophisticated as shown in Fig. 1.4 if we add Wi-Fi capability so that the temperature can be monitored and controlled remotely from anywhere on the Earth. As you can see, because the microcontrollers are programmable, it is very easy to make the final system as simple or as complicated as we like. It is obvious from this simple example that as the system becomes more complex, it becomes necessary to divide the system into several interrelated tasks and then use a multitasking kernel to achieve the required control and synchronization between these tasks.

Microcontrollers are classified by the number of bits they process. Although the 8-bit microcontrollers have been very popular in the past, the 32-bit microcontrollers, such as the STM32 family are becoming very popular, especially in complex applications that may require high speed, precision, large amounts of data and program memories, and many other resources.

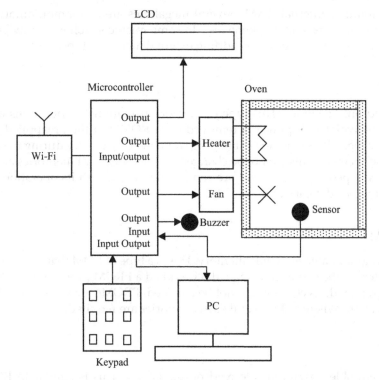

FIGURE 1.4   **Temperature control system with Wi-Fi capability.**

The simplest microcontroller architecture consists of a microprocessor, memory, and input-output. The microprocessor consists of a central processing unit (CPU), and the control unit (CU). The CPU is the brain of the microcontroller and this is where all of the arithmetic and logic operations are performed. The control unit controls all the internal operations of the microprocessor and sends out control signals to other parts of the microcontroller to carry out the required instructions. For example, in a simple addition operation, the control unit fetches data from the memory and loads into the arithmetic and logic unit for the addition to be performed. The result is then sent back to the memory under the control of the CU.

Memory is an important part of all microcontroller systems. Depending upon the type used, we can classify memories into two groups: program memory, and data memory. Program memory stores the program written by the programmer and this memory is usually nonvolatile, that is, data is not lost after the removal of power. Data memory is where the temporary data used in a program are stored and this memory is usually volatile, that is, data is lost after the removal of power.

There are basically six types of memories as summarized below.

1.2.1 RAM

RAM means random access memory. It is a general-purpose memory which usually stores the user data in a program. RAM memory is volatile in the sense that it cannot retain data in the absence of power, that is, data is lost after the removal of power. Most microcontrollers have some amount of internal RAM. Several megabytes are a common amount, although some microcontrollers have more, some less. In some microcontrollers it may be possible to extend the available RAM memory by adding external memory chips.

1.2.2 ROM

ROM is read only memory. This type of memory usually holds programs or fixed user data. ROM is nonvolatile. If power is removed from ROM and then reapplied, the original data will still be there. ROM memories are programmed at the factory during the manufacturing process and their contents cannot be changed by the user. ROM memories are only useful if you have developed a program and are completely happy with its operation and wish to order several thousand copies of it.

1.2.3 PROM

PROM is programmable read only memory. This is a type of ROM that can be programmed in the field, often by the end user, using a device called a PROM programmer. Once a PROM has been programmed, its contents cannot be changed. PROMs are usually used in low production applications where only several such memories are required.

1.2.4 EPROM

EPROM is erasable programmable read only memory. This is similar to ROM, but the EPROM can be programmed using a suitable programming device. EPROM memories have a small clear glass window on top of the chip where the data can be erased under strong ultraviolet light. Once the memory is programmed, the window can be covered with dark tape to prevent accidental erasure of the data. An EPROM memory must be erased before it can be reprogrammed. In the past, many development versions of microcontrollers were manufactured with EPROM memories where the user programs could be stored. These memories have recently been replaced with flash memories. EPROM memories are erased and reprogrammed until the user is satisfied with the program. Some versions of EPROMs, known as OTP (one time programmable), can be programmed using a suitable programmer device but these memories cannot be erased. OTP memories cost much less than the EPROMs. OTP is useful after a project has been developed completely and it is required to make many copies of the memory chips.

1.2.5 EEPROM

EEPROM is electrically erasable programmable read only memory, which is a nonvolatile memory. These memories can be erased and also be reprogrammed using suitable programming devices. EEPROMs are used to save configuration information, maximum, and minimum values, identification data, passwords, etc. EEPROM memories are usually very slow and their cost is much higher than that of an EPROM chip. Many microcontrollers nowadays offer some amount of on-chip EEPROM memories.

1.2.6 Flash EEPROM

This is another version of EEPROM type memory. This memory has become popular in microcontroller applications and is used to store the user program. Flash EEPROM is nonvolatile and is usually very fast. The data can be erased and then reprogrammed using a suitable programming device. Some microcontrollers have only several kilobytes of flash EEPROM while some others have several megabytes or even more. All microcontrollers nowadays have built-in flash EEPROM type memories.

1.3 Microcontroller features

Microcontrollers from different manufacturers have different architectures and different capabilities. Some may suit a particular application while others may be totally unsuitable for the same application. The basic hardware features of microcontrollers in general are described in this section.

1.3.1 Supply voltage

Most microcontrollers operate with the standard logic voltage of +5V or +3.3V. Some microcontrollers can operate at as low as +2.7V and some will tolerate +6V without any problems. You should check the manufacturers' data sheets about the allowed limits of the power supply voltage.

A voltage regulator circuit is usually used to obtain the required power supply voltage when the device is to be operated from a mains adaptor or batteries. For example, a 3.3V regulator is required if the microcontroller is to be operated using a 9V supply (e.g., a battery).

1.3.2 The clock

All microcontrollers require a clock (or an oscillator) to operate. The clock is usually provided by connecting external timing devices to the microcontroller. Most microcontrollers will generate clock signals when a crystal and two small capacitors are connected. Some will operate with resonators or external resistor-capacitor pair. Some microcontrollers have built-in timing circuits and they do not require any external timing components. If your application is not time sensitive, you should use external or internal (if available) resistor-capacitor timing components for simplicity and low cost. For applications that may require accurate timing, it is recommended to use an external crystal to generate the timing pulses. An instruction is executed by fetching it from the memory and then decoding it. This usually takes several clock cycles and is known as the *instruction cycle*. The STM32 family of microcontrollers can operate at up to 168 MHz clock.

1.3.3 Timers

Timers are important parts of any microcontroller system. A timer is basically a counter which is driven either from an external clock pulse or from the internal oscillator of the microcontroller. A timer can be 8-bits,16-bits, or 32-bits wide. Some microcontrollers have only a few timers, while some others have ten or more timers. Data can be loaded into a timer under program control and the timer can be stopped or started under program control. Most timers can be configured to generate internal interrupts when they reach a certain count (usually when they overflow or underflow). The interrupts can be used by the user programs to carry out accurate timing-related operations inside the microcontroller.

Some microcontrollers offer one or more capture and compare facilities, where a timer value can be read when an external event occurs, or the timer value can be compared to a preset value and an interrupt can be generated when this value is reached.

1.3.4 Watchdog

Most microcontrollers have at least one watchdog facility. The watchdog is basically a timer which is refreshed by the user program and a reset occurs if the program fails to refresh the watchdog. The watchdog timer is used to detect a system problem, such as the program being stuck in an endless loop. A watchdog is a safety feature that prevents runaway software and stops the microcontroller from executing meaningless and unwanted code. Watchdog facilities are commonly used in real-time systems where it is required to regularly check the successful termination of one or more activities.

1.3.5 Reset input

A reset input is used to reset a microcontroller externally. Resetting puts the microcontroller into a known state such that the program execution usually starts from address 0 of the program memory. An external reset action is usually achieved by connecting a push-button switch to the reset input such that the microcontroller can be reset when the switch is pressed.

1.3.6 Interrupts

Interrupts are very important concepts in microcontrollers. An interrupt causes the microcontroller to respond to external and internal (e.g., a timer) events very quickly. When an interrupt occurs the microcontroller leaves its normal flow of program execution and jumps to a special part of the program, known as the *interrupt service routine* (ISR). The program code inside the ISR is executed and upon return from the ISR the program resumes its normal flow of execution.

The ISR starts from a fixed address of the program memory. This address is also known as the *interrupt vector address*. Some microcontrollers with multi-interrupt features have just one interrupt vector address, while some others have unique interrupt vector addresses, one for each interrupt source. Interrupts can be nested such that a new interrupt can suspend the execution of another interrupt. Another important feature of a microcontroller with multi-interrupt capability is that different interrupt sources can be given different levels of priorities, and higher priority interrupts can grab the CPU from lower priority interrupts.

1.3.7 Brown-out detector

Brown-out detectors are also common in many microcontrollers and they reset a microcontroller if the supply voltage falls below a nominal value. Brown-out detectors are safety features and they can be employed to prevent unpredictable operation at low voltages, especially to protect the contents of EEPROM type memories.

1.3.8 Analog-to-digital converter

An analog-to-digital converter (ADC) is used to convert an analog signal such as voltage to a digital form so that it can be read and processed by a microcontroller. Most microcontrollers nowadays have built-in ADC converters. It is also possible to connect an external ADC converter to any type of microcontroller. ADC converters are usually 10 or 12 bits, having 1024–4096 quantization levels.

The ADC conversion process must be started by the user program and it may take several hundreds of microseconds for a conversion to complete. ADC converters usually generate interrupts when a conversion is complete so that the user program can read the converted data as quickly as possible. ADC converters are very useful in control and monitoring applications since most sensors in real life (e.g., temperature sensor, pressure sensor, force sensor, etc.) produce analog output voltages.

1.3.9 Serial input-output

Serial communication (also called RS232 communication) enables a microcontroller to be connected to another microcontroller or to a PC using a serial cable. Some microcontrollers have built-in hardware called USART (universal synchronous-asynchronous receiver-transmitter) to implement a serial communication interface. The baud rate and the data format can usually be selected by the user program. If any serial input-output hardware is not provided, it is easy to develop software to implement serial data communication using any I/O pin of a microcontroller.

The original RS232 protocol was based on using ±12V for logic signal levels. Nowadays, TTL-based RS232 signals are used commonly where the original data transmission protocol remains the same but the logic signal level is reduced to ±5V or ±3.3V to make it compatible with the microcontroller inputs.

1.3.10 SPI and I²C

Nowadays, most microcontrollers incorporate SPI (serial peripheral interface), I²C (integrated inter connect). SPI and I²C protocols are mainly used in multisensor- and/or multiactuator-based applications to receive data from a number of sensors or to activate actuators.

1.3.11 LCD drivers

LCD drivers enable a microcontroller to be connected to an external LCD display directly. These drivers are not common since most of the functions provided by them can be implemented in software using general-purpose microcontrollers.

1.3.12 Analog comparator

Analog comparator modules are used where it is required to compare two external analog voltages. These modules are usually implemented in most medium to high-end microcontrollers.

1.3.13 Real-time clock

Real-time clock (RTC) enables a microcontroller to have absolute date and time information continuously and independent of the processor. Built-in real-time clock modules are not common in most microcontrollers since they can easily be implemented by either using a dedicated real-time clock chip, or by writing a program. STM32 family of microcontrollers offers internal real-time clock nodules.

1.3.14 Sleep mode

Some microcontrollers offer power management functions such as built-in sleep modes, where executing this instruction puts the microcontroller into a mode where the internal oscillator is stopped and the power consumption is reduced to an extremely low level. The main reason for using the sleep mode is to conserve battery power when the microcontroller is not doing anything useful. The microcontroller usually wakes up from the sleep mode by an external reset or by a watchdog time-out.

1.3.15 Power-on reset

Some microcontrollers have built-in power-on reset circuits which keep the microcontroller in the reset state until all the internal circuitry has been initialized correctly. This feature is very useful as it starts the microcontroller from a known state on power-up. An external reset can also be provided where the microcontroller can be reset when an external button is pressed.

1.3.16 Low power operation

Low power operation is especially important in portable applications where the microcontroller-based equipment is operated from batteries. Some microcontrollers can operate with less than 2 mA with 5V supply, and around 15 µA at 3 V supply. Some other microcontrollers, especially microprocessor-based systems where there could be several chips may consume several hundred milliamperes of current or even more.

1.3.17 Current sink/source capability

It is important to know the current sink/source capability of a microcontroller input-output port pin before connecting an external device to the microcontroller. The current capability can in general be increased by connecting external transistor switching circuits or relays to the output port pins.

1.3.18 USB interface

USB is currently a very popular computer interface specification used to connect various peripheral devices to computers and microcontrollers. Some microcontrollers offer USB ports that can be used to interface them to other USB compatible devices, for example, to PCs.

STM32 family of microcontroller development systems have USB interfaces to enable them to be connected to a PC for programming purposes.

1.3.19 CAN interface

CAN bus is a very popular bus system, used mainly in automation applications. Some microcontrollers offer built-in CAN modules so that they can be connected to other CAN compatible devices. If a built-in CAN module is not available, it is possible to connect an external CAN module to the input-output ports.

1.3.20 Ethernet interface

Some microcontrollers provide Ethernet interface capabilities that enable them to be connected to the Ethernet directly for network-based applications.

1.3.21 Wi-Fi and/or Bluetooth interface

Some microcontrollers offer Wi-Fi and/or Bluetooth modules so that they can easily be connected to Wi-Fi routers, or communicate with other Bluetooth compatible devices, such as with PCs or mobile phones.

1.4 Microcontroller architectures

Usually, two types of architectures are used in microcontrollers (see Fig. 1.5): *Von Neumann* architecture and *Harvard* architecture. Von Neumann architecture is used by a large percentage of microcontrollers and here all memory space is on the same bus and instruction and data use the same bus. In the Harvard architecture, code and data are on separate busses and this allows the code and data to be fetched simultaneously, resulting in improved performance and simpler chip design.

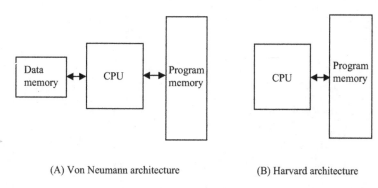

(A) Von Neumann architecture   (B) Harvard architecture

FIGURE 1.5   **Von Neumann and Harvard architectures.**

1.4.1 RISC and CISC

RISC (reduced instruction set computer) and CISC (complex instruction computer) refer to the instruction set of a microcontroller. In an 8-bit RISC microcontroller, data is 8-bit wide but the instruction words are more than 8-bit wide (usually 12-, 14- or 16-bits) and the instructions occupy one word in the program memory. Thus, the instructions are fetched and executed in one cycle, resulting in improved performance.

In a CISC microcontroller both data and instructions are 8-bit wide. CISC microcontrollers usually have over 200 instructions. Data and code are on the same bus and cannot be fetched simultaneously.

1.5 Summary

In this chapter we have looked at the main differences between microprocessors and microcontrollers. Additionally, we have briefly covered the various basic components of typical microcontrollers.

In the next chapter we shall be looking briefly at the architecture of the ARM family of microcontrollers, especially we will concentrate on the highly popular STM32F407 family of ARM microcontrollers since this is the microcontroller used in all the projects in this book.

Further readings

[1] D. Ibrahim, Advanced PIC Microcontroller Projects in C, Newnes, Oxford, UK, (2008) ISBN: 978-0-7506-8611-2.
[2] R. Toulson, T. Wilmshurst, Fast and Effective Embedded Systems Design, Newnes, Oxford, UK, (2017) ISBN: 978-0-08-100880-5.
[3] D. Ibrahim, Designing Embedded Systems With 32-Bit PIC Microcontrollers and MikroC, Newnes, Oxford, UK, (2014) ISBN: 978-0-08-097786-7.
[4] G. Grindling, B. Weiss, Introduction to Microcontrollers, 2007. Available from: https://ti.tuwien,ac.at/ecs/teaching/courses/mclu/theory-material/Microcontroller.pdf.

Architecture of ARM microcontrollers

2.1 Overview

It is important to learn the basic architecture, advantages, disadvantages, and limitations of a microcontroller before it is used in a project. This concept is more important if one is going to use assembler programming. It is still important to know the basic internal block diagram and the input-output structure if one is going to program using a high-level language. In this book we shall be using the highly popular 32-bit ARM microcontroller, the STM32F407VGT6 in all the projects, together with the *mikroC Pro for ARM* high-level language. This microcontroller is a member of the STM32 family of ARM microcontrollers. A brief description of the architecture of this microcontroller is given in this chapter and its basic features are described so that we can develop projects easily and efficiently.

Clock configuration and input-output ports are important parts of every microcontroller and are used almost in all projects. As a result, these are described in detail in this chapter.

2.2 ARM microcontrollers

There are over a thousand different types of microcontrollers manufactured by many companies. The choice of the best microcontroller for a particular application has become rather difficult as the user is faced with many options. Briefly, this choice depends on many factors, such as:

- Cost
- Speed
- Power consumption
- Working voltage
- Size
- Data width (8, 16, 32 bit?)
- Program and data memory capacity
- Number of general purpose digital input-output ports
- Number of analog input ports (ADC) and their precisions
- Number of digital-to-analog converter (DAC) ports and their precisions
- Interrupt support

ARM-Based Microcontroller Multitasking Projects. http://dx.doi.org/10.1016/B978-0-12-821227-1.00002-5

- Number of timers and their precisions
- UART support
- Special bus support (I2C, SPI, CAN USB, etc.)
- Availability of development boards
- Availability of compilers, simulators, debuggers, and programmers (e.g., integrated development environment)
- Hardware and software support available
- Compatibility with commonly available external devices and components (e.g., sensors, actuators, Wi-Fi modules, Bluetooth modules, etc.)
- Availability of the chosen microcontroller
- Reliability of the chosen microcontroller (e.g., temperature range, operation under vibration and shock, failure rate, etc.)

For example, if the microcontroller is to be used in a battery-operated children's toy then the two most important requirements are the low cost and low power consumption. High performance is not normally a requirement in such applications unless the toy is a fast graphical game. If on the other hand the microcontroller is to be used in a flight controller equipment, then the performance, reliability, and data width are some of the most important factors to consider while making a choice. Similarly, reliability, safety, and power consumption are important factors in most portable medical applications. In games-based applications with graphical displays and keyboards, very high speed and low power consumption are the two most important factors. If the application is to control the temperature of a chemical plant then the important factors could be the reliability, precision of the ADC and the DAC, timer support, and interrupt support. In most hobby type application, one can in general choose a general purpose microcontroller that satisfies the following criteria: low cost, adequate speed, enough number of input-output ports, required numbers of ADC and DAC, and support for special bus support modules such as SPI and/or I2C. The size, memory capacity, timer support, interrupt support, data width, and working voltage are not important factors since almost all microcontrollers provide enough support for these items. In general, as the clock speed goes up so does the power consumption and the cost, and as a result a trade-off should be made in choosing a microcontroller for a specific application.

ARM has been designing high performance and low-cost 32-bit microcontrollers for over 20 years and in the last few years they have also started to offer 64-bit designs in addition to their 32-bit systems It is important to know that ARM does not manufacture or sell any processors or chips. In fact, they design the core processor architecture and make money by licensing their designs to various chip manufacturers. The manufacturers use the core ARM processors (the core CPU) and integrate them with their own peripherals to create complete microcontrollers. For example, manufacturers add their memory modules, input-output, interrupt modules, timer modules, ADC and DAC, etc. to the core CPU processors to make a complete working microcontroller. ARM's core architecture does not include graphics controllers, wireless connectivity, or any other form of peripheral modules. ARM is then given royalty fees for each chip manufactured by the third party companies. Companies that use ARM core CPU processors include, Atmel, Broadcom, Apple, Freescale Semiconductors, Analog Devices, Texas Instruments, NXP, Samsung Electronics, Nvidia, Qualcomm, Renesas, STMicroelectronics, and many others.

ARM was originally known as the Acorn Computers and they have developed the first Acorn RISC Machine (ARM) architecture in the 1980s to use in their personal computers. The first ARM processors were coprocessor modules used in the old and famous BBC Micro series. After failing to find suitable high-performance microprocessor chips in the market, Acorn decided to design and use their own processors. In 1990, the research section of Acorn formed ARM Ltd. Today, known as the ARM Holdings Ltd, their headquarters are based in Cambridge (UK) and is owned by the Japanese telecommunications company SoftBank Group. As in the year 2010, ARM market share was over 95% in the smartphone market, 10% in mobile computers, 35% in smart TVs. In the year 2014, over 50 billion chips with the ARM core processors were manufactured in the world.

The main feature of the ARM core processors is their low power consumption, which makes them ideal processors in battery-operated portable applications. Nowadays, almost all mobile phones contain ARM core processors as their main CPUs. Recently, the highly popular Raspberry Pi single-board computer uses ARM processors in all of their CPUs. The low power consumption, small size, and low cost make ARM an ideal processor in embedded applications. ARM processors are based on an instruction set called Thumb. This instruction set cleverly takes 32-bit instructions and compresses them down to 16-bits, thus reducing the hardware size and consequently the overall cost. Although Thumb is easy to learn and use, almost all applications make use of a high-level language, such as C, C++, Python, etc. Complex multistage pipelined architecture is used inside the processors in order to increase the throughput significantly.

ARM processors have the RISC (reduced instruction set computer) architecture where only a small number of instructions is used in their instruction sets. Compared to CISC (complex instruction set computer) architectures, RISC results in higher speed since the unimportant and not frequently used instructions are removed and the data ways are optimized to result in superior performance.

ARM has developed many 32-bit processors over the last several decades. Around the year 2003, ARM decided to improve their market share by developing a new family of high-performance processors. These processors were aimed for general purpose microcontroller-based industrial, domestic, and the consumer market applications. As a result, the highly popular Cortex family of processors was created. Depending on the throughput and complexity of the core processor, this family consists of three processor families: Cortex-M, Cortex-R, and Cortex-A. Brief details of these family of processors are given below.

2.2.1 Cortex-M

Cortex-M series has been targeted specifically for the crowded MCU market where there are already many types of microcontrollers. This family was first released in 2004 and soon gained popularity. Cortex-M has become the most popular 32-bit microcontroller in the market since its introduction and one can easily say that it has become the industry standard microcontroller. There are basically five processor families within the Cortex-M family: Cortex-M7, Cortex-M4, Cortex-M3, and Cortex-M0, and Cortex-M0+. Brief details of these families are given below.

2.2.1.1 Cortex-M7

This is the highest performance Cortex-M processor. With the built-in floating point unit, the power consumption is reduced and thus the battery life is extended. The processor is based on 6-stage pipeline with branch prediction. The performance is 3.23 DMIPS/MHz, consuming 33 μW/MHz.

2.2.1.2 Cortex-M4

Cortex-M4 is built using the ARMv7-M architecture. These are high-performance micro-controllers having DSP and floating point arithmetic capabilities with high throughputs. The performance is 1.95 DMIPS/MHZ with a 3-stage pipeline, and clock speeds up to 200 MHz. The processor consumes 32.82 μW/MHz. This family uses the Thumb-2 instruction set with special instructions for handling DSP algorithms and floating point operations. If the application requires floating point maths then Cortex-M4 is probably one of the best choices. The STM32F407 microcontroller used in this book is based on the Cortex-M4 architecture.

2.2.1.3 Cortex-M3

Cortex-M3 is also based on the ARMv7-M architecture and its architecture is very similar to Cortex-M4. The performance and clock speed of Cortex-M3 is slightly lower than the Cortex-M4. The performance of Cortex-M3 is 1.89 DMIPS/MHz and it consumes 31 μW/MHz. The significant difference between Cortex-M4 and Cortex-M3 is that Cortex-M3 does not include a DSP processor or a floating point module. If the application does not need to use the DSP functionality, then it may be more appropriate to choose a member of the Cortex-M3 family.

2.2.1.4 Cortex-M0+

The smallest members of the Cortex-M family are Cortex-M0+ and Cortex-M0. The performance of Cortex-M0+ is 1.35 DMIPS/MHZ, but it is still compatible with other Cortex-M family members. The processor consumes only 9.85 μW/MHz. Cortex-M0+ uses a subset of the Thumb-2 instruction set (Thumb) and is based on a 2-stage pipeline architecture. Although the performance is lower, there is overall power saving compared to its bigger brothers. Cortex-M0+ also features advanced debug options.

2.2.1.5 Cortex-M0

This is the smallest processor in the Cortex-M family, having a gate count of only 12K, consuming 12.5 μW/MHz. The processor reduces memory requirements where the on-chip flash memory is optimized to save cost, reduce power, and increase performance. The processor uses 3-stage pipeline with a subset of the Thumb-2 instruction set (Thumb). The performance is 1.27 DMIPS/MHZ. The low cost of the processor enables the developers to achieve 32-bit performance at an 8-bit price.

2.2.2 Cortex-R

Cortex-R family are real-time higher performance processors than the Cortex-M family. Some members of this family are designed to operate at clock speeds in excess of 1 GHz.

The main application areas of these processors are hard-disk controllers, automotive applications, network devices, and specialized high-speed applications. Early members of this family, Cortex-R4 and Cortex-R5, operate at clock speeds of up to 600 MHz. Cortex-R7 incorporates 11-stage pipeline and it can operate with clock speeds in excess of 1 GHz. Although the Cortex-R processors are high performance, their architectures are complex and they consume high power, making them unsuitable for use in mobile battery-powered devices. The performance of Cortex-R7 is 3.77 DMIPS/MHz. Cortex-R52 is a faster member of the family, having a performance of 5.07 DMIPS/MHz.

2.2.3 Cortex-A

Cortex-A family is the highest performance ARM processor family used in real-time operating systems, mainly in mobile applications, such as in mobile phones, tablets, GPS devices, electronic games, and so on. These processors support advanced features required for the design of mobile operating systems, such as ioS, Android, Linux, etc. Additionally, advanced memory management is supported by these processors with virtual memory. Early members of the family include processors such as Cortex-A5 to Cortex-A17, based on the ARMv7-A architecture. Latest members of the family are the Cortex-A50 and Cortex-A72 series designed for lower power and very high-performance mobile applications. These processors are built using the ARMv8-A architecture which offers 64-bit energy efficient operation with the capability of more than 4 GB of physical memory.

2.2.4 Cortex-M processor comparison

Table 2.1 shows a comparison of various Cortex-M family of processors. As can be seen from this table, Cortex-M0 and Cortex-M0+ are used at low speed and low power consumption applications. Cortex-M1 is optimized for use in programmable gate array applications. Cortex-M3 and Cortex-M4 are medium power processors used in microcontroller applications with the Cortex-M4 supporting DSP and floating point arithmetic operations. Cortex-M7 is a

TABLE 2.1   Cortex-M processor comparison.

Cortex processor	Description
Cortex-M0	Low power consumption, low to medium performance, smallest ARM processor
Cortex-M0+	Lower power consumption and higher performance than Cortex-M0
Cortex-M1	Designed mainly for gate array applications
Cortex-M3	Very popular, low power consumption, medium performance, debug features, used in microcontroller type applications
Cortex-M4	Similar architecture to Cortex-M3 but includes DSP and floating point arithmetic, used in high end microcontroller type applications
Cortex-M7	High performance processor, used in applications where Cortex-M4 is not fast enough, supports DSP and single and double precision arithmetic

high-performance member of the family which is used in applications requiring higher performance than the Cortex-M4.

2.2.5 Cortex-M compatibility

Processors in the Cortex family are upward compatible with each other. Cortex-M0 and Cortex-M0+ are based on the ARMv6-M architecture, using the Thumb instruction set. Cortex-M4 and Cortex-M7 are based on the ARMv7-M architecture, using the Thumb-2 instruction set which is a superset of Thumb. Although the architectures are different, software developed on the Cortex-M0 and Cortex-M0+ processors can run on Cortex-M3, Cortex-M4, and Cortex-M7 processors without any modifications provided the required memory and input-output ports are available.

2.2.6 Processor performance measurement

Processor performance is usually measured using benchmark programs. There are many benchmark programs available and one should exercise care when comparing the performance of various processors as the performance depends on many external factors, such as the efficiency of the compiler used, and the type of operation performed for the measurement.

Many attempts were made in the past to measure the performance of a processor and quote it as a single number. For example, MOPS, MFLOPS, Dhrystone, DMIPS, BogoMIPS, and so on. Nowadays, CoreMark is one of the most commonly used benchmark programs used to indicate the processor performance. CoreMark is developed by Embedded Microprocessor Benchmark Consortium (EEMBC, www.eembc.org/coremark) and is currently one of the most reliable performance measurement tools available.

Table 2.2 shows the CoreMark results for some of the commonly used microcontrollers. As can be seen from this table, Cortex-M7 achieves 5.01 CoreMark/MHz, while the medium range PIC18 microcontroller achieves only 0.04 CoreMark/MHz.

TABLE 2.2   CoreMark/MHz for some commonly used microcontrollers.

Processor	CoreMark/MHz
Cortex-M7	5.01
Cortex-A9	4.15
Cortex-M4	3.40
Cortex-M3	3.32
Cortex-M0+	2.49
Cortex-M0	2.33
dsPIC33	1.89
MSP430	1.11
PIC24	1.88
PIC18	0.04

2.3 The STM32F407VGT6 microcontroller

The STM32 family of 32-bit microcontrollers is based on ARM Cortex and there are over 300 compatible devices in the family. As described below, the family includes microcontrollers with the Cortex-M4, Cortex-M3, and Cortex-M0 architectures.

In this book we shall be using the highly popular ARM-based microcontroller STM32F407VGT6 together with the *Clicker 2 for STM32* development board (details are given in a later chapter). In the remaining sections of this chapter, we shall be looking at the features of the STM32F407VGT6 microcontroller. The internal architecture of this microcontroller is very complex and we shall only look at the important modules used in most projects, such as I/O, timers, ADC and DAC converters, interrupts, I²C, USART, and so on. Interested readers can get detailed information from manufacturers' data sheets and application notes available for download on the Internet.

2.3.1 Basic features of the STM32F407VGT6

The STM32F407VGT6 microcontroller is based on the Cortex-M4 architecture and has the following basic features:

- ARM Cortex-M4 32-bit RISC architecture
- Included floating point unit (FPU) and digital signal processor (DSP)
- Up to 168 MHz maximum operating frequency
- Single-cycle multiplication and hardware division
- Up to 1 Mb of flash memory
- Up to 192 Kb of SRAM
- 1.8–3.6 V power supply
- −40°C to +105°C operation
- Clock PLL
- 4–26 MHz external crystal
- Internal 16 MHz RC clock
- Internal 32 kHz oscillator for RTC
- Low power with sleep, stop, and standby modes
- 3 × 12-bit 24 channel ADC converters with 0–3.6 V reference voltage
- Sample and hold capability
- Temperature sensor
- 2 × 12-bit DAC converters
- Up to 17 timers
- Up to 140 I/O ports (138 of them +5V tolerant)
- 16 stream DMA controller
- 2 × CAN bus interface (2.0B)
- 6 × USART interface (with LIN and IrDA capabilities)
- 3 × SPI interface (42 Mbits/s)
- 3 × I²S interface
- 3 × I²C interface
- 2 × USB interface

- 2 × Watchdog timer
- 2 × 16 bit motor control PWM
- SDIO interface
- 1 × 10/100 Ethernet interface
- 8–14 bit parallel camera interface
- Nested vectored interrupt controller
- Random number generator
- Serial wire debug and JTAG interface
- Cyclic redundancy check (CRC) calculation unit

The basic features of the STM32F407VGT6 microcontroller are summarized in Fig. 2.1.

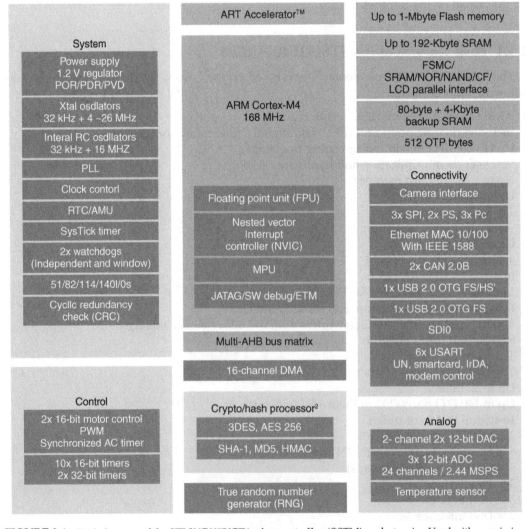

FIGURE 2.1   Basic features of the STM32F407VCT6 microcontroller. (©STMicroelectronics. Used with permission)

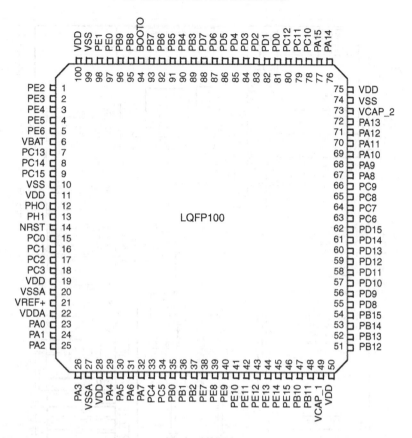

FIGURE 2.2 **Pin layout of the STM32F407VGT6 microcontroller.** (©STMicroelectronics. Used with permission)

Fig. 2.2 shows the pin layout (100 pin package) of the STM32F407VGT6 microcontroller. Detailed information on the STM32F407VCT6 microcontroller can be obtained from the following document:

RM0090, Reference manual, STM32F405/415, STM32F407/417, STM32F427/437 and STM32F429/439 advanced Arm-based 32-bit MCUs
RM0090 Rev 18, STMicroelectronics.

2.3.2 Internal block diagram

The internal block diagram of the microcontroller is shown in Fig. 2.3. At the top left corner is the 168 MHz Cortex-M4 processor with flash memory and SRAM, with DMA channels, USB and Ethernet modules just below the processor. The camera interface, voltage regulator, and external crystal inputs are shown at the top right-hand corner of the figure. The internal AHB (advanced high-speed bus) bus has two sections AHB1 and AHB2. AHB1 is divided into 84 MHz high-speed bus APB2 (advanced peripheral bus 2) and 42 MHz low-speed bus APB1 (advanced peripheral bus 1). APB2 supports some timers, SPI bus, USARTs, and ADC

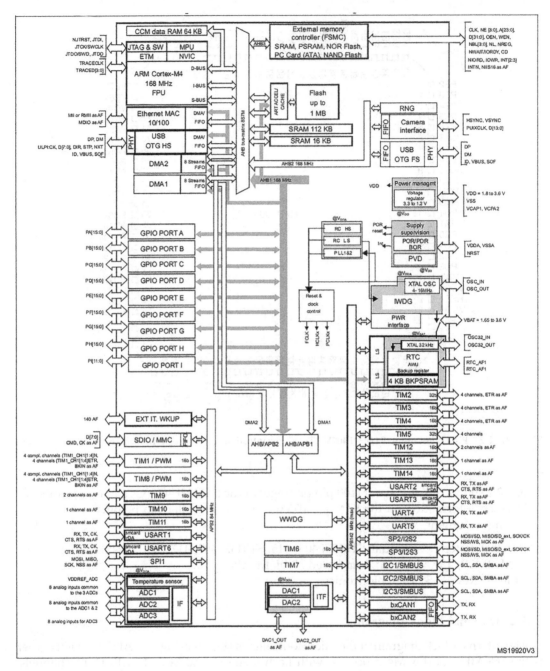

FIGURE 2.3 Internal block diagram of the STM32F407VGT6 microcontroller. (©STMicroelectronics. Used with permission)

channels. The low-speed APB1 bus supports some timers, USARTs, I²C bus, CAN modules, DAC, and the watchdog timer. Clocks to the GPIO ports are driven from the high-speed 168 MHz AHB1 bus in the middle of the figure. AHB2 bus drives the camera interface and the USB port. Memories are shown in the top middle part of the figure.

2.3.3 The power supply

The microcontroller is powered from VDD pins with a voltage in the range of 1.8–3.6 V. VDDA is the external analog power supply for the ADC and some other parts of the chip. A minimum of 1.8 V must be applied to VDDA when the ADC converter is used. VDDA and VSSA can be connected to VDD and VSS, respectively. V_{BAT} is the external battery voltage for the RTC, 32 kHz oscillator and backup registers when the VDD is not present. This voltage must be in the range 1.65–3.6 V.

2.3.4 Low power modes

The STM32F407VGT6 microcontroller can be operated in one of three modes in low-power operations:

Sleep mode: In this mode, the CPU is stopped but all peripherals continue to operate. The CPU wakes up when an interrupt occurs.
Stop mode: All clocks are stopped and this mode provides the lowest power consumption while retaining the contents of CPU registers and SRAM.
Standby mode: In this mode oscillators and the voltage regulator are switched off and thus it provides the lowest power consumption. All register contents and SRAM contents are lost (except for registers in the backup circuitry).

2.3.5 The clock circuit

The clock circuit of the STM32F407VGT6 microcontroller is very powerful and at the same time very complex. Correct configuration of the clock circuit is very important as it controls all the timing within the microcontroller. In this section we shall be looking at the various clock options and also see how to configure the clock.

On reset, the 16 MHz internal RC oscillator is selected as the default CPU clock. The application program can then select either the RC oscillator or an external 4–26 MHz crystal-based clock source as the system clock. This clock can be monitored for failure and if a failure is detected, the system automatically switches back to the internal RC oscillator. This clock source is input to a PLL, thus allowing to increase the frequency up to 168 MHz. There are several prescalers that allow configuration of the clock for the required speed.

Basically, there are two types of clock sources that can be used to drive the system clock: *external* clock, and *internal* clock (Fig. 2.4).

Fig. 2.5 shows the block diagram of the clock circuit.

2.3.5.1 *External clock sources*

High-speed external (HSE): This can be an external crystal or resonator device, or an external clock signal. The frequency range of the crystal or resonator should be 4–26 MHz. Fig. 2.6

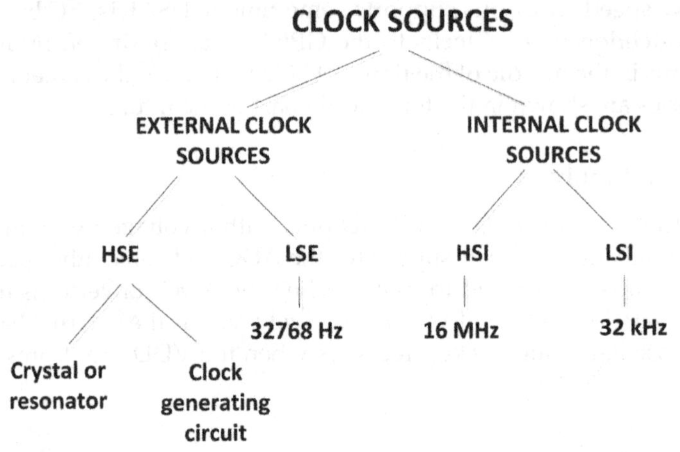

CLOCK SOURCES

FIGURE 2.4   STM32F407VGT6 clock sources.

shows a typical crystal connection. It is recommended to use two capacitors in the range of 4–25 pF with the crystal circuit.

When using a clock generator circuit, the waveform can be square, sine, or triangular and must be symmetrical, that is, 50% ON and 50% OFF times. The clock signal must be fed to the OSC_IN pin of the microcontroller (Fig. 2.7).

If external clock circuitry is used, the HSE oscillator should be bypassed to avoid any conflict.

Low speed external (LSE): This is a 32,768 Hz clock driven from an external crystal and feeding the internal real-time clock (RTC) module.

2.3.5.2 *Internal clock sources*

High-speed internal (HIS): This is an accurate 16 MHz internal clock with a factory-calibrated tolerance of 1%.

Low-speed internal (LSI): This clock source is not very accurate and is around 32 kHz. Although the LSI can be used to feed the RTC, it is not recommended as it is not very accurate. The LSI is normally used as a clock source for the independent watchdog (IWDG).

2.3.5.3 *Configuring the clock*

As shown in Fig. 2.5, the clock circuit consists of a number of multiplexers, prescalers, and a phase locked loop (PLL). The multiplexers are used to select the required clock source. The prescalers are used to divide the clock frequency by a constant. Similarly, the PLL is used to multiply the clock frequency with a constant in order to operate the chip at higher frequencies.

Configuring the clock by programming the internal clock registers is a complex task and detailed knowledge of the clock circuitry is required. Luckily, STMicroelectronics provides an Excel file tool to help configure the clock easily. Fig. 2.8 shows this Excel configuration tool (see web site: http://www.st.com/web/catalog/tools/FM147/CL1794/SC961/SS1533/PF257927#) in wizard mode. Using this tool one can easily configure the clock for the required speed.

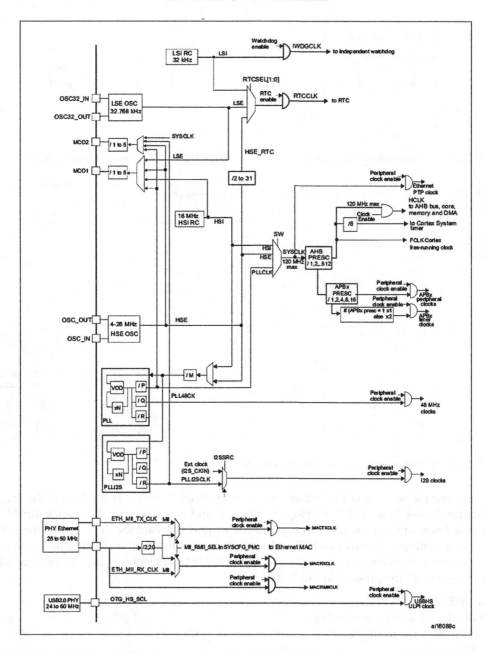

FIGURE 2.5   STM32F407VGT6 microcontroller clock circuit. (©STMicroelectronics. Used with permission)

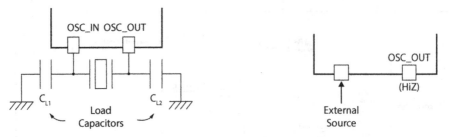

FIGURE 2.6 Crystal oscillator connection.   FIGURE 2.7 Using clock generator circuit.

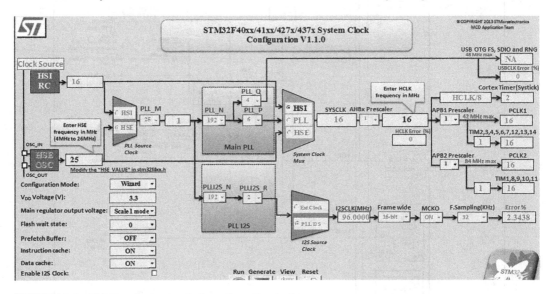

FIGURE 2.8 STMicroelectronics clock configuration tool.

As an example, assuming that we are using an external 25 MHz crystal (this is the crystal used in the Clicker 2 for STM32 development board) and the required CPU clock is 168 MHz, the above Excel tool can be used in *expert mode* to find the various clock parameters. You should enable macros in excel and click the run button at the bottom of the display to configure the clock. The configuration settings for 168 MHz CPU clock are as follows (this is the settings used in all the projects in this book):

- Use HSE clock
- Set crystal frequency to 25 MHz
- Select HSE in the multiplexer
- Set PLL to 25
- Set PLL_N to 336
- Set PLL_P to 2
- Set PLL_Q to 8
- Select PLL
- Set AHBx prescaler to 1

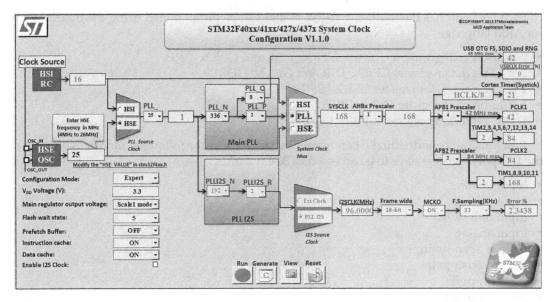

FIGURE 2.9   **Configuring the clock.**

As shown in Fig. 2.9, the CPU clock will be set to 168 MHz, APB1 clock to 42 MHz, and APB2 clock to 84 MHz.

2.4 General purpose inputs and outputs

General purpose inputs and outputs (GPIO) ports are arranged into five ports, each port 16-pin wide, and named as A, B, C, D, and E. Each port has a separate clock. Each port has the following basic features:

- Most of the port pins are +5V tolerable when used as inputs (except the analog input pins)
- Port outputs can be configured as push-pull, open-drain or pull-up, pull-down
- The speed of each port can be configured in software
- Port inputs can be configured as pull-up or pull-down, analog, or floating
- Port pins can be digital I/O or they can have alternative functions, such as DAC, SPI, USB, PWM, etc.)
- Each port pin can be used with one of 15 alternate functions (AF)
- Bit manipulations can be performed on each port pin

After hardware or software reset, the default values of the port pins are:

- Input
- Push-pull
- 2 MHz speed
- No pull-up or pull-down

Each I/O port has the following registers that can be programmed using the mikroC Pro for ARM language:

- 2 × 32-bit configuration registers GPIOx_CRL and GPIOx_CRH
- 2 × 32-bit data registers GPIOx_IDR and GPIOx_ODR
- 1 × 32-bit set/reset register GPIOx_BSRR
- 1 × 16-bit reset register GPIOx_BRR
- 1 × 32-bit locking register GPIOx_LCKR

Port pins can be individually configured by software in the following modes. Notice that the I/O port registers have to be accessed as 32-bit words:

- Input floating
- Input pull-up
- Input pull-down
- Input analog
- Output open-drain
- Output push-pull
- AF push-pull
- AF open-drain

Set/reset registers are used for read/modify accesses to any port pin without being interrupted by the system interrupt controller module.

Fig. 2.10 shows the structure of a push-pull output port pin which is the most commonly used structure. Similarly, an open-drain output port pin is shown in Fig. 2.11. Input pull-up and pull-down circuits are shown in Fig. 2.12 and Fig. 2.13, respectively.

The basic structure of an I/O port pin is shown in Fig. 2.14. The push-pull transistors and pull-up and pull-down resistors can be seen from the figure. Notice that protection diodes are used at the port inputs to protect the input circuitry from high voltages.

Port configuration registers GPIOx_CRL and GPIOx_CRH are used to configure the following parameters of a port:

- Analog mode
- Floating input mode
- Input with pull-up/pull-down
- Output with push-pull

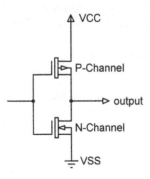

FIGURE 2.10   Push-pull output pin.

FIGURE 2.11   Open-drain output pin.

FIGURE 2.12 **Pull-up pin.**   FIGURE 2.13 **Pull-down pin.**

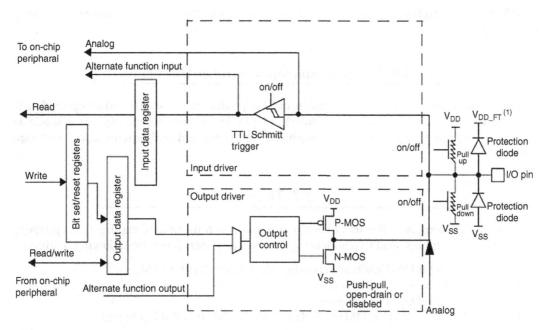

FIGURE 2.14   **Structure of an I/O pin.** (©STMicroelectronics. Used with permission)

- Output with open-drain
- AF output with push-pull
- AF output with open-drain
- Output speed

Port data registers GPIOx_IDR and GPIOx_ODR are used to read and write data to a port respectively.

Port bit set/reset register GPIOx_BSRR or GPIOx_BRR are used in read/modify operations. Using these registers to modify a port pin protects the operation from interrupts. Thus, there is no need for the software to disable interrupts during port read/write operations.

Port locking register GPIOx_LCKR allows the input-output configuration of a port to be frozen until the microcontroller is reset. The locking operation is useful when the ports are configured and it is required to protect this configuration from accidental changes.

Port pins can be programmed for AF. For AF inputs, the port must be configured in the required input mode. Similarly, for AF outputs, the port must be configured in AF output mode. When a port is configured as an AF, the pull-up and pull-down resistors are disabled, the output is set to operate in push-pull or in open-drain mode.

Most of the port input pins are +5V tolerant which means that devices giving +5V outputs can directly be connected to the microcontroller input port pins without having to lower their voltages. A +5V tolerant input is shown as "FT" in data sheets.

2.5 Nested vectored interrupt controller (NVIC)

STM32F407 includes a nested vectored interrupt controller that can manage 16 priority levels and handle 82 maskable interrupts.

2.6 External interrupt controller (EXTI)

The external interrupt controller consists of 23 edge detected lines used to accept and generate interrupts. Each line can be configured independently to select the triggering mode as a rising edge, falling edge, or both, and each line can be masked individually under software control.

2.7 Timers

STM32F407 microcontroller includes two advanced-control timers, eight general purpose timers, two basic timers, and two watchdog timers. The timers have the following features:

TIM1, TIM8: 16-bit Up/Down advanced-control timers (with PWM)
TIM3, TIM4: 16-bit Up/Down timers
TIM2, TIM5: 32-bit Up/Down timers
TIM6, TIM7, TIM9, TIM10, TIM11, TIM12, TIM13, TIM14: 16-bit Up timers

2.8 Analog-to-digital converters (ADCs)

$3 \times$ 12-bit ADC are included with each ADC sharing up to 16 external channels, each having 4096 levels of quantization. Conversion can be done as single-shot or in scan mode. Scan mode is the most commonly used option where automatic conversion is performed on the selected channels. Sample and hold functionality is available with the ADC channels which are used to hold the input signal just before a conversion takes place. The ADC can be triggered by any of TIM1, TIM2, TIM3, TIM4, or TIM8 timer.

2.9 Built-in temperature sensor

A built-in temperature sensor is provided on the microcontroller chip whose output voltage varies linearly with the chip temperature. The temperature sensor is internally connected to analog port ADC1_IN16. The temperature sensor is not accurate and can only be used to detect temperature changes instead of reading the absolute temperatures.

2.10 Digital-to-analog converter

2×12-bit DAC channels are provided with 8-bit or 12-bit outputs, offering 256 or 4096 levels of quantization. The converted data can be aligned left or right and each channel has DMA capability. The DAC channels additionally feature noise-wave generation or triangular-wave generation.

2.11 Reset

There are three types of reset: system reset, power reset, and backup domain reset. A system reset sets all registers to their default reset values. This reset is generated by one of the following events:

- Low-level signal on NRST pin (external reset)
- Watchdog timeout
- Software reset
- Low-power management reset

Low-power management reset is triggered when entering the Standby mode or when entering the Stop mode.

Power reset is generated when power is applied to the microcontroller or when exiting the Standby mode. Backup domain reset sets all RTC registers to their reset values. This type of reset is generated when a software reset is triggered by setting a bit in the backup domain control register, or if V_{DD} or V_{BAT} become ON if they were both previously OFF.

2.12 Electrical characteristics

It is important to know the absolute maximum and typical ratings of a microcontroller before it is used in a project. Stresses above the absolute maximum ratings for extended periods may affect device reliability and may even damage the device. Some of the absolute maximum ratings of the STM32F407VCT6 microcontroller are shown in Table 2.3. Notice from

TABLE 2.3 Absolute maximum ratings.

Symbol	Description	Absolute maximum ratings
Vdd-Vss	External supply voltage	4.0 V
Vin	Input voltage on +5V tolerant pin	Vdd + 4.0
Vin	Input voltage on non +5V tolerant pin	4.0 V
Ivdd	Total current into Vdd power lines (source)	240 mA
Ivss	Total current out of Vss ground lines (sink)	240 mA
Io	Output current sunk by any I/O pin	25 mA
Io	Output current sourced by any I/O pin	25 mA
Tstg	Storage temperature	$-65°C$ to $+150°C$
Tj	Maximum junction temperature	150°C

TABLE 2.4 Typical operating conditions.

Symbol	Description	Min	Max
fhclk	Internal AHB clock frequency	0	168 MHz
fpclk1	Internal APB1 clock frequency	0	42 MHz
fpclk2	Internal APB2 clock frequency	0	84 MHz
Vdd	Operating voltage	1.8 V	3.6 V
Vdda	ADC operating voltage	1.8 V	3.6 V
V_{BAT}	Backup voltage	1.8 V	3.6 V
Pd	Power dissipation (LQFP100 package)	–	465 mW
Id	Supply current in Run mode, code in flash (at 168 MHz with all peripherals enabled)	–	87 mA
Id	Supply current in Run mode, code in flash (at 168 MHz with all peripherals disabled)	–	40 mA

this table that the output current sunk and sourced by any I/O pin is specified as maximum 25 mA (the typical value is 8 mA, but for relaxed I/O voltages this current can be increased to 20 mA) and thus, direct LED drive is possible. To drive larger loads, it will be necessary to use BJT- or MOSFET-based transistor switching circuits or even relays for higher voltages. The total current sourced from all I/O pins plus the run consumption of the CPU should not exceed 240 mA. Care should be taken when driving CMOS circuits that operate with +5V since the output voltage of an I/O pin of the microcontroller will not be high enough to drive a CMOS input, even with pull-up resistors. In such circumstances it is recommended to use 3–5 V level converter circuits, for example, transistor switches or voltage converter integrated circuits.

Table 2.4 shows the typical operating conditions of the STM32F407VCT6 microcontroller. The values given in this table should be considered in normal operating conditions.

2.13 Summary

In this chapter the basic features of the Cortex-M processors have been described. In addition, the architecture of the STM32F407VCT6 microcontroller has been described in some detail since this is the microcontroller that is used in all the projects in this book. The clock configuration options and general purpose input-output structure of the STM32F407VCT6 microcontroller are given in this chapter.

In the next chapter we shall be looking at the basic features of some of the commonly used ARM Cortex based development boards.

Further readings

[1] J. Yiu, The Definitive Guide to the ARM Cortex-M3, second ed. Newnes, Oxford, 2010.
[2] D. Ibrahim, Programming With STM32 Nucleo Boards, Elektor, Netherlands, (2014) ISBN: 978-1-907920-68-4.
[3] T. Martin, The Designer's Guide to the Cortex-M Processor Family, Elsevier, Oxford, (2013).
[4] T. Wilmhurst, An Introduction to the Design of Small-scale Embedded Systems, Palgrave, London, (2001).

CHAPTER

3

ARM Cortex microcontroller development boards

3.1 Overview

Microcontroller development boards (or kits) help the system designers to develop projects easily and speedily. These boards incorporate the target microcontroller with usually additional memory, input-output ports, some LEDs, some switches, device programmer, and some other peripheral interfaces such as UART, I2C, SPI, etc. Because the hardware of the development boards has been tested by the manufacturers, the designer can concentrate on the software of the application, knowing that the hardware is in working order. In this chapter we shall be looking at the basic features of some of the popular ARM Cortex-based microcontroller development boards.

3.2 LPC1768

This is an Mbed compatible microcontroller, based on the Cortex-M3 processor (Fig. 3.1), having a form-factor of 40-pin DIP with 0.1 in. of spacing, and manufactured by NXP. The basic features of this development board are:

- 32-bit 96 MHz processor
- 32 KB SRAM, 512 KB flash
- 12-bit ADC
- 10-bit DAC
- Ethernet
- SPI, I2C, UART, PWM, CAN interfaces
- breadboard compatible
- USB or external power supply

ARM-Based Microcontroller Multitasking Projects. http://dx.doi.org/10.1016/B978-0-12-821227-1.00003-7

FIGURE 3.1   **LPC1768 development board.** *(Pololu Robotics & Electronics, pololu.com)*

3.3 STM32 Nucleo family

The family of STM32 Nucleo consists of many ARM Cortex-based Mbed compatible development boards with different specifications. For example, Nucleo-L476RG is one of the low-cost and very popular development boards (Fig. 3.2) in this family, having the following specifications:

- 32-bit Cortex-M4 CPU
- 80 MHz max CPU frequency
- 1 MB Flash, 128 KB SRAM
- 13 × Timers
- 2 × Watchdog
- 3 × SPI
- 3 × I2C
- 3 × USART, 2 × UART
- CAN bus
- 2 × SAI
- 51 GPIO ports with external interrupt capability
- 12 Channel capacitive sensing
- 3 × 12-bit ADC with 16 channels
- 12-bit DAC with 2 channels
- 2 × analog comparators
- 2 × Opamps
- user LED and User push-button

FIGURE 3.2   Nucleo-L476RG development board. *(©STMicroelectronics. Used with permission)*

The Nucleo family of microcontrollers is supported by a large number of compatible and plug-in boards, such as Wi-Fi, Bluetooth, DC and stepper motor controller, temperature sensor, distance sensor, etc.

3.4 EasyMX Pro V7 For STM32

EasyMx PRO v7 for STM32 is a development board for STM32 ARM Cortex-M3 and Cortex-M4, M7, M0 architectures. It contains many on-board modules necessary for device development, including multimedia, Ethernet, USB, RS232, CAN interface, and others. On-board mikroProg programmer and debugger supports the programming and debugging of over 180 ARM-based microcontrollers. The board is fully supported and is compatible with the mikroC Pro for ARM compiler and IDE. EasyMx Pro V7 for STM32 is delivered with the microcontroller card containing the STM32F107VCT6. This development board, manufactured by mikroElektronika is a full-size board (Fig. 3.3), having the following specifications:

- STM32F107VCT6 microcontroller
- 72 MHz clock
- 256 KB Flash, 64 KB SRAM
- 5 × USB UART
- Piezo buzzer
- analog and digital temperature sensors
- Ethernet
- CAN
- 2 × 12-bit ADC
- 2 × 12-bit DAC

FIGURE 3.3   **EasyMX Pro V7 for STM32 development board.** *(www.mikroe.com)*

- 2 × I2C
- 2 × SPI
- 2 × CAN
- microSD card slot
- stereo MP3 Codec
- 8 Mbit serial flash
- 8 × 256 Bytes EEPROM
- 320 × 240 pixel Graphics TFT board
- 128 × 64 pixel graphics LCD
- 2 × microbus connectors
- touch screen controller
- 67 LEDs and 67 push-buttons
- navigation switch
- on-board programmer/debugger

3.5 STM32F4DISCOVERY board

This is another highly popular ARM-based development board used in many applications. This development board (Fig. 3.4) is based on the STM32F407VGT6 32-bit ARM Cortex-M4-based CPU, and it has the following basic specifications:

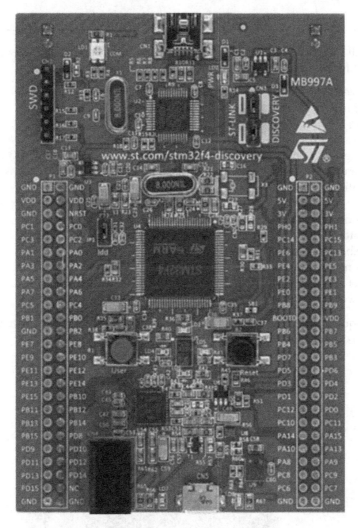

FIGURE 3.4   **STM32FDISCOVERY board.** *(©STMicroelectronics. Used with permission)*

- 1 Mb flash 192 KB SRAM
- MEMS 3-axis accelerometer
- MEMS audio sensor omnidirectional digital microphone
- audio DAC with integrated class D speaker driver
- 8 LEDs
- 2 push-buttons
- USB OTG FS with micro-AB connector
- USB ST-LINK with re-enumeration capability, debug port, virtual com port, and mass storage

3.6 mbed application board

This is a small size, but popular 32-bit ARM microcontroller (Fig. 3.5) based development board, designed for rapid prototyping, having the following specifications:

- credit card sized
- 128 × 32 graphics LCD
- 5-way joystick
- 3-axis MEMS accelerometer
- temperature sensor
- 2 × potentiometers
- 5-way navigation switch
- RGB LED
- miniature loudspeaker
- 2 × servo motor headers
- headers for Xbee Zigbee module
- mini USB connector
- RJ-45 Ethernet socket
- 6–9 V DC power socket

The board requires the LPC1768 processor to operate, and with this processor it offers all the specifications of the LPC1768 (see Section 3.2).

FIGURE 3.5   mbed Application board. *(From SparkFun Electronics, Photo taken by Juan Peña)*

3.7 EasyMx Pro V7 for Tiva

EasyMx PRO v7 for Tiva C Series is a full-featured development board (Fig. 3.6) for TI's Tiva C Series ARM Cortex M4 microcontrollers. It contains many on-board modules necessary for developing a variety of applications, including multimedia, Ethernet, USB, RS232, CAN, and others. On-board mikroProg programmer and debugger supports over 55 TI Tiva C series microcontroller programming and debugging. The board is delivered with a microcontroller socket containing the TM4C129XNCZAD type Tiva microcontroller. The basic features of this board are:

- 32-bit Cortex-M4 processor
- 120 MHz clock
- 1 MB flash, 256 KB SRAM
- 6 KB EEPROM
- 2 mikroBus sockets
- 2 × USB UART
- buzzer
- 2 × CAN
- 2 × 12-bit ADC
- 8 × UART
- 8 Timers
- 2 × Watchdog timer
- 16 × digital comparator
- 8 M bit flash
- Ethernet
- 256 × 8 I2C EEPROM
- stereo MP3 Codec
- mikro SD card slot
- 67 LEDs and 67 push buttons
- 320 × 240 pixel graphics TFT
- analog and digital temperature sensors
- all I/O ports at headers

FIGURE 3.6   **EasyMx Pro V7 for Tiva.** *(www.mikroe.com)*

3.8 MINI-M4 for STM32

This is a small ARM Cortex-M4-based development board (Fig. 3.7) containing the STM-32F415RG type microcontroller. It is equipped with 16 MHz crystal oscillator, and 32.768 KHz crystal which can be used for its internal RTCC module. It has a reset button and three signal LEDs. The board is preprogrammed with fast USB Bootloader, so no external programmers are needed for programming the microcontroller and for program development. The board is fully compatible with the mikroc Pro for ARM compiler and the IDE. The basic features of this board are:

- 32-bit ARM Cortex-M4 processor
- 1 MB flash, 192 + 4 KB SRAM
- Up to 168 MHz operation

FIGURE 3.7   **MINI-M4 for STM32 board.** *(www.mikroe.com)*

- 7 × analog inputs
- CAN
- 4 × PWM channels
- 2 × SPI
- I2C
- 2 × UART
- 3 × 12-bit ADC
- 2 × 12-bit DAC
- 17 × Timers

3.9 Clicker 2 for MSP432

This board is based on the MSP432 32-bit Cortex-M4–based processor (Fig. 3.8). The board supports two mikroBUS sockets so that up to two Click Boards can be plugged-in to the board. The basic features of this development board are:

- 48 MHz clock
- 256 KB flash, 64 KB SRAM

FIGURE 3.8   **Clicker 2 for MSP432.** *(www.mikroe.com)*

- 6 timers
- SPI
- I2C
- 2 LEDs
- 2 push-button switches
- 52 general purpose GPIO
- 2 × mikroBUS sockets
- on-chip Bootloader
- mikro-USB connector
- power management

3.10 Tiva EK-TM4C123GXL LaunchPad

This is a low-cost development board (Fig. 3.9) based on ARM Cortex-M4, using the TM-4C123GH6PMI microcontroller. The basic features of this board are:

- 32-bit ARM processor

FIGURE 3.9 **Tiva EK-TM4C123GXL.** *(Courtesy of Texas Instruments Inc.)*

- 80 MHz clock
- 256 KB flash, 32 KB SRAM
- 2 × CAN modules
- 8 × UARTs with IrDA
- 2 × 12-bit ADC with 12 channels
- 2 × analog, 16 × digital comparators
- 12 × 16-bit Timers
- 43 × general purpose GPIO
- RGB LED
- reset switch
- motion control PWM

3.11 Fusion for ARM V8

This is an advanced state-of-the-art development board designed for ARM-based micro-controllers (Fig. 3.10). The board supports over 1600 types of ARM-based processors and it has the unique feature that it can be used and programmed/debugged remotely over a Wi-Fi link. The board is suitable for all kinds of microcontroller-based project development as it provides a large number of switches, LEDs, LCD, and graphical TFT sockets, CAN bus, UARTs, etc. By default, the board is distributed with the STM32F407ZG microcontroller. The basic features of this board are (with the default processor):

- 32-bit ARM processor support
- 1 MB flash, 192 + 4 KB SRAM
- 168 MHz clock

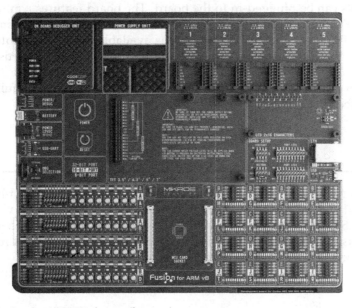

FIGURE 3.10 **Fusion for ARM V8.** (*www.mikroe.com*)

- 3 × 12-bit ADC with 24 channels
- 2 × 12-bit DAC
- 17 Timers
- up to 140 I/O ports
- 3 × I2C
- 4 × UART
- 3 × SPI
- 2 × CAN
- up to 800 × 480 pixel TFT support
- 1 × 16 pin LCD connector
- 5 × mikroBUS connectors
- CODEGRIP programmer/debugger, enabling programming, and debugging over a Wi-Fi link
- large number of configurable LEDs and push-button switches
- UART connectivity over USB-C
- Up-pull-down switches
- 2 × 5-pin I/O headers

The novelty of this board is that at the time of writing this book, this was the first development board that could be programmed/debugged over a Wi-Fi link.

3.12 Clicker 2 for STM32

This is a low-cost highly popular development board based on the 32-bit ARM processor STM32F407VGT6. This board is equipped with two mikroBUS sockets so that up to two Click Boards can be plugged-in to the board. The board features a mini USB port for connection to a PC. A Bootloader program is preloaded in the program memory of the microcontroller. A PC-based Bootloader program is available from the manufacturer (www.mikroe.com) so that the processor can easily be programmed with the user application program.

This is the development board used in all the projects in this book and full details of this board are described in Chapter 4.

3.13 Summary

In this chapter we have looked at some of the popular ARM processor-based development boards and studied the basic features of these boards. In this book we will be using the Clicker 2 for STM32 development board in all the projects. In the next chapter we will be looking at the basic architecture of the Clicker 2 for STM32 development board and the STM-32F407VGT6 processor used on this board.

Further readings

[1] LPC1768 development board, Pololu Robotics & Electronics. Available from: www.pololu.com.

[2] Nucleo-L476RG development board, STMiroelectronics. Available from: www.st.com.

[3] EasyMX Pro V7 for STM32 development board. Available from: www.mikroe.com.

[4] STM32FDISCOVERY board, STMiroelectronics. Available from: www.st.com.

[5] mbed Application board, SparkFun Electronics. Available from: www.sparkfun.com.

[6] EasyMx Pro V7 for Tiva development board. . Available from: www.mikroe.com.

[7] MINI-M4 for STM32 development board. Available from: www.mikroe.com.

[8] Clicker 2 for MSP432 development board. Available from: www.mikroe.com

[9] Tiva EK-TM4C123GXL development board, Texas Instruments Inc. Available from: www.ti.com.

[10] Fusion for ARM V8 development board. Available from: www.mikroe.com.

4

Clicker 2 for STM32 development board

4.1 Overview

In the last chapter we had a look at some of the popular ARM processor development boards. In this chapter we shall be looking in detail the features of the Clicker 2 for STM32 development board which is used in all the projects in this book.

4.2 Clicker 2 for STM32 hardware

The Clicker 2 for STM32 is a very powerful microcontroller development board using the STM32F407VGT6 32-bit ARM Cortex-M4-based microcontroller operating at up to 168 MHz. The board is called *Clicker 2* since it has two mikroBUS sockets mounted on it. The board incorporates 1 MB of flash memory and over 192 KB of SRAM memory. The board (see Fig. 4.1) is developed and manufactured by mikroElektronika (www.mikroe.com), and it has the following basic features:

- STM32F407VGT6 microcontroller (100 pins)
- 168 MHz operation speed
- 1 MB flash memory
- over 192 KB SRAM
- 25 MHz and 32.768 kHz external crystals
- 52 programmable GPIO pins
- 16-bit and 32-bit timers
- 3 × 12-bit analog-to-digital converters
- SPI, I2C, UART, USART, RTC, Ethernet interfaces
- 2 mikroBUS sockets to accept Click boards
- USB mini connector
- 2 LEDs
- 2 push-button switches
- 2 × 26 connection pads

ARM-Based Microcontroller Multitasking Projects. http://dx.doi.org/10.1016/B978-0-12-821227-1.00004-9

Key features

1 ON/OFF Switch

2 Pads for connecting external ON/OFF Switch

3 Jumper for enabling RTC power supply

4 25 MHz crystal oscillator

5 32.768 KHz crystal oscillator

6 2x26 connection pads

7 mikroBUS^m sockets1and 2

8 Pushbuttons

9 Additionals LEDs

10 LTC3586 USB power manager IC

11 Indication LEDs

12 RESET button

13 USB mini-B connector

14 STM32F407VGT6

15 Battery connector

16 JTAG programmer connector

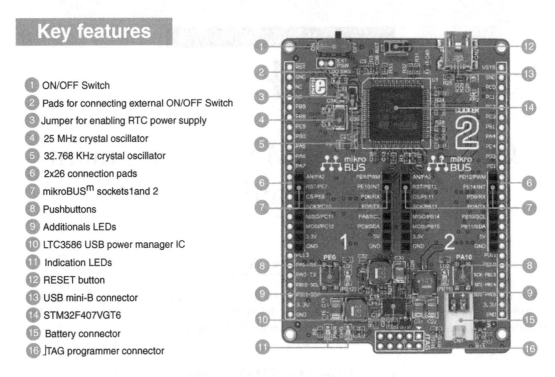

FIGURE 4.1   Clicker 2 for STM32 development board.

- power manager IC
- reset button
- external battery connector

The Clicker 2 for STM32 board has 2 × 26 header type connectors at both ends. The board can therefore be plugged-in on a suitable size breadboard so that the input-output pins can easily be accessed during project development. This is the recommended method to use the board for project development.

4.2.1 On-board LEDs

There are two on-board LEDs, LD1 and LD2, connected to port pins **PE12** and **PE15**, respectively. The cathodes of the LEDs are connected to ground via 2.2K current limiting resistors and their anodes are connected directly to the corresponding port pins. Thus, the LEDs are turned ON when logic 1 is applied to the corresponding output ports of the microcontroller.

4.2.2 On-board push-button switches

There are two on-board push-button switches, T2 and T3, connected to port pins **PE0** and **PA10**, respectively. The switches are connected to port pins and are normally pulled HIGH

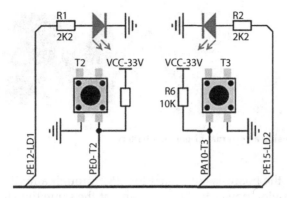

FIGURE 4.2   LED and push-button connections.

through 10K resistors. Pushing a switch forces its output to logic 0 so that the corresponding port pins read logic 0.

Fig. 4.2 shows the LED and push-button connections on the board.

4.2.3 Reset switch

A reset switch is provided on the board. Pressing this switch resets the microcontroller, forcing it to enter into the Bootloader mode for about 5 s. If there is no connection request from a corresponding Bootloader program on a PC then the processor initializes its registers into default reset state and then starts to execute the user program.

4.2.4 Power supply

The board can be powered either from a PC or from an external suitable 5V DC supply through its mini USB port (see Fig. 4.3), or using an external 3.7V Li-polymer battery (see Fig. 4.4). Battery charging current and charging voltage are 300 mA and 4.2 V, respectively.

FIGURE 4.3   Powering from the mini USB port.

FIGURE 4.4   Powering using an external Li-polymer battery.

In normal operations, the board is connected to a PC through a mini USB cable where this interface is used to provide power to the board and at the same time to program the micro-controller on the board.

4.2.5 On-board mikroBUS sockets

There are two mikroBUS sockets on-board (labeled mikroBUS 1 and mikroBUS 2) for connecting any type of Click board to the processor. Click boards are manufactured by mikro-Elektronika (www.mikroe.com) and there are over 800 Click boards available (at the time of writing this book, since the number is increasing all the time) that can be plugged-in to the mikroBUS compatible sockets. mikroBUS interface provides connectivity for the commonly used protocols such as SPI, I²C, UART, analog input, etc. Click boards simplify the task of overall system development. There are Click boards for various analog and digital sensors, displays, relays, communication boards, and so on. Some example Click boards are:

- temperature and humidity sensor
- accelerometer
- gyrator
- pressure sensor
- gas sensor
- GPS
- Wi-Fi
- Ethernet
- ZigBee
- CAN bus
- 7-segment LED
- Mini LCD
- OLED
- buzzer
- bar graph LED
- EEPROM
- line follower
- RF transmitter/receiver
- heart rate sensor
- ADC and DAC

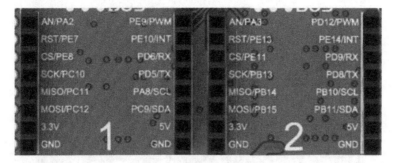

FIGURE 4.5   mikroBUS pin configurations.

- DC motor controller
- stepper motor controller
- and many more

mikroBUS sockets have 16 pins, organized as 2 × 8 pins in a dual-in-line type socket. Pin 1 is located at the top left-hand side of the socket. Fig. 4.5 shows the pin configuration of the two mikroBUS sockets on the Clicker 2 for the STM32 development board.

4.2.6 Input-output pins

Fig. 4.6 shows the Clicker 2 for STM32 development board input-output pin names as viewed from the back of the board. The input-output pins can be categorized as follows:
Digital input-output
PB5,PB6,PB7,PC7,PC8,PC13,PD7,PD10,PD11,PD13,PD14,PD15,PE1,PE2,PE3,PE4,PE6,
Analog inputs
PC0.PC1,PC2,PC3,PB1,PA4,PC4
Interrupt lines
PD0,PD1,PD2,PD3
UART lines
PA0 (TX), PA1(RX)
I2C lines
PB10 (SCL), PB11(SDA)
SPI lines
PB13 (SCK), PB14 (SDI), PB15 (SDO)
Power and ground
+3.3V and +5V power and ground lines are provided on the mikroBUS sockets. Additionally, the mainboard provides +3.3V power and ground lines.

In addition, the board is equipped with the following:

- reset push-button (RST)
- on-off slide switch
- GND and +3.3V power pins
- power management and battery charger module

FIGURE 4.6   Input-output pins.

- JTAG programming interface
- mini USB socket

4.2.7 Oscillators

In addition to the internal 16 MHz RC oscillator, the board is equipped with a 25 MHz and a 32,768 Hz crystal-based oscillators for accurate processor timing and accurate RTC applications (see Fig. 4.7).

4.2.8 Programming the on-board microcontroller

The microcontroller on the development board can be programmed using one of the following methods:

- A Bootloader program is preloaded in the program memory of the on-board microcontroller. By downloading the compatible mikroBootloader program to our PC, we can program the on-board microcontroller. This method is described in detail in the next chapter.
- Using an external ST-LINK V2 programmer device (Fig. 4.8).
- Using the mikroProg for STM32 programmer device (Fig. 4.9).

Figure 6-2:
25MHz crystal
oscillator
module (X1)

FIGURE 4.7   On-board 25 MHz and 32,768 Hz crystals.

FIGURE 4.8   ST-LINK V2 programmer.

FIGURE 4.9   **mikroProg for STM32 programmer.**

The Bootloader programming method is used in all the projects in this book as it does not require any additional external programming devices, and it is also the cheapest and the fastest way of programming the on-board microcontroller.

4.3 Summary

In this chapter we had a look at the basic features of the Clicker 2 for the STM32 development board. Since this board is used in all the projects in the book, it is important that the reader has an understanding of its basic features.

In the next chapter we shall be looking at the various ARM microcontroller programming tools including the mikroC Pro for ARM compiler and the IDE used in all the projects in this book.

Further reading

[1] Clicker 2 for STM32 development board. Available from: www.mikroe.com.

Programming the ARM-based microcontrollers

5.1 Overview

In the last chapter we have seen the features of the Clicker 2 for STM32 development board which is used in all the projects in this book. This chapter is about the software development tools (integrated development environments [IDEs], or toolchains) that can be used to develop ARM microcontroller-based programs, and also to upload the developed code to the program memory of the target processor. Brief specifications of the popular ARM processor-based program development tools are given in this chapter.

5.2 IDEs supporting the ARM-based microcontrollers

The ARM-based microcontrollers are supported by several IDEs, consisting of text editors, compilers, debuggers, simulators, and tools to upload the executable code to the program memory of the target processor. The compiler is usually a version of the popular C/C++, developed specifically for embedded processors. In this book we are only interested in the STM32 family of ARM microcontrollers. Some of the popular IDEs supporting the STM32 family of ARM microcontrollers are:

- Embedded Workbench for ARM (EWARM) by IAR systems
- ARM Mbed
- MDK-ARM by Keil
- TrueStudio for STM32
- System Workbench for STM32 (SW4STM32) by AC6
- mikroC Pro for ARM by mikroElektronika

In this book we will be using the highly popular mikroC Pro for ARM IDE. Brief details of all the other popular IDEs are given in the following sections.

ARM-Based Microcontroller Multitasking Projects. http://dx.doi.org/10.1016/B978-0-12-821227-1.00005-0

5.2.1 EWARM

EWARM is a professional compiler based on the popular C/C++ language, developed by IAR systems, and supporting ARM Cortex-M0, Cortex-M0+, Cortex-M3, Cortex-M4, and Cortex-M7–based processors. Two free evaluation versions of this IDE are available: code size limited and time limited. Both versions can be used to develop small to medium-sized programs for the ARM-based processors. The differences between the two versions are:

- Size-limited version
  - total code size is limited to 32 KB
  - source code for runtime libraries is not included
  - there is no support for MISRA C
  - only limited technical support is available
- 30-day time-limited version
  - the license expires after 30 days
  - there is no support for MISRA C
  - C-RUN is limited to 12 KB of code
  - source code for runtime libraries is not included
  - there is limited technical support
  - the IDE must not be used for commercial product development

Users are requested to register before using this IDE. At the time of writing this book the latest version of the IDE was 8.20, and it can be downloaded from the following website. Full documentation and application notes on EWARM are available on the Internet:

https://www.iar.com/iar-embedded-workbench/tools-for-arm/arm-cortex-m-edition/

5.2.2 ARM Mbed

Mbed is an online IDE that can be used to develop programs for the 32-bit ARM Cortex family of processors. It is supported by over 60 partners in many countries and with a community of over 200,000 developers. Mbed consists of a text editor and a compiler. User programs are compiled online on the cloud using a version of the popular C/C++ compiler. The executable code can easily be uploaded to the program memory of the target processor as a drag and drop operation (or a simple copy operation). Mbed supports large numbers of ARM-based microcontroller development boards and provides an extensive software library to make programming an easy task. Many application notes and example programs are available on the Internet. Users must register before they are allowed to use Mbed. Registration is done using the following website:

https://os.mbed.com/account/login

5.2.3 MDK-ARM

This is a professional IDE developed by Keil. Three versions of this IDE are available: *MDK-Professional*, *MDK-Plus*, and *MDK-Lite*. MDK-Professional and MDK-Plus can be downloaded and used for a time period of 7 days without a license. MDK-Lite is a 32 KB code size limited version of the IDE and is available free of charge, intended for product evaluation, for the development of small to medium-sized projects, and for educational purposes. A debugger is also provided for code sizes up to 32 KB.

MDK-Lite has the following limitations:

- code size is limited to 32 KB
- disassembly listing is not generated by the compiler
- position independent code is not generated
- the assembler and linker output files cannot be linked with third-party linker utilities

There are many example projects and documentation available on the Internet for using the MDK_ARM. The lite version occupies around 800 MB of disk space and can be downloaded from the following website:

http://www2.keil.com/mdk5/editions/lite

5.2.4 TrueStudio for STM32

TrueStudio for STM32 is a professional IDE used to develop STM32 processor-based projects. This IDE supports a highly optimizing compiler, editor, assembler, and linker. Additionally, the following features are provided:

- single- and multi-core debug
- trace and profiling
- memory analyzer
- hard fault analysis
- stack analyzer
- project management
- version control

Interested readers should be able to find many example projects using the TrueStudio on the Internet. The IDE is free of charge and can be downloaded from the following website:

https://atollic.com/truestudio

5.2.5 System Workbench for STM32 by AC6

The *System Workbench for STM32* (SW4STM32) toolchain, called SW4STM32, is a free of charge development environment-based on Eclipse and it supports the full range of STM32 microcontrollers. The key features of the SW4STM32 are:

- full support of all STM32 processors and most development boards
- free of charge with no code size limit or no time limit
- Eclipse IDE with teamwork management
- compatible with the Eclipse plug-ins
- ST-LINK support
- C/C++ compiler and debugger

Users have to register before downloading and using this IDE. The IDE can be downloaded from the following website:

http://www.openstm32.org/HomePage

5.2.6 MikroC Pro for ARM

MikroC Pro for ARM is a professional IDE developed by mikroElektronika (www.mikroe. com). This IDE supports almost all types of Cortex-based ARM microcontrollers and it has the following features:

- supports for over 1300 types of ARM-based processors
- supports for Cortex-M0, M0+, M4, and M7 microcontrollers
- supports for over 1200 library functions
- over 400 example programs
- C type compiler, developed for embedded design
- free code limited version
- supports for FreeRTOS real-time multitasking kernel
- supports for LCD, GLCD, and TFT graphics
- supports for Library Manager, Interrupt Assistant, Project Explorer, Quick Converter
- supports for bitmap editor and 7-segment LED editor
- supports for UDP, UART, and HID terminals
- ASCII chart
- active comments editor
- advanced statistics
- supports for simulator and debugger
- supports for hardware in-circuit debugger
- code assistant
- comprehensive documentation
- uploading the executable code to the target processor via a development board or a programmer device
- online technical support

A free 2K code size limited version of the IDE is available that can be used to try the IDE to develop small projects, or for educational purposes, or for learning the features of the IDE. A USB-based dongle is available at a charge to enable licensed users to develop large programs. Alternatively, users can request license codes or site licenses without the need to use a dongle. The IDE without a dongle or a license can be downloaded from the following website (the same IDE is used with a dongle or a license):

https://www.mikroe.com/mikroc-arm

MikroC Pro for ARM is the IDE that will be used in all the projects in this book. The FreeRTOS real-time multitasking kernel is included in the latest version of the compiler. The IDE includes the Visual TFT software package and the TFT library which supports over 17 TFT controllers for developing TFT-based graphics projects. The TFT library includes a large number of built-in functions for drawing various shapes, drawing lines, drawing graphs, displaying text at different sizes, and many more functions. Users can easily switch between the graphical screens and the compiler. The developed graphical programs can be compiled and uploaded to the program memory of the target processor.

The Libstock website (https://libstock.mikroe.com) is a collection of large numbers of example projects, developed by general users of the public, and by the programmers of mikroElektronika. These projects have been developed to be compatible for use with all types of compilers of mikroElektronika. Additionally, libraries and SDK (software development kit) are included for all the Click boards to ease using and programming the Click boards. The example programs and the libraries can easily be installed to the user environments with a single click. The Libstock website provides example programs for almost all of the 800 Click boards developed and manufactured by mikroElektronika.

5.3 Summary

In this chapter we have briefly looked at the various IDEs that can be used to develop STM32 ARM-based projects. The mikroC Pro for ARM will be used in all of the projects in this book. In the next chapter we shall be looking at a simple project using the Clicker 2 for STM32 development board described in Chapter 4, and learn how to use the mikroC Pro for STM32 to create a project, to compile the code, and then to upload the executable code to the program memory of the target microcontroller.

Further readings

[1] D. Ibrahim, Programming With STM32 Nucleo Boards, Elektor, Netherlands, 2014, ISBN: 978-1-907920-68-4.
[2] D. Norris, Programming with STM32, Getting Started with the Nucleo Board and C/C++, McGraw Hill, USA, 2014, ISBN: 978-1-260-03131-7.

Programming using the mikroC Pro for ARM

6.1 Overview

In the last chapter we had a look at the various Integrated Development Environments (IDEs) that can be used to program the ARM-based microcontrollers. In this book we shall be using the mikroC Pro for ARM in all the projects. This chapter describes the basic features of this IDE and gives an example project to illustrate how a program can be created, compiled, and then uploaded to the program memory of the Clicker 2 for STM32 development board. The example given in this chapter is based on the STM32F407VCT6 microcontroller since this is the processor used on the Clicker 2 for STM32 development board.

6.2 MikroC Pro for ARM

MikroC Pro for ARM (simply called mikroC from now onwards) is very similar to the standard C language but it has been developed specifically for programming ARM-based microcontrollers. mikroC allows a programmer to:

- Write source code using the built-in text editor
- Include the required library to speed up the development process
- Manage your project easily
- Monitor program structure, variables, and functions
- Generate assembly, HEX, and list files for programming the target processor
- Use the integrated simulator to debug code on your PC
- Use the integrated hardware debugger to speed up program development and testing
- Get detailed reports on memory usage, calling tree, assembly listings, and more
- Program the target processor using the integrated programming software (not available for the Clicker 2 for STM32 development board since this board is programmed using a Bootloader program).

ARM-Based Microcontroller Multitasking Projects. http://dx.doi.org/10.1016/B978-0-12-821227-1.00006-2

mikroC includes libraries on hardware, digital signal processing, ANSI C, and others. Some more commonly used libraries are (there are over 60 libraries):

- ADC library
- CAN library
- EEPROM library
- Ethernet library
- GPIO library
- LCD and graphics LCD library
- Keypad library
- Sound library
- UART library
- TFT display library
- Touch panel library
- USB library
- Digital filter libraries (FIR and IIR)
- FFT library
- Matrices library
- ANSI C Math library
- Button library
- Conversions library
- Time library
- Trigonometry library

mikroC includes a built-in integrated Help facility that helps programmers to learn the format of various library statements and also to check the syntax of program statements. The advantage of this help utility is that not like the paper documentation, the help utility is up to date. mikroC organizes applications into project folders, consisting of a single project file, one or more source files, and header files, all in the same folder. The IDE helps programmers to create multiple projects. Project folders consist of the following:

- Project name
- Target microcontroller device
- Device clock
- List of project source files
- Header files
- Binary files
- Image files
- Other files

Fig. 6.1 shows the structure of a mikroC program written for the Clicker 2 for STM32 development board (as mentioned earlier, readers should note that this development board uses the STM32F407VGT6 microcontroller). Although comments are optional in a program, it is highly recommended as it makes a program easier to understand and maintain in the future. This very simple program (program: **LED.c**) flashes the on-board LED connected to port pin PE12 every second. We shall see in this chapter some of the STM32F407VCT6 specific features of the mikroC language. Most of the features described in this chapter are applicable to other members of the STM32 family.

```
/**************************************************************************
                              FLASHING LED
                              ============

In this project the on-board LED connected to PE12 of the Clicker 2 for
STM32 development board is flashed every second

Author: Dogan Ibrahim
File   : LED.c
Date   : September, 2019

**************************************************************************/
#define LED GPIOE_ODR.B12

void main()
{

  GPIO_Digital_Output(&GPIOE_BASE, _GPIO_PINMASK_12);    // Set PE12 as digital output

  while(1)                                               // Do Forever
  {
      LED = 1;                                           // LED ON
      Delay_ms(1000);                                    // 1 second delay
      LED = 0;                                           // LED OFF
      Delay_ms(1000);                                    // 1 second delay
  }
}
```

FIGURE 6.1   A simple program that flashes an LED.

People familiar with the standard C language will notice in Fig. 6.1 that there is no library *include* files (i.e., header files) at the beginning of the program. This is because all library files are automatically included by the compiler when a new file is created.

In the remainder of this chapter, the important GPIO library (which is used in almost all projects) and some STM32 specific features of the mikroC are described. In addition, the steps to create, compile, and upload a program to the Clicker 2 for STM32 development board are described.

6.3 The general purpose input-output library

The mikroC general purpose input-output (GPIO) library includes a set of routines for easier handling of the GPIO pin functions. The library contains the following functions (only the STM32 processor-specific features are described in this section):

- GPIO_Clk_Enable
- GPIO_Clk_Disable
- GPIO_Config
- GPIO_Set_Pin_Mode

- GPIO_Digital_Input
- GPIO_Digital_Output
- GPIO_Analog_Input
- GPIO_Alternate_Function_Enable

6.3.1 GPIO_Clk_Enable

This function enables the clock on the desired port. In the following example code, clock is enabled on PORTE:

GPIO_Clock_Enable(&GPIO_BASE)

6.3.2 GPIO_Clk_Disable

This function disables the clock on the desired port. In the following example code, clock is disabled on PORTE:

GPIO_Clock_Disable(&GPIO_BASE)

6.3.3 GPIO_Config

This function is used to configure port pins according to the parameters specified. The function has the following format:

void GPIO_Config(unsigned long *port, unsigned int pin_mask, unsigned long config)

where *port* is the PORT we wish to use, *pin_mask* is the pin we wish to configure, and *config* is the desired configuration of the port pin.

The function returns a 0 if there are no errors. In the following example, PORTA pins 0 and 7 are configured as digital inputs with no pull-up or pull-down resistors:

GPIO_Config(&GPIOA_BASE,_GPIO_PINMASK_0 | _GPIO_PINMASK_7,

_GPIO_CFG_MODE_INPUT | _GPIO_CFG_PULL_NO);

Similarly, the following example configures all pins of PORTB as digital outputs with push-pull output transistors:

GPIO_Config(&GPIOB_BASE,_GPIO_PINMASK_ALL,

_GPIO_CFG_MODE_OUTPUT | _GPIO_CFG_OTYPE_PP);

The following example configures PORTB pin 1 as digital output:

GPIO_Config(&GPIOB_BASE,_GPIO_PINMASK_1,

_GPIO_CFG_MODE_OUTPUT);

pin_mask can take the following values:

_GPIO_PINMASK_0	pin 0 mask
_GPIO_PINMASK_1	pin 1 mask
....	
_GPIO_PINMASK_15	pin 15 mask
_GPIO_PINMASK_LOW	low 8 port pins
_GPIO_PINMASK_HIGH	high 8 port pins
_GPIO_PINMASK_ALL	all pins masked

config can take different values depending upon the port usage. The following values are valid:

Basic

_GPIO_CFG_PULL_UP	configure pins as pull-up
_GPIO_CFG_PULL_DOWN	configure pins as pull-down
_GPIO_CFG_PULL_NO	configure pins as floating (no pull-up/down)
_GPIO_CFG_MODE_ALT_FUNCTION	pins have alternate functions (non GPIO)
_GPIO_CFG_MODE_ANALOG	configure pins for analog
_GPIO_CFG_OTYPE_OD	configure pins as open-drain
_GPIO_CFG_OTYPE_PP	configure pins as push-pull
_GPIO_CFG_SPEED_400KHZ	configure pins for 400 kHz clock
_GPIO_CFG_SPEED_2MHZ	configure pins for 2 MHz clock
_GPIO_CFG_SPEED_10MHZ	configure pins for 10 MHz clock
_GPIO_CFG_SPEED_25MHZ	configure pins for 25 MHz clock
_GPIO_CFG_SPEED_40MHZ	configure pins for 40 MHz clock
_GPIO_CFG_SPEED_50MHZ	configure pins for 50 MHZ clock
_GPIO_CFG_SPEED_100MHZ	configure pins for 100 MHZ clock
_GPIO_CFG_SPEED_MAX	configure pins for maximum clock
_GPIO_CFG_DIGITAL_OUTPUT	configure pins as digital output
_GPIO_CFG_DIGITAL_INPUT	configure pins as digital input
_GPIO_CFG_ANALOG_INPUT	configure pins as analog input

Timer

These are timer functions and the function name changes depending upon the timer used. For example, for Timer 1 the following functions are available (similar functions are available for other timers, see the HELP file for more details):

_GPIO_CFG_AF_TIM1	Timer 1 alternate function mapping
_GPIO_CFG_AF2_TIM2	Timer 1 alternate function 2 mapping
_GPIO_CFG_AF6_TIM1	Timer 1 alternate function 6 mapping
_GPIO_CFG_AF11_TIM1	Timer 1 alternate function 11 mapping

I2C

The following functions are available for I²C operation:

_GPIO_CFG_AF_I2C1	Alternate function mapping
_GPIO_CFG_AF4_I2C1	Alternate function 4 mapping

_GPIO_CFG_AF_I2C2	Alternate function mapping
_GPIO_CFG_AF4_I2C2	Alternate function 4 mapping
_GPIO_CFG_AF_I2C3	Alternate function mapping

SPI
Some SPI functions are (see the HELP file for more details):

_GPIO_CFG_AF_SPI1	SPI1 alternate function mapping
_GPIO_CFG_AF5_API1	SPI1 alternate function 5 mapping

USART
Some USART functions are (see the HELP file for more details):

_GPIO_CFG_AF_USART1	USART1 alternate function mapping
_GPIO_CFG_AF7_USART1	USART1 alternate function 7 mapping

CAN
Some CAN functions are (see the HELP file for more details):

_GPIO_CFG_AF_CAN1	CAN1 alternate function mapping
_GPIO_CFG_AF_CAN2	CAN2 alternate function 7 mapping

USB
Some USB functions are (see the HELP file for more details):

_GPIO_CFG_AF_USB	USB alternate function mapping
_GPIO_CFG_AF14_USB	USB alternate function 14 mapping

I2S
Some I^{2}S functions are (see the HELP file for more details):

_GPIO_CFG_AF5_I2S1	I2S alternate function 5 mapping
_GPIO_CFG_AF6_I2S1	I2S alternate function 6 mapping

TSC
Some TSC functions are (see the HELP file for more details):

_GPIO_CFG_AF3_TSC_G1	TSC Group 1 alternate function 3 mapping
_GPIO_CFG_AF3_TSC_G2	TSC Group 2 alternate function 3 mapping

RTC
RTC functions are:

_GPIO_CFG_AF_RTC_50 Hz	RTC 50Hz alternate function mapping
_GPIO_CFG_AF_RTC_AF1	RTC alternate function mapping
_GPIO_CFG_AF_TAMPER	TAMPER alternate function mapping

MCO
MCO functions are:

_GPIO_CFG_AF_MCO	MCO1 and MCO2 alternate function mapping
_GPIO_CFG_AF0_TSC_G2	MCO1 and MCO2 alternate function 0 mapping
_GPIO_CFG_AF_MCO1	MCO1 alternate function mapping

DEBUG

DEBUG functions are:

_GPIO_CFG_AF_SWJ	SWJ alternate function mapping
_GPIO_CFG_AF_TRACE	TRACE alternate function mapping
_GPIO_CFG_AF0_TRACE	TRACE alternate function 0 mapping

MISC

Some other functions are (see HELP file for more details):

_GPIO_CFG_AF_WKUP	Wakeup alternate function mapping
_GPIO_CFG_AF_LCD	LCD alternate function mapping
_GPIO_CFG_ETH	ETHERNET alternate function mapping

6.3.4 GPIO_Set_Pin_Mode

This function configures the desired pin according to the parameters used. The function has the following format:

GPIO_Set_Pin_Mode(port_base : ^dword; pin : word; config : dword;)

where *port_base* is the port to be used, *pin* is the pin we wish to configure, and *config* is the desired pin configuration.

pin can take the following values:

_GPIO_PIN_0	pin 0
_GPIO_PIN_1	pin 1
....	
_GPIO_PIN_15	pin 15

config can take the following values:

_GPIO_CFG_MODE_INPUT	set pin as input
_GPIO_CFG_MODE_OUTPUT	set pin as output
_GPIO_CFG_PULL_UP	configure pin as pull-up
_GPIO_CFG_PULL_DOWN	configure pin as pull-down
_GPIO_CFG_PULL_NO	configure pin as floating
_GPIO_CFG_MODE ALT_FUNCTION	pin has alternate function (non GPIO)
_GPIO_CFG_MODE_ANALOG	configure pin for analog input
_GPIO_CFG_OTYPE_OD	configure pin as open-drain
_GPIO_CFG_OTYPE_PP	configure pin as push-pull
_GPIO_CFG_SPEED_400KHZ	configure pin for 400 kHz clock
_GPIO_CFG_SPEED_2MHZ	configure pin for 2 MHz clock
_GPIO_CFG_SPEED_10MHZ	configure pin for 10 MHz clock
_GPIO_CFG_SPEED_25MHZ	configure pin for 25 MHz clock
_GPIO_CFG_SPEED_50MHZ	configure pin for 50 MHz clock
_GPIO_CFG_SPEED_100MHZ	configure pin for 100 MHz clock
_GPIO_CFG_SPEED_MAX	configure pin for maximum clock

In the following example, PORTE pin 0 is configured as digital output with push-pull driver transistors:

```
GPIO_Set_Pin_Mode(&GPIOE_BASE, _GPIO_PIN_0,
_GPIO_CFG_MODE_OUTPUT |
_GPIO_CFG_PULL_UP)
```

6.3.5 GPIO_Digital_Input

This function configures the desired port pins as digital inputs. The format of this function is:

void GPIO_Digital_Input(**unsigned long** *port, **unsigned long** pin_mask)

where *port* is the port to be configured and *pin_mask* is the mask as defined in Section 6.3.3. In the following example, PORTC pins 0 and 1 are configured as digital inputs:

```
GPIO_Digital_Input(&GPIOC_BASE, _GPIO_PINMASK_0 |

_GPIO_PINMASK_1);
```

6.3.6 GPIO_Digital_Output

This function configures the desired port pins as digital outputs. The format of this function is:

void GPIO_Digital_Output(**unsigned long** *port, **unsigned long** pin_mask)

where *port* is the port to be configured and *pin_mask* is the mask as defined in Section 6.3.3. In the following example, PORTC pins 0 and 1 are configured as digital outputs:

```
GPIO_Digital_Output(&GPIOC_BASE, _GPIO_PINMASK_0 |
_GPIO_PINMASK_1);
```

6.3.7 GPIO_Analog_Input

This function configures the desired port pins as analog inputs. The format of this function is:

void GPIO_Analog_Input(**unsigned long** *port, **unsigned long** pin_mask)

In the following example, PORTC pin 0 is configured as analog input:

```
GPIO_Analog_Input(&GPIOC_BASE, _GPIO_PINMASK_0);
```

6.3.8 GPIO_Alternate_Function_Enable

This routine enables desired alternative function on GPIO pins using a predefined internal module pinout as a parameter. The format of this function is:

void GPIO_Alternate_Function_Enable(**const** Module_Struct *module)

where *Module Struct* is the desired module pinout (see the mikroC Pro for ARM HELP file for a list of predefined module pinouts).

6.4 Memory type specifiers

Each variable in mikroC may be assigned to a specific memory space by using a memory type specifier. A list of the memory type specifiers is given below:

- code
- data
- sfr
- ccm

code is used to allocate constants in the program memory. In the following example, character array *Dat* is placed in the program memory:

const code char Dat[] = "Test";

data is used to store variables in the data RAM. An example is given below:

data char count;

sfr allows users to access special function registers. An example is given below:

extern sfr char tst;

ccm allows users to allocate variables in the Core Coupled Memory (for Cortex-M4 only). An example is given below:

ccm unsigned char cnt;

6.5 PORT input-output

PORT output and input data are accessed using the GPIOx_ODR and GPIOx_IDR registers, respectively. For example, PORTA can be set to all HIGH with the statement:

GPIOA_ODR = 0xFFFF;

Similarly, for example, PORTA data can be read and stored in variable Cnt with the statement:

Cnt = GPIOA_IDR;

6.6 Accessing individual bits

mikroC allows us to access individual bits of variables. B0–B15 (or F0–F15) are used to access bits 0–15 of a variable, respectively. **sbit** data type provides access to registers, SFRs, variables, etc. **at** is used to make alias to a variable. In the following example, LED can be used to access bit 3 of PORTA:

sbit LED **at** GPIOA_ODR.B3;

similarly, the **#define** statement can be used to access for example bit 3 of PORTA:

#define LED GPIOA_ODR.B3

6.7 Bit data type

mikroC provides a **bit** data type that can be used to define single bits in programs. An example is shown below:

bit x;

Notice that bit variables cannot be initialized and they cannot be members of structures or unions.

6.8 Interrupts and exceptions

Cortex-M3 supports Nested Vector Interrupt Controller (NVIC) with a number of exceptions and a number of external interrupts (IRQs). Depending upon the processor type used, a large number of external interrupts (e.g., up to 240) with many priority levels (e.g., up to 250) can be declared. The vector table contains the addresses of exception handlers and interrupt service routines (ISRs).

6.8.1 Exceptions

Based on their priority levels, on Cortex-M3 processors interrupts/exceptions are divided into two types: configurable and unconfigurable.

Unconfigurable exceptions

The unconfigurable exceptions have fixed priorities and consist of the following types:

- **Reset**: this has the highest priority (-3) and when asserted execution restarts from the address provided by the reset entry point in the vector table.
- **NMI**: Nonmaskable interrupt (NMI) has the highest priority exception (-2) other than Reset. NMI cannot be masked or prevented by other exceptions.
- **Hard Fault:** These exceptions have priority -1 and they occur because an exception cannot be handled properly.

Configurable exceptions

You can assign a priority level from 0 to 255 to an interrupt. Hardware priority decreases with increasing interrupt number. Thus, priority level 0 is the highest priority level, and priority 255 is the lowest priority level. When multiple interrupts occur with the same priority numbers, the interrupt with the lowest interrupt number (highest priority) takes precedence.

Configurable exceptions have programmable priorities and they consist of the following types:

- **Memory management**: This exception occurs when a memory protection fault has happened. The priority level is programmable.
- **Bus fault**: This exception occurs because of a memory fault or because of an error on the bus.

- **Usage fault**: This type of exception occurs because of a fault in an instruction such as undefined instruction, illegal access, invalid state on instruction execution, or an error on exception return. For example, division by zero.
- **SVCall**: The Supervisor Call (SVC) exception occurs by an application using the SVC instruction to access kernel functions or device drivers.
- **PendSV**: This is an interrupt driven request for system-level services.
- **SysTick**: This exception is generated by the system timer when it reaches zero.
- **Interrupts (IRQ)**: This type of exception is triggered by a peripheral, or generated by software.

6.8.2 Interrupt service routine

ISRs are defined as functions in the following format (e.g., for Timer 7 interrupts):

void interrupt() iv IVT_INT_TIM7 ics ICS_OFF

{

interrupt service routine here…

}

where
iv is a reserved word to inform the compiler that this is an ISR
IVT_INT_TIM7 is the Interrupt Vector for Timer 7 (different interrupt sources have different vector names)
ics is the Interrupt Context Saving, which can have the values:

ICS_OFF: no context saving
ICS_AUTO: compiler chooses whether the context saving will be done

The **Interrupt Assistant** utility of mikroC can be used to create ISR templates. To use the Interrupt Assistant, start the mikroC IDE and click on *Tools -> Interrupt Assistant*. You should see a form as in Fig. 6.2. Enter the desired ISR function name (e.g., *button*), choose the type of interrupt source (e.g., *INT_TIM2*), choose the ICS parameter (e.g., *AUTO*) and then click OK (see Fig. 6.3). The following ISR code template will be automatically generated:

void button() iv IVT_INT_TIM2 ics ICS_AUTO {
}

FIGURE 6.2   Interrupt Assistant form.

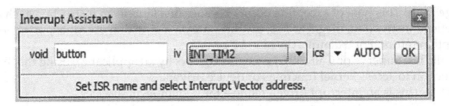

FIGURE 6.3   Interrupt Assistant example.

6.9 Creating a new project

The aim of the project created in this section is to show how to develop a project, then how to compile and upload the executable code to the program memory of the target processor. In this section, we will flash the LED connected to port pin PE12 of the Clicker 2 for STM32 development board every second. In this project we shall be using the external 25 MHz crystal as the timing source.

The steps in creating a new mikroC project are given below:

- **Step 1**: Start the mikroC Pro for ARM IDE by clicking on its icon. Fig. 6.4 shows parts of the IDE screen.
- **Step 2:** Create a new project by clicking *New Project*. Select *Standard project* and click *Next*. As shown in Fig. 6.5, give a name to your project (e.g., LED) and specify a folder (e.g., D:\ARM). Choose the device name as STM32F407VG and set the device clock to 168MHz. Click *Next*. Click *Finish* and you should see the main IDE window shown in Fig. 6.6.

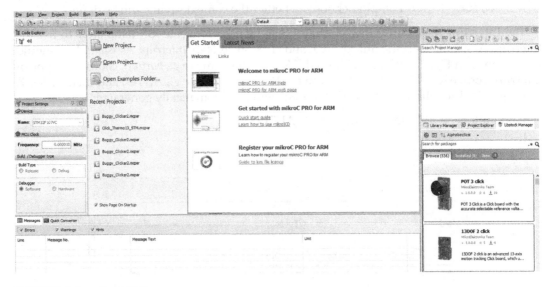

FIGURE 6.4   mikroC IDE screen.

New Project Wizard			✕

Steps:

1. Project type
2. **Project settings**
3. Add files

Project Settings:

Project Name: LED

Project folder: D:\ARM\   Browse

Device name: STM32F407VG

Device clock: 168.000000 MHz

Open Edit Project window to set Configuration bits ☐

Enter project name, project folder, select device name and enter a device clock (for example: 80.000).

Checking 'Open Edit Project' option will open 'Edit Project' window after closing this wizard. This enables you to easily setup your device and project.

Note: Project name and project folder must not be left empty.

◆ Back   Next ◆   Cancel

FIGURE 6.5   Create a new project.

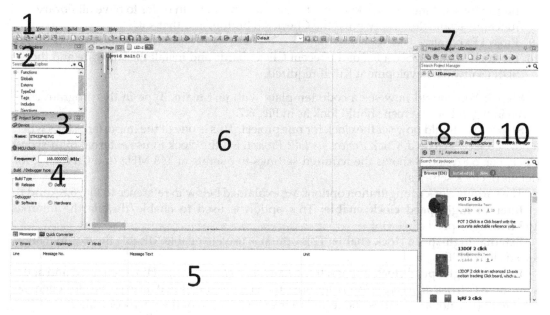

FIGURE 6.6   Main IDE window.

The parts of the screen are as follows:

1. Top Menu Bar. There are icons just at the bottom of the Menu Bar for quick access to various features and tools of the IDE.
2. The Code Explorer is located at the top left corner of the screen. You can see a list of functions, weblinks, and active comments in the project you opened.
3. Project Settings. In this section, you have the name of the device you are using, and the frequency of the microcontroller clock. The frequency of the clock determines the speed of the microcontroller.
4. Select the build or debugger type. You should select **Release** for the Build Type.
5. Messages. In case that errors were encountered during compiling, the compiler will report them in the Message box, and a hex file will not be generated. The compiler also reports warnings, but these do not affect the output; only errors can interfere with the generation of a successful hex file.
6. The Code Editor features adjustable Syntax Highlighting, Code Folding, Code Assistant, Parameters Assistant, Auto Correct for common typos, and Code Templates.
7. The Project Manager is an IDE feature which allows you to manage multiple projects. It shows source and header files in each project. Several projects can be open at the same time, but only one of them may be active at any one time. To set a project in an active mode you need to double click on the desired project in the Project Manager.
8. The Library Manager allows you to work with the libraries in a simple and easy way. The Library Manager window lists all libraries. The desired library is added to the project by selecting the checkbox next to the library name. In order to have all library functions available, simply press the Check All button, and that's it.
9. Project Explorer.
10. Libstock Manager. See a list of the recent Click boards and install the software and the SDK (Software Development Kit) if required.

Step 3: You should now see a code template with just **main**. Type in the program code given in Fig. 6.1. The screen should look as in Fig. 6.7.

Step 4: We should now set the clock for our project. This is one of the important steps when a new project is created. Click *Project -> Edit Project*. Set the clock to use external high-speed clock. Fig. 6.8A and B shows the required settings to operate at 168 MHz (see Chapter 2 for details of clock settings).

The various clock configuration options are explained below in reference to Fig. 6.8A and B.

Internal high-speed clock enable: This option is used to enable/disable the internal 16 MHz high-speed clock HSI.

External high-speed clock enable: This option is used to enable/disable the external high-speed clock HSE.

External high-speed clock bypass: If the *External high-speed clock* HSE is enabled and at the same time *External high-speed clock is bypassed,* then it is assumed that an external clock generator circuit (i.e., not a crystal) is connected to the OSC_IN pin of the microcontroller.

Clock security system enable: This option is used to enable/disable the clock security system. When enabled, if there is an error in the HSE oscillator, the HIS oscillator automatically starts running and generates a clock for the microcontroller. At the same time, an interrupt is generated.

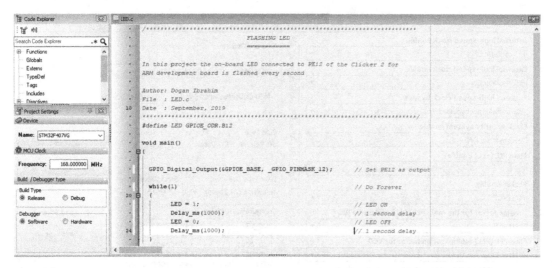

FIGURE 6.7   Write your program.

Main PLL enable: This option enables/disables the PLL block.

PLLI2S enable: This option enables/disables the PLLI2S block.

Division factor for the man PLL and Audio PLL (PLLI2S) input clock: This option selects the main PLL division factor. This is shown as **PLL_M** in Fig. 6.8.

Main PLL (PLL) multiplication factor for VCO: This option is used to select the main PLL multiplication factor for VCO. This is shown as **PLL_N** in Fig. 6.8.

Main PLL (PLL) division factor for main system clock: This option is used to select the AHB prescaler. It is shown as **PLL_P** in Fig. 6.8.

Main PLL (PLL) and audio PLL (PLLI2S) entry clock source: This option is used to select the PLL block that provides clock to the Main PLL and to the I2S. The HSE or HIS clocks can be selected from here. This is shown as **PLL Source Clock** in Fig. 6.8.

Main PLL (PLL) division factor for USB OTG FS, SDIO and random number generator clocks: Select the division factor for USB, SDIO and random number generator. This is shown as **PLL_Q** in Fig. 6.8.

System clock switch: This is used to select the system clock either from HIS, HSE, or PLL.

Set and cleared by software to control the division factor of the AHB clock: This is used to select the division factor to derive the AHB clock from the system clock SYSCLK. This is shown as **AHBx Prescaler** in Fig. 6.8.

APB low-speed prescaler (APB1): This is used to select the low-speed APB1 clock (PCLK1). It is shown as **APB1 Prescaler** in Fig. 6.8.

APB high-speed prescaler (APB2): This is used to select the high-speed APB2 clock (PCLK2). It is shown as **APB2 Prescaler** in Fig. 6.8.

HSE division factor for RTC clock: This option is used to select the division factor for the RTC clock.

Microcontroller clock output 1: This option is used to select the microcontroller clock output (MCO1) from either HIS, HSE, LSE, or PLL.

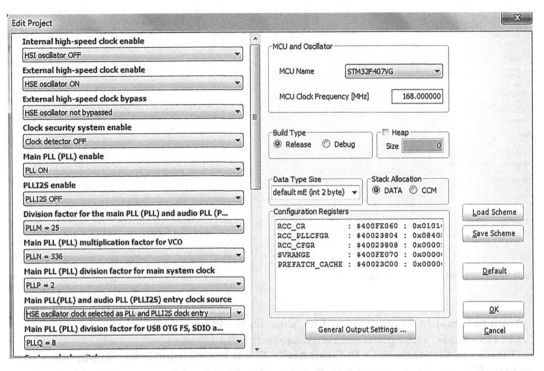

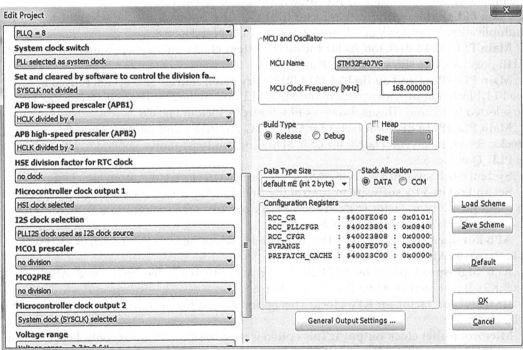

FIGURE 6.8 (A) Clock selection. (B) Clock selection.

I2S clock selection: This option is used to select the I²S clock source. The PLLI2S or external clock source connected to the I2S_CKIN pin can be selected.

MCO1 prescaler: This option is used to select the MCO1 output clock prescaler.

MCO2PRE: This option is used to select the MCO2 prescaler.

Microcontroller clock output 2: This option is used to select the microcontroller clock 2 output (MCO2) either from SYSCLK, PLLI2S, HSE, or PLL.

Voltage range: Use this option to select voltage range.

Prefetch and cache option: This option is used to enable or disable the prefetch and cache if we wish to store data in the flash memory area.

It is important that the following rules are obeyed while configuring the clock:

- The frequency to the input of the PLL modules must be between 1 and 2 MHz.
- The frequency at the output of the PLL modules must be between 64 and 432 MHz.
- The USB frequency must be 48 MHz.
- Make sure that PLL_N > 1, PLL_Q > 1, and PLL_P = 2, 4, 6, or 8.
- AHB frequency must not be greater than 168 MHz.
- APB1 frequency must not be greater than 42 MHz.
- APB2 frequency must not be greater than 84 MHz.

An example is given below to illustrate how the clock configuration can be done in a new project.

Example

It is required to configure the clock to use the internal high-speed clock (16 MHz) and operate the STM32F407VGT6 microcontroller with 168 MHz. Assume that the RTC, USB, or I²S are not used in this application.

Solution

The required clock settings are:

Internal high-speed clock:	ON
External high-speed clock:	OFF
External high-speed clock bypass:	HSE oscillator not bypassed
Clock security system enable:	Clock detector OFF
Main PLL (PLL) enable:	PLL ON
PLLI2S enable:	PLLI2S OFF
Division factor for the main PLL and…:	PLLM = 16
Main PLL (PLL) multiplication factor:	PLLN = 336
Main PLL (PLL) division factor for main..:	PLLP = 2
Main PLL (PLL) and Audio PLL (PLLI2S):	HSI oscillator clock selected as PLL…
Main PLL (PLL) division factor for USB..:	(not important here)
System clock switch:	PLL selected as system clock
Set and cleared by software to control the…:	SYSCLK not divided
APB low-speed prescaler (APB1):	HCLK divided by 4
APB high-speed prescaler (APB2):	HCLK divided by 2
HSE division factor for RTC clock:	no clock
Microcontroller clock output 1:	(not important here)
I2S clock selection:	(not important here)

MCO1 prescaler:	(not important here)
MCO2PRE:	(not important here)
Microcontroller clock output 2:	(not important here)
Voltage range:	2.7–3.6 V
Prefetch and cache option:	(not important here)

In this example the internal 16 MHZ HSI clock is divided by 16 to give 1 MHZ and is then multiplied by 336 to give the 336 MHz and divided by 2 to give the 168 MHz system clock.

Step 5: We are now ready to compile the program. Click *Build- > Build* or click the *Build* icon (see Fig. 6.9). Your program should compile with no errors as shown in Fig. 6.10. Notice that memory usage and compilation time are given at the bottom of the screen inside the message window. The compiler generates various files, such as the assembly listing, HEX file, configuration file and so on (some of these files are generated optionally). The important file is the HEX file as it is used to upload the program memory of the target microcontroller.

6.9.1 Uploading the executable code

The microcontroller on the Clicker 2 for STM32 development board can be programmed using the Bootloader firmware which has already been loaded to the microcontroller memory by the manufacturers. We need to install the mikroBootloader software to our PC so that we

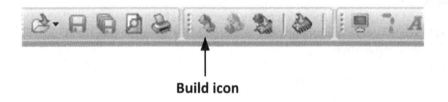

Build icon

FIGURE 6.9   Build icon.

Message Text

Used RX: 16 (100%)   Free RX: 0 (0%)

Static RAM (bytes): 8   Dynamic RAM (bytes): 131061

Used ROM (bytes): 2392 (0%) Free ROM (bytes): 1046184 (100%)

Project Linked Successfully

Linked in 281 ms

Project 'LED.mcpar' completed: 484 ms

Finished successfully: 17 Aug 2019, 10:24:25

FIGURE 6.10   Program compiled with no errors.

can upload our executable code to the program memory of the target processor. The steps to install the mikroBootloader are as follows:

- Go to web site: https://www.mikroe.com/clicker-2-stm32f4
- Click on *clicker 2 STM32 Bootloader* at the bottom of the screen
- Copy the software to a folder of your choice (e.g., to Desktop)

The steps to upload the executable code to the microcontroller memory are as follows:

- Connect the Clicker 2 for STM32 development board to your PC using a mini USB cable, and turn on the power switch. You should see the green power LED to turn ON.
- Start the mikroBootloader on your PC.
- Press and release the red Reset button next to the power switch on your development board.
- Click the *Connect* button on the mikroBootloader application as soon as possible (you should do this within 5 s, otherwise the microcontroller performs a hardware reset and starts executing the previously loaded user program—if there is already one). You should see the **Connected** message (see Fig. 6.11).

FIGURE 6.11   Connect the mikcroBootloader to the development board.

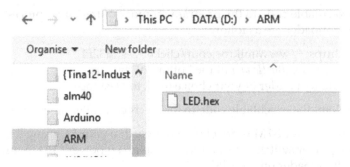

FIGURE 6.12 Select the HEX file of your application.

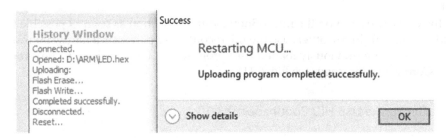

FIGURE 6.13 Uploading the executable code to target processor.

- Click the **Browse for HEX** button and select the HEX file of your application program (Fig. _6.12). You should see a message similar to:
- Opened: D:\ARM\LED.hex
- Click *Begin uploading* to start uploading the executable code to the program memory of the microcontroller on your development board. You should see a successful upload message as shown in Fig. 6.13.
- If everything went well then you should see the red LED on the development board flashing every second.

6.10 Simulation

Simulation is a useful tool during program development as it helps to detect programming errors at an early stage before the code is loaded to the program memory of the target microcontroller. Simulation is normally carried out on a PC and it can be used to single-step through a program, to set breakpoints, and to view and modify processor registers and variables used in the program. In this section we will be seeing how to simulate the simple LED flashing program developed in the previous section.

The steps to simulate our program are given below:

Step 1: Click *Run -> Start Debugger*. The simulation window will open on the right-hand side as shown in Fig. 6.14. The blue bar across the screen shows where the program step is currently located and it should be at the beginning of the program by default.

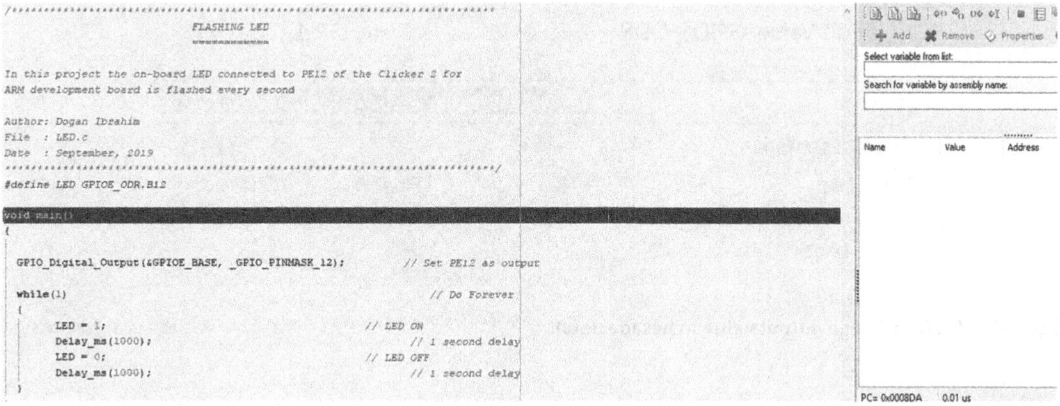

```
/********************************************************************
                    FLASHING LED
                    ============

In this project the on-board LED connected to PE12 of the Clicker 2 for
ARM development board is flashed every second

Author: Dogan Ibrahim
File  : LED.c
Date  : September, 2019
********************************************************************/
#define LED GPIOE_ODR.B12

void main()
{

  GPIO_Digital_Output(&GPIOE_BASE, _GPIO_PINMASK_12);    // Set PE12 as output

  while(1)                                               // Do Forever
  {
    LED = 1;                        // LED ON
    Delay_ms(1000);                          // 1 second delay
    LED = 0;                    // LED OFF
    Delay_ms(1000);                          // 1 second delay
  }
}
```

PC= 0x0008DA   0.01 us

FIGURE 6.14   Simulation window.

Step 2: Let us view the contents of PORTE as the program is run in single-step mode. Select PORTE output register GPIOE_ODR and click *Add* (the + sign). PORTE will be added to the window (see Fig. 6.15) so that we can view its values as the program is run. Its value is shown as 0 at the moment.

Step 3: Keep pressing F8 to single-step through the program. You should see the blue bar moving through the program as the key is pressed.

Step 4: You should see the data at PORTE changing when the port value is toggled. Click on the *value* in the simulation window to change the output data from decimal to binary (see Fig. 6.16). You should see the port value displayed as 0000 0000 0000 0000 0001 0000 0000 0000, as shown in Fig. 6.17 where PE12 is set to 1.

Step 5: As you single-step through the program, port PE12 value will change between 0 and 1. Simulation timing statistics are shown at the bottom of the simulation window (see Fig. 6.18)

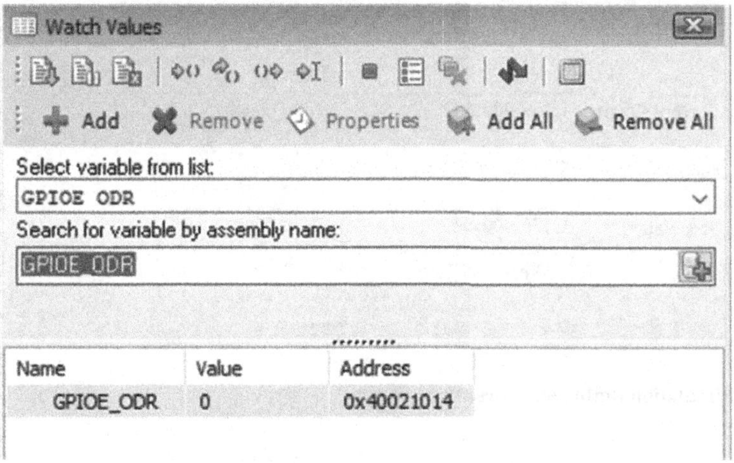

FIGURE 6.15   Add GPIOE_ODR to the simulation window.

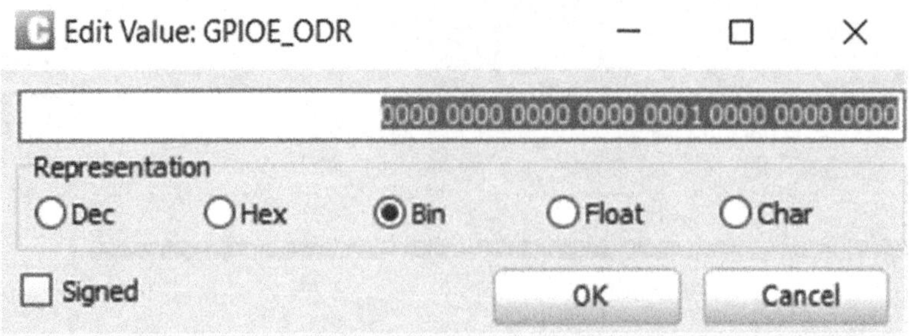

Edit Value: GPIOE_ODR   —   □   ✕

0000 0000 0000 0000 0001 0000 0000 0000

Representation
○ Dec   ○ Hex   ◉ Bin   ○ Float   ○ Char

☐ Signed   OK   Cancel

FIGURE 6.16 Change output value to hexadecimal.

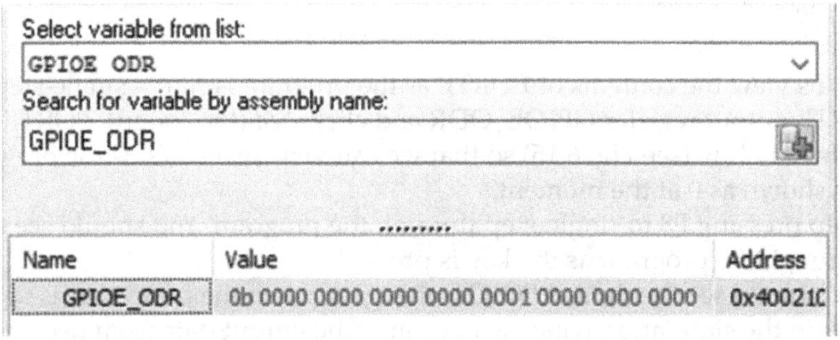

Select variable from list:
GPIOE ODR   ∨
Search for variable by assembly name:
GPIOE_ODR

Name	Value	Address
GPIOE_ODR	0b 0000 0000 0000 0000 0001 0000 0000 0000	0x400210

FIGURE 6.17 Port value changing to 0xFFFF.

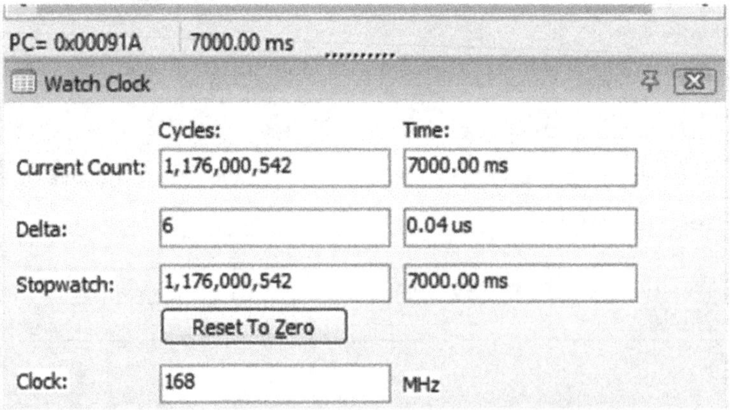

PC= 0x00091A   7000.00 ms

Watch Clock   ⏻ ☒

	Cycles:	Time:
Current Count:	1,176,000,542	7000.00 ms
Delta:	6	0.04 us
Stopwatch:	1,176,000,542	7000.00 ms
	Reset To Zero	
Clock:	168	MHz

FIGURE 6.18 Simulation timing statistics.

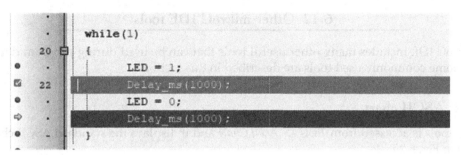

FIGURE 6.19 Setting a breakpoint.

6.10.1 Setting break points

Breakpoints are useful especially while testing large and complex programs. By setting a breakpoint in a program, we allow the program to run up to the breakpoint and then we can examine or modify the values of various registers and variables. An example is given in this section to show how a breakpoint can be set and variables examined in our program.

Step 1: Start the simulator as described in the previous section.

Step 2: Let us set a breakpoint at the instruction Delay_ms(1000). Put the cursor on this instruction and then click *Run -> Toggle Breakpoint* (or click F5). You should see a red bar at the breakpoint (see Fig. 6.19) and also a small arrow on the left-hand side of the instruction where the breakpoint is placed.

Step 3: Now run the program by clicking *Run -> Run/Pause Debugger* (or click F6). The program will run-up to the breakpoint and then stop. You can now view the output data of PORTE as shown earlier.

Step 4: You can remove the breakpoint by clicking *Run -> Toggle Breakpoint* or by clicking on the small arrow on the left-hand side of the instruction where the breakpoint is placed.

6.11 Debugging

Debugging is similar to simulation but is carried out on the target hardware. The hardware to be debugged usually consists of the complete project hardware including all the peripheral devices. By debugging we try to find errors in a program or in associated hardware (although only a limited number of hardware errors can be detected by the process of debugging).

In a typical debugging session, the developed program is uploaded to the program memory of the target microcontroller and then the actual debugging takes place while the program runs in real-time on the target microcontroller. As in simulation, the code can be single-stepped and breakpoints can be inserted into the code and registers and variables can easily be examined or modified as desired.

Unfortunately, we cannot run the debugger with the Clicker 2 for STM32 development board as it requires a hardware programmer device to be connected to the development board. But the steps for debugging are similar to the steps for simulation. The Build/Debugger type panel should be set to Debug and Hardware before the debugger can be started.

6.12 Other mikroC IDE tools

mikroC IDE includes many other useful tools that can be used during program development. Some commonly used tools are described in this section.

6.12.1 ASCII chart

This tools is accessed from *Tools -> Ascii Chart* and it displays the standard ASCII chart as shown in Fig. 6.20.

Ascii Chart

	0	1	2	3	4	5	6	7	8	9	A	B	C	D	E	F
0	NUL 0	SOH 1	STX 2	ETX 3	EOT 4	ENQ 5	ACK 6	BEL 7	BS 8	HT 9	LF 10	VT 11	FF 12	CR 13	SO 14	SI 15
1	DLE 16	DC1 17	DC2 18	DC3 19	DC4 20	NAK 21	SYN 22	ETB 23	CAN 24	EM 25	SUB 26	ESC 27	FS 28	GS 29	RS 30	US 31
2	SPC 32	! 33	" 34	# 35	$ 36	% 37	& 38	' 39	(40	) 41	* 42	+ 43	, 44	- 45	. 46	/ 47
3	0 48	1 49	2 50	3 51	4 52	5 53	6 54	7 55	8 56	9 57	: 58	; 59	< 60	= 61	> 62	? 63
4	@ 64	A 65	B 66	C 67	D 68	E 69	F 70	G 71	H 72	I 73	J 74	K 75	L 76	M 77	N 78	O 79
5	P 80	Q 81	R 82	S 83	T 84	U 85	V 86	W 87	X 88	Y 89	Z 90	[91	\ 92	] 93	^ 94	_ 95
6	` 96	a 97	b 98	c 99	d 100	e 101	f 102	g 103	h 104	i 105	j 106	k 107	l 108	m 109	n 110	o 111
7	p 112	q 113	r 114	s 115	t 116	u 117	v 118	w 119	x 120	y 121	z 122	{ 123	| 124	} 125	~ 126	DEL 127
8	€ 128	129	‚ 130	ƒ 131	„ 132	… 133	† 134	‡ 135	^ 136	‰ 137	Š 138	‹ 139	Œ 140	141	Ž 142	143
9	144	' 145	' 146	" 147	" 148	• 149	– 150	— 151	~ 152	™ 153	š 154	› 155	œ 156	157	ž 158	Ÿ 159
A	160	¡ 161	¢ 162	£ 163	¤ 164	¥ 165	¦ 166	§ 167	¨ 168	© 169	ª 170	« 171	¬ 172	- 173	® 174	175
B	° 176	± 177	² 178	³ 179	´ 180	µ 181	¶ 182	· 183	¸ 184	¹ 185	º 186	» 187	¼ 188	½ 189	¾ 190	¿ 191
C	À 192	Á 193	Â 194	Ã 195	Ä 196	Å 197	Æ 198	Ç 199	È 200	É 201	Ê 202	Ë 203	Ì 204	Í 205	Î 206	Ï 207
D	Ð 208	Ñ 209	Ò 210	Ó 211	Ô 212	Õ 213	Ö 214	× 215	Ø 216	Ù 217	Ú 218	Û 219	Ü 220	Ý 221	Þ 222	ß 223
E	à 224	á 225	â 226	ã 227	ä 228	å 229	æ 230	ç 231	è 232	é 233	ê 234	ë 235	ì 236	í 237	î 238	ï 239
F	ð 240	ñ 241	ò 242	ó 243	ô 244	õ 245	ö 246	÷ 247	ø 248	ù 249	ú 250	û 251	ü 252	ý 253	þ 254	ÿ 255

CHR: NAK
DEC: 21
HEX: 0x15
BIN: 0001 0101

FIGURE 6.20   ASCII chart tool.

6.12.2 GLCD bitmap editor

This tool is accessed from *Tools -> GLCD Bitmap Editor* and it helps to design a bitmap for the GLCD displays. Fig. 6.21 shows the editor tool.

6.12.3 HID terminal

This tool is accessed from *Tools -> HID terminal* and it is useful while developing USB based applications. Fig. 6.22 shows this tool.

6.12.4 Interrupt assistant

This tool helps to create an ISR template as described in an earlier section.

6.12.5 LCD custom character

This tool is accessed from *Tools -> LCD Custom Character* and it can be used to create code for custom characters for standard LCD displays. Fig. 6.23 shows this tool.

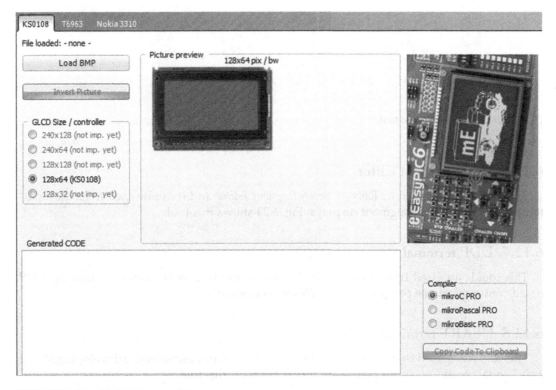

FIGURE 6.21   GLCD bitmap editor.

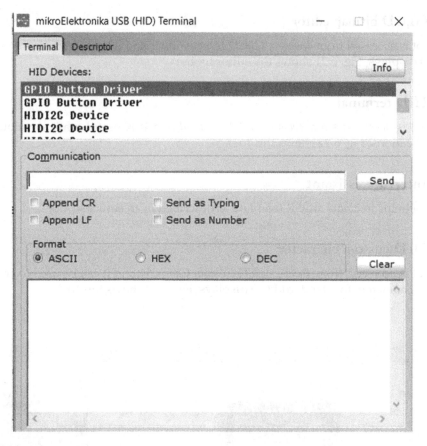

FIGURE 6.22   HID terminal tool.

6.12.6 Seven segment editor

This tool is accessed from *Tools -> Seven Segment Editor* and it can be used to create a pattern for standard seven-segment displays. Fig. 6.24 shows this tool.

6.12.7 UDP terminal

This tool is accessed from *Tools -> UDP Terminal* and it is useful while developing UDP based communications programs. Fig. 6.25 shows this tool.

6.12.8 USART terminal

This tool is accessed from *Tools -> USART Terminal* and it is useful while developing RS232 based serial communications programs. Fig. 6.26 shows this tool.

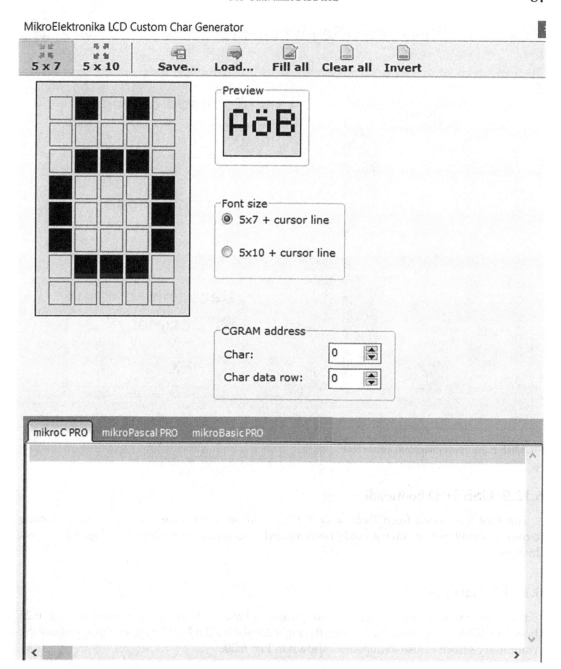

FIGURE 6.23   LCD custom character tool.

MikroElektronika Seven Segment Editor

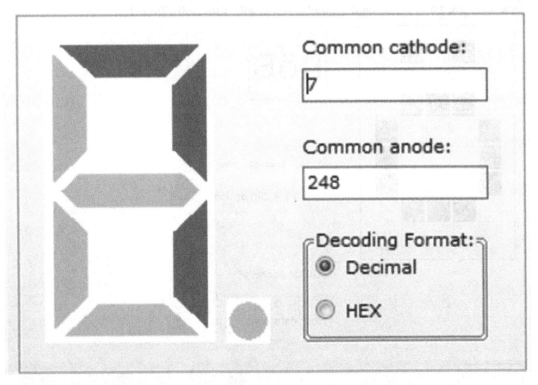

FIGURE 6.24   Seven segment editor tool.

6.12.9 USB HID bootloader

This tool is accessed from *Tools -> USB HID Bootloader* and it can be used to upload code to microcontrollers that have already been loaded with bootloader programs. Fig. 6.27 shows this tool.

6.12.10 Statistics

Program statistics can be seen by using the tool *View -> Statistics*. For example, Fig. 6.28 shows the RAM usage statistics. Similarly, Fig. 6.29 shows the ROM memory usage statistics. A summary screen is also available as shown in Fig. 6.30.

6.12.11 The library manager

A list of the library functions included in a project can be seen using the menu option *View -> Library Manager*. Additional libraries can be added to a project if desired by clicking

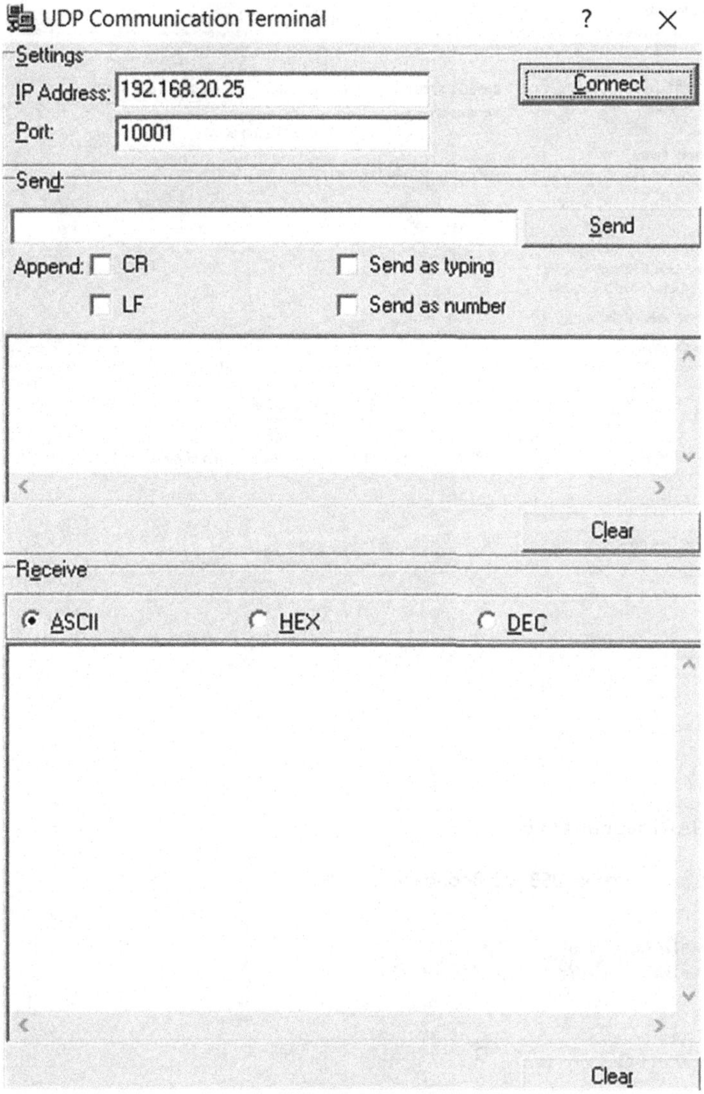

FIGURE 6.25   UDP terminal tool.

at the left hand side of the desired library name in the Library Manager. Fig. 6.31 shows part of the library manager screen.

6.12.12 Assembly listing

The assembly listing of the program can be displayed by clicking *View- > Assembly* as shown in Fig. 6.32.

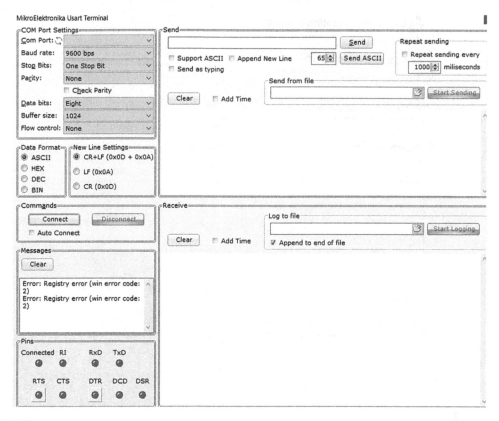

FIGURE 6.26   USART terminal tool.

FIGURE 6.27   USB HID bootloader tool.

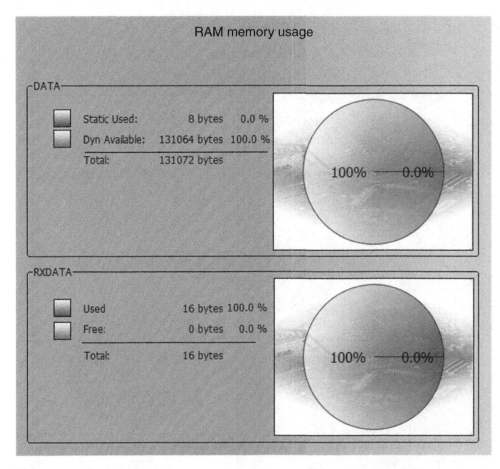

FIGURE 6.28 RAM usage statistics.

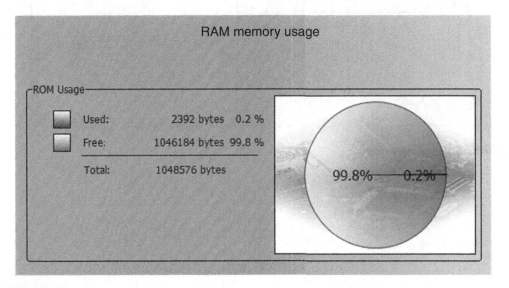

FIGURE 6.29 ROM usage statistics.

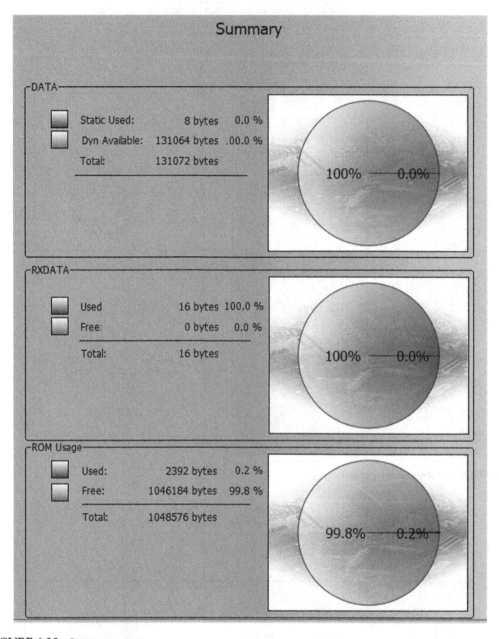

FIGURE 6.30   Summary screen.

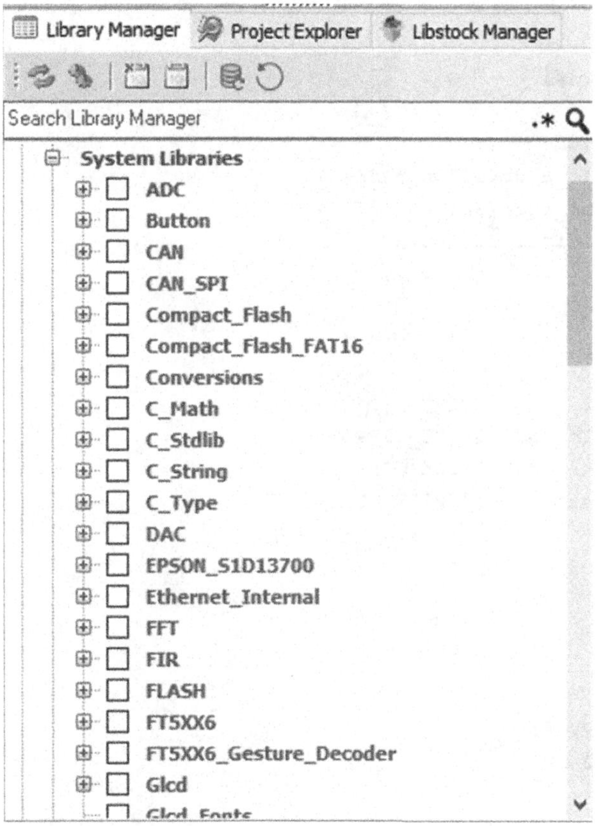

FIGURE 6.31   The library manager.

6.12.13 Output files

A list of the output files generated by the compiler can be seen by clicking *Output Files* in the Project Manager window as shown in Fig. 6.33. The most important output file is the HEX file since this is the file which is uploaded to the microcontroller program memory.

6.12.14 Options window

Clicking the *Options* icon displays various IDE options that can be set by the user. An example is shown in Fig. 6.34.

```
_main:
;LED.c,14 ::                      void main()
SUB         SP, SP, #4
;LED.c,17 ::                      GPIO_Digital_Output(&GPIOE_BASE, _GPIO_PINMASK_12,
MOVW        R1, #4096
MOVW        R0, #lo_addr(GPIOE_BASE+0)
MOVT        R0, #hi_addr(GPIOE_BASE+0)
BL          _GPIO_Digital_Output+0
;LED.c,19 ::                      while(1)
L_main0:
;LED.c,21 ::                      LED = 1;                            /.
MOVS        R1, #1
SXTB        R1, R1
MOVW        R0, #lo_addr(GPIOE_ODR+0)
MOVT        R0, #hi_addr(GPIOE_ODR+0)
_SX         [R0, ByteOffset(GPIOE_ODR+0)]
;LED.c,22 ::                      Delay_ms(1000);
MOVW        R7, #32254
MOVT        R7, #854
NOP
NOP
L_main2:
SUBS        R7, R7, #1
BNE         L_main2
NOP
```

FIGURE 6.32   Assembly listing.

FIGURE 6.33   Output files.

FIGURE 6.34   Options window.

6.13 Summary

This chapter has described the features of the mikroC Pro for ARM programming language and IDE. The ARM Cortex-M4 specific features of this language have been given briefly with examples where appropriate. The chapter has also shown how to create a new project using the IDE, and then how to compile and upload the generated HEX code to the Clicker 2 for STM32 development board program memory. Additionally, the steps in simulating a program in software have been described in detail. Finally, some of the useful tools of the mikroC IDE are shown with their screen views.

Next Chapter makes an introduction to multitasking which is the main topic of this book. The chapter describes the basic principles of some of the commonly used multitasking scheduling algorithms.

Further readings

[1] mikroC User Manual. Available from: www.mikroe.com.

[2] D. Ibrahim, Advanced PIC Microcontroller Projects in C, Newnes, Oxon, UK, 2008, ISBN: 978-0-7506-8611-2.

[3] D. Ibrahim, Designing Embedded Systems With 32-Bit PIC Microcontrollers and MikroC, Newnes, Oxon, UK, 2014, ISBN: 978-0-08-097786-7.

Introduction to multitasking

7.1 Overview

Microcontrollers are nowadays used in many electronic devices in an endless variety of ways. It is estimated that there are more than 50 microcontrollers used in intelligent appliances in a modern house in Europe. Some typical application areas are in microwave ovens, mobile phones, tablets, cookers, washing machines, dishwashers, MP3 players, Hi-Fi equipment, TVs, computers, games consoles, watches, clocks, and so on. Some microcontroller-based systems are required to respond to external events in the shortest possible time and such systems are often referred to as real-time systems. It is important to understand that not all systems are real-time. For example, most automotive and aerospace systems can be classified as real-time systems. Various specialized control functions in a vehicle, such as engine control, brake, and clutch control are examples of real-time systems. Similarly, the engine control, wing control, and other dynamic controls in an aeroplane are real-time. All digital signal processing applications require immediate response of a microcontroller and therefore can be classified as real-time systems.

Most complex real-time systems require a number of tasks (or programs) to be processed almost at the same time. For example, consider an extremely simple real-time system which is required to flash an LED at required intervals, and at the same time to look for a key input from a keyboard. One solution would be to scan the keyboard in a loop at regular intervals while flashing the LED at the same time. Although this approach may work for a simple example, in most complex real-time systems a multitasking approach should be implemented.

The term multitasking means that several tasks (or programs) are processed in parallel on the same CPU. However, it is not possible for several tasks to run on a single CPU at the same time. Therefore, task switching is done where the tasks share the CPU time. In many applications, tasks cannot run independently of each other and they are expected to co-operate in some way. For example, the execution of a task may depend upon the completion of another task, or a task may need some data from another task. In such circumstances, the tasks involved must be synchronized using some form of inter-task communication methods.

Real-time systems are time responsive systems where the CPU is never overloaded. In such systems tasks usually have priorities that are obeyed strictly. A task with a higher priority can grab the CPU from a lower priority task and then use the CPU exclusively until it releases the CPU. When the higher priority task completes its processing, or if it is waiting for

ARM-Based Microcontroller Multitasking Projects. http://dx.doi.org/10.1016/B978-0-12-821227-1.00007-4

a resource to be available, then the lower priority task can grab the CPU and resume processing from the point where it was interrupted. Real-time systems are also expected to react to events as quickly as possible. External events are usually processed using external interrupts and the interrupt latency of such systems is expected to be very short so that the interrupt service routine is executed as soon as an interrupt occurs.

In this chapter we shall be looking at the different multitasking algorithms and discuss their advantages and disadvantages briefly.

7.2 Multitasking kernel advantages

- Without a multitasking kernel, multiple tasks can be executed in a loop, but this approach results in very poorly controlled real-time performance where the execution times of the tasks cannot be controlled.
- It is possible to code the various tasks as interrupt service routines. This may work in practice, but if the application has many tasks then the number of interrupts grow, making the code less manageable.
- A multitasking kernel allows new tasks to be added or some of the existing tasks to be removed from the system without any difficulty.
- The testing and debugging of a multitasking system with a multitasking kernel are easy compared to a multitasking system without a kernel.
- Memory is better managed using a multitasking kernel.
- Inter-task communication is easily handled using a multitasking kernel.
- Task synchronization is easily controlled using a multitasking kernel.
- CPU time is easily managed using a multitasking kernel.
- Most multitasking kernels provide memory security where a task cannot access the memory space of another task.
- Most multitasking kernels provide task priority where higher priority tasks can grab the CPU and stop the execution of lower priority tasks. This allows important tasks to run whenever it is required.

7.3 Need for an RTOS

An RTOS (real-time operating system) is a program that manages system resources, schedules the execution of various tasks in a system, synchronizes the execution of tasks, manages resource allocations, and provides inter-task communication and messaging between the tasks. Every RTOS consists of a kernel that provides the low-level functions, mainly the scheduling, task creation, inter-task communication, resource management, etc. Most complex RTOSs also provide file-handling services, disk read-write operations, interrupt servicing, network management, user management, etc.

A task is an independent thread of execution in a multitasking system, usually with its own local set of data. A multitasking system consists of a number of tasks, each running its own code, and communicating and synchronizing with each other in order to have access to shared resources. The simplest RTOS consists of a scheduler that determines the execution order of the tasks in the system. Each task has its own context consisting of the state of the CPU and its associated registers. The scheduler switches from one task to another one by performing a context switching where the context of the running task is stored and the context of the next task is loaded appropriately so that execution can continue properly with the next task. The time taken for the CPU to perform context switching is known as the context switching time and is usually negligible compared to the actual execution times of the tasks.

7.4 Task scheduling algorithms

Although there are many variations of scheduling algorithms in use today, three most commonly used algorithms are:

- Co-operative scheduling
- Round-robin scheduling
- Preemptive scheduling

The type of scheduling algorithm to be used depends on the nature of the application and in general, most applications use either one of the above algorithms, or a combination of them, or a modified version of these algorithms.

7.4.1 Co-operative scheduling

Co-operative scheduling, also known as nonpreemptive scheduling, shown in Fig. 7.1, is perhaps the simplest algorithm where tasks voluntarily give up the CPU usage when they have nothing useful to do or when they are waiting for some resources to become available. This algorithm has the main disadvantage that certain tasks can use excessive CPU times, thus not allowing some other important tasks to run when needed. Co-operative scheduling is only used in simple multitasking systems where there are no time-critical tasks.

State machines, also called finite-state machine (FSM) are probably the simplest ways of implementing co-operative scheduling. A **while** loop can be used to execute the tasks one after the other one as shown below for a three task application. In the code below, a task is represented with a function:

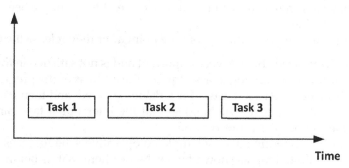

FIGURE 7.1   Co-operative scheduling.

```
Task1()
{
   Task 1 code
}
Task2()
{
   Task 2 code
}
Task3()
{
   Task 3 code
}
while(1)
{
   Task1();
   Task2();
   Task3();
}
```

The tasks are executed one after the other one inside the main infinite loop formed using a while statement. In this simple approach, the tasks can communicate with each other using global variables declared at the beginning of the program. It is important that the tasks in a co-operative scheduler should satisfy the following requirements for successful running of the overall system:

- Tasks must not block the overall execution, for example, by using delays or waiting for some resources and not releasing the CPU.
- The execution time of each tasks should be acceptable to other tasks.
- Tasks should exit as soon as they complete their processings.
- Tasks do not have to run to completion and they can exit for example before waiting for a resource to be available.
- Tasks should resume their operations from the point after they release the CPU.

The last requirement listed above is very important and is not satisfied in the simple scheduler example given above. Resuming a task requires the address of the program counter and important variables when the task releases the CPU to be saved, and then restored when the task resumes (also called context switching) so that the interrupted task can continue normally as if there has not been any interruption.

Another way of implementing a very simple co-operative scheduling is using a switch statement inside an infinite loop as shown below. Notice here that as before, the task states are not saved in this simple example:

```
Task1()
{
   Task 1 code
}
Task2()
{
   Task 2 code
}
Task3()
{
   Task 3 code
}
nxt = 1;
while(1)
{
   switch(nxt)
   {
      case 1:
         Task1();
         nxt = 2;
         break;
      case 2:
         Task2();
         nxt = 3;
         break;
      case 3:
         Task3();
         nxt = 1;
         break;
   }
}
```

Simple scheduling can also be implemented using timer interrupts. Here, the tasks can run in the background where the duration of each task can be organized by timer interrupts. An example program is given below to show how timer interrupts can be used in a simple co-operative scheduling based application.

Example

Write a program to flash the two LEDs on the Clicker 2 for STM32 development board at different rates. LD1 (at port PE12) should flash every second, while LD2 (at port PE15) should flash every 0.2 s (i.e., 200 ms).

Solution

The required program listing is shown in Fig. 7.2 (program: **multiled.c**). You should set the microcontroller clock frequency to 168 MHz as described in Section 6.9. At the beginning of

```
/*************************************************************************
                    TWO LEDS FLASHING AT DIFFERENT RATES LED
                    ============================================

In this project the on-board LEDs PE12 and PE15 are used. The program
establishes two tasks called TASK1() and TASK2(). TAsk1() flashes LED
PE12 every 200ms. Similarly, TASK2() flashes LED PE15 every second.

Author: Dogan Ibrahim
File   : multiled.c
Date   : September, 2019
*************************************************************************/
#define LD1 GPIOE_ODR.B12
#define LD2 GPIOE_ODR.B15

int count1 = 0, count2 = 0;
int LD1flag = 0, LD2flag = 0;

//
// Define the interrupt parameetrs so that Timer 2 interrupts at every 100ms
//
void InitTimer2()
{
  RCC_APB1ENR.TIM2EN = 1;
  TIM2_CR1.CEN = 0;
  TIM2_PSC = 279;
  TIM2_ARR = 59999;
  NVIC_IntEnable(IVT_INT_TIM2);
  TIM2_DIER.UIE = 1;
  TIM2_CR1.CEN = 1;
}

//
// This is the interrupt service routine The program jumps here every 100ms
//
void Timer2_interrupt() iv IVT_INT_TIM2
{
  count1++;
  count2++;

  if(count1 == 2)                       // If 200ms
  {
    count1 = 0;                         // Reset counter
    LD1flag = 1;                        // Set flag for LD1
  }

  if(count2 == 10)                      // Of 1000ms (1 sec)
  {
    count2 = 0;                         // Reset counter
    LD2flag = 1;                        // Set flag for LD2
  }
  TIM2_SR.UIF = 0;                      // Clear interrupt flag
}

//
// This is Task1. If LD1flag is set then toggle the LD1
//
TASK1()
{
    if(LD1flag == 1)
```

FIGURE 7.2   Program listing.

```
    {
        LD1flag = 0;
        LD1 = ~LD1;                         // Toggle LD1
    }
}

//
// This is Task2. If LD2flag is set then toggle the LD2
//
TASK2()
{
    if(LD2flag == 1)
    {
        LD2flag = 0;
        LD2 = ~LD2;                         // Toggle LD2
    }
}

//
// Start of main program. Configure PE12 and PE15 as outputs
//
void main()
{
    int nxt = 1;
    GPIO_Digital_Output(&GPIOE_BASE, _GPIO_PINMASK_12 | _GPIO_PINMASK_15);
    InitTimer2();

    while(1)
    {
        switch(nxt)
        {
            case 1:
                    TASK1();
                    nxt = 2;
                    break;
            case 2:
                    TASK2();
                    nxt = 1;
                    break;
        }
    }
}
```

FIGURE 7.2 (Cont.)

the program, ports PE12 and PE15 are defined as LD1 and LD2, respectively. Inside the main program, I/O ports PE12 and PE15 are configured as digital outputs. The program is based on a timer interrupt where Timer 2 is used to generate interrupts at every 100 ms. The interrupt service routine is the function **Timer2_interrupt**. There are two tasks in the program: **Task1()** and **Task2()**. Each task is assigned a counter with the names **count1** and **count2**, respectively. Additionally, the two tasks have flags **LD1flag** and **LD2flag**. Inside the interrupt service routine, the two counts are incremented by one each time an interrupt occurs. When **count1** reaches 2 (i.e., 200 ms elapsed) then flag **LD1flag** is set. Similarly, when **count2** reaches 10 (i.e., 1000 ms) then flag **LD2flag** is set. **Task1()** toggles LED LD1 when **LD1flag** is set. Similarly, **Task2()** toggles LED LD2 when flag **LD2flag** is set. The result is that LED LD1 flashes every 200 ms and LED LD2 flashes every second.

Timer 2 interrupts are enabled by calling to function **InitTimer2**. The **Timer Calculator** utility developed by mikroElektronika was used to set the timer interrupt parameters. This utility can be downloaded from the following link:

- https://www.mikroe.com/timer-calculator

You should install the **Timer Calculator** utility on your PC before using it. The steps to find the Timer 2 parameters for generating interrupts at every 100 ms are as follows (see Fig. 7.3):

- Start the Timer Calculator utility
- Select device STM32F2xx/3xx/4xx
- Set MCU frequency to 168 MHz
- Choose Timer 2
- Set the interrupt time to 100 ms
- Click calculate
- Copy function **InitTimer2** to your program to initialize the timer. Also, copy the interrupt service routine function **Timer2_interrupt** to your program.

It is clear from this example that multitasking, even for a very simple two task application can be complex when timer interrupts are used.

7.4.2 Round-robin scheduling

Round-robin scheduling (see Fig. 7.4) allocates each task an equal share of the CPU time. Tasks are in a circular queue and when a task's allocated CPU time expires, the task is removed

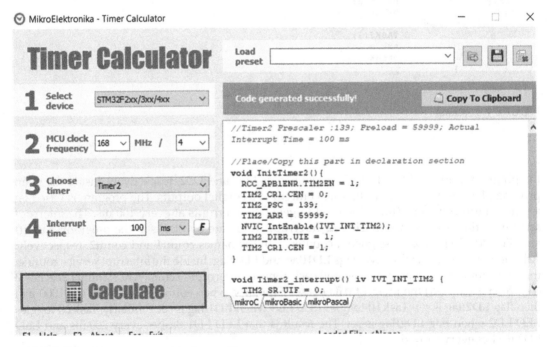

FIGURE 7.3 Using the Timer Calculator utility.

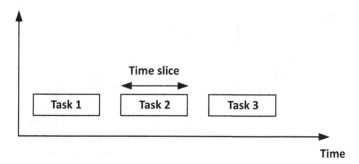

FIGURE 7.4 Round-robin scheduling.

and placed at the end of the queue. This type of scheduling cannot be satisfactory in any real-time application where each task can have varying amount of CPU requirements depending on the complexity of the processing involved. Round-robin scheduling requires the context of the running task to be saved on stack when a task is removed from the queue so that the task can resume from the point it was interrupted when it becomes active again. One variation of the pure round-robin-based scheduling is to provide a priority-based scheduling, where tasks with the same priority levels receive equal amounts of CPU time.

Round-robin scheduling has the following advantages:

- It is easy to implement.
- Every task gets an equal share of the CPU.
- Easy to compute the average response time.

The disadvantages of round-robin scheduling are:

- It is not generally good to give the same CPU time to each task.
- Some important tasks may not run to completion.
- Not suitable for real-time systems where tasks usually have different processing requirements.

7.4.3 Preemptive scheduling

Preemptive scheduling is the most commonly used scheduling algorithm in real-time systems. Here, the tasks are prioritized and the task with the highest priority among all other tasks gets the CPU time (see Fig. 7.5). If a task with a priority higher than the currently executing task becomes ready to run, the kernel saves the context of the current task and switches to the higher priority task by loading its context. Usually, the highest priority task runs to completion or until it becomes noncomputable, for example, waiting for a resource to become available, or calling a function to delay. At this point, the scheduler determines the task with the highest priority that can run and loads the context of this task and starts executing it. Although the preemptive scheduling is very powerful, care is needed as a programming error can place a high priority task in an endless loop and thus not release the CPU to other tasks. Some multitasking systems employ a combination of round-robin and preemptive scheduling. In such systems, time-critical tasks are usually prioritized and run under preemptive scheduling, whereas the nontime critical tasks run under round-robin scheduling, sharing the left CPU time among themselves.

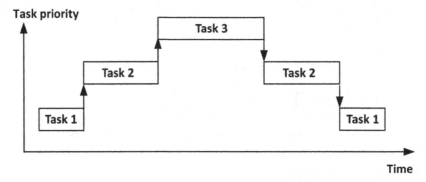

FIGURE 7.5   Preemptive scheduling.

It is important to realize that in a preemptive scheduler, tasks at the same priorities run under round-robin. In such a system, when a task uses its allocated time, a timer interrupt is generated by the scheduler which saves the context of the current task and gives the CPU to another task with equal priority that is ready to run, provided that there are no other tasks with higher priorities which are ready to run.

The priority in a preemptive scheduler can be static or dynamic. In a static priority system tasks used the same priority all the time. In a dynamic priority-based scheduler, the priority of the tasks can change during their courses of execution.

So far, we have said nothing about how various tasks work together in an orderly manner. In most applications, data and commands must flow between various tasks so that the tasks can co-operate and work together. One very simple way of doing this is through shared data held in RAM where every task can access. Modern RTOS systems, however, provide local task memories and inter-task communication tools such as mailboxes, pipes, and queues to pass data securely and privately between various tasks. In addition, tools such as event flags, semaphores, and mutexes are usually provided for inter-task communication and synchronization purposes and for passing data between tasks.

The main advantage of a preemptive scheduler is that it provides an excellent mechanism where the importance of every task may be precisely defined. On the other hand, it has the disadvantage that a high priority task may starve the CPU such that lower priority tasks can never have the chance to run. This can usually happen if there are programming errors such that the high priority task runs continuously without having to wait for any system resources and never stops.

7.4.4 Scheduling algorithm goals

It can be said that a good scheduling algorithm should possess the following features:

- Be fair such that each process gets a fair share of the CPU.
- Be efficient by keeping the CPU busy. The algorithm should not spend too much time to decide what to do.
- Maximize throughput by minimizing the time users have to wait.
- Be predictable so that same tasks take the same time when run multiple times.
- Minimize response time.
- Maximize resource use.
- Enforce priorities.
- Avoid starvataion.

TABLE 7.1 Differences between preemptive and nonpreemptive scheduling.

Nonpreemptive scheduling	Preemptive scheduling
Tasks have no priorities	Tasks have priorities
Tasks cannot be interrupted	A higher priority task interrupts a lower priority one
Waiting and response times are longer	Waiting and response times are shorter
Scheduling is rigid	Scheduling is flexible
Tasks do not have priorities	High priority tasks run to completion
Not suitable for real-time systems	Suitable for real-time systems

7.4.5 Difference between preemptive and nonpreemptive scheduling

Some differences between a preemptive and nonpreemptive scheduling algorithm are summarized in Table 7.1.

7.4.6 Some other scheduling algorithms

There are many other types of scheduling algorithms used in practice. Most of these algorithms are a combination or a derivation of the basic three algorithms described in this chapter. Bried details of some other scheduling algorithms are outlined in this section.

7.4.6.1 First come first served

This is one of the simplest scheduling algorithms, also known as the FIFO scheduling. In this algorithm, tasks are run in the order they become ready. Some features of this algorithm are:

- Throughput is low since long processes can hold the CPU, causing short processes to wait for a long time.
- There is no proritization and thus real-time tasks cannot be executed quickly.
- It is non-preemptive.
- The context switching occurs only on task termination and therefore the overhead is minimal.
- Each process gets the chance to be executed even if they have to wait for long time.

7.4.6.2 Shortest remaining time first

In this algorithm, the scheduler arranges the tasks with the least estimated processing time remaining to be next in the queue. Some features of this algorithm are:

- If a shorter task arrives then the currently running task is interrupted, thus causing overhead.
- Waiting time of tasks requiring long processing times can be very long.
- If there are too many small tasks in the system, longer tasks may never get the chance to run.

7.4.6.3 Longest remaining time first

In this algorithm, the scheduler arranges the tasks with the longest processing times to be next in the queue. Some features of this algorithm are:

- If a longer task arrives then the currently running task is interrupted, thus causing overhead.

- Waiting time of tasks requiring short processing times can be very long.
- If there are too many long tasks in the system, shorter tasks may never get the chance to run.

7.4.6.4 *Multilevel queue scheduling*

In this type of scheduling, tasks are classified into different groups, such as interactive (foreground) and batch (background). Each group has its own scheduling algorithm, foreground tasks are given higher priorities since the background tasks can always wait.

7.4.6.5 *Dynamic priority scheduling*

In dynamic priority scheduling, although the tasks have priorities, their priorities can change, that is, the priority can be lower or higher than it was earlier. Dynamic priority algorithms achieve high processor utilization, and they can adapt to dynamic environments, where task parameters are unknown. On the contrary, it is not advisable to use dynamic priority in real-time systems because of the uncertainty that an important task may not run in time.

7.5 Choosing a scheduling algorithm

When designing a multitasking system with several tasks, a programmer must consider which scheduling algorithm will perform the best for the application to be developed. In simple terms, most real-time systems should be based on preemptive scheduling with fixed priorities where time-critical tasks grab and use the CPU until they complete their processings or wait for a resource to be available. If there are several time critical tasks then all such tasks should run at the same higher priorities. In general, tasks at the same priorities run as round-robin and share the available CPU time. Then, all the other tasks which are not time critical should run at lower priorities. If the time taken for a task to complete is not critical then simple co-operative scheduler algorithms can be employed.

7.6 Summary

In this chapter we have made an introduction to basic multitasking and have learned some of the basic features of multitasking systems, including the concepts of various task scheduling algorithms.

The projects in this book are based on using the FreeRTOS multitasking kernel. In the next chapter we shall be making an introduction to FreeRTOS multitasking kernel and learn how to install it on the mikroC Pro for ARM IDE and the compiler so that we can use it in our projects.

Further readings

[1] D. Ibrahim, Designing Embedded Systems With 32-Bit PIC Microcontrollers and MikroC, Newnes, Oxon, UK, 2014, ISBN: 978-0-08-097786-7.
[2] T.W. Schultz, C and the 8051: Vol. 1: Hardware, Modular Programming & Multitasking, Prentice Hall, New Jersey, USA, 1997.
[3] D. Ibrahim, Designing Embedded Systems with 32-Bit PIC Microcontrollers and MikroC, Newnes, Oxon, UK, 2014, ISBN: 978-0-08-097786-7.

Introduction to FreeRTOS

8.1 Overview

FreeRTOS was originally developed by Richard Barry around 2003 and was then further developed and maintained by Richard's own company Real Time Engineers Ltd. in close partnership with the world's leading chip manufacturers over a decade. FreeRTOS is a real-time kernel (or real-time scheduler) that is well suited to embedded microcontroller-based multi-tasking applications where more than one task shares the CPU. FreeRTOS is a professionally developed high-quality software with strict quality control that is freely available even in commercial applications. FreeRTOS is so popular that it supports over 35 architectures and is reported that (www.freertos.org) in 2018 it was downloaded every 175 s. In 2017 Real Time Engineers Ltd. passed the stewardship of the FreeRTOS project to Amazon Web Services (AWS).

In this chapter we shall be making a brief introduction to FreeRTOS and see how it can be used with the microC Pro for ARM compiler and the IDE on the Clicker 2 for STM32 micro-controller development board.

FreeRTOS has the following standard features. Do not worry if you don't understand some of the terminology at this stage:

- Preemptive or co-operative operation
- Task management
- Task notifications
- Heap memory management
- Flexible task priority assignment
- Queue management
- Software timer management
- Interrupt management
- Resource management
- Binary and counting semaphores
- Mutexes
- Event groups
- Stack overflow checking
- Trace recording
- Task run-time statistics gathering
- Optional commercial licensing and support

ARM-Based Microcontroller Multitasking Projects. http://dx.doi.org/10.1016/B978-0-12-821227-1.00008-6

Detailed information on FreeRTOS and its functions can be obtained from the following sources:

1. **Mastering the FreeRTOS Real Time Kernel: A Hands-On Tutorial Guide**, by Richard Barry, web site:

   a. https://www.freertos.org/wp-content/uploads/2018/07/161204_Mastering_the_ FreeRTOS_Real_Time_Kernel-A_Hands-On_Tutorial_Guide.pdf

2. **The FreeRTOS Reference Manual**, web site:

   b. https://www.freertos.org/wp-content/uploads/2018/07/FreeRTOS_Reference_ Manual_V10.0.0.pdf

3. https://www.freertos.org/documentation

8.2 FreeRTOS distribution

It is important to understand the FreeRTOS distribution structure before it can be used successfully. FreeRTOS is supplied as a set of C source files and these files are built with your application code to make up your project. A demo folder is provided as part of the distribution, containing sample application programs and these programs should help the beginners in developing their own programs.

The latest official release is available as a standard zip file (.zip), or as a self-extracting zip file (.exe). The steps to install FreeRTOS are given below:

- Go to FreeRTOS web site:

  - https://www.freertos.org/a00104.html

- Click **Download Source Code and Projects** (see Fig. 8.1).

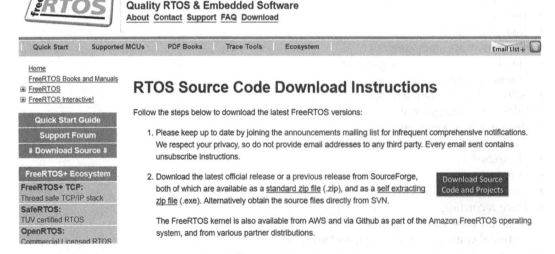

FIGURE 8.1   Installing FreeRTOS.

- Double click on FreeRTOS installation file and choose a drive to install the files (e.g., C:\). In this book, the files are installed on the C:\ drive, but they can equally be installed into a different drive. At the time of writing this book, the filename was **FreeRTOSv10.2.1.exe**.

8.3 Installing from MikroElektronika web site

Alternatively, you can copy all the necessary FreeRTOS files for mikroC Pro for ARM compiler from the mikroElektronika Libstock web site. The advantage of doing this way is that the files are configured correctly for the mikroC Pro for ARM and the demo files work without any changes. This is the method used in this book and is the recommended procedure. The steps to install FreeRTOS for the MikroC are given below:

- Open the following mikeoElektronika **Libstock** web site:

  - https://libstock.mikroe.com/projects/view/2083/freertos-v9-0-0-mikroc-examples

- Click to open the files for the mikroC Pro for ARM.
- Create the following directories on your C:\ drive and copy all the files from the corresponding folders in the Libstock folders. You should have the following folders and files on your C:\ drive:

C:\
  FreeRTOS
    Source
      croutine.c
      event_groups.c
      list.c
      queue.c
      stream_buffer.c
      tasks.c
      timers.c
      include
        header files (.h)
      portable
        MikroC
          ARM_CM4F
            port.c
            portmacro.h
          ARM_CM3
            port.c
            portmacro.h
      MemMang
        heap_1.c
        heap_2.c
        heap_3.c
        heap_4.c
        heap_5.c

Common
   mpu_wrappers.c
Demo
   STM32F407_MikroC
   LedBlinking
      main.h
      main.c
      FreeRTOS_STM32F407_LedBlinking.mcpar
      FreeRTOS_STM32F407_LedBlinking.cfg
      FreeRTOS_STM32F407_LedBlinking.hex
      FreeRTOS_STM32F407_LedBlinking.bin
      FreeRTOSConfig.h

FreeRTOS is configured using the header file **FreeRTOSConfig.h**. This file is located in the same folder as the application program being built by the user. The file contains various constants and application specific definitions, such as **configCPU_CLOCK_Hz**, **configTICK_RATE_HZ**, **configSYSTICK_CLOCK_DIVIDER**, and many more. Source files specific to a compiler are contained within the folder: **FreeRTOS/Source/portable**.

Constants that start with **INCLUDE_** are used to include or exclude a FreeRTOS API function. For example, setting **INCLUDE_vTaskPrioritySet** to 1 will include **vTaskPrioritySet()** API function, and clearing it to 0 will exclude it from the API. If a function is excluded from the FreeRTOS API then it cannot be called by an application program. Excluding a function from the API has the advantage that it reduces the overall code size.

Constants that start with **config** define attributes of the kernel, or include or exclude features of the kernel. Detailed information on the contents of configuration file **FreeRTOSConfig.h** can be obtained from the references given in the Overview section of this chapter. The author will describe the meanings and uses of the important parameters in this file as they are used in programs in later chapters.

FreeRTOS also requires heap memory allocation and heap memory manager if **configSUP-PORT_DYNAMIC_ALLOCATION** is set to 1 in **FreeRTOSConfig.h**. Five heap allocation schemes are provided: heap_1, heap_2, heap_3, heap_4, and heap_5 and are implemented by files such as **heap_1.c, heap_2.c, heap_3.c, heap_4.c**, and **heap_5.c**. The heap allocation schemes are contained in folder **FreeRTOS/Source/portable/MemMang**. User application programs are in a file called **main.c**.

8.4 Developing project files

Perhaps the easiest approach to develop new application programs is to use a template file and modify this file as required for different projects. In this book, all the example programs will be stored in the DEMO folder as in the above directory structure. Fig. 8.2 shows a template file that can be used for the programs in this book (this template file is a modified version of the **main.c** file in the LedBlinking folder supplied in Libstock and it will be modified and used in all the projects in this book). Do not worry if you do not understand some of the statement in this template file as all will be clear soon in the next chapter when we look at the FreeRTOS API functions.

```
/*=====================================================================
                            TEMPLATE FILE
                            =============

This template file will be used in all the projects in this book. This
heading and the contents of the file will be modified as required. This
template file is shown with only one task which does nothing useful

Author: Dogan Ibrahim
Date:    September, 2019
=====================================================================*/

#include "main.h"

//
// Define all your TASK functions here
// ===================================
//

// Task 1
void task1(void *pvParameters)
{
    while (1)
    {
    }
}

//
// Start of MAIN program
// =====================
//
void main()
{

//
// Create all the TASKS here
// =========================
//

// Create Task 1
    xTaskCreate(
        (TaskFunction_t)task1,
        "Task 1",
        configMINIMAL_STACK_SIZE,
        NULL,
        10,
        NULL
    );
```

FIGURE 8.2 Template program.

```
//
// Start the RTOS scheduler
// =========================
//
    vTaskStartScheduler();

//
// We will never reach here
// =========================
//
    while (1);
}
```

FIGURE 8.2   *(Cont.)*

8.5 FreeRTOS headers files path and source files path

The compiler IDE must be configured to include the header files and the source files paths correctly so that the compiler can find these files. In mikroC Pro for ARM IDE, you should click **Project -> Edit Search Paths** and then configure the paths as described in the following steps (see Fig. 8.3):

Headers path:
- Click the "..." at the bottom right of **Headers Path** and select folder: **C:\FreeRTOS\Source\include**.
- Click **Add** at the bottom left corner.
- Select and add folder: **C:\FreeRTOS\Source\portable\MikroC\ARM_CM4F**.
- Also, select and add folder **C:\FreeRTOS\Demo\STM32F407\LedBlinking**.

Sources path:
- Click the "..." at the bottom right of **Sources Path** and select folder **C:\FreeRTOS\Source**.
- Click Add to add the folder.
- Select and add folder: **C:\Source\portable\MemMang**.
- Select and add folder: **C:\Users\Public\Documents\Mikroelektronika\mikroC Pro for ARM\Packages\Memory manager dmalloc\Uses**.
- Also, select and add folder **C:\FreeRTOS\Source\portable\MikroC\ARM_CM4F**.

8.6 Compiler case sensitivity

The case sensitivity of the mikroC Pro for ARM must be enabled before compiling programs otherwise you will get compilation errors. The steps are as follows:

- Open mikroC Pro for ARM
- Click **Tools -> Options** and select the **Output** tab
- Click **Output Settings**
- Click **Case sensitive** under **Compiler** (see Fig. 8.4)

FIGURE 8.3   Configure the compiler search paths.

8.7 Compiling the template program

At this stage, you should compile the template program file by clicking the Build icon (see Fig. 8.5) and ensure that the program file is compiled. Make sure that the compilation is successful and there are no error messages in the message board at the bottom part of the IDE screen. If there are any compilation errors, you are advised to go back and check the installation instructions. Always make sure that you save your project program files after a successful compilation.

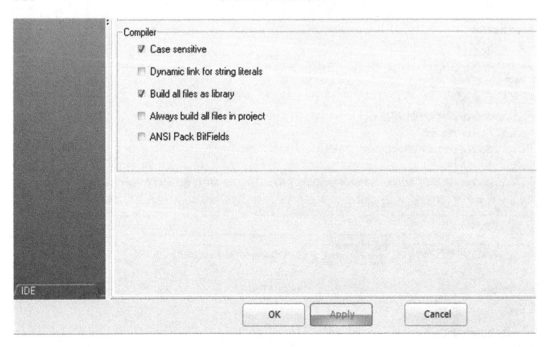

FIGURE 8.4   Enable case sensitivity in the compiler.

Build icon

FIGURE 8.5   Compile by clicking the Build icon.

8.8 Summary

In this chapter we have made an introduction to the FreeRTOS kernel and have seen how to install the kernel files on our computer for use by the mikroC Pro for ARM compiler and IDE.

In the next chapter we shall be looking in detail at the various API functions of FreeRTOS and learn how to use them in programs.

Further readings

[1] R. Barry. Mastering the FreeRTOS Real Time Kernel: A Hands-On Tutorial Guide. Available from: https://www.freertos.org/wp-content/uploads/2018/07/161204_Mastering_the_FreeRTOS_Real_Time_Kernel-A_Hands-On_Tutorial_Guide.pdf.

[2] The FreeRTOS Reference Manual. Available from: https://www.freertos.org/wp-content/uploads/2018/07/FreeRTOS_Reference_Manual_V10.0.0.pdf.

[3] https://www.freertos.org/documentation

9

Using the FreeRTOS functions

9.1 Overview

In the last chapter we made an introduction to FreeRTOS and have seen how to install the FreeRTOS distribution files to our computer for the mikroC Pro for ARM compiler and IDE. In this chapter we shall be learning how to use the various functions of FreeRTOS.

Further information on FreeRTOS functions and features can be obtained from the following sources:

- www.freertos.org/documentation
- Mastering the FreeRTOS Real Time Kernel—a Hands On Tutorial Guide, by Richard Barry
- FreeRTOS Reference Manual, Amazon Web Services, Weblink: https://www.freertos.org/wp-content/uploads/2018/07/FreeRTOS_Reference_Manual_V10.0.0.pdf
- Using the FreeRTOS Real Time Kernel: A Practical Guide, by Richard Barry
- Using the FreeRTOS Real Time Kernel: ARM Cortex-M3 Edition, by Richard Barry

FreeRTOS contains a very large number of functions. Only some of the most commonly used FreeRTOS functions are described in this chapter. Interested readers should refer to the FreeRTOS Reference Manual whose details are given above.

9.2 FreeRTOS data types

Header file **portmacro.h** contains definitions for data types **TickType_t** and **BaseType_t**.

TickType_t: A periodic interrupt called the tick interrupt is used by FreeRTOS. The tick count is the number of tick interrupts that have occurred since the FreeRTOS application started and this is used as a measure of time. The time interval between two tick interrupts is called the tick period and times are specified as multiples of tick periods. **TickType_t** is the data type used to hold the tick count value and it can be either an unsigned 16-bit or an unsigned 32-bit type depending on the setting of **configUSE_16_BIT_TICKS** in file **FreeRTOSConfig.h**. Setting **configUSE_16_BIT_TICKS** to 1 or 0 defines **TickType_t** to 16 or 32-bits, respectively. Although setting to 16-bit can improve the efficiency, it is recommended to set it to 32-bit on a 32-bit CPU.

ARM-Based Microcontroller Multitasking Projects. http://dx.doi.org/10.1016/B978-0-12-821227-1.00009-8

BaseType_t: This is a 32-bit type on a 32-bit CPU and 16-bit type on a 16-bit CPU. **BaseType_t** is used for return types that can take only a very limited range of values and for pdTRUE/pdFALSE type Boolean variables.

9.3 FreeRTOS variable names

Prefixes are used to identify variable types as follows:

c	char
s	int16_t (short)
l	int32_t (long)
x	BaseType and any other nonstandard types
u	unsigned variable type
p	pointer variable type

9.4 FreeRTOS function names

Function names are prefixed with the type they return and the file they are defined within. Some examples are:

vTaskPrioritySet()	returns a void and is defined within file **tasks.c**
xQueueReceive()	returns a variable of type BaseType and is defined within file
	queue.c
pvTimerGetTimerID()	returns a pointer to void and is defined within file **timers.c**

9.5 Common macro definitions

The following macro definitions are used in FreeRTOS:

pdTRUE	1
pdFALSE	0
pdPASS	1
pdFAIL	0

9.6 Task states

Tasks in FreeRTOS can be in one of four states at any time: Running, Ready, Suspended, and Blocked. Fig. 9.1 shows the possible task states and also shows how a task can move from one state to another state.

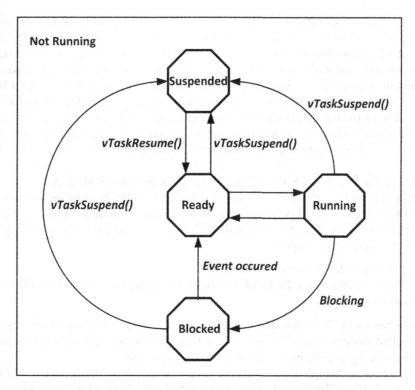

FIGURE 9.1 **Task states.**

Running state: A task is said to be in running state if it is currently using the CPU and is not waiting for any resources and there no other tasks that can run at higher priorities.

Ready state: A task is in ready state if it is not waiting for any resources so that it is ready to run. The scheduler always selects the highest priority task from the tasks which are in the ready state. If a higher priority task is not ready to run (e.g., it is waiting for some resources to become available) then the scheduler selects the lower priority task which is in the ready state that can run.

Suspended state: Tasks that are in suspended state are not available to the scheduler and therefore they cannot run. A task is put into suspended state by calling API function **vTask-Suspend()**. A suspended task can come out of this state and become ready to run by calling the API function **vTaskResume()**, or **xTaskResumeFromISR()**.

Blocked state: A task that is waiting for a resource (e.g., an event) is said to be in the blocked state. A task may be blocked because of the following:

- A task may be waiting for a timer-related event to occur (e.g., delay expiring or absolute time being reached)
- A task may be waiting for synchronization, for example, to receive data in a queue
- Queues, semaphores, mutexes, event groups, and direct task notifications can all block a task

All the tasks in the examples in this book are run using the preemptive scheduling algorithm where parameter configUSE_PREEMPTION and configUSE_TIME_SLICING are both set to 1 in the FreeRTOSConfig.h configuration file. Therefore, tasks having the same priorities will run with time slicing and share the CPU time (i.e., run under Round-robin) between themselves. A time slice is equal to the time between two FreeRTOS tick interrupts. Notice that Round-robin scheduling does not guarantee that tasks having same priorities will have exactly same CPU times, but it guarantees that Ready state tasks having same priorities will enter the running state in turn. This is the configuration used in most applications, that is, preemptive scheduling with time slicing for tasks having equal priorities.

It is also possible to configure the scheduler for preemptive scheduling without time slicing by setting parameter configUSE_TIME_SLICING to 0. This is same as described earlier, but the CPU time is not shared between tasks having equal priorities. In this case, when the scheduler selects a Ready task, this task will grab the CPU and carry on executing until one of the following conditions happen:

- A higher priority task enters the Ready state
- The executing task enters the Blocked or Suspended state, for example, waiting for a resource to become available

When the time slicing is turned off, the scheduler has to do less context switches and this reduces the scheduler overhead. But at the same time, it becomes very difficult to assess when other tasks having equal priorities will have the chance to run.

It is also possible to change the scheduling algorithm to be co-operative by setting parameter configUSE_PREEMPTION to 0. Parameter configUSE_TIME_SLICING can be set to any value when co-operative scheduling algorithm is used. In co-operative scheduling, a task that becomes executable will run until one of the following conditions happen:

- The running task enters the Blocked or Suspended state, for example, waiting for a resource to become available
- The running task requests a context switch by manually calling function taskYIELD(). That is, the running tasks decide when the context switching should be done.

Since there is no preemption, time slicing cannot be used with the co-operative scheduling algorithm.

Parameter configUSE_TICKLESS_IDLE also affects the scheduling algorithm as this parameter can turn off the tick interrupts. This is an advances parameter that can be used in applications that are required to minimize the processor power consumption. Parameter configUSE_TICKLESS_IDLE is set to 0, which is the default setting if it is left undefined in the configuration file.

9.7 Task-related functions

In this section we will look at some of the commonly used task-related FreeRTOS functions and see how they can be used in simple projects. In later chapters we will be looking at other important functions and learn how they can be used in projects.

9.7.1 Creating a new task

The following function creates an instance of a new task:

xTaskCreate(TaskFunction_t pvTaskCode,
   const char* const pcName,
   unsigned short usStackDepth,
   void *pvParameters,
   UBaseType_t uxPriority,
   TaskHandle_t *pxCreatedTask);

A task can be created before or after the scheduler is started. When a task is created, the required RAM is automatically allocated from the FreeRTOS heap. A newly created task is initially in the Ready state, but possibly moves to the Running state if there are no other higher priority tasks that are able to run, or if the currently running task has the same priority as this task and the running task gives up the CPU.

Parameters

pvTaskCode: This parameter is the function name that implements the task.

pcName: This is the name given to the task, used to facilitate debugging, but can also be used in a call to xTaskGetHandle() to obtain a task handle. The application-defined constant configMAX_TASK_NAME_LEN in the configuration file FreeRTOSConfig.h defines the maximum length of the task name in characters.

usStackDepth: Each task has its own unique stack that is allocated by the kernel to the task when the task is created, and the usStackDepth value tells the kernel how large to make the stack. This value specifies the number of words (not the bytes) the stack can hold. Constant configMINIMAL_STACK_SIZE in the configuration file defines the minimum size of the stack. If a task requires more stack space, then a larger value should be assigned to the task.

pvParameters: Task functions accept a parameter of type "pointer to void"(void*). The value assigned to pvParameters will be the value passed into the task. For example, integer types can be passed into a task function by casting the integer to a void pointer at the point the task is created. Then, by casting the void pointer parameter back to an integer in the task function, the parameter is passed to the function.

uxPriority: This parameter defines the priority at which the task will run. Priorities can be assigned from 0, which is the lowest priority, to (configMAX_PRIORITIES –1), which is the highest priority. Using a uxPriority value above (configMAX_PRIORITIES –1) will result in the priority assigned to the task being capped silently to the maximum legitimate value.

pxCreatedTask: This parameter is used as a handle to the task where the handle can be used to reference the task in API calls (e.g., to change task priority, to delete the task, etc.).

Return values

There are two return values:

pdPASS: This return value indicates that the task has been creates successfully

errCOULD_NOT_ALLOCATE_REQUIRED_MEMORY: This return value indicates that the task could not be created because there was insufficient heap memory available for FreeRTOS to allocate the task data structures and stack. **FreeRTOSConfig.h** parameter configSUPPORT_DYNAMIC_ALLOCATION must be set to 1 or simply left undefined for this function to be available

9.7.2 Delaying a task

The following function blocks a task temporarily by delaying it for a specified time.

`vTaskDelay(TickType_t xTicksToDelay);`

This function blocks the calling task for a fixed number of tick interrupts.

Parameters

xTicksToDelay: This is the number of tick interrupts that the calling task is blocked. For example, if the tick count is 100 and a task calls vTaskDelay(10), then the task will be placed in Blocked state until the tick count reaches 110.

The macro pdMS_TO_TICKS() can be used to convert milliseconds into ticks so that the task can be blocked by the specified number of milliseconds.

INCLUDE_vTaskDelay must be set to 1 in in file **FreeRTOSConfig.h** for the vTaskDelay API function to be available to a program.

Return value

This function has no return value.

9.7.3 Project 1—flashing an LED every second

Description: This project flashes the LED at port PE12 of the Clicker for STM32 development board every second.

Aim: The aim of this project is to show how the FreeRTOS API functions vTaskCreate(), xTicksToDelay(), and macro pdMS_TO_TICKS() can be used in a program. There is only one task in this project.

Block diagram: Fig. 9.2 shows the project block diagram.

Program listing: The program listing is shown in Fig. 9.3 (program: **LED1.c**). Before compiling the program make sure that the clock of the CPU is set correctly to 168 MHz (see Fig. 6.8A and B). There is only one task in this program called **Task 1** and it is created using the following API function call:

LED at port PE12

FIGURE 9.2   Block diagram of the project.

```
/*==============================================================================
                            FLASH AN LED
                            ============

This program flashes the LED connected to port pin PE12 of the Clicker 2 for
STM32 development board every second. The program uses only one task.

Author: Dogan Ibrahim
Date   : September, 2019
File   : LED1.c
==============================================================================*/
#include "main.h"

//
// Define all your Task functions here
// ===================================
//

// Task 1 - Flashes LED at port pin PE12 every second
void task1(void *pvParameters)
{
    GPIO_Digital_Output(&GPIOE_BASE, _GPIO_PINMASK_12);    // Set PE12 output

    while (1)
    {
        vTaskDelay(pdMS_TO_TICKS(1000));                   // 1 second delay
        GPIOE_ODR.B12 = ~GPIOE_ODR.B12;                    // Toggle LED
    }
}


//
// Start of MAIN program
// =====================
//
void main()
{
//
// Create all the TASKS here
// =========================
//
    // Create Task 1
    xTaskCreate(
        (TaskFunction_t)task1,
        "Task 1",
        configMINIMAL_STACK_SIZE,
        NULL,
        10,
        NULL
    );

//
// Start the RTOS scheduler
//
    vTaskStartScheduler();

//
// Will never reach here
//
    while (1);
}
```

FIGURE 9.3   LED1.c program listing.

```
xTaskCreate(
  (TaskFunction_t)task1,
  "Task 1",
  configMINIMAL_STACK_SIZE,
  NULL,
  10,
  NULL
  );
```
where,
Task function: task1
Task name: Task 1
Stack size: minimal stack size
Parameters: none
Task priority: 10
Task handle: none

Task function task1 configures port pin PE12 as digital output and then toggles this pin every second so that the LED connected to this port flashes every second. The code for task1 is simply:

```
void task1(void *pvParameters)
{
  GPIO_Digital_Output(&GPIOE_BASE, _GPIO_PINMASK_12);
  while (1)
  {
    vTaskDelay(pdMS_TO_TICKS(1000));
    GPIOE_ODR.B12 = ~GPIOE_ODR.B12;
  }
}
```
The scheduler is started with the function call:

vTaskStartScheduler();

It is recommended to check the return status when an API function is called to ensure that the function has completed successfully. The task creation code in Fig. 9.3 can be modified by checking the return status as follows:

```
If(xTaskCreate(
  (TaskFunction_t)task1,
  "Task 1",
  configMINIMAL_STACK_SIZE,
  NULL,
  10,
  NULL
  ) != pdPASS)
{
      // Task could not be created – not sufficient heap memory
}
else
{
// Task created successfully – carry on with the remainder of the program
}
```

LED1 at   **LED2 at**
port PE12   **port PE15**

FIGURE 9.4   Block diagram of the project.

9.7.4 Project 2—flashing two LEDs, one every second, other one every 200 ms

Description: Two LEDs are used in this project. One of the LEDs (LED at port PE12) flashes every second, while the other one (LED at port PE15) flashes every 200 ms.

Aim: The aim of this project is to show how FreeRTOS API functions vTaskCreate(), xTicksToDelay(), and macro pdMS_TO_TICKS() can be used in a program. There are two tasks in this project.

Block diagram: Fig. 9.4 shows the project block diagram.

Program listing: The program listing is shown in Fig. 9.5 (program: **LED2.c**). The code for task1 is same as in Fig. 9.3. task2 configures port pin PE15 as digital output and then toggles the port pin every 200 ms. The code for this task is:

```
void task2(void *pvParameters)
{
  GPIO_Digital_Output(&GPIOE_BASE, _GPIO_PINMASK_15);
  while (1)
  {
    vTaskDelay(pdMS_TO_TICKS(200));
    GPIOE_ODR.B15 = ~GPIOE_ODR.B15;
  }
}
```

Task1 is to create as in Fig. 9.3. The creation of task2 is similar and is shown below:

```
xTaskCreate(
  (TaskFunction_t)task2,
  "Task 2",
  configMINIMAL_STACK_SIZE,
  NULL,
  10,
  NULL
);
```

```
/*=============================================================================
                           FLASH TWO LEDs
                           ==============

This program flashes the two LEDs connected to port pins PE12 and PE15 of the
Clicker 2 for STM32 development board. LED at PE12 flashes every second, while
the LED at port PE15 flashes every 200ms.

Author: Dogan Ibrahim
Date   : September, 2019
File   : LED2.c
=============================================================================*/
#include "main.h"

//
// Define all your Task functions here
// ===================================
//

// Task 1 - Flashes LED at port pin PE12 every second
void task1(void *pvParameters)
{
    GPIO_Digital_Output(&GPIOE_BASE, _GPIO_PINMASK_12);        // Set PE12 output

    while (1)
    {
        vTaskDelay(pdMS_TO_TICKS(1000));                       // 1 second delay
        GPIOE_ODR.B12 = ~GPIOE_ODR.B12;                        // Toggle LED
    }
}

 // Task 2 - Flashes LED at port pin PE15 every 200ms
void task2(void *pvParameters)
{
    GPIO_Digital_Output(&GPIOE_BASE, _GPIO_PINMASK_15);        // Set PE15 output

    while (1)
    {
        vTaskDelay(pdMS_TO_TICKS(200));                        // 200ms delay
        GPIOE_ODR.B15 = ~GPIOE_ODR.B15;                        // Toggle LED
    }
}
//
// Start of MAIN program
// =====================
//
void main()
{
//
// Create all the TASKS here
// =========================
//
    // Create Task 1
    xTaskCreate(
        (TaskFunction_t)task1,
        "Task 1",
        configMINIMAL_STACK_SIZE,
        NULL,
        10,
        NULL
```

FIGURE 9.5   LED2.c program listing.

```
    );

      // Create Task 2
    xTaskCreate(
        (TaskFunction_t)task2,
        "Task 2",
        configMINIMAL_STACK_SIZE,
        NULL,
        10,
        NULL
    );
//
// Start the RTOS scheduler
//
    vTaskStartScheduler();

//
// Will never reach here
//
    while (1);
}
```

FIGURE 9.5 (*Continued*)

9.7.5 Suspending a task

A suspended task is not available to run unless it is resumed. A task is suspended by calling to API function vTaskSuspend() as follows:

vTaskSuspend(TaskHandle_t pxTaskToSuspend);

Parameter
pxTaskToSuspend: This is the handle of the task being suspended. The handle of a task is specified during its creation. The task name can be supplied to function xTaskGetHandler() to get its handle.
Return value
This function has no return value.

The API function vTaskSuspendAll() suspends the scheduler. It has the following format:

vTaskSuspendAll(void);

This function has no parameters and no return values. Suspending the scheduler prevents context switching occurring, but leaves interrupts enabled. Any interrupts requesting a context switching while the scheduler is suspended is held pending until the scheduler is resumed by the API call xTaskResumeAll(). Calls to xTaskSuspendAll() can be nested and the same number of calls must be made to xTaskResumeAll() as have been made to vTaskSuspendAll() before the scheduler will leave the suspended state. xTaskResumeAll() must be called from an executing task. Any other FreeRTOS API functions must not be called while the scheduler is suspended.

9.7.6 Resuming a suspended task

A suspended task can be resumed and placed in the Ready state by calling to function vTaskResume() as follows:

vTaskResume(TaskHandle_t pxTaskToResume);

Parameter
pxTaskToResume: This is the handle of the task to be resumed. The handle of a task is specified during its creation. The task name can be supplied to function xTaskGetHandler() to get its handle.
Return value
This function has no return value.
The API function xTaskResumeAll() resumes the scheduler activity after the function call vTaskSuspendAll(). The format of this function is:

xTaskResumeAll(void);

This function has no parameters, but have the following return values:
pdTRUE: The scheduler moved to Active state.
pdFALSE: Either the scheduler moved into the Active state and the transition did not cause a context switch to occur, or the scheduler was left in the Suspended state due to nested calls to vTaskSuspendAll()
Since calls to vTaskSuspendAll() can be nested, the same number of calls must be made to xTaskResumeAll() before the scheduler leaves the Suspended state and moves into Active state. Function xTaskResumeAll() must be called from an executing task.

9.7.7 Project 3—suspending and resuming a task

Description: There are two tasks in this project. Task 1 flashes the LED at port PE12 every second. Task 2 flashes the LED at port PE15 every 200 ms as in the previous project. Task 2 is suspended by Task 1 after Task 1 makes 10 flashes, and as a result Task 2 stops flashing the LED. Task 2 is then resumed after Task 1 makes 15 flashes at which point Task 2 LED starts to flash again.

Aim: The aim of this project is to show how FreeRTOS API functions vTaskCreate(), xTicksToDelay(), vTaskSuspend(), vTaskResume(), and macro pdMS_TO_TICKS() can be used in a program. There are two tasks in this project.

Block diagram: The block diagram of the project is same as in Fig. 9.4.

Program listing. Fig. 9.6 shows the program listing (program: **LED3.c**). The code of this program is similar to the one given in Fig. 9.5. Here, the handle of task2 is stored in a variable pointed to by **xT2Handle**. This handle is then used in task1 to suspend and then resume task2. When variable **cnt** is equal to 10, task2 is suspended. This task is then resumed when **cnt** becomes equal to 15. The code to suspend and resume task2 is as follows:

```
void task1(void *pvParameters)
{
  GPIO_Digital_Output(&GPIOE_BASE, _GPIO_PINMASK_12);
  while (1)
  {
    vTaskDelay(pdMS_TO_TICKS(1000));
```

```
/*==============================================================================
                    FLASH TWO LEDs - Suspend and Resume
                    ===================================

This program flashes the two LEDs connected to port pins PE12 and PE15 of the
Clicker 2 for STM32 development board. LED at PE12 (Task 1) flashes every second,
while the LED at port PE15 (Task 2) flashes every 200ms. Task 2 is suspended
after Task 1 makes 10 flashes. When Task 2 is suspended it stops flashing.
Task 2 is then resumed after Task 1 makes 15 flashes. At this point Task 2
starts flashing again

Author: Dogan Ibrahim
Date  : September, 2019
File  : LED3.c
==============================================================================*/
#include "main.h"
TaskHandle_t xT2Handle;
unsigned int cnt = 0;

//
// Define all your Task functions here
// ===================================
//

// Task 1 - Flashes LED at port pin PE12 every second
void task1(void *pvParameters)
{
    GPIO_Digital_Output(&GPIOE_BASE, _GPIO_PINMASK_12);    // Set PE12 output

    while (1)
    {
        vTaskDelay(pdMS_TO_TICKS(1000));                   // 1 second delay
        GPIOE_ODR.B12 = ~GPIOE_ODR.B12;                    // Toggle LED
        cnt++;
        if(cnt == 10)vTaskSuspend(xT2Handle);              // Suspend task2
        if(cnt == 15)vTaskResume(xT2Handle);               // Resume task2
    }
}

 // Task 2 - Flashes LED at port pin PE15 every 200ms
void task2(void *pvParameters)
{
    GPIO_Digital_Output(&GPIOE_BASE, _GPIO_PINMASK_15);    // Set PE15 output

    while (1)
    {
        vTaskDelay(pdMS_TO_TICKS(200));                    // 200ms delay
        GPIOE_ODR.B15 = ~GPIOE_ODR.B15;                    // Toggle LED
    }
}
//
// Start of MAIN program
// =====================
//
void main()
{
//
// Create all the TASKS here
// =========================
//
```

FIGURE 9.6 LED3.c program listing.

```
      // Create Task 1
      xTaskCreate(
          (TaskFunction_t)task1,
          "Task 1",
          configMINIMAL_STACK_SIZE,
          NULL,
          10,
          NULL
      );

       // Create Task 2
      xTaskCreate(
          (TaskFunction_t)task2,
          "Task 2",
          configMINIMAL_STACK_SIZE,
          NULL,
          10,
          &xT2Handle
      );
  //
  // Start the RTOS scheduler
  //
      vTaskStartScheduler();

  //
  // Will never reach here
  //
      while (1);
  }
```

FIGURE 9.6   (*Continued*)


```
      GPIOE_ODR.B12 = ~GPIOE_ODR.B12;
      cnt + +;
      if(cnt == 10)vTaskSuspend(xT2Handle);
      if(cnt == 15)vTaskResume(xT2Handle);
    }
  }
```

9.7.8 Deleting a task

A deleted task is removed from the system and it can no longer run. API function vTask-Delete() is used to delete a task:

vTaskDelete(TaskHandle_t pxTask);

Parameter
pxTask: This is the handle of the task to be deleted. A task can delete itself by passing NULL in place of a valid task handle
Return value
This function has no return value.

9.7.9 Project 4—flashing LEDs and deleting a task

Description: There are two tasks in this project. Task 1 flashes the LED at ort PE12 every second. Task 2 flashes the LED at port PE15 every 200 ms as in the previous project. Task 2 is deleted by Task 1 after Task 1 makes 10 flashes. After this point only Task 1 remains in the system and runs.

Aim: The aim of this project is to show how FreeRTOS API functions vTaskCreate(), xTicksToDelay(), vTaskDelete(), and macro pdMS_TO_TICKS() can be used in a program. There are two tasks in this project.

Block diagram: The block diagram of the project is same as in Fig. 9.4.

Program listing: Fig. 9.7 shows the program listing (program: **LED4.c**). This program is similar to the one given in Fig. 9.6, but here task2 is deleted after task1 makes 10 flashes. The code to delete task2 is shown below:

```
void task1(void *pvParameters)
{
  GPIO_Digital_Output(&GPIOE_BASE, _GPIO_PINMASK_12);
  while (1)
  {
    vTaskDelay(pdMS_TO_TICKS(1000));
    GPIOE_ODR.B12 = ~GPIOE_ODR.B12;
    cnt + +;
    if(cnt == 10)vTaskDelete(xT2Handle);
  }
}
```

9.7.10 Getting the task handle

The task handle is defined during the creation of a task. We can use the API function call xTaskGetHandle() to return the handle of a task.

xTaskGetHandle(const char *pcNameToQuery);

<u>Parameter</u>

pcNameToQuery: This is the name of the task whose handle is to be returned, where the name is specified as a standard Null terminated C string.

Parameter INCLUDE_xTaskGetHandle must be set to 1 in FreeRTOSConfig.h for function xTaskGetHandle() to be available to a program.

<u>Return value</u>

The task handle is returned. If there is no task with the specified name, then a NULL is returned. This function can take a long time to complete and therefore it is not recommended to use it only once for each task.

Considering the example program in Fig. 9.7, task1 can get the handle of task2 and then delete it as shown in the following code. As in the previous program, in the code below, task2 is deleted after 10 flashes of task1. Notice here that the code checks whether or not the handle is valid before deleting the task:

```
TaskHandle_t xT2Handle, xHandle;
void task1(void *pvParameters)
{
  const char *pcNameToQuery = "Task 2";
  GPIO_Digital_Output(&GPIOE_BASE, _GPIO_PINMASK_12);
  while (1)
```

```
/*==============================================================================
                    FLASH TWO LEDs - Deleta a Task
                    ==============================

This program flashes the two LEDs connected to port pins PE12 and PE15 of the
Clicker 2 for STM32 development board. LED at PE12 (Task 1) flashes every second,
while the LED at port PE15 (Task 2) flashes every 200ms. Task 2 is deleted
after Task 1 makes 10 flashes. At this point only Task 1 flashes the LED

Author: Dogan Ibrahim
Date  : September, 2019
File  : LED4.c
==============================================================================*/
#include "main.h"
TaskHandle_t xT2Handle;
unsigned int cnt = 0;


//
// Define all your Task functions here
// ====================================
//

// Task 1 - Flashes LED at port pin PE12 every second
void task1(void *pvParameters)
{
    GPIO_Digital_Output(&GPIOE_BASE, _GPIO_PINMASK_12);      // Set PE12 output

    while (1)
    {
        vTaskDelay(pdMS_TO_TICKS(1000));                     // 1 second delay
        GPIOE_ODR.B12 = ~GPIOE_ODR.B12;                      // Toggle LED
        cnt++;
        if(cnt == 10)vTaskDelete(xT2Handle);                 // Delete task2
    }
}

 // Task 2 - Flashes LED at port pin PE15 every 200ms
void task2(void *pvParameters)
{
    GPIO_Digital_Output(&GPIOE_BASE, _GPIO_PINMASK_15);      // Set PE15 output

    while (1)
    {
        vTaskDelay(pdMS_TO_TICKS(200));                      // 200ms delay
        GPIOE_ODR.B15 = ~GPIOE_ODR.B15;                      // Toggle LED
    }
}
//
// Start of MAIN program
// =====================
//
void main()
{
//
// Create all the TASKS here
// =========================
//
    // Create Task 1
    xTaskCreate(
        (TaskFunction_t)task1,
```

FIGURE 9.7   LED4.c program listing.

```
            "Task 1",
            configMINIMAL_STACK_SIZE,
            NULL,
            10,
            NULL
        );

        // Create Task 2
        xTaskCreate(
            (TaskFunction_t)task2,
            "Task 2",
            configMINIMAL_STACK_SIZE,
            NULL,
            10,
            &xT2Handle
        );
//
// Start the RTOS scheduler
//
        vTaskStartScheduler();

//
// Will never reach here
//
        while (1);
    }
```

FIGURE 9.7 (*Continued*)

```
    {
        vTaskDelay(pdMS_TO_TICKS(1000));
        GPIOE_ODR.B12 = ~GPIOE_ODR.B12;
        cnt + +;
        if(cnt == 10)
        {
            xHandle = xTaskGetHandle(pcNameToQuery)
            if(xHandle != NULL) vTaskDelete(xHandle);
        }
    }
}
```

The API function call xTaskGetIdleTaskHandle() returns the task handle of the *Idle* task. The Idle task is created automatically by the scheduler and it runs at the lowest possible priority in the background. This function has no parameter and its format is:

xTaskGetIdleTaskHandle(void);

Parameter INCLUDE_xTaskGetIdleTaskHandle must be set to 1 in file FreeRTOSConfig.h for this function to be available.

The API function xTaskGetCurrentTaskHandle() returns the handle of the task which is currently running. This function has no parameters.

Parameter INCLUDE_xTaskGetCurrentTaskHandle must be set to 1 in file FreeRTOSConfig.h for xTaskGetCurrentTaskHandle() to be available.

9.7.11 Running at fixed intervals

The API function vTaskDelayUntil() can be used to place a task into constant execution frequency. This function blocks a task until an absolute time is reached and can be used to run the task at regular intervals.

vTaskDelayUntil(TickType_t *pxPreviousWakeTime, TickType_t xTimeIncrement);

Parameters
pxPreviousWakeTime: This parameter holds the time at which the task last left the Blocked state. This time is used as a reference point to calculate the time at which the task should next leave the Blocked state. The variable pointed to by pxPreviousWakeTime is updated automatically within the vTaskDelayUntil() function.

xTimeIncrement: Assuming that the function is being used to implement a task that executes periodically and with a fixed frequency, the frequency of the repeat interval is set by this parameter.

Parameter INCLUDE_vTaskDelayUntil must be set to 1 in FreeRTOSConfig.h for the vTaskDelay() API function to be available.

Return value
This function has no return value.

9.7.12 Tick count

The tick count is the total number of tick interrupts that have occurred since the scheduler was started. API function xTaskGetTickCount() returns the current tick count. After some time, the tick count overflows and returns to zero, but this does not affect the internal operation of the kernel. The actual time that one tick period represents depends on the value assigned to parameter configTICK_RATE_HZ in file FreeRTOSConfig.h.

xTaskGetTickCount(void);

Parameters
None.

Return value
The function returns the current tick count at the time it is called.

9.7.13 Project 5—flashing an LED using function vTaskDelayUntil()

Description: In this project the LED connected to port pin PE12 is used only. The program flashes the LED at every 500 ms.

Aim: The aim of this project is to show how FreeRTOS API functions vTaskCreate(), vTaskDelayUntil(), xTaskGetTickCount(), and macro pdMS_TO_TICKS can be used in a program. There is only one task in this project.

Block diagram: The block diagram of the project is same as in Fig. 9.2.

Program listing: Fig. 9.8 shows the program listing (program: **LED5.c**). Only one task is used in this program. Inside this task, the period of repetition is set to 500 ms and stored in xPeriod, the current tick count is obtained and stored in xPreviousWakeTime. Function vTaskDelayUntil() is called with the xPreviousWakeTime and xPeriod. The net result is that the code inside the loop is executed at every 500 ms, flashing the LED.

```
/*===========================================================================
                    FLASH AN LED USING vTaskDeleteUntil()
                    ====================================

This program flashes the LED connected to port pin PE12 every 500ms, using the
API function vTaskDelayUntil().

Author: Dogan Ibrahim
Date   : September, 2019
File   : LED5.c
=============================================================================*/
#include "main.h"

//
// Define all your Task functions here
// ==================================
//

// Task 1 - Flashes LED at port pin PE12 every 500ms
void task1(void *pvParameters)
{
    TickType_t xPreviousWakeTime;
    const TickType_t xPeriod = pdMS_TO_TICKS(500);              // 500ms

    GPIO_Digital_Output(&GPIOE_BASE, _GPIO_PINMASK_12);        // Set PE12 output
    xPreviousWakeTime = xTaskGetTickCount();

    while (1)
    {
        vTaskDelayUntil(&xPreviousWakeTime, xPeriod);
        GPIOE_ODR.B12 = ~GPIOE_ODR.B12;                        // Toggle LED
    }
}

//
// Start of MAIN program
// =====================
//
void main()
{
//
// Create all the TASKS here
// =========================
//
    // Create Task 1
    xTaskCreate(
        (TaskFunction_t)task1,
        "Task 1",
        configMINIMAL_STACK_SIZE,
        NULL,
        10,
        NULL
    );

//
// Start the RTOS scheduler
//
    vTaskStartScheduler();

//
// Will never reach here
//
    while (1);
}
```

FIGURE 9.8 LED5.c program listing.

9.7.14 Task priorities

Task priorities range from 0 (lowest priority) to configMAX_PRIORITIES-1 (highest priority). Parameter configMAX_PRIORITIES is defined in file FreeRTOSConfig.h. A high priority task can grab the CPU and block the execution of a lower priority task. Upon completion of the higher priority task, or when the higher priority task waits for a resource then the lower priority task can become executable.

vTaskSetPriority()

The priority of a task can be defined during its creation. API function vTaskSetPriority() can be used to change the priority of a task. This function must be called from a running task. Its format is:

vTaskPrioritySet(TaskHandle_t pxTask, UBaseType_t uxNewPriority);

<u>**Parameters**</u>

pxTask: This is the handle of the task whose priority is to be changed. A task can change its own priority by passing NULL in place of its handle.

uxNewPriority: The priority to which the subject task will be set. In the FreeRTOSConfig.h file used in this book, the value of configMAX_PRIORITIES is 16, so that the priorities can be specified from 0 to 15. Specifying a value greater than 15 will set it to 15.

<u>**Return value**</u>

This function has no return value.

uxTaskPriorityGet()

API function uxTaskPriorityGet() can be called to return the priority of a task at the time the call is made. This function has the following format:

uxTaskPriorityGet(TaskHandle_t pxTask);

<u>**Parameter**</u>

pxTask: This is the handle of the task whose priority is being queried. A task may query its own priority by passing NULL in place of a valid task handle.

<u>**Return value**</u>

The priority of the task queried is returned.

9.7.15 Project 6—flashing LED and push-button switch at different priorities

Description: In this project the LED connected to port pin PE12 is used in Task 1. Additionally, the push-button switch connected to port pin PE0 is used in Task 2. The priorities of the tasks are changed and the results are noted as follows:

Task 1	Task 2
Turn ON the LED continuously	Turn OFF the LED

Task 1 runs continuously without having to wait for a resource. Task 2 polls the push-button switch and turns OFF the LED when the button is pressed. We have the following three cases as far as the priorities are concerned:

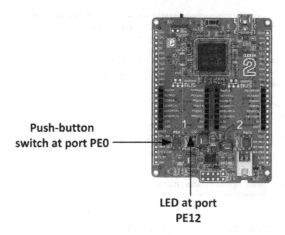

Push-button
switch at port PE0

LED at port
PE12

FIGURE 9.9   Block diagram of the project.

Task 1 has higher priority than Task 2: The LED is turned ON continuously. Pressing the button has no effect on the LED since Task1 is at higher priority and is not releasing the CPU.

Task 1 and Task 2 have the same priorities: Both Task1 and Task2 share the CPU. The LED is ON continuously. Pressing the button dims the LED brightness slightly.

Task 1 has lower priority than Task 2: Task1 never runs and the LED remains OFF since Task2 never releases the CPU.

Aim: The aim of this project is to show how two tasks with different priorities can operate.

Block diagram: The block diagram of the project is shown in Fig. 9.9.

Program listing: Fig. 9.10 shows the program listing (program: **LED6.c**). The priorities of the tasks are changed and the programs are compiled and tested for each of the above three cases. Notice that the output state of the push-button switch at logic 1 and goes to logic 0 when the button is pressed.

9.7.16 Project 7—getting/setting task priorities

Description: In this project the LED connected to port pin PE12 is used in Task 1. Additionally, the push-button switch connected to port pin PE0 is used in Task 2. Initially both tasks are given the same priority of 10 during their creations. As a result, the LED is ON all the time and pressing the button dims the LED brightness slightly. When the button is pressed, Task 2 gets the priority of Task 1, checks it, and if it is 10 changes it to 8. As a result, Task 2 grabs the CPU and the LED remains OFF forever.

Aim: The aim of this project is to show how the priority of a task can be obtained and also how it can be changed. API functions xTaskCreate(), vTaskPrioritySet(), uxTaskPriorityGet are used in this program.

Block diagram: The block diagram of the project is as shown in Fig. 9.9.

Program listing: Fig. 9.11 shows the program listing (program: **LED7.c**). The two tsks are created with both having priorities of 10. When the button is pressed, Task2 gets the priority of Task1 by calling function uxTaskPriorityGet() and stores in variable uxTask1Priority. If the

```
/*=============================================================================
                    TWO TASKS AT DIFFERENT PRIORITIES
                    ================================

This program has two tasks: Task1 turns ON the LED connected to port pin PE12
continuously. In Task 2 a push-button switch is used. Pushing the button is
supposed to turn OFF the LED.

Author: Dogan Ibrahim
Date  : September, 2019
File  : LED6.c
=============================================================================*/
#include "main.h"

//
// Define all your Task functions here
// ===================================
//

// Task 1 - Turn ON the LED at port pin PE12 continuously
void Task1(void *pvParameters)
{
    GPIO_Digital_Output(&GPIOE_BASE, _GPIO_PINMASK_12);      // Set PE12 output

    while (1)
    {
        GPIOE_ODR.B12 = 1;                                   // LED ON
    }
}

// Task 2 - Push-button switch at port pin PE0. Turn OFF the LED
void Task2(void *pvParameters)
{
    GPIO_Digital_Output(&GPIOE_BASE, _GPIO_PINMASK_12);      // Set PE12 output
    GPIO_Digital_Input(&GPIOE_BASE, _GPIO_PINMASK_0);        // Set PE0 as input

    while (1)
    {
        while(GPIOE_IDR.B0 == 1);                            // Wait for switch
        GPIOE_ODR.B12 = 0;                                   // Turn OFF LED
    }
}

//
// Start of MAIN program
// =====================
//
void main()
{
//
// Create all the TASKS here
// =========================
//
    // Create Task 1
    xTaskCreate(
        (TaskFunction_t)Task1,
        "Task 1",
        configMINIMAL_STACK_SIZE,
        NULL,
        1,
```

FIGURE 9.10   LED6.c program listing.

```
        NULL
    );

    // Create Task 2
    xTaskCreate(
        (TaskFunction_t)Task2,
        "Task 2",
        configMINIMAL_STACK_SIZE,
        NULL,
        10,
        NULL
    );

//
// Start the RTOS scheduler
//
    vTaskStartScheduler();

//
// Will never reach here
//
    while (1);
}
```

FIGURE 9.10 (*Continued*)

priority is 10, then it is changed to 8 by calling to function vTaskPrioritySet() and passing the handle of Task1 as well as the new priority 8.

9.8 Using an LCD

In this section we will learn how to use an LCD to display various text outputs from our FreeRTOS projects. Before going into the details of LCD-based projects, it is worthwhile to review the basic features of character-based LCDs.

In microcontroller systems the output of a measured variable is usually displayed using LEDs, 7-segment displays, or LCD type displays. LCDs have the advantages that they can be used to display alphanumeric or graphical data. Some LCDs have 40 or more character lengths with the capability to display several lines. Some other LCD displays can be used to display graphics images. Some modules offer color displays while some others incorporate backlighting so that they can be viewed in dimly lit conditions.

There are basically two types of LCDs as far as the interface technique is concerned: parallel LCDs and serial LCDs. Parallel LCDs (e.g., Hitachi HD44780) are connected to a microcontroller using more than one data line and the data is transferred in parallel form. It is common to use either 4 or 8 data lines. Using a 4 wire connection saves I/O pins but it is slower since the data is transferred in two stages. Serial LCDs are connected to the microcontroller using only one data line and data is usually sent to the LCD using the standard RS-232 asynchronous data communication protocol. Serial LCDs are much easier to use but they cost more than the parallel ones.

The programming of a parallel LCD is usually a complex task and requires a good understanding of the internal operation of the LCD controllers, including the timing diagrams. Fortunately, most high-level languages provide special library commands for displaying data on

```
/*==============================================================================
                    GET/SET TASK PRIORITIES
                    =======================

This program has two tasks: Task1 turns ON the LED connected to port pin PE12
continuously. In Task 2 a push-button switch is used. When the button is
pressed, Task2 gets the priority of Task1 and changes it to 8 so that Task2 has
a higher priority. As a result, the LED turns OFF forever.

Author: Dogan Ibrahim
Date  : September, 2019
File  : LED7.c
==============================================================================*/
#include "main.h"
TaskHandle_t xHandle;

//
// Define all your Task functions here
// ====================================
//

// Task 1 - Turn ON the LED at port pin PE12 continuously
void Task1(void *pvParameters)
{
    GPIO_Digital_Output(&GPIOE_BASE, _GPIO_PINMASK_12);     // Set PE12 output

    while (1)
    {
        GPIOE_ODR.B12 = 1;                                  // LED ON
    }
}

// Task 2 - Push-button switch at port pin PE0. Turn OFF the LED
void Task2(void *pvParameters)
{
    UBaseType_t uxTask1Priority;

    GPIO_Digital_Output(&GPIOE_BASE, _GPIO_PINMASK_12);     // Set PE12 output
    GPIO_Digital_Input(&GPIOE_BASE, _GPIO_PINMASK_0);       // Set PE0 as input

    while (1)
    {
        while(GPIOE_IDR.B0 == 1);                            // Wait for switch
        uxTask1Priority = uxTaskPriorityGet(xHandle);       // Get Task1 priority
        if(uxTask1Priority == 10) vTaskPrioritySet(xHandle, 8);
        GPIOE_ODR.B12 = 0;                                  // Turn OFF LED
    }
}

//
// Start of MAIN program
// =====================
//
void main()
{
//
// Create all the TASKS here
// =========================
//
    // Create Task 1
```

FIGURE 9.11   LED7.c program listing.

```
xTaskCreate(
    (TaskFunction_t)Task1,
    "Task 1",
    configMINIMAL_STACK_SIZE,
    NULL,
    10,
    &xHandle
);

// Create Task 2
xTaskCreate(
    (TaskFunction_t)Task2,
    "Task 2",
    configMINIMAL_STACK_SIZE,
    NULL,
    10,
    NULL
);

//
// Start the RTOS scheduler
//
    vTaskStartScheduler();

//
// Will never reach here
//
    while (1);
}
```

FIGURE 9.11 *(Continued)*

alphanumeric as well as on graphical LCDs. All the user has to do is connect the LCD to the microcontroller, define the LCD connection in the software, and then send special commands to display data on the LCD.

9.8.1 HD44780 LCD module

HD44780 is one of the most popular alphanumeric LCD modules used in industry and also by hobbyists. This module is monochrome and comes in different sizes. Modules with 8, 16, 20, 24, 32, and 40 columns are available. Depending on the model chosen, the number of rows varies between 1, 2, or 4. The display provides a 14-pin (or 16-pin) connector to a microcontroller. Table 9.1 gives the pin configuration and pin functions of a 14-pin LCD module. Below is a summary of the pin functions:

V_{SS} is the 0 V supply or ground. The V_{DD} pin should be connected to the positive supply. Although the manufacturers specify a 5 V d.c. supply, the modules will usually work with as low as 3 V or as high as 6 V.

Pin 3 is named V_{EE} (or V_O) and this is the contrast control pin. This pin is used to adjust the contrast of the display and it should be connected to a variable voltage supply. A 10 K potentiometer is normally connected between the power supply lines with its wiper arm connected to this pin so that the contrast can be adjusted.

Pin 4 is the Register Select (RS) and when this pin is LOW, data transferred to the display is treated as commands. When RS is HIGH, character data can be transferred to and from the module.

TABLE 9.1   Pin configuration of HD44780 LCD module.

Pin no.	Name	Function
1	V_{SS}	Ground
2	V_{DD}	+ve supply
3	V_{EE}	Contrast
4	RS	Register select
5	R/W	Read/write
6	E	Enable
7	D0	Daat bit 0
8	D1	Data bit 1
9	D2	Data bit 2
10	D3	Data bit 3
11	D4	Data bit 4
12	D5	Data bit 5
13	D6	Data bit 6
14	D7	Data bit 7

Pin 5 is the Read/Write (R/W) line. This pin is pulled LOW in order to write commands or character data to the LCD module. When this pin is HIGH, character data or status information can be read from the module.

Pin 6 is the Enable (E) pin which is used to initiate the transfer of commands or data between the module and the microcontroller. When writing to the display, data is transferred only on the HIGH to LOW transition of this line. When reading from the display, data becomes available after the LOW to HIGH transition of the enable pin and this data remains valid as long as the enable pin is at logic HIGH.

Pins 7–14 are the eight data bus lines (D0 to D7). Data can be transferred between the microcontroller and the LCD module using either a single 8-bit byte or as two 4-bit nibbles. In the latter case only the upper four data lines (D4–D7) are used. 4-bit mode has the advantage that four less I/O lines are required to communicate with the LCD. In this book we shall be using a character-based LCD in 4-bit interface mode.

Some LCDs have A and K pins which are used for the backlight. The K pin should be connected to ground, while the A pin should be connected to +5 V supply through a 220 Ω resistor.

9.8.2 Connecting the LCD to the Clicker 2 for STM32 development board

The following LCD data pins are used in 4-bit mode in addition to the power and ground pins:

D4:D7
E
R/S

The R/W pin of the LCD is connected to ground in 4-bit interface mode.

In this book we shall be connecting the LCD to our Clicker 2 for STM32 microcontroller development board as in the following table, using only the mikroBUS 1 connector pins on the development board:

LCD pin	Microcontroller pin
D4	PA2
D5	PE7
D6	PE8
D7	PC10
R/S	PC11
E	PC12
Vss	GND
Vdd	+5 V

9.8.3 LCD functions

mikroC Pro for ARM compiler supports the following LCD functions:

Lcd_Init()	Initialize the LCD library
Lcd_Out(r, c, text)	Display the given text at row r, column c of the LCD
Lcd_Out_Cp(text)	Display the given text at current cursor position
Lcd_Chr(r, c, ch)	Display the given character at row r, column c of the LCD
Lcd_Chr_Cp(ch)	Display the given character at the current cursor position
Lcd_Cmd(cmd)	Send a command to the LCD

Function Lcd_Init describes the interface between the LCD and the microcontroller system in use. This function must be called before any other LCD function is used.

The following LCD commands are valid:

LCD command	Purpose
_LCD_FIRST_ROW	Move cursor to the 1st row
_LCD_SECOND_ROW	Move cursor to the 2nd row
_LCD_THIRD_ROW	Move cursor to the 3rd row
_LCD_FOURTH_ROW	Move cursor to the 4th row
_LCD_CLEAR	Clear display
_LCD_RETURN_HOME	Return cursor to home position, returns a shifted display to its original position. Display data RAM is unaffected
_LCD_CURSOR_OFF	Turn off cursor
_LCD_UNDERLINE_ON	Underline cursor on
_LCD_BLINK_CURSOR_ON	Blink cursor on
_LCD_MOVE_CURSOR_LEFT	Move cursor left without changing display data RAM
_LCD_MOVE_CURSOR_RIGHT	Move cursor right without changing display data RAM

LCD command	Purpose
_LCD_TURN_ON	Turn LCD display on
_LCD_TURN_OFF	Turn LCD display off
_LCD_SHIFT_LEFT	Shift display left without changing display data RAM
_LCD_SHIFT_RIGHT	Shift display right without changing display data RAM

9.8.4 Project 8—displaying text on the LCD

Description: In this project an LCD is connected to the Cliker 2 for STM32 microcontroller development board as described in Section 9.8.2. The text **FreeRTOS** is displayed starting from row 0, column 5 of the LCD.

Aim: The aim of this project is to show how an LCD can be used in a microcontroller-based project.

Block diagram: The block diagram of the project is as shown in Fig. 9.12.

Construction: The project was constructed on a breadboard and is shown in Fig. 9.13. The figure shows the Clicker 2 for STM32 development board, LCD, potentiometer to adjust the contrast, wiring, and the breadboard. Wiring between the development board and the LCD was done using jumper wires.

Circuit diagram: The circuit diagram of the project is shown in Fig. 9.14. The connections between the LCD and the Clicker 2 for STM32 microcontroller development board are as described earlier in this section.

Program listing: Fig. 9.15 shows the program listing (program: **LCD1.c**). Only one task is used in this program. At the beginning of the program the interface between the LCD and the microcontroller development board is defined. The LCD is then initialized in Task 1 and text FreeRTOS is displayed at row 0, column 5 of the LCD. You should adjust the contrast of the LCD using the potentiometer until a sharp and clear image is obtained.

Notice that the LCD library must be enabled in the mikroC Pro for ARM Library Manager window before a program using an LCD can be compiled.

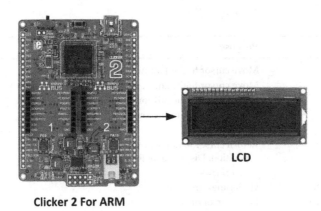

Clicker 2 For ARM

FIGURE 9.12   Block diagram of the project.

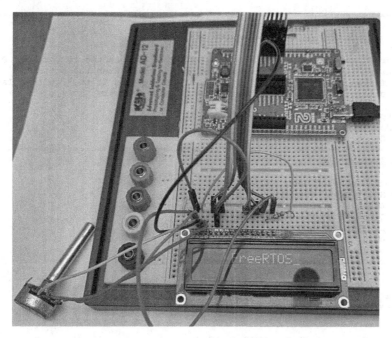

FIGURE 9.13   Project constructed on a breadboard.

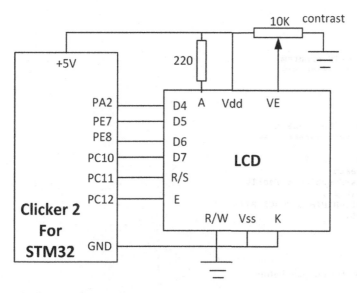

FIGURE 9.14   Circuit diagram of the project.

```
/*================================================================================
                    GET/SET TASK PRIORITIES
                    =======================

This program has two tasks: Task1 turns ON the LED connected to port pin PE12
continuously. In Task 2 a push-button switch is used. When the button is
pressed, Task 2 gets the priority of Task 1 and changes it to 8 so that Task2 has
a higher priority. As a result, the LED turns OFF forever.

Author: Dogan Ibrahim
Date  : September, 2019
File  : LCD1.c
================================================================================*/
#include "main.h"

// LCD module connections
sbit LCD_RS at GPIOC_ODR.B11;
sbit LCD_EN at GPIOC_ODR.B12;
sbit LCD_D4 at GPIOA_ODR.B2;
sbit LCD_D5 at GPIOE_ODR.B7;
sbit LCD_D6 at GPIOE_ODR.B8;
sbit LCD_D7 at GPIOC_ODR.B10;
// End LCD module connections

//
// Define all your Task functions here
// ====================================
//

// Task 1 - Display text FreeRTOS on LCD
void Task1(void *pvParameters)
{
    Lcd_Init();                                      // Initialize LCD
    Lcd_Cmd(_LCD_CLEAR);                             // Clear LCD
    Lcd_Out(0, 5, "FreeRTOS");                       // Display text

    while (1)
    {
    }
}

//
// Start of MAIN program
// ======================
//
void main()
{
//
// Create all the TASKS here
// =========================
//
    // Create Task 1
    xTaskCreate(
        (TaskFunction_t)Task1,
        "Task 1",
        configMINIMAL_STACK_SIZE,
        NULL,
        10,
        NULL
    );
```

FIGURE 9.15 LCD1.c program listing.

```
//
// Start the RTOS scheduler
//
    vTaskStartScheduler();

//
// Will never reach here
//
    while (1);
}
```

FIGURE 9.15 (*Continued*)

9.9 Task name, number of tasks, and tick count

The API function pcTaskGetName() returns the name of a task in standard NULL-terminated C string format. The format of this function is:

pcTaskGetName(TaskHandle_t xTaskToQuery);

Parameter
xTaskToQuery: This is the handle of the task being queried. A task may query its own name by passing NULL in place of a valid task handle.

Return value
The task name is returned bypassing its handle.

The API function uxTaskGetNumberOfTasks() returns the number of tasks that exist at the time of calling this function. The format of this function is:

uxTaskGetNumberOfTasks(void);

Parameter
None.

Return value
The function returns the total number of tasks under the control of FreeRTOS at the time the call is made. The number includes the Suspended tasks, Blocked tasks, Ready tasks, idle task, plus the Running task.

API function xTaskGetTickCount() returns the total number of tick interrupts that have occurred since the scheduler was started. The format of this function is:

xTaskGetTickCount(void);

Parameter
None.

Return value
The tick count is returned by the function. One tick period is set by parameter configTICK_RATE_HZ in file FreeRTOSConfig.h. The tick count overflows after a while and returns to zero, but this does not affect the internal operation of the kernel.

9.10 Project 9—displaying a task name, number of tasks, and tick count on the LCD

Description: In this project an LCD is connected to the Clicker 2 for STM32 microcontroller development board as in the previous project. There are three tasks in this project in addition to the *Idle* task. The LCD displays the task name of a calling task, number of tasks in the system, and the tick count at the time of calling the function.

Aim: The aim of this project is to show how an LCD can be used to display a task name, number of tasks, and the tick count at the time of calling the relevant API functions.

Program listing: Fig. 9.16 shows the program listing (program: **LCD2.c**). At the beginning of the program the interface between the LCD and the microcontroller development board is defined. Task 2 and Task 3 are dummy tasks and do not do anything useful. Task 1 initializes the LCD and clears it. The task name of this task is then obtained by using NULL in place of the task handle. This is displayed on the LCD. The program then gets the number of tasks under the control of FreeRTOS and displays it on the LCD. The Tick count is then obtained and displayed on the LCD.

Fig. 9.17 shows the LCD display. Notice that the task name was **Task 1** as expected, there were **4** tasks under the control of FreeRTOS including the Idle task, and the Tick count was **232** at the time the LCD display was updated

The Idle task

Notice that even though we have created three tasks in this project, the task count is displayed as 4. This is because of the Idle task. The Idle task is created automatically at the lowest possible priority when the FreeRTOS scheduler is started to ensure there is always at least one task that is able to run. This task does not use any CPU since all the other tasks are assumed to have higher priorities. The Idle task is responsible for freeing the memory allocated by FreeRTOS to tasks that have been deleted.

9.11 Yield to another task of equal priority

The API function taskYield() yields to another task of equal priority, where a task volunteers to leave the CPU without being preempted, and before its time slice has been fully utilized. The format of this function is:

taskYIELD(void);

This function has no parameters and no return value, and it must be called from an executing task. When this function call is made, the scheduler selects another Ready state task of equal priority and places it in the Running state. If there are no other tasks of equal priority that are eligible to run, then the task will be put back into Running state.

9.12 Aborting delay

The API function call xTaskAbortDelay() can be called to abort a delay set by the function call vTaskDelay() and then move the function from Blocked state to Ready state. vTaskDelay blocks the calling task until the set timeout elapses, after which time the task will come out of

```
/*=============================================================================
                    DISPLAY TASK NAME,NUMBER OF TASKS,TICK COUNT
                    =================================================

This program displays the task name of the calling task, number of tasks under
the control of FreeRTOS, and the tick count on the LCD.

Author: Dogan Ibrahim
Date  : September, 2019
File  : LCD2.c
=============================================================================*/
#include "main.h"
TaskHandle_t xHandle;

// LCD module connections
sbit LCD_RS at GPIOC_ODR.B11;
sbit LCD_EN at GPIOC_ODR.B12;
sbit LCD_D4 at GPIOA_ODR.B2;
sbit LCD_D5 at GPIOE_ODR.B7;
sbit LCD_D6 at GPIOE_ODR.B8;
sbit LCD_D7 at GPIOC_ODR.B10;
// End LCD module connections

//
// Define all your Task functions here
// ====================================
//

// Task 1 - Display Task name, Number of tasks, Tick count on LCD
void Task1(void *pvParameters)
{
    char *TaskName;
    char TaskCount;
    char Txt[7];
    int Tcount;

    Lcd_Init();                                    // Initialize LCD
    Lcd_Cmd(_LCD_CLEAR);                           // Clear LCD
    TaskName = pcTaskGetName(NULL);                // Current Task name
    Lcd_Out(1, 1, TaskName);                       // Display Task name

    TaskCount = uxTaskGetNumberOfTasks(void);      // Number of Tasks
    ByteToStr(TaskCount, Txt);                     // Convert to text
    Lcd_Out(1, 10, Txt);                           // Display Task cnt

    Tcount = xTaskGetTickCount(void);              // Get tick count
    IntToStr(Tcount, Txt);                         // Convert to text
    Lcd_Out(2, 1, Txt);                            // Display tick cnt

    while (1)
    {
    }
}

// Task 2 - Dummy task
void Task2(void *pvParameters)
{
    while (1)
    {
    }
```

FIGURE 9.16 LCD2.c program listing.

```
    }

    // Task 3 - Dummy task
    void Task3(void *pvParameters)
    {
        while (1)
        {
        }
    }


    //
    // Start of MAIN program
    // =====================
    //
    void main()
    {
    //
    // Create all the TASKS here
    // =========================
    //
        // Create Task 1
        xTaskCreate(
            (TaskFunction_t)Task1,
            "Task 1",
            configMINIMAL_STACK_SIZE,
            NULL,
            10,
            NULL
        );

        // Create Task 2
        xTaskCreate(
            (TaskFunction_t)Task2,
            "Task 2",
            configMINIMAL_STACK_SIZE,
            NULL,
            10,
            NULL
        );

        // Create Task 3
        xTaskCreate(
            (TaskFunction_t)Task3,
            "Task 3",
            configMINIMAL_STACK_SIZE,
            NULL,
            10,
            NULL
        );


    //
    // Start the RTOS scheduler
    //
        vTaskStartScheduler();

    //
    // Will never reach here
    //
        while (1);
    }
```

FIGURE 9.16   (*Continued*)

FIGURE 9.17   **LCD display.**

the Blocked state. A blocked task is not eligible to run and will not consume any CPU time. The format of xTaskAbortDelay() function is:

xTaskAbortDelay(TaskHandle_t xTask);

<u>Parameter</u>
xTask: This is the handle of the task that will be moved out of the Blocked state.
<u>Return values</u>
pdPASS: The task was removed from the Blocked state
pdFAIL: The task was not removed from the Blocked state since it was not blocked

9.13 Project 10—7-segment 2-digit multiplexed LED display counter

Description: In this project a 7-segment 2-digit multiplexed LED display is used as a counter to count up every second from 0 to 99. Multidigit 7-segment displays require continuous refreshing of their digits so that the human eye sees the digits as steady and nonflashing. The general technique used is to enable each digit for a short time (e.g., 10 ms) so that the human eye sees both digits ON at any time. This process requires the digits to be enabled alternately and continuously. As a result of this, the processor cannot perform any other tasks and has to be busy refreshing the digits. One technique used in nonmultitasking systems is to use timer interrupts and refresh the digits in the timer interrupt service routines. In this project, we will be employing a multitasking approach to refreshing the display digits.

Aim: The aim of this project is to show how the digits of a multiplexed 2-digit 7-segment LED display can be refreshed in a task, while another task sends data to the display to count up from 0 to 99 in seconds.

7-Segment LED displays: 7-Segment LED displays are used frequently in electronic circuits to show numeric or alphanumeric values. As shown in Fig. 9.18, a 7-segment LED display basically consists of 7 LEDs connected such that numbers from 0 to 9 and some letters can be displayed. Segments are identified by letters from **a** to **g** and Fig. 9.19 shows the segment names of a typical 7-segment display.

Fig. 9.20 shows how numbers from 0 to 9 can be obtained by turning ON different segments of the display.

7-Segment LED displays are available in two different configurations: **common cathode** and **common anode**. As shown in Fig. 9.21, in common cathode configuration all the cathodes of all segment LEDs are connected together to ground. The segments are turned ON

FIGURE 9.18   Some 7-segment displays.

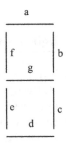

FIGURE 9.19   Segment names of a 7-segment display.

by applying a logic 1 to the required segment LED via current limiting resistors. In common cathode configuration the 7-segment LED is connected to the microcontroller in current sourcing mode.

In a common anode configuration, the anode terminals of all the LEDs are connected together as shown in Fig. 9.22. This common point is then normally connected to the supply voltage. A segment is turned ON by connecting its cathode terminal to logic 0 via a current limiting resistor. In common anode configuration the 7-segment LED is connected to the microcontroller in current sinking mode.

In multiplexed LED applications (for example, see Fig. 9.23 for a 2-digit LED), the LED segments of all the digits are tied together and the common pins of each digit is turned ON separately by the microcontroller. By displaying each digit for several milliseconds the eye can not differentiate that the digits are not ON all the time. This way we can multiplex any number of 7-segment displays together. For example, to display number 53, we have to send 5 to the first digit and enable its common pin. After a few milliseconds, number 3 is sent to

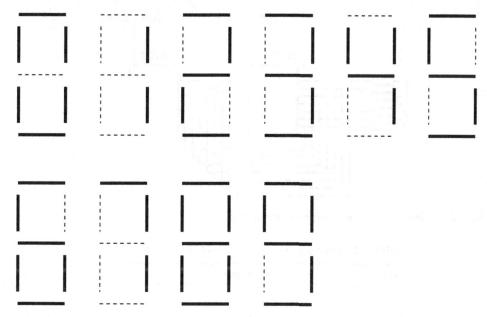

FIGURE 9.20 Displaying numbers 0–9.

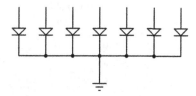

FIGURE 9.21 Common cathode 7-segment LED display.

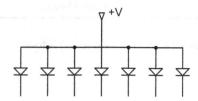

FIGURE 9.22 Common anode 7-segment LED display.

the second digit and the common point of the second digit is enabled. When this process is repeated continuously the user sees as if both displays are ON continuously.

Some manufacturers provide multiplexed multidigit displays in single packages. For example, we can purchase 2,4, or 8 digit multiplexed displays in a single package. The display used in this project is the DC56-11EWA which is a red color 0.56–in. height common-cathode two-digit display having 18 pins and the pin configuration as shown in Table 9.2. This display can be controlled from the microcontroller as follows:

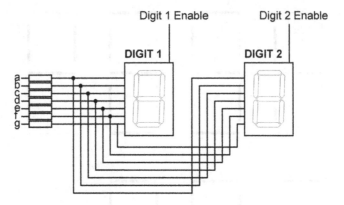

FIGURE 9.23   2-Digit multiplexed 7-segment LED display.

TABLE 9.2   Pin configuration of DC56-11EWA dual display.

Pin no.	Segment
1,5	e
2,6	d
3,8	c
14	digit 1 Enable
17,7	g
15,10	b
16,11	a
18,12	f
13	digit 2 Enable
4	decimal Point1
9	decimal Point 2

- Send the segment bit pattern for digit 1 to segments a to g
- Enable digit 1
- Wait for a few milliseconds
- Disable digit 1
- Send the segment bit patter for digit 2 to segments a to g
- Enable digit 2
- Wait for a few milliseconds
- Disable digit 2
- Repeat the above process continuously

The segment configuration of DC56-11EWA display is shown in Fig. 9.24. In a multiplexed display application, the segment pins of corresponding segments are connected together. For example, pins 11 and 16 are connected as the common **a** segment. Similarly, pins 15 and 10 are connected as the common **b** segment and so on.

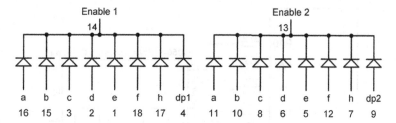

FIGURE 9.24 DC56-11EWA display segment configuration.

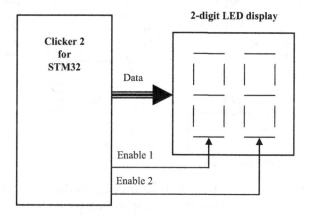

FIGURE 9.25 Block diagram of the project.

Block diagram: Fig. 9.25 shows the block diagram of the project.

Circuit diagram: The circuit diagram of the project is shown in Fig. 9.26. In this project, the following pins of the Clicker 2 for STM32 development board are used to interface with the 7-segment display:

7-Segment display pin	Clicker 2 for STM32 port pin
a	PA0
b	PA1
c	PA2
d	PA3
e	PA4
f	PA5
g	PA6
E1	PD12 (via transistor)
E2	PE14 (via transistor)

7-Segment display segments are driven from the port pins through 220 Ω current limiting resistors. Digit enable pins E1 and E2 are driven from port pins PD12 and PE14, respectively, through two BC108 type NPN transistors (any other NPN transistor can be used

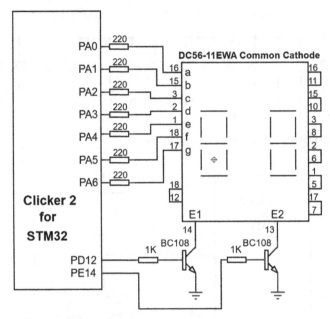

FIGURE 9.26　Circuit diagram of the project.

here), used as switches. The collectors of these transistors drive the segment digits. The segments are enabled when the base of the corresponding transistor is set to logic 1. Notice that the following pins of the display are connected together to form a multiplexed display:

16 and 11, 15 and 10, 3 and 8, 2 and 6, 1 and 5, 17 and 7, 18 and 12

Program listing: Before driving the display, we have to know the relationship between the numbers to be displayed and the corresponding segments to be turned ON, and this is shown in Table 9.3. For example, to display number 3 we have to send the hexadecimal number 0x4F to PORTA which turns ON segments **a,b,c,d**, and **g**. Similarly, to display number 9 we have to send the hexadecimal number 0x6F to PORTA which turns ON segments **a,b,c,d,f**, and **g**.

Fig. 9.27 shows the program listing (program: **Seg7-2.c**). The program consists of two tasks having equal priorities: task1 increments a common variable called **Cnt** every second. When

TABLE 9.3　Displayed number and data sent to PORTA.

Number	x g f e d c b a	PORTA data
0	0 0 1 1 1 1 1 1	0x3F
1	0 0 0 0 0 1 1 0	0x06
2	0 1 0 1 1 0 1 1	0x5B
3	0 1 0 0 1 1 1 1	0x4F
4	0 1 1 0 0 1 1 0	0x66
5	0 1 1 0 1 1 0 1	0x6D
6	0 1 1 1 1 1 0 1	0x7D
7	0 0 0 0 0 1 1 1	0x07
8	0 1 1 1 1 1 1 1	0x7F
9	0 1 1 0 1 1 1 1	0x6F

x is not used, taken as 0.

```
/*===============================================================================
                7-SEGMENT 2-DIGIT MULTIPLEXED DISPLAY COUNTER
                =============================================

This is a 7-segment 2-digit multiplexed LED counter program. The program counts
up every second from 0 to 99 continuously. Task 1 increment variable Cnt, and
Task 2 refreshes the display.

Author: Dogan Ibrahim
Date  : September, 2019
File  : SEG7-2.c
===============================================================================*/
#include "main.h"
TaskHandle_t xHandle;
int Cnt = 0;

//
// Define all your Task functions here
// ===================================
//

// Task 1 - Increment variable Cnt every second and display it on 7-segment LED
void Task1(void *pvParameters)
{
    while (1)
    {
      Cnt++;                                       // Increment Cnt
      if(Cnt == 100)Cnt = 0;                       // If 100,back to 0
      vTaskDelay(pdMS_TO_TICKS(1000));             // Delay 1 sec
    }
}

// Task 2 - Refresh the 7-segment LED and display data in variable Cnt
void Task2(void *pvParameters)
{
    #define DIGIT1 GPIOD_ODR.B12                   // DIGIT1 at PD12
    #define DIGIT2 GPIOE_ODR.B14                   // DIGIT2 at PE14

    unsigned char Pattern;
    unsigned char MSD, LSD;
    unsigned char SEGMENT[] = {0x3F,0x06,0x5B,0x4F,0x66,0x6D,
                               0x7D,0x07,0x7F,0x6F};

    GPIO_Config(&GPIOA_BASE, _GPIO_PINMASK_ALL, _GPIO_CFG_MODE_OUTPUT);
    GPIO_Config(&GPIOD_BASE, _GPIO_PINMASK_12, _GPIO_CFG_MODE_OUTPUT);
    GPIO_Config(&GPIOE_BASE, _GPIO_PINMASK_14, _GPIO_CFG_MODE_OUTPUT);

    DIGIT1 = 0;                                    // Disable digit 1
    DIGIT2 = 0;                                    // Disable digit 2

    while (1)
    {
       if(Cnt > 9)
       {
           MSD = Cnt / 10;                         // Get MSD digit
           GPIOA_ODR = SEGMENT[MSD];               // Output bit pattern
           DIGIT2 = 1;                             // Enable DIGIT2
           vTaskDelay(pdMS_TO_TICKS(10));          // Delay 10ms
       }
       DIGIT2 = 0;                                 // Disable DIGIT2
```

FIGURE 9.27   Seg7-2.c program listing.

```
        LSD = Cnt % 10;                    // Get LSD digit
        GPIOA_ODR = SEGMENT[LSD];          // Output bit pattern
        DIGIT1 = 1;                        // Enable DIGIT1
        vTaskDelay(pdMS_TO_TICKS(10));     // Delay 10ms
        DIGIT1 = 0;                        // Disable DIGIT1
    }
}


//
// Start of MAIN program
// =====================
//
void main()
{
//
// Create all the TASKS here
// =========================
//
    // Create Task 1
    xTaskCreate(
        (TaskFunction_t)Task1,
        "Task 1",
        configMINIMAL_STACK_SIZE,
        NULL,
        10,
        NULL
    );

    // Create Task 2
    xTaskCreate(
        (TaskFunction_t)Task2,
        "Task 2",
        configMINIMAL_STACK_SIZE,
        NULL,
        10,
        NULL
    );

//
// Start the RTOS scheduler
//
    vTaskStartScheduler();

//
// Will never reach here
//
    while (1);
}
```

FIGURE 9.27 (*Continued*)

Cnt reaches 100, it is reset back to 0. task2 displays the contents of variable **Cnt** on the 7-seg-
ment 2-digit display. The bit pattern corresponding to each digit (i.e., Table 9.3) is stored in
an array called **SEGMENT**. Initially both digits are disabled by setting both **DIGIT1** and
DIGIT2 to 0. The MSD digit of the **Cnt** is extracted and **DIGIT2** is enabled so that this digit is
displayed. After a delay of 10 ms the LSD digit is extracted and **DIGIT2** disabled, **DIGIT1** is
enabled so that this digit is displayed. The delay is done using API function call vTaskDelay()
with macro pdMS_TO_TICKS set to 10. Each digit is displayed for 10 ms and this process is
repeated. As a result, the human eye sees both digits to be ON continuously. Notice that the

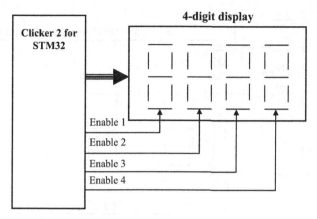

FIGURE 9.28 **Block diagram of the project.**

MSD digit is blanked if **Cnt** is less than 10. Therefore, for example, number 5 is displayed just as 5 and not as 05.

9.14 Project 11—7-segment 4-digit multiplexed LED display counter

Description: This project is similar to the previous one, but here a 4-digit multiplexed 7-segment LED display is used so that numbers from 0 to 9999 can be displayed instead of from 0 to 99 as was the case in the previous project.

Aim: The aim of this project is to show how a 4-digit 7-segment multiplexed LED display can be designed.

Block diagram: Fig. 9.28 shows the block diagram of the project.

Circuit diagram: The circuit diagram of the project is shown in Fig. 9.29. As in the previous project PORTA of the microcontroller is used to send data to the display. 4 NPN type transistors are used to control each digit individually. In this project, the following pins of the Clicker 2 for STM32 development board are used to interface with the 7-segment display:

7-Segment display pin	Clicker 2 for STM32 port pin
a	PA0
b	PA1
c	PA2
d	PA3
e	PA4
f	PA5
g	PA6
E1	PD12 (via transistor)
E2	PE14 (via transistor)
E3	PD9 (via transistor)
E4	PD8 (via transistor)

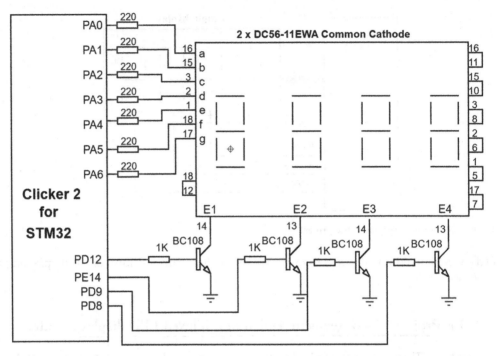

FIGURE 9.29   Circuit diagram of the project.

Because DC56-11EWA is a 2-digit display, two such modules were used to make a 4-digit display. The following pins of the displays were connected together to form a multiplexed 4-digit display as in the previous project:

16 and 11, 15 and 10, 3 and 8, 2 and 6, 1 and 5, 17 and 7, 18 and 12

Program listing: The bit pattern shown in Table 9.3 to control the LED segments is also used in this project. Fig. 9.30 shows the program listing (program: **Seg7-4.c**). The program consists of two tasks having equal priorities. task1 increments a common variable called **Cnt** every second. When **Cnt** reaches 10,000, it is reset back to 0. task2 displays the contents of variable **Cnt** on the 7-segment 4-digit display. The bit pattern corresponding to each digit (i.e., Table 9.3) is stored in an array called **SEGMENT**. Initially all digits are disabled by setting **DIGIT1**, **DIGIT2**, **DIGIT3**, and **DIGIT4** to 0. The MSD digit of the **Cnt** is extracted and **DIGIT4** is enabled so that this digit is displayed. After a delay of 5 ms the other digits are extracted, their corresponding digits are enabled in turn. Each digit is displayed for 5 ms using API function call vTaskDelay() with macro pdMS_TO_TICKS set to 5. As a result, the human eye sees all digits to be ON continuously. Notice that the MSD digits are not blanked if they are 0. Therefore, for example, number 5 is displayed just as 0005 and not as 5. Similarly, number 200 is displayed as 0200 and not as 200.

```
/*==============================================================================
                7-SEGMENT 4-DIGIT MULTIPLEXED DISPLAY COUNTER
                =============================================

This is a 7-segment 4-digit multiplexed LED counter program. The program counts
up every second from 0 to 9999 continuously. Task 1 increment variable Cnt, and
Task 2 refreshes the display.

Author: Dogan Ibrahim
Date   : September, 2019
File   : SEG7-4.c
==============================================================================*/
#include "main.h"
TaskHandle_t xHandle;
int Cnt = 0;

//
// Define all your Task functions here
// ====================================
//

// Task 1 - Increment variable Cnt every second and display it on 7-segment LED
void Task1(void *pvParameters)
{
    while (1)
    {
      Cnt++;                                        // Increment Cnt
      if(Cnt == 10000)Cnt = 0;                      // If 10000,back to 0
      vTaskDelay(pdMS_TO_TICKS(1000));              // Delay 1 sec
    }
}

// Task 2 - Refresh the 7-segment LED and display data in variable Cnt
void Task2(void *pvParameters)
{
    #define DIGIT1 GPIOD_ODR.B12                    // DIGIT1 at PD12
    #define DIGIT2 GPIOE_ODR.B14                    // DIGIT2 at PE14
    #define DIGIT3 GPIOD_ODR.B9                     // DIGIT3 at PD9
    #define DIGIT4 GPIOD_ODR.B8                     // DIGIT4 at PD8

    unsigned char Pattern;
    unsigned char MSD, LSD;
    unsigned int D1, D2, D3, D4, D5, D6;
    unsigned char SEGMENT[] = {0x3F,0x06,0x5B,0x4F,0x66,0x6D,
                               0x7D,0x07,0x7F,0x6F};

    GPIO_Config(&GPIOA_BASE, _GPIO_PINMASK_ALL, _GPIO_CFG_MODE_OUTPUT);
    GPIO_Config(&GPIOD_BASE, _GPIO_PINMASK_12 | _GPIO_PINMASK_8 | _GPIO_PINMASK_9,
            _GPIO_CFG_MODE_OUTPUT);
    GPIO_Config(&GPIOE_BASE, _GPIO_PINMASK_14, _GPIO_CFG_MODE_OUTPUT);

    DIGIT1 = 0;                                     // Disable digit 1
    DIGIT2 = 0;                                     // Disable digit 2
    DIGIT3 = 0;                                     // Disable digit 3
    DIGIT4 = 0;                                     // Disable digit 4

    while (1)
    {
        D1 = Cnt / 1000;                            // Get MSD digit
        GPIOA_ODR = SEGMENT[D1];                    // Output bit pattern
```

FIGURE 9.30 Seg7-4-2.c program listing.

```
            DIGIT4 = 1;                                    // Enable DIGIT4
            vTaskDelay(pdMS_TO_TICKS(5));                   // Delay 5ms
            DIGIT4 = 0;                                     // Disable DIGIT4

            D2 = Cnt % 1000;                                // Get next digit
            D3 = D2 / 100;
            GPIOA_ODR = SEGMENT[D3];                        // Output bit pattern
            DIGIT3 = 1;                                     // Enable DIGIT3
            vTaskDelay(pdMS_TO_TICKS(5));                   // Delay 5ms
            DIGIT3 = 0;                                     // Disable DIGIT3

            D4 = D2 % 100;                                  // Get next digit
            D5 = D4 / 10;
            GPIOA_ODR = SEGMENT[D5];                        // Output bit pattern
            DIGIT2 = 1;                                     // Enable DIGIT2
            vTaskDelay(pdMS_TO_TICKS(5));                   // Delay 5ms
            DIGIT2 = 0;                                     // Disable DIGIT2

            D6 = D4 % 10;                                   // Get next digit
            GPIOA_ODR = SEGMENT[D6];                        // Output bit pattern
            DIGIT1 = 1;                                     // Enable DIGIT1
            vTaskDelay(pdMS_TO_TICKS(5));                   // Delay 5ms
            DIGIT1 = 0;                                     // Disable DIGIT1
    }
}


//
// Start of MAIN program
// =====================
//
void main()
{
//
// Create all the TASKS here
// =========================
//
    // Create Task 1
    xTaskCreate(
        (TaskFunction_t)Task1,
        "Task 1",
        configMINIMAL_STACK_SIZE,
        NULL,
        10,
        NULL
    );

    // Create Task 2
    xTaskCreate(
        (TaskFunction_t)Task2,
        "Task 2",
        configMINIMAL_STACK_SIZE,
        NULL,
        10,
        NULL
    );

//
// Start the RTOS scheduler
//
    vTaskStartScheduler();

//
// Will never reach here
//
    while (1);
}
```

FIGURE 9.30   (*Continued*)

The program in Fig. 9.30 can be modified so that the leading zeroes are blanked so that for example number 20 is displayed as 20 and not as 0020. The modified program listing (program: **Seg7-4-2.c**) is shown in Fig. 9.31.

9.15 Project 12—7-segment 4-digit multiplexed LED display event counter

Description: This project is similar to the previous one, but here a 4-digit multiplexed 7-segment LED display is used to count external events. An external event is assumed to occur when port pin PE0 changes from logic 1 to logic 0. This is same as pressing the pushbutton switch connected to port pin PE0. In real event counter projects one can, for example, use visible or infrared light beams and light detectors to detect the occurrence of external events. The program counts the external events and displays the total on the 7-segment 4-digit LED display.

Aim: The aim of this project is to show how an event counter can be designed to count external events and display the total count on a 4-digit 7-segment multiplexed LED display.

Block diagram: Fig. 9.32 shows the block diagram of the project. Here, for simplicity, pressing button PE0 is assumed to create an external event.

Circuit diagram: The circuit diagram of the project is same as in Fig. 9.29.

Program listing: Notice that mechanical switches usually have contact bouncing problems. When a switch is actuated, its contacts touch one another and they are supposed to establish a crisp movement. In practice this is not the case and due to the mass of the contacts and the mechanical action, the contacts bounce for a period of a few milliseconds before coming to a full rest. A few milliseconds is very long time for a microcontroller and during this bouncing period wrong switch state can be read by the microcontroller input port. In some applications the switch contact bounce may not be a problem, but there are many applications where it is required to eliminate this bouncing problem. There are several hardware and software methods used in practise to eliminate the contact bouncing problem. Some of the commonly used methods are:

- Modify the design of the mechanical switch by reducing its kinetic energy when the switch is closed or opened.
- Use a resistor-capacitor filter circuit with a time constant of around 20 ms to avoid contact bouncing.
- Use a digital Schmitt trigger gate to reduce or eliminate contact bouncing.
- Use a cross-coupled NAND gate circuit to eliminate contact bouncing
- Use a D-type flip-flop to eliminate contact bouncing.
- Introduce a small delay in software after reading the state of the switch.

Fig. 9.33 shows the state of a typical mechanical switch when it is closed (assuming that its output is normally at logic 1, and goes to logic 0 when it is closed).

The program of this project is similar to the one given in Fig. 9.31, only the code for Task 1 is different and this is shown in Fig. 9.34. The program consists of two tasks with

```
/*=====================================================================
               7-SEGMENT 4-DIGIT MULTIPLEXED DISPLAY COUNTER
               =============================================

This is a 7-segment 4-digit multiplexed LED counter program. The program counts
up every second from 0 to 9999 continuously. Task 1 increment variable Cnt, and
Task 2 refreshes the display. In this modified version of the program the
leading zeroes are blanked.

Author: Dogan Ibrahim
Date  : September, 2019
File  : SEG7-4-2.c
=====================================================================*/
#include "main.h"
TaskHandle_t xHandle;
int Cnt = 0;


//
// Define all your Task functions here
// ====================================
//

// Task 1 - Increment variable Cnt every second and display it on 7-segment LED
void Task1(void *pvParameters)
{
    while (1)
    {
      Cnt++;                                            // Increment Cnt
      if(Cnt == 10000)Cnt = 0;                          // If 10000,back to 0
      vTaskDelay(pdMS_TO_TICKS(1000));                  // Delay 1 sec
    }
}

// Task 2 - Refresh the 7-segment LED and display data in variable Cnt
void Task2(void *pvParameters)
{
    #define DIGIT1 GPIOD_ODR.B12                        // DIGIT1 at PD12
    #define DIGIT2 GPIOE_ODR.B14                        // DIGIT2 at PE14
    #define DIGIT3 GPIOD_ODR.B9                         // DIGIT3 at PD9
    #define DIGIT4 GPIOD_ODR.B8                         // DIGIT4 at PD8

    unsigned char Pattern;
    unsigned char MSD, LSD;
    unsigned int D1, D2, D3, D4, D5, D6;
    unsigned char SEGMENT[] = {0x3F,0x06,0x5B,0x4F,0x66,0x6D,
                               0x7D,0x07,0x7F,0x6F};

    GPIO_Config(&GPIOA_BASE, _GPIO_PINMASK_ALL, _GPIO_CFG_MODE_OUTPUT);
    GPIO_Config(&GPIOD_BASE, _GPIO_PINMASK_12 | _GPIO_PINMASK_8 | _GPIO_PINMASK_9,
            _GPIO_CFG_MODE_OUTPUT);
    GPIO_Config(&GPIOE_BASE, _GPIO_PINMASK_14, _GPIO_CFG_MODE_OUTPUT);

    DIGIT1 = 0;                                         // Disable digit 1
    DIGIT2 = 0;                                         // Disable digit 2
    DIGIT3 = 0;                                         // Disable digit 3
    DIGIT4 = 0;                                         // Disable digit 4

    while (1)
    {
        D1 = Cnt / 1000;                                // Get MSD digit
```

FIGURE 9.31 Seg7-4-2.c program listing.

```
            if(Cnt > 999)
            {
                    GPIOA_ODR = SEGMENT[D1];          // Output bit pattern
                    DIGIT4 = 1;                       // Enable DIGIT4
                    vTaskDelay(pdMS_TO_TICKS(5));     // Delay 5ms
                    DIGIT4 = 0;                       // Disable DIGIT4
            }

            D2 = Cnt % 1000;                          // Get next digit
            D3 = D2 / 100;
            if(Cnt > 99)
            {
                    GPIOA_ODR = SEGMENT[D3];          // Output bit pattern
                    DIGIT3 = 1;                       // Enable DIGIT3
                    vTaskDelay(pdMS_TO_TICKS(5));     // Delay 5ms
                    DIGIT3 = 0;                       // Disable DIGIT3
            }

            D4 = D2 % 100;                            // Get next digit
            D5 = D4 / 10;
            if(Cnt > 9)
            {
                    GPIOA_ODR = SEGMENT[D5];          // Output bit pattern
                    DIGIT2 = 1;                       // Enable DIGIT2
                    vTaskDelay(pdMS_TO_TICKS(5));     // Delay 5ms
                    DIGIT2 = 0;                       // Disable DIGIT2
            }

            D6 = D4 % 10;                             // Get next digit
            GPIOA_ODR = SEGMENT[D6];                  // Output bit pattern
            DIGIT1 = 1;                               // Enable DIGIT1
            vTaskDelay(pdMS_TO_TICKS(5));             // Delay 5ms
            DIGIT1 = 0;                               // Disable DIGIT1
    }
}


//
// Start of MAIN program
// =====================
//
void main()
{
//
// Create all the TASKS here
// =========================
//
    // Create Task 1
    xTaskCreate(
        (TaskFunction_t)Task1,
        "Task 1",
        configMINIMAL_STACK_SIZE,
        NULL,
        10,
        NULL
    );

    // Create Task 2
    xTaskCreate(
        (TaskFunction_t)Task2,
```

FIGURE 9.31   (*Continued*)

```
        "Task 2",
        configMINIMAL_STACK_SIZE,
        NULL,
        10,
        NULL
    );

//
// Start the RTOS scheduler
//
    vTaskStartScheduler();

//
// Will never reach here
//
    while (1);
}
```

FIGURE 9.31   (*Continued*)

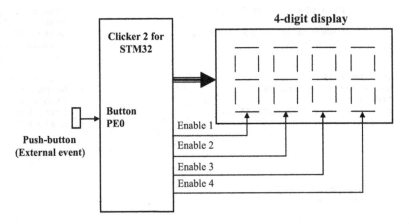

FIGURE 9.32   Block diagram of the project.

FIGURE 9.33   Typical switch bouncing problem.

equal priorities: task 1 increments variable **Cnt** when an external event occurs (i.e., when the push-button is pressed). task2 displays the total count on the 7-segment 4-digit multiplexed display. The button input in task1 is configured as digital input. Up to 9999 events can be counted by this program. Notice that switch debouncing hardware is not used in this project.

```
// Task 1 - Increment variable Cnt when the puch-button is pressed
void Task1(void *pvParameters)
{
    #define Button GPIOE_IDR.B0

    GPIO_Config(&GPIOE_BASE, _GPIO_PINMASK_0, _GPIO_CFG_MODE_INPUT);

    while (1)
    {
        while(Button == 1);                    // Wait for button
        while(Button == 0);                    // Wait for release
        Cnt++;                                 // Increment Cnt
    }
}
```

FIGURE 9.34   Modified Task 1.

Instead, the state of the button is checked: if the button is not pressed, the task waits. When the button is pressed, the program waits until the button is released before the count **Cnt** is incremented.

9.16 Project 13—traffic lights controller

Description: In this project a simple traffic lights controller is designed for a junction. The junction is located at the intersection of two roads: East Street and North Street. There are traffic lights at each end of the junction. Additionally, there is a 2-digit 7-segment LED at the top end of the traffic lights at the south end of North Street. The display here counts down and indicates the time left for the Red and Green lights to change. There are push-button switches located near the traffic lights on North Street. Pressing a pedestrian button turns all lights to red at the end of their cycles. A buzzer is then sounded to indicate that the pedestrians can cross the road safely. In addition, an LCD is connected to the system to see the status of the lights at the junction for safety and monitoring purposes. Fig. 9.35 shows the layout of the equipment at the junction.

In this project, the following fixed times are given to each traffic light duration, and also to the duration of the pedestrian buzzer. For simplicity, both roads of the junction are assumed to have the same timings:

Red time:	21 s
Amber time:	4 s
Green time:	15 s
Amber + Red time:	2 s
Pedestrian time:	10 s

The total cycle time of the lights in this example project is set to be 42 s.

The sequence of traffic lights is assumed to be as follows (different countries may have different sequences):

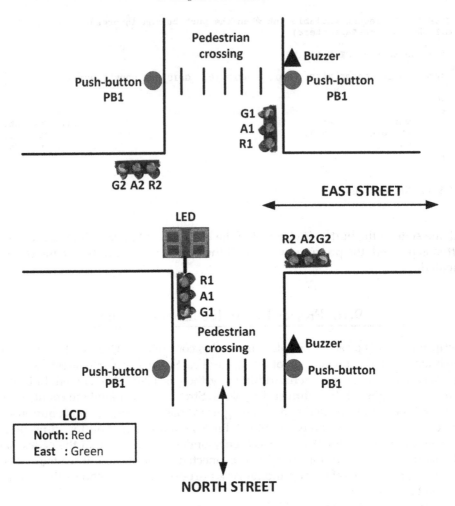

FIGURE 9.35   Layout of the equipment at the junction.

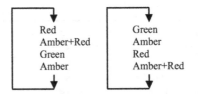

Aim: The aim of this project is to show how a simple traffic lights controller can be designed for a junction using a multitasking approach.

Block diagram: Fig. 9.36 shows the block diagram of the project.

Circuit diagram: The circuit diagram of the project is shown in Fig. 9.37. Red (R), Amber (A), and Green (G) LEDs are used in this project to represent the real traffic lights. The

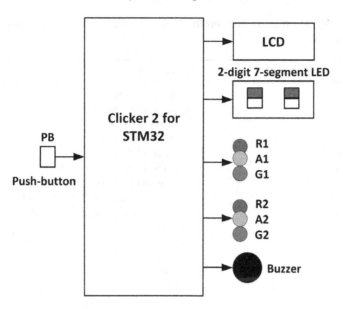

FIGURE 9.36   Block diagram of the project.

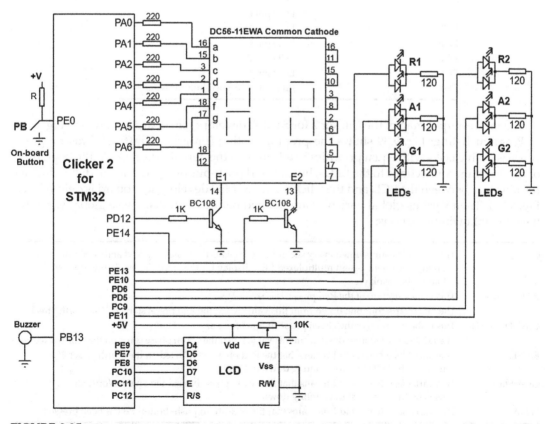

FIGURE 9.37   Circuit diagram of the project.

following connections are made between the Clicker 2 for STM32 development board and the traffic road equipment:

Clicker 2 for STM32	Equipment
PA0	7-Segment LED pin a
PA1	7-Segment LED pin b
PA2	7-Segment LED pin c
PA3	7-Segment LED pin d
PA4	7-Segment LED pin e
PA5	7-Segment LED pin f
PA6	7-Segment LED pin g
PD12	7-Segment LED pin E1 (via transistor)
PE14	7-Segment LED pin E2 (via transistor)
PE13	LED R1
PE10	LED A1
PD6	LED G1
PD5	LED R2
PC9	LED A2
PE11	LED G2
PB13	Buzzer
PE9	LCD pin D4
PE7	LCD pin D5
PE8	LCD pin D6
PC10	LCD pin D7
PC11	LCD pin E
PC12	LCD pin R/S
PE0	PB (on-board push-button switch)

The input-output map of the Clicker 2 for STM32 development board is shown in Fig. 9.38.

Program listing: Fig. 9.39 shows the program listing (program: **Traffic.c**). This program consists of five tasks with equal priorities in addition to the default Idle task. At the beginning of the program connections to the LEDs, buzzer, and push-button switch are all defined. Then the interface between the LCD and the Clicker 2 for STM32 development board is defined (see Fig. 9.37). Then various global variables are defined before the tasks. These global variables have the following functions:

Cnt	This variable counts down every second and displays the remaining Red and Green timings on the 7-segment 2-digit multiplexed LED display for the North Street. Setting it to 99 blanks the display
RedDuration	This is the duration of the Red phase. It is set to 21 s.
	The LCD starts counting down from this value when the Red phase starts on the North Street
GreenDuration	This is the duration of the Green phase. It is set to 15 s.
	The LCD starts counting down from this value when the Green phase starts on the North Street
RedStart	This variable, when set to 1 means that the Red phase has started on the North Street. It is used by the LCD to start counting down
GreenStart	This variable, when set to 1 means that the Green phase has started on the North Street. It is used by the LCD to start counting down
PedMode	This variable, when set to 1 indicates that the pedestrian push- button PB has been pressed

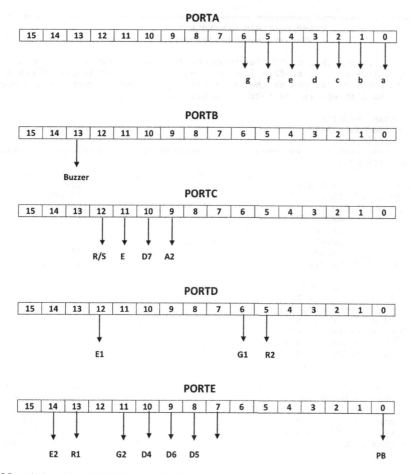

FIGURE 9.38   Clicker 2 for STM32 input-output map.

Task 1

This task displays the state of the lights on the LCD at any time for the North Street and the East Street. When the light is green and there is no Amber, the display shows Green. Similarly, when the light is Red and there is no Amber, the display shows Red. The LCD display is refreshed every second. A typical display on the LCD is as follows:

North Str: Green
East Str : Red

Task 2

This is the 7-segment LED controller task. If variable RedStart is set to 1 then the duration of the red light (21 s) is stored in variable Cnt. Similarly, if variable GreenStart is set to 1 then the duration of the green light (15 s) is stored in variable Cnt. The value of Cnt is then decremented every second until it reaches 0. This value is displayed by the 7-segment task (Task 3). When Cnt is 0, it is set to 99 so that the 7-segment display is blank.

```
/*==============================================================================
                        TRAFFIC LIGHTS CONTROLELR
                        =========================

This is a traffic lights controller program. In this program a junction with two
roads is considered with traffic lights in each road. Additionally, there are
pedestrian crossings in one of the roads with a push-button switch and a buzzer
(refer to the drawings in the text for details)

Author: Dogan Ibrahim
Date  : September, 2019
File  : Traffic.c
==============================================================================*/
#include "main.h"

#define Buzzer GPIOB_ODR.B13                              // Buzzer port
#define PB GPIOE_IDR.B0                                   // PB port
#define R1 GPIOE_ODR.B13                                  // R1 port
#define A1 GPIOE_ODR.B10                                  // A1 port
#define G1 GPIOD_ODR.B6                                   // G1 port
#define R2 GPIOD_ODR.B5                                   // R2 port
#define A2 GPIOC_ODR.B9                                   // A2 port
#define G2 GPIOE_ODR.B11                                  // G2 port

// LCD module connections
sbit LCD_RS at GPIOC_ODR.B12;
sbit LCD_EN at GPIOC_ODR.B11;
sbit LCD_D4 at GPIOE_ODR.B9;
sbit LCD_D5 at GPIOE_ODR.B7;
sbit LCD_D6 at GPIOE_ODR.B8;
sbit LCD_D7 at GPIOC_ODR.B10;
// End LCD module connections

unsigned char Cnt = 99;                                   // 99 to disable 7-seg
unsigned char RedDuration = 20;                           // Red duration
unsigned char GreenDuration = 15;                         // Green duration
unsigned char RedStart = 0;                               // Start of Red
unsigned char GreenStart = 0;                             // Start of Green
unsigned char PedMode = 0;                                // Pedestrian mode

//
// Define all your Task functions here
// ====================================
//

// Task 1 - This is the LCD controller task. The state of the lights are dislayed
void Task1(void *pvParameters)
{
    Lcd_Init();                                           // Initialize LCD
    Lcd_Cmd(_LCD_CLEAR);                                  // Clear LCD
    Lcd_Out(1, 1, "North Str:");                          // Display text
    Lcd_Out(2, 1, "East Str :");                          // Display text

    while (1)
    {
      if(G1 == 1 && A1 == 0)                              // If North Str=Green
            Lcd_Out(1, 12, "Green");
      else
            if(R1 == 1 && A1 == 0)Lcd_Out(1, 12, "Red  ");  // If North Str=Red
```

FIGURE 9.39 Traffic.c program listing.

```
        if(G2 ==1 && A2 == 0)                              // If East Str=Green
            Lcd_Out(2, 12,  "Green");
        else
            if(R2 == 1 && A2 == 0)Lcd_Out(2, 12, "Red  ");    // If EastStr=Red

        vTaskDelay(pdMS_TO_TICKS(1000));                   // 1 second delay
    }
}

// Task 2 - LED controller
void Task2(void *pvParameters)
{
    unsigned char Flag = 0;

    while (1)
    {
        if(RedStart == 1)                                  // If Red start
        {
            RedStart = 0;
            Cnt = RedDuration;                             // Get Red duration
            Flag = 1;
        }
        else if(GreenStart == 1)                           // If Green start
        {
            GreenStart = 0;
            Cnt = GreenDuration;                           // Get Green duration
            Flag = 1;
        }

        if(Flag == 1)
        {
            vTaskDelay(pdMS_TO_TICKS(1000));               // Delay 1 second
            Cnt--;                                         // Decremen Cnt
            if(Cnt == 0)                                   // If end
            {
                Cnt=99;                                    // Disable LCD
                Flag = 0;
            }
        }
    }
}


// Task 3 - 7-segment 2-digit multiplexed LED controller
void Task3(void *pvParameters)
{
    #define DIGIT1 GPIOD_ODR.B12                           // DIGIT1 at PD12
    #define DIGIT2 GPIOE_ODR.B14                           // DIGIT2 at PE14

    unsigned char Pattern;
    unsigned char MSD, LSD;
    unsigned char SEGMENT[] = {0x3F,0x06,0x5B,0x4F,0x66,0x6D,
                               0x7D,0x07,0x7F,0x6F};

    GPIO_Config(&GPIOA_BASE, _GPIO_PINMASK_ALL, _GPIO_CFG_MODE_OUTPUT);
    GPIO_Config(&GPIOD_BASE, _GPIO_PINMASK_12, _GPIO_CFG_MODE_OUTPUT);
    GPIO_Config(&GPIOE_BASE, _GPIO_PINMASK_14, _GPIO_CFG_MODE_OUTPUT);

    DIGIT1 = 0;                                            // Disable digit 1
    DIGIT2 = 0;                                            // Disable digit 2
```

FIGURE 9.39 (*Continued*)

```
    while (1)
    {
        if(Cnt != 99)
        {
          MSD = Cnt / 10;                               // Get MSD digit
          GPIOA_ODR = SEGMENT[MSD];                     // Output bit pattern
          DIGIT2 = 1;                                   // Enable DIGIT2
          vTaskDelay(pdMS_TO_TICKS(10));                // Delay 10ms

          DIGIT2 = 0;                                   // Disable DIGIT2
          LSD = Cnt % 10;                               // Get LSD digit
          GPIOA_ODR = SEGMENT[LSD];                     // Output bit pattern
          DIGIT1 = 1;                                   // Enable DIGIT1
          vTaskDelay(pdMS_TO_TICKS(10));                // Delay 10ms
          DIGIT1 = 0;                                   // Disable DIGIT1
        }
    }
}


// Task 4 - Main program control loop
void Task4(void *pvParameters)
{
    GPIO_Config(&GPIOD_BASE, _GPIO_PINMASK_5 | _GPIO_PINMASK_6,
                _GPIO_CFG_MODE_OUTPUT);
    GPIO_Config(&GPIOC_BASE, _GPIO_PINMASK_9, _GPIO_CFG_MODE_OUTPUT);
    GPIO_Config(&GPIOE_BASE, _GPIO_PINMASK_13 | _GPIO_PINMASK_10 | _GPIO_PINMASK_11,
                _GPIO_CFG_MODE_OUTPUT);
    GPIO_Config(&GPIOB_BASE, _GPIO_PINMASK_13, _GPIO_CFG_MODE_OUTPUT);

    while (1)
    {
        RedStart = 0; GreenStart = 0;
        R1 = 0; A1 = 0; G1 = 1; R2 = 1; A2 = 0; G2 = 0;   // East Street Green
        GreenStart = 1;
        vTaskDelay(pdMS_TO_TICKS(15000));
        G1 = 0; A1 = 1;                                   // East Street Amber
        vTaskDelay(pdMS_TO_TICKS(2000));
        A1 = 0; R1 = 1; A2 = 1;                           // North Street Red
        RedStart = 1;
        vTaskDelay(pdMS_TO_TICKS(2000));
        A2 = 0; R2 = 0; G2 = 1;                           // East Street Green
        vTaskDelay(pdMS_TO_TICKS(15000));
        G2 = 0; A2 = 1;                                   // East Street Amber
        vTaskDelay(pdMS_TO_TICKS(2000));
        A2 = 0; A1 = 1; R2 = 1;                           // East Street Red
        vTaskDelay(pdMS_TO_TICKS(2000));

        if(PedMode == 1)                                  // Ped button active
        {
          G1 = 0; R1 = 1; A1 = 0; G2 = 0; R2 = 1; A2 = 0;
          PedMode = 0;
          Buzzer = 1;                                     // Buzzer ON
          vTaskDelay(pdMS_TO_TICKS(10000));               // 10 sec delay
          Buzzer = 0;                                     // Buzzer OFF
        }
    }
}
```

FIGURE 9.39   (*Continued*)

```
// Task 5 - Pedestrian controller
void Task5(void *pvParameters)
{
    GPIO_Config(&GPIOE_BASE, _GPIO_PINMASK_0, _GPIO_CFG_MODE_INPUT);

    while (1)
    {
        if(PB == 0)                              // If button pressed
        {
            PedMode = 1;                         // Set Ped mode
        }
    }
}


//
// Start of MAIN program
// =====================
//
void main()
{
//
// Create all the TASKS here
// =========================
//
    // Create Task 1
    xTaskCreate(
        (TaskFunction_t)Task1,
        "LCD Controller",
        configMINIMAL_STACK_SIZE,
        NULL,
        10,
        NULL
    );

    // Create Task 2
    xTaskCreate(
        (TaskFunction_t)Task2,
        "LED Controller",
        configMINIMAL_STACK_SIZE,
        NULL,
        10,
        NULL
    );

    // Create Task 3
    xTaskCreate(
        (TaskFunction_t)Task3,
        "7-seg LED Controller",
        configMINIMAL_STACK_SIZE,
        NULL,
        10,
        NULL
    );

    // Create Task 4
    xTaskCreate(
        (TaskFunction_t)Task4,
```

FIGURE 9.39   (*Continued*)

```
            "Main program loop",
            configMINIMAL_STACK_SIZE,
            NULL,
            10,
            NULL
        );

        // Create Task 5
        xTaskCreate(
            (TaskFunction_t)Task5,
            "Pedestrian Controller",
            configMINIMAL_STACK_SIZE,
            NULL,
            10,
            NULL
        );


    //
    // Start the RTOS scheduler
    //
        vTaskStartScheduler();

    //
    // Will never reach here
    //
        while (1);
    }
```

FIGURE 9.39 (*Continued*)

Task 3

This is the 7-segment 2-digit multiplexed display controller task. This task displays the value of variable Cnt when it is not 99. If Cnt is set to 99 then the display is blank.

Task 4

This is the main program task which controls the LEDs so that correct timings are given to each LED. Inside this routine, variable GreenStart is set to 1 when the green phase starts on North Street. Similarly, variable RedStart is set to 1 when the red phase starts on North Street. At the end of a complete cycle the program checks whether or not the pedestrian push-button PB was pressed. This is identified by the variable PedMode having the value 1. If PedMode is set to 1 then all the red lights are turned ON, the buzzer is activated for 10 s to tell the pedestrians that it is now safe to cross the road. At the end of 10 s the buzzer is de-activated.

Task 5

This is the pedestrian controller cycle. Pedestrians can press button PB at any time to request to cross the road. When button PB is pressed, this task sets variable PedMode to 1. PedMode is used by Task 4 at the end of a cycle to give access to the pedestrians.

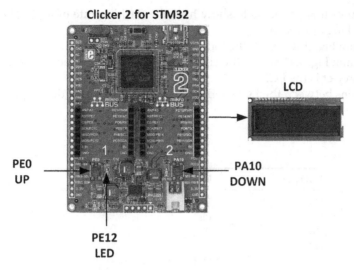

FIGURE 9.40 Block diagram of the project.

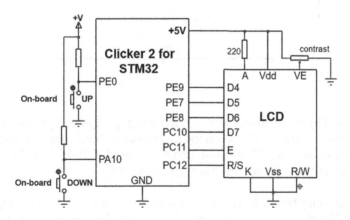

FIGURE 9.41 Circuit diagram of the project.

9.17 Project 14—changing LED flashing rate

Description: In this project the LED connected to port pin PE12 is used. Additionally, the two push-buttons at port pins PE0 and PA10 are used. The LED starts flashing at a rate of 1 s. Every time button PE0 (here called the UP button) is pressed, the flashing rate will increment by 1 s. Similarly, every time button PA10 (here called the DOWN button) is pressed, the flashing rate will decrement by 1 s. The minimum and maximum flashing rates can be set as 1 and 60 s, respectively (this can easily be changed if desired).

Aim: The aim of this project is to show how the flashing rate of an LED can be changed using a multitasking approach.

Block diagram: Fig. 9.40 shows the block diagram of the project.

Circuit diagram: Fig. 9.41 shows the circuit diagram of the project. The only external component in this project is the LCD.

The connections between the LCD and the Clicker 2 for STM32 development board are as follows:

LCD pin	Clicker 2 for STM32 pin
D4	PE9
D5	PE7
D6	PE8
D7	PC10
E	PC11
R/S	PC12
R/W	GND
Vdd	+5 V
K	GND
Vss	GND
A	+5 V (through a resistor)
VE	Potentiometer

Program listing: Fig. 9.42 shows the program listing (program: **UpDown.c**). At the beginning of the program the interface between the LCD and the development board is defined, the push-button switches and the LED are assigned the names UP, DOWN and LED, respectively. The program consists of three tasks excluding the Idle task.

<u>Task 1</u>

This is the LCD controller task. This task displays the current LED flashing rate, which is stored in variable FlashRateSecs in seconds. A heading is also displayed in the first row of the LCD. The LCD display below shows when the flashing rate was set to 5 s:

Flashing Rate:

5 s

```
/*=============================================================================
                        CHANGING LED FLASHING RATE
                        ==========================

In this program the LED connected to port pin PE12 is flashed. The flashing rate
is chaned by using button connected to port pin PE0 (UP) and to PA10 (DOWN).
pressing the UP button increments the flashing rate, while pressing the DOWN
button decrements the flashing rate. Current flashing rate is displayed on the
LCD.

Author: Dogan Ibrahim
Date  : September, 2019
File  : UpDown.c
=============================================================================*/
#include "main.h"

#define LED GPIOE_ODR.B12                               // LED port
#define UP GPIOE_IDR.B0                                 // UP button
#define DOWN GPIOA_IDR.B10                              // DOWN button

unsigned char FlashRateSecs = 1;                        // Flash rate sec
unsigned long FlashRateMs = 1000;                       // Flash rate ms

// LCD module connections
sbit LCD_RS at GPIOC_ODR.B12;
sbit LCD_EN at GPIOC_ODR.B11;
sbit LCD_D4 at GPIOE_ODR.B9;
sbit LCD_D5 at GPIOE_ODR.B7;
sbit LCD_D6 at GPIOE_ODR.B8;
sbit LCD_D7 at GPIOE_ODR.B10;
// End LCD module connections

//
// Define all your Task functions here
// ====================================
//

// Task 1 - LCD controller
void Task1(void *pvParameters)
{
    unsigned char Txt[4];

    Lcd_Init();                                         // Initialize LCD
    Lcd_Cmd(_LCD_CLEAR);                                // Clear LCD
    Lcd_Cmd(_LCD_CURSOR_OFF);                           // LCD Cursor OFF
    Lcd_Out(1, 1, "Flashing Rate:");                    // Heading

    while (1)
    {
        ByteToStr(FlashRateSecs, Txt);                  // Convert to string
        Ltrim(Txt);                                     // Remove leading spaces
        Lcd_Out(2, 1, Txt);                             // Display flash rate
        Lcd_Chr_CP('s');                                // Display s
        Lcd_Chr_CP(' ');
    }
}


// Task 2 - LED Controller
void Task2(void *pvParameters)
```

FIGURE 9.42 UpDown.c program listing.

```
    {
        GPIO_Config(&GPIOE_BASE, _GPIO_PINMASK_12, _GPIO_CFG_MODE_OUTPUT);

        while (1)
        {
            LED = 0;                                    // LED OFF
            vTaskDelay(pdMS_TO_TICKS(FlashRateMs));     // Delay
            LED = 1;                                    // LED ON
            vTaskDelay(pdMS_TO_TICKS(FlashRateMs));     // Delay
        }
    }


    // Task 3 - Button Controller
    void Task3(void *pvParameters)
    {
        GPIO_Config(&GPIOE_BASE, _GPIO_PINMASK_0, _GPIO_CFG_MODE_INPUT);
        GPIO_Config(&GPIOA_BASE, _GPIO_PINMASK_10, _GPIO_CFG_MODE_INPUT);

        while (1)
        {
            if(UP == 0)                                 // UP button pressed
            {
                FlashRateSecs++;                        // Increment flash rate
                if(FlashRateSecs > 60) FlashRateSecs = 1;
                FlashRateMs = 1000 * FlashRateSecs;     // Convert to ms
                while(UP == 0);                         // Wait to release
            }

            if(DOWN == 0)                               // DOWN button pressed
            {
                FlashRateSecs--;                        // Decrement flash rate
                if(FlashRateSecs < 1) FlashRateSecs = 1;
                FlashRateMs = 1000 * FlashRateSecs;     // Convert to ms
                while(DOWN == 0);                       // Wait to release
            }
        }
    }

    //
    // Start of MAIN program
    // ======================
    //
    void main()
    {
    //
    // Create all the TASKS here
    // =========================
    //
        // Create Task 1
        xTaskCreate(
            (TaskFunction_t)Task1,
            "LCD Controller",
            configMINIMAL_STACK_SIZE,
            NULL,
            10,
            NULL
        );

        // Create Task 2
```

FIGURE 9.42   (*Continued*)

```
    xTaskCreate(
        (TaskFunction_t)Task2,
        "LED Controller",
        configMINIMAL_STACK_SIZE,
        NULL,
        10,
        NULL
    );

    // Create Task 3
    xTaskCreate(
        (TaskFunction_t)Task3,
        "Button Controller",
        configMINIMAL_STACK_SIZE,
        NULL,
        10,
        NULL
    );

//
// Start the RTOS scheduler
//
    vTaskStartScheduler();

//
// Will never reach here
//
    while (1);
}
```

FIGURE 9.42   (*Continued*)

Task 2

This task is the LED controller. The LED is flashed at the rate specified by variable Flash-RateMs. This variable is derived from FlashRateSecs by multiplying it by 1000 to convert from seconds into milliseconds. API function vTaskDelay() is used with macro pdMS_TO_TICKS() to set the required delay time in milliseconds.

Task 3

This is the button controller task. Push-buttons PE0 and PA10 are configured as digital outputs at the beginning of this task. The program then checks if a button is pressed. If the UP button is pressed, then variable FlashRateSecs is incremented by one. When this variable reaches 60 it is reset back to 1. The flashing rate is also converted into milliseconds inside this task. Similarly, if the DOWN button is pressed, then variable FlashRateSecs is decremented by one. When this variable is 0 it is reset back to 1.

Notice that the items Lcd and Lcd_Constants must be enabled in the mikroC Pro for ARM Library Manager before the program is compiled.

9.18 Project 15—sending data to a PC over USB serial link

Description: There are applications where we may want to send data to a PC over a USB serial link, for example displaying the status of an equipment, displaying log data, etc. In this project a small USB UART board is connected to our Clicker 2 for STM32 development

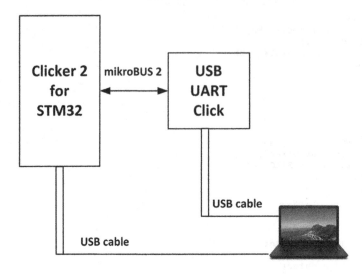

FIGURE 9.43   Block diagram of the project.

board. This board can be connected to a PC using its USB port. Data can then be sent to and read from the PC through this USB UART board. In this project the text FreeRTOS is sent to the PC every second. The text can be displayed on the PC screen using a terminal emulation program such as Putty or HyperTerm, or any other terminal emulation program. Also, data can be received from the PC keyboard via the terminal emulation software and then sent to the development board.

Aim: The aim of this project is to show how a small USB UART board can be connected to or Clicker 2 for STM32 development board to send and receive data from the PC using a terminal emulation software on the PC.

Block diagram: Fig. 9.43 shows the block diagram of the project.

Circuit diagram: In this project the USB UART Click board from mikroElektronika (see www.mikroe.com, part: MIKROE-1203) is used. This board is mikroBUS compatible and it can therefore be directly plugged in one of the mikroBUS sockets of the Clicker 2 For STM32 development board. In this project the USB UART Click board is connected to mikroBUS 2 socket of the development board. The USB UART Click board uses the following pins of the development board:

USB UART Click board pin	Clicker 2 for STM32 development board
TX	PD9
RX	PD8
3.3 V	3.3 V
GND	GND

PD8 and PD9 are the UART 3 receive (RX) and transmit (TX) pins, respectively.

USB UART Click board adds serial UART communication via USB cable. It features FT232RL USB-to-UART interface module. As shown in Fig. 9.44, the board contains RX and

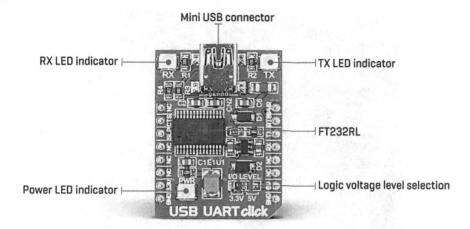

FIGURE 9.44   USB UART Click board.

TX LED diodes that indicate the transmit and receive data via USB. The basic features of this board are:

- IC module: FT232RL
- Interface: UART
- Power supply: 3.3 or 5 V (jumper selectable)
- Power LED
- TX and RX LED
- USB mini B type connector

The Baud Rate Generator on the USB UART Click board provides a 16x clock input to the UART Controller from the 48 MHz reference clock. It consists of a 14-bit prescaler and 3 register bits which provide fine-tuning of the baud rate—used to divide by a number plus a fraction. This determines the baud rate of the UART, which is programmable from 183 baud to 3 Mbaud. Also, nonstandard baud rates are supported. The baud rate is automatically calculated by the FTDI driver, so it is enough to simply forward the desired baud rate to the driver, usually done by selecting the baud rate via the GUI interface (e.g., using a terminal emulation software) of the PC terminal application.

Fig. 9.45 shows the USB UART Click board connected to mikroBUS socket 2 of the Clicker 2 for STM32 development board.

Program listing: This program consists of one task only. At the beginning of the task, function UART3_Init_Advanced() is used (see later in this section) to initialize UART 3 to 9600 baud, 8 data bits, 1 stop bit, no parity bit, and pins PD8 and PD9 being the UART TX and RX pins, respectively. After the initialization of the UART, text message FreeRTOS is sent to out via the UART.

The Putty program can be used to display the data on the PC. This program is available free of charge from the following link:

https://www.putty.org

FIGURE 9.45   USB UART Click connected to mikroBUS 2 socket.

Before using the Putty we have to know the serial port number assigned to our USB UART Click board. This can be found in the Device Manager window. The steps to find the serial port number are as follows:

- Plug-in the USB UART Click board to mikroBUS 2 socket
- Plug-in the USB cable to your Clicker 2 for STM32 development board and turn the board power switch to ON position
- Connect the USB UART Click board to your PC using a mini USB cable
- Open the Run dialog box by pressing and holding the Windows key, then press the **R** key
- Type **devmgmt.msc** and click OK
- Click to expand Ports
- You should see the serial port number assigned to your USB UART Click board as shown in Fig. 9.46. In this example the required serial port is **COM3**
- Close the Device Manager window

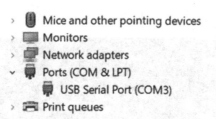

FIGURE 9.46   Serial port assigned to the USB UART Click board.

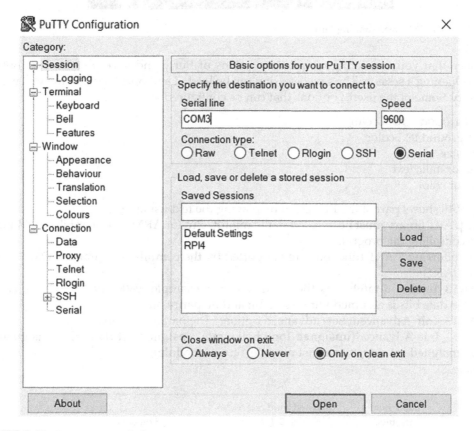

FIGURE 9.47   Putty startup window.

You are now ready to use the Putty. The steps are as follows:

- Start Putty by clicking on Putty.exe
- Click Serial, set the Speed to 9600, and select the Serial line as described earlier (in this example, as shown in Fig. 9.46 COM3 was selected)
- Click Open to start the terminal emulator window (see Fig. 9.47)

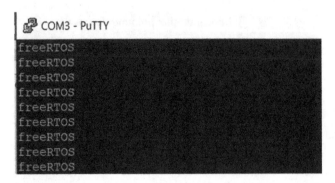

FIGURE 9.48 **PC screen running Putty.**

Notice that you can configure various options of Putty and save your session options before Opening a session. The saved session can be loaded and opened next time you wish to use Putty. Some of the useful options that can be configured are:

- Background screen color
- Foreground text color
- Text size
- Bold or italic text
- Cursor color

Fig. 9.48 shows part of the PC screen displaying the text using Putty.

The UART library must be enabled in the mikroC Pro for ARM compiler Library Manager before compiling the program.

The following UART functions are supported by the compiler (assuming COM2 is used for the UART):

UART3_Init(baud-rate): Sets the baud rate. For example, 9600, 19,200, 38,400, etc. By default, 8 data bits is assumed with 1 stop bit and no parity bit

UART3_Init_Advanced: Sets advanced options. The parameters are:

UART2_Init_Advanced(**unsigned long** baud_rate, **unsigned int** data_bits, **unsigned int** parity, **unsigned int** stop_bits, **const** module_Struct* module);

where,

baud_rate:	Required baud rate	
data_bits:	_UART_8_BIT_DATA	8 bit data
	_UART_9_BIT_DATA	9 bit data
parity:	_UART_NOPARITY	No parity
	_UART_EVENPARITY	Even parity
	_UART_ODDPARITY	Odd parity
stop_bits:	_UART_HALF_STOPBIT	Half stop bit
	_UART_ONE_STOPBIT	One stop bit

module: Appropriate module pinout. The following UART s are available on the Clicker 2 for STM32 development board (first pin is TX and the second pin is RX):

PC10, 11	UART 4
PC12, PD2	UART 5
PA9, 10	UART 1
PB6, 7	UART 1
PB2, 3	UART 2
PD5, PA3	UART 2
PD5, 6	UART 2
PB10, 11	UART 3
PC10, 11	UART 3
PD8, 9	UART 3
PC6, 7	UART 6
PG9, 14	UART 6

The UART must be initialzies before any of the following functions can be used.

UART3_Data_Ready():	This function checks if there is data available in the receive buffer. 1 is returned if data is available and 0 if there is no data in the receive buffer
UART3_TX_Idle():	This function is used to check if the transmit buffer is empty or not. 1 is returned if data has been transmitted and the buffer is empty. 0 is returned if the buffer is not empty. It is recommended to call this function and check before sending data to the UART
UART3_Read():	This function receives a byte (character) from the UART. It is recommended to call function: UART3_Data_Ready() before attempting to read
UART3_Read_Text():	This function reads text from UART until a specified Delimeter is encountered. The format of the function is:

void UARTx_Read_Text(**char** *Output, **char** *Delimiter, **char** Attempts);
where,
Output is the received text
Delimiter is the sequence of characters that identify the end of a received string
Attempts defines the number of received characters in which Delimiter sequence is expected.
If Attempts is set to 255, this routine will continually try to detect the Delimiter sequence
UART3_Write(): This function transmits a byte to UART
UART_Write_Text(): This function sends text via UART. The text should be zero-terminated and not be larger than 255 bytes
UART_Set_Active(): This function sets the active UART module to be used
The format of this function call is:

void UART_Set_Active(**unsigned** (*read_ptr)(), **void** (*write_ptr)(**unsigned char** _data), **unsigned** (*ready_ptr)(), **unsigned** (*tx_idle_ptr)());

where,
read_ptr is the UART3_Read handler
write_ptr is the UART3_Write handler
ready_ptr is the UART3_Data_Ready handler
tx_idle_ptr is the UART3_Tx_IDLE handler
UART3_Enable(): This function enables UART3
UART3_Disable() This function disables UART3
Fig. 9.49 shows the program listing (program: **UART.c**). Only one task is used in this program for simplicity as the aim was here to show how data can be sent to a PC.

```
/*===============================================================================
                    SENDING DATA TO A PC
                    ====================

In this program the USB UART Click board is plugged in to mikroBUS socket 2 of
the Clicker 2 for STM32 development board. UART 3 is used on the development
board to send text FreeRTOS to the PC. A terminal emulator can be used on the
PC to display the received data.

Author: Dogan Ibrahim
Date   : September, 2019
File   : UART.c
===============================================================================*/
#include "main.h"

//
// Define all your Task functions here
// ===================================
//

// Task 1 - UART Controller
void Task1(void *pvParameters)
{
    UART3_Init_Advanced(9600,_UART_8_BIT_DATA,_UART_NOPARITY,_UART_ONE_STOPBIT,
                        &_GPIO_MODULE_USART3_PD89);
    while (1)
    {
        UART3_Write_Text("freeRTOS\n\r");                // Send text to UART
        vTaskDelay(pdMS_TO_TICKS(1000));                 // Wait 1 second
    }
}

//
// Start of MAIN program
// ======================
//
void main()
{
//
// Create all the TASKS here
// =========================
//
    // Create Task 1
    xTaskCreate(
        (TaskFunction_t)Task1,
        "UART Controller",
        configMINIMAL_STACK_SIZE,
        NULL,
        10,
        NULL
    );

//
// Start the RTOS scheduler
//
    vTaskStartScheduler();

//
// Will never reach here
//
    while (1);
}
```

FIGURE 9.49   UART.c program listing.

Notice that item UART must be enabled in the Library Manager of mikroC Pro for ARM compiler before the program is compiled.

9.19 Project 16—changing LED flashing rate from the PC keyboard

Description: In this project the on-board LED connected to port pin PE12 is used. Additionally, the USB UART Click board is used as in the previous project. The LED flash rate is read from the PC keyboard in seconds as an integer number, and this number is used to change the flashing rate while the LED is flashing. There are two tasks in this project in addition to the Idle task.

Aim: The aim of this project is to show how data can be read from a PC keyboard using the USB UART Click board. This is a multitasking program where the LED keeps flashing while the user is prompted to enter the flashing rate via the PC keyboard.

Block diagram: The block diagram of this project is same as in Fig. 9.43, but here additionally the LED at port PE12 is used. The USB UART Click board is plugged to mikroBUS 2 socket of the Clicker 2 for STM32 development board.

Program listing: Fig. 9.50 shows the program listing (program: **UARTFlash.c**). The program consists of two tasks with the following functions:

Task 1

This is the UART Controller task. At the beginning of the task UART 3 is initialized to operate at 9600 baud as in the previous project. Then, the user is prompted to enter the required flashing rate and the following text is displayed on the PC screen

Enter LED Flash Rate (Seconds):

The program reads the flashing rate as numeric data and stores the total number in seconds in variable called Total. The user number is terminated when the Enter key is pressed on the keyboard. Variable Total is then converted into milliseconds by multiplying with 1000 and is stored in variable called FlashRateMs, which is used by Task 2 to flash the LED. The following text is then displayed on the PC screen:

Flashing Rate Changed...

Task 2

This task implements the LED flashing function. The LED keeps flashing as the user enters data from the keyboard. The flashing rate is read from global variable FlashRateMs in milliseconds and is used in API function vTaskDelay().

Fig. 9.51 shows a typical run of the program where the flashing rate was set to 10 s.

9.20 Task list

API function vTAskList() creates a table in a buffer that describes the state of each task at the time the call is made. The function format is:

vTaskList(char* pcWriteBuffer);

```
/*===============================================================================
                CHANGE LED FLASHING RATE FROM THE PC KEYBOARD
                ==============================================

In this program the USB UART Click board is plugged in to mikroBUS socket 2 of
the Clicker 2 for STM32 development board. The LED connected to port pin PE12 is
used in this project. Commands are received from the PC keyboard to change the
LED flashing rate in seconds.

Author: Dogan Ibrahim
Date   : September, 2019
File   : UARTFlash.c
================================================================================*/
#include "main.h"
unsigned long FlashRateMs = 1000;
unsigned int N, Total;

//
// Define all your Task functions here
// ====================================
//

// Task 1 - UART Controller
void Task1(void *pvParameters)
{
    unsigned char Buffer[20];

    UART3_Init_Advanced(9600,_UART_8_BIT_DATA,_UART_NOPARITY,_UART_ONE_STOPBIT,
                      &_GPIO_MODULE_USART3_PD89);
    while (1)
    {
        UART3_Write_Text("\n\r\n\rEnter LED Flash Rate (Seconds): ");
        N = 0;
        Total = 0;

        while(1)
        {
            N = UART3_Read();                            // Read a number
            UART3_Write(N);                              // Echo the number
            if(N == '\r') break;                         // If Enter
            N = N - '0';                                 // Pure number
            Total = 10*Total + N;                        // Total number
        }
        FlashRateMs = Total * 1000;                      // Flash rate
        UART3_Write_Text("\n\rFlashing Rate Changed...");  // Send message
    }
}

// Task 2 - LED Controller
void Task2(void *pvParameters)
{
    #define LED GPIOE_ODR.B12

    GPIO_Config(&GPIOE_BASE, _GPIO_PINMASK_12, _GPIO_CFG_MODE_OUTPUT);

    while (1)
    {
        LED = 0;                                         // LED OFF
        vTaskDelay(pdMS_TO_TICKS(FlashRateMs));          // Delay
        LED = 1;                                         // LED ON
```

FIGURE 9.50   UARTFlash.c program listing.

```
        vTaskDelay(pdMS_TO_TICKS(FlashRateMs));         // Delay
    }
}

//
// Start of MAIN program
// =====================
//
void main()
{
//
// Create all the TASKS here
// =========================
//
    // Create Task 1
    xTaskCreate(
        (TaskFunction_t)Task1,
        "UART Controller",
        configMINIMAL_STACK_SIZE,
        NULL,
        10,
        NULL
    );


    // Create Task 2
    xTaskCreate(
        (TaskFunction_t)Task2,
        "LED Controller",
        configMINIMAL_STACK_SIZE,
        NULL,
        10,
        NULL
    );

//
// Start the RTOS scheduler
//
    vTaskStartScheduler();

//
// Will never reach here
//
    while (1);
}
```

FIGURE 9.50 (*Continued*)

```
Enter LED Flash Rate (Seconds): 10
Flashing Rate Changed...

Enter LED Flash Rate (Seconds): ▊
```

FIGURE 9.51   Setting the flashing rate to 10 s.

Parameter

pcWriteBuffer: This is the character buffer into which the table data is written. The buffer must be large enough to hold the table as there is no boundary checking.

Return value

The function has no return value.

The task table is in the following format:

Name	State	Priority	Stack	Num
LCD	R	10	300	25
LED	R	10	320	18
IDLE	R	0	60	0

Where,

Name: This is the name given to the task when it was created.

State: This is the state of the task at the time of calling the function. This can take the following values:

X:	the task is executing (this is the task calling the function)
B:	the task is in Blocked state
R:	the task is in Ready state
S:	the task is in Suspended state without timeout
D:	the task has been deleted (the Idle task has not freed the memory used by the task)

Priority: the priority assigned to the task at the time of making the function call.

Stack: This is the minimum amount of free stack that has been available during the lifetime of the task (the value becomes closer to zero if the task has come to overflow its stack).

Num: This is a unique number assigned to each task. It can be used to identify a task if the same name is assigned to more than one task.

Function vTaskList() is provided for convenience only and the function will disable interrupts for the duration of its execution.

Parameters configUSE_TRACE_FACILITY and configUSE_STATS_FORMATTING_FUNCTIONS must both be set to 1 in file FreeRTOSConfig.h for vTaskList() to be available.

A project is given in the next section that displays the task list on the PC screen.

9.21 Project 17—displaying the task list on the PC screen

Description: In this project the task list is displayed on a PC screen. The project uses the USB UART Click board as in the previous project. Some dummy tasks are created for display purposes.

Aim: The aim of this project is to show how the Task List can be displayed on the PC screen.

Block diagram: The block diagram of this project is same as in Figure 9.43.

Program listing: Fig. 9.52 shows the program listing (program: **Tasks.c**). The program consists of three tasks (excluding the Idle task) which do not do anything useful. At the beginning of task MAIN, a buffer is created, UART 3 is initialized to operate at 9600 baud, and function

```
/*==============================================================================
                        DISPLAY THE TASK LIST
                        =====================

In this program the USB UART Clicker board is connected to mikroBUS socket 2 of
the Clicker 2 for STM32 development board. The program displays the Task List
at the time of making the API function call vTaskList().

Author: Dogan Ibrahim
Date   : September, 2019
File   : Tasks.c
==============================================================================*/
#include "main.h"

//
// Define all your Task functions here
// ===================================
//

// Task 1 - Dummy task - Display the Task List
void Task1(void *pvParameters)
{
    static char Buffer[512];

    UART3_Init_Advanced(9600,_UART_8_BIT_DATA,_UART_NOPARITY,_UART_ONE_STOPBIT,
                        &_GPIO_MODULE_USART3_PD89);
    vTaskList(Buffer);
    UART3_Write_Text(Buffer);

    while (1)
    {
    }
}

// Task 2 - Dummy TAsk
void Task2(void *pvParameters)
{
    while (1)
    {
    }
}


// Task 3 - Dummy TAsk
void Task3(void *pvParameters)
{
    while (1)
    {
    }
}

//
// Start of MAIN program
// =====================
//
void main()
{
//
// Create all the TASKS here
// =========================
```

FIGURE 9.52   Tasks.c program listing.

```
//
    // Create Task 1
    xTaskCreate(
        (TaskFunction_t)Task1,
        "Main",
        configMINIMAL_STACK_SIZE,
        NULL,
        10,
        NULL
    );


    // Create Task 2
    xTaskCreate(
        (TaskFunction_t)Task2,
        "Dummy2",
        configMINIMAL_STACK_SIZE,
        NULL,
        10,
        NULL
    );


     // Create Task 3
    xTaskCreate(
        (TaskFunction_t)Task3,
        "Dummy3",
        configMINIMAL_STACK_SIZE,
        NULL,
        10,
        NULL
    );


//
// Start the RTOS scheduler
//
    vTaskStartScheduler();

//
// Will never reach here
//
    while (1);
}
```

FIGURE 9.52 *(Continued)*

vTaskList() is called. Fig. 9.53 shows the task list on the PC screen using the Putty terminal emulator software as described in the previous project. Notice that all the tasks have priorities 10 except the Idle task which has the lowest priority of 0.

Library function sprint must be enabled in the mikroC Pro for ARM compiler Library Manager before the program is compiled.

Dummy3	R	10	115	3
Main	R	10	98	1
Dummy2	R	10	116	2
IDLE	R	0	116	4

FIGURE 9.53 **Task List on the PC screen.**

9.22 Task info

This function gets the structure of a single task and populates a TaskStatus_t type structure with this information. The format of the function is:

void vTaskGetTaskInfo(TaskHandle_t xTask,TaskStatus_t *pxTaskStatus,BaseType_t xGetFreeStackSpace, eTaskState eState);

where,

xTask: This is the handle of the task being queried.

pxTaskStatus: This points to a variable of type TaskStatus_t which is filled with the information about the task being queried.

xGetFreeStackSpace: Setting this parameter TRUE includes the minimum amount of stack space of the task.

eState: Setting this parameter to eInvalid includes the task state in the structure TaskStatus_t.

Parameter configUSE_TRACE_FACILITY must be defined as 1 in file FreeRTOSConfig.h for vTaskGetTaskInfo() to be available.

A project is given in the next section that displays the task list on the PC screen.

9.23 Project 19—displaying the task info on the PC screen

Description: In this project the task information for a task is displayed on the PC screen. The project uses the USB UART Click board as in the previous project. There are three tasks (excluding the Idle task) in this project. The display shows the task information of task called Dummy2.

Aim: The aim of this project is to show how the Task Info can be displayed on the PC screen.

Block diagram: The block diagram of this project is same as in Fig. 9.43.

Program listing: Fig. 9.54 shows the program listing (program: **Taskinfo.c**). The program consists of three tasks (excluding the Idle task) which do not do anything useful. Inside Task 1, UART 3 is initialized to 9600 baud. The handle of Task 2 (Task name: Dummy2) is then stored in xHandle. The program then calls function vTaskGetTaskInfo() with this handle. The task information is populated to the structure of type TaskStatus_t called xTaskInfo. The program then displays the Task Name, Current task priority, Base task Priority, and the Task Number.

Structure TaskStatus_t has the following members:

code const unsigned char ***pcTaskName**
UBaseType_t **xTaskNumber**
eTaskState **eCurrentState**
UBaseType_t **uxCurrentPriority**
UBaseType_t **uxBasePriority**
Uint32_t **ulRunTimeCounter**
StackType_t ***pxStackBase**
Uint16_t **usStackHighWaterMark**

Notice that a carriage-return, line-feed pair is output after displaying each parameter so that each parameter starts on a new line. Parameters Current Priority, Base Priority, and Task Number are converted into strings using the mikroC Pro for ARM compiler built-in function ByteToStr(), leading spaces removed using function Ltrim(), and then sent to UART.

```
/*=============================================================================
                        DISPLAY TASK INFORMATION
                        ========================

In this program the USB UART Clicker board is connected to mikroBUS socket 2 of
the Clicker 2 for STM32 development board. The program displays the Task Info
of the task called Dummy2 (Task 2).

Author: Dogan Ibrahim
Date  : September, 2019
File  : Taskinfo.c
=============================================================================*/
#include "main.h"
TaskHandle_t xHandle;
TaskStatus_t xTaskInfo;

//
// Define all your Task functions here
// ===================================
//

// Task 1 - Dummy task - Display the Task List
void Task1(void *pvParameters)
{
    unsigned char Txt[4];
    UART3_Init_Advanced(9600,_UART_8_BIT_DATA,_UART_NOPARITY,_UART_ONE_STOPBIT,
                        &_GPIO_MODULE_USART3_PD89);

    xHandle = xTaskGetHandle("Dummy2");
    vTaskGetTaskInfo(xHandle, &xTaskInfo, pdTRUE, eInvalid);

    UART3_Write_Text("Task Name: "); UART3_Write_Text(xTaskInfo.pcTaskName);
    UART3_Write('\n'); UART3_Write('\r');

    ByteToStr(xTaskInfo.uxCurrentPriority, Txt); Ltrim(Txt);
    UART3_Write_Text("Current Priority: "); UART3_Write_Text(Txt);
    UART3_Write('\n'); UART3_Write('\r');

    ByteToStr(xTaskInfo.uxBasePriority, Txt); Ltrim(Txt);
    UART3_Write_Text("Base Priority: "); UART3_Write_Text(Txt);
    UART3_Write('\n'); UART3_Write('\r');

    ByteToStr(xTaskInfo.xTaskNumber, Txt); Ltrim(Txt);
    UART3_Write_Text("Task Number: "); UART3_Write_Text(Txt);
    UART3_Write('\n'); UART3_Write('\r');

    while (1)
    {
    }
}

// Task 2 - Dummy TAsk
void Task2(void *pvParameters)
{
    while (1)
    {
    }
}
```

FIGURE 9.54   Taskinfo.c program listing.

```
// Task 3 - Dummy Task
void Task3(void *pvParameters)
{
    while (1)
    {
    }
}

//
// Start of MAIN program
// =====================
//
void main()
{
//
// Create all the TASKS here
// =========================
//
    // Create Task 1
    xTaskCreate(
        (TaskFunction_t)Task1,
        "Main",
        configMINIMAL_STACK_SIZE,
        NULL,
        10,
        NULL
    );


    // Create Task 2
    xTaskCreate(
        (TaskFunction_t)Task2,
        "Dummy2",
        configMINIMAL_STACK_SIZE,
        NULL,
        10,
        NULL
    );


     // Create Task 3
    xTaskCreate(
        (TaskFunction_t)Task3,
        "Dummy3",
        configMINIMAL_STACK_SIZE,
        NULL,
        10,
        NULL
    );


//
// Start the RTOS scheduler
//
    vTaskStartScheduler();

//
// Will never reach here
//
    while (1);
}
```

FIGURE 9.54 *(Continued)*

```
Task Name: Dummy2
Current Priority: 10
Base Priority: 10
Task Number: 2
```

FIGURE 9.55 **Typical output on the PC screen.**

Library function sprint must be enabled in the mikroC Pro for ARM compiler Library Manager before the program is compiled.

The data is displayed on the PC screen using the Putty terminal emulation software as in the previous project. Fig. 9.55 shows a typical output on the PC screen.

9.24 Task state

API function eTaskGetState() returns the state of a function whose handle is supplied. The format of the function is:

eTaskGetState(TaskHandle_t pxTask);

Parameter

pxTask: This is the handle of the task whose state is required.

Return values

The following enumerated values are returned by the function:

Task state	Returned enumerated value
Running	eRunning (the running task is calling the function)
Ready	eReady
Blocked	eBlocked
Suspended	eSuspended
Deleted	eDeleted (the task's structures are waiting to be cleaned up)

Parameter INCLUDE_eTaskGetState must be set to 1 in file FreeRTOSConfig.h for the eTaskGetState() API function to be available.

An example project using function eTaskGetState() is given in the next section.

9.25 Project 20—displaying the task state on the PC screen

Description: In this project the task state for a task is displayed on the PC screen. The project uses the USB UART Click board as in the previous project. The display shows the task state of task called Dummy2.

Aim: The aim of this project is to show how the Task State can be displayed on the PC screen.

Block diagram: The block diagram of this project is same as in Fig. 9.43.

Program listing: Fig. 9.56 shows the program listing (program: **Taskstate.c**). In Task 1, UART 3 is initialized to 9600 baud. The handle of Task 2 (Task name: Dummy2) is then stored

```
/*==============================================================================
                        DISPLAY TASK STATE
                        ==================

In this program the USB UART Clicker board is connected to mikroBUS socket 2 of
the Clicker 2 for STM32 development board. The program displays the Task State
of the task called Dummy2 (Task 2).

Author: Dogan Ibrahim
Date  : September, 2019
File  : Taskstate.c
===============================================================================*/
#include "main.h"
TaskHandle_t xHandle;
eTaskState xTask;
//
// Define all your Task functions here
// ===================================
//

// Task 1 - Dummy task - Display the Task List
void Task1(void *pvParameters)
{
    unsigned char Txt[4];
    UART3_Init_Advanced(9600,_UART_8_BIT_DATA,_UART_NOPARITY,_UART_ONE_STOPBIT,
                        &_GPIO_MODULE_USART3_PD89);

    xHandle = xTaskGetHandle("Dummy2");
    xTask = eTaskGetState(xHandle);

    switch (xTask)
    {
        case eReady:
                    UART3_Write_Text("Ready");
                    break;
        case eRunning:
                    UART_Write_Text("Running");
                    break;
        case eBlocked:
                    UART_Write_Text("Blocked");
                    break;
        case eSuspended:
                    UART_Write_Text("Blocked");
                    break;
        case eDeleted:
                    UART_Write_Text("Deleted");
                    break;
    }

    while (1)
    {
    }
}

// Task 2 - Dummy Task
void Task2(void *pvParameters)
{
    while (1)
    {
    }
```

FIGURE 9.56   Taskstate.c program listing.

```
    }


    //
    // Start of MAIN program
    // ====================
    //
    void main()
    {
    //
    // Create all the TASKS here
    // =========================
    //
        // Create Task 1
        xTaskCreate(
            (TaskFunction_t)Task1,
            "Main",
            configMINIMAL_STACK_SIZE,
            NULL,
            10,
            NULL
        );


        // Create Task 2
        xTaskCreate(
            (TaskFunction_t)Task2,
            "Dummy2",
            configMINIMAL_STACK_SIZE,
            NULL,
            10,
            NULL
        );

    //
    // Start the RTOS scheduler
    //
        vTaskStartScheduler();

    //
    // Will never reach here
    //
        while (1);
    }
```

FIGURE 9.56   (*Continued*)

in xHandle. The program then calls function eTaskGetState() with this handle. The task state is then displayed using a switch statement. In this example, string Ready is displayed on the PC screen since this task was in the Ready state at the time it was called.

9.26 Task parameters

We have seen earlier that one of the parameters when a new task is created is pvParameters. A function accepts a parameter of type pointer to void. That is, (void*). The value assigned to pvParameters is the value passed into the task.

As an example, assume that we wish to pass the following string to a task:

This is for Task 1

The string should be defined as a constant to ensure that it remains valid when the tasks are executing. Thus, define the string as follows:

static const char *pcTaskText = "This is for Task 1"

We can then pass this string to a task when the task is created as follows:
xTaskCreate(vTaskFunction,
   "Task 1",
   1000,
   (void*)pcTaskText,
   10,
   NULL);

9.27 Summary

In this chapter we have learned how to use most of the important FreeRTOS task functions. Tested and working examples in the form of projects are given to show how the functions can be used in application programs.

In the next chapter we shall be looking at the Queue Management functions and give examples to show how they can be used in practical applications.

Further readings

[1] R. Barry. Mastering the FreeRTOS Real Time Kernel: A Hands-On Tutorial Guide. Available from: https://www.freertos.org/wp-content/uploads/2018/07/161204_Mastering_the_FreeRTOS_Real_Time_Kernel-A_Hands-On_Tutorial_Guide.pdf.

[2] The FreeRTOS Reference Manual. Available from: https://www.freertos.org/wp-content/uploads/2018/07/FreeRTOS_Reference_Manual_V10.0.0.pdf.

[3] https://www.freertos.org/documentation.

CHAPTER
10

Queue management

10.1 Overview–global variables

In the last chapter, we have developed several FreeRTOS based projects, each project having multiple tasks. You will notice that in those projects we used global variables (variables declared at the beginning of a program before any task) to pass data between tasks. Although global variables can be safe and easy to use in small programs, in general, it is not recommended to use global variables in complex programs because of the following reasons:

- Global variables can be changed by any part of the code, for example, by any task in a multitasking environment. This can make it difficult to keep track of these variables.
- Using global variables causes very tight coupling of code.
- Global variables have no access control.
- Testing a program using global variables can be very difficult as it is difficult to decouple them.
- If global variables can be accessed by multiple tasks at the same time, then synchronization of these tasks may be required.

There are no problems of using global variables in small programs as long as these global variables names are prefixed by some letters so that they cannot be mixed with local variables with similar names. For example, instead of using Cnt as a global variable, use GblCnt instead.

10.2 Why queues?

Queues are important parts of any multitasking operating systems. Queues are used for intertask communication in multitasking operating systems. They can be used to send messages and data between tasks and between interrupt service routines and tasks. It is recommended to use queues instead of global variables in complex programs when it is required to pass data or messages between tasks in a multitasking program. A queue is basically a FIFO (First In First Out) type buffer such that new data is sent to the back of the queue and the first data that is sent to the queue is the first one that is received by the receiving task. Notice that in FreeRTOS it is possible to send data to the front of the queue. You may think a queue to be like

ARM-Based Microcontroller Multitasking Projects. http://dx.doi.org/10.1016/B978-0-12-821227-1.00010-4

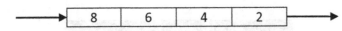

FIGURE 10.1 **A queue with 4 cells.**

a table having only one row but many columns. Data is put into the table columns from the left and extracted from the right. For example, consider a queue having four storage cells. Assuming that numbers 2, 4, 6, and 8 are put into the queue, the queue will look like in Fig. 10.1

In FreeRTOS, messages are passed to queues by copy which means that the data itself is copied into the queue and not the reference to the data. As a result of this, the data is available for re-use. The kernel allocates memory for the use of queues. Small messages and data (e.g., characters, integers, small structures, etc.) can be sent into a queue directly without having to allocate buffer for them. Large data can be passed to a queue by defining a queue to hold pointers and copy just a pointer to the message into the queue. A single queue can be used to receive different message types, and messages from multiple locations, by defining the queue to hold a structure that has a member that holds the message type, and another member that holds the message data.

In this chapter, we shall be looking at the various FreeRTOS queue functions and see how they can be used in application programs. Only the commonly used queue functions are described in this Chapter. Interested readers can get further details on all available queue functions from the following link:

https://www.freertos.org/wp-content/uploads/2018/07/FreeRTOS_Reference_Manual_ V10.0.0.pdf

10.3 Creating a queue, sending and receiving data using queues

The API function xQueueCreate() is used to create a new queue. The RAM memory required by the queue is automatically allocated by the kernel. The format of this function is:

xQueueCreate(UBaseType_t uxQueueLength, UBaseType_t uxItemSize);

Parameters
uxQueueLength: This is the maximum number of items that the queue can hold at any time.
uxItemSize: The size (in bytes) of each data item that can be stored in the queue.
Return values
NULL: The queue cannot be created (e.g. because there is insufficient heap memory available for FreeRTOS to allocate to the queue).
Any other value: The queue was created successfully. The returned value is a handle by which the created queue can be referenced.

The parameter configSUPPORT_DYNAMIC_ALLOCATION must be set to 1 in file FreeRTOSConfig.h, or simply left undefined, for this function to be available

The API function xQueueReceive() is used to receive (read) data from a queue. The format of this function is:

xQueueReceive(QueueHandle_t xQueue, void *pvBuffer, TickType_t xTicksToWait);

Parameters

xQueue: The handle of the queue from which the data is being received (read). The queue handle will have been returned from the call to xQueueCreate().

pvBuffer: A pointer to the memory into which the received data will be copied to. The length of the buffer must be at least equal to the queue item size. The item size will have been set by the uxItemSize parameter of the call to xQueueCreate().

xTicksToWait: This is the maximum amount of time the task should remain in the Blocked state to wait for data to become available on the queue, if the queue is empty. If xTicksToWait is zero, then xQueueReceive() will return immediately if the queue is already empty. The block time is specified in tick periods, the pdMS_TO_TICKS() macro can be used to convert a time specified in milliseconds to a time specified in ticks. Setting xTicksToWait to portMAX_DELAYwill cause the task to wait indefinitely (without timing out) provided INCLUDE_vTaskSuspend is set to 1 file FreeRTOSConfig.h.

Return values

pdPASS: Returned if data was successfully read from the queue. If a block time was specified (xTicksToWait was not zero), then it is possible that the calling task was placed into the Blocked state, to wait for data to become available on the queue, but data was successfully read from the queue before the block time expired.

errQUEUE_EMPTY: Returned if data cannot be read from the queue because the queue is already empty. If a block time was specified (xTicksToWait was not zero) then the calling task will have been placed into the Blocked state to wait for another task or interrupt to send data to the queue, but the block time expired before this happened

The API functions to send data to a queue are:

xQueueSend(QueueHandle_t xQueue, const void * pvItemToQueue, TickType_t xTicksToWait);
xQueueSendToFront(QueueHandle_t xQueue, const void * pvItemToQueue, TickType_t xTicksToWait);
xQueueSendToBack(QueueHandle_t xQueue, const void * pvItemToQueue, TickType_t xTicksToWait);

API functions xQueueSend() and xQueueSendToBack() are identical and they both send (write) data to the back of a queue. Function xQueueSendToFront() sends data to the front of a queue.

Parameters

xQueue: The handle of the queue to which the data is being sent (written). The queue handle is returned from a call to create a queue.

pvItemToQueue: A pointer to the data to be copied into the queue. The size of each item the queue can hold is set when the queue is created, and that many bytes will be copied from pvItemToQueue into the queue storage area.

xTicksToWait: The maximum amount of time the task should remain in the Blocked state to wait for space to become available on the queue, should the queue already be full.

xQueueSend(): xQueueSendToFront() and xQueueSendToBack() will return immediately if xTicksToWait is zero and the queue is already full. The block time is specified in tick periods. The pdMS_TO_TICKS() macro can be used to convert a time specified in milliseconds to a time specified in ticks. Setting xTicksToWait to portMAX_DELAYwill cause the task to

wait indefinitely (without timing out), provided INCLUDE_vTaskSuspend is set to 1 in file
FreeRTOSConfig.h.

Return values

pdPASS: Returned if data was successfully sent to the queue. If a block time was specified (xTicksToWait was not zero), then it is possible that the calling task was placed into the
Blocked state, to wait for space to become available in the queue before the function returned,
but data was successfully written to the queue before the block time expired.

errQUEUE_FULL: Returned if data could not be written to the queue because the queue
was already full. If a block time was specified (xTicksToWait was not zero) then the calling
task will have been placed into the Blocked state to wait for another task or interrupt to make
room in the queue, but the specified block time expired before that happened.

An example project is given in the next section to shows how a queue can be created in
practise and how inter-task communication can take place using this queue.

10.4 Project 21–changing LED flashing rate from the PC keyboard

Description: This project is similar to Project 16 described in Chapter 9, where global variable called FlashRateMs was received from the PC keyboard and it was used as the delay
parameter to change the LED flashing rate. In this program, a queue is created instead of
using a global variable, and the LED flashing rate is passed to the task controlling the LED
using this queue. There are two tasks in this project in addition to the Idle task.

Aim: The aim of this project is to show how a queue can be created and data can be sent
from one task to another one using this queue.

Block diagram: The block diagram of this project is same as in Fig. 9.43, but here additionally the LED at port PE12 is used. The USB UART Click board is plugged to mikroBUS socket
2 of the Clicker 2 for STM32 development board as in Project 16.

Program listing: Fig. 10.2 shows the program listing (program: **QueueLED.c**). The program consists of two tasks excluding the Idle task. The queue handle is named xQueue and
is passed to both tasks as task parameters during the creation of the tasks. Task 1 is created
as shown below:

```
    xTaskCreate(
        (TaskFunction_t)Task1,
        "UART Controller",
        configMINIMAL_STACK_SIZE,
        (void*)xQueue,
        10,
        NULL
    );
```

The queue length (QueueLength) was set to 1 since only one variable was to be sent via
the queue. The queue size (QueueSizeBytes) was set to 8 since the variable was a long which
consists of 8 bytes. The operation of the two tasks are summarized below:

Task 1

This is the UART Controller task. At the beginning of the task the queue handle is obtained
from the task parameter, UART 3 uses ports PD8 and PD9 of the development board and it

```
/*=================================================================================
                    CHANGE LED FLASHING RATE FROM THE PC KEYBOARD
                    =============================================

In this program the USB UART Click board is plugged in to mikroBUS socket 2 of
the Clicker 2 for STM32 development board. The LED connected to port pin PE12 is
used in this project. Commands are received from the PC keyboard to change the
LED flashing rate in seconds.

In this program a Queue is used to send the flashing rate to the LED Controller
task

Author: Dogan Ibrahim
Date  : September, 2019
File  : QueueLED.c
=================================================================================*/
#include "main.h"

//
// Define all your Task functions here
// ====================================
//

// Task 1 - UART Controller
void Task1(void *pvParameters)
{
    unsigned N;
    unsigned long Total;
    QueueHandle_t xQueue;
    xQueue = (QueueHandle_t) pvParameters;

    UART3_Init_Advanced(9600,_UART_8_BIT_DATA,_UART_NOPARITY,_UART_ONE_STOPBIT,
                        &_GPIO_MODULE_USART3_PD89);

    while (1)
    {
        UART3_Write_Text("\n\r\n\rEnter LED Flash Rate (Seconds): ");
        N = 0;
        Total = 0;

        while(1)
        {
            N = UART3_Read();                          // Read a number
            UART3_Write(N);                            // Echo the number
            if(N == '\r') break;                       // If Enter
            N = N - '0';                               // Pure number
            Total = 10*Total + N;                      // Total number
        }

        Total = Total * 1000;                          // Flash rate (ms)
        xQueueSend(xQueue, &Total, pdMS_TO_TICKS(10)); // Send via Queue
        UART3_Write_Text("\n\rFlashing Rate Changed..."); // Write on screen
    }
}

// Task 2 - LED Controller
void Task2(void *pvParameters)
{
    #define LED GPIOE_ODR.B12
    unsigned long FlashRateMs;
```

FIGURE 10.2 QueueLED.c program listing.

```
      QueueHandle_t xQueue;
      xQueue = (QueueHandle_t) pvParameters;

      GPIO_Config(&GPIOE_BASE, _GPIO_PINMASK_12, _GPIO_CFG_MODE_OUTPUT);
      FlashRateMs = 1000;                                    // Default rate

      while (1)
      {
            xQueueReceive(xQueue, &FlashRateMs, 0 );         // Receive data
            LED = 0;                                         // LED OFF
            vTaskDelay(pdMS_TO_TICKS(FlashRateMs));          // Delay
            LED = 1;                                         // LED ON
            vTaskDelay(pdMS_TO_TICKS(FlashRateMs));          // Delay
      }
}

//
// Start of MAIN program
// =====================
//
void main()
{

    #define QueueLength 1                                    // Queue length
    #define QueueSizeBytes 8                                 // item size (bytes)
    QueueHandle_t xQueue;

    xQueue = xQueueCreate(QueueLength, QueueSizeBytes);      // Create a Queue

//
// Create all the TASKS here
// =========================
//
    // Create Task 1
    xTaskCreate(
        (TaskFunction_t)Task1,
        "UART Controller",
        configMINIMAL_STACK_SIZE,
        (void*)xQueue,                                       // Pass Queue handle
        10,
        NULL
    );


    // Create Task 2
    xTaskCreate(
        (TaskFunction_t)Task2,
        "LED Controller",
        configMINIMAL_STACK_SIZE,
        (void*)xQueue,                                       // Pass Queue handle
        10,
        NULL
    );

//
// Start the RTOS scheduler
//
    vTaskStartScheduler();

//
// Will never reach here
//
    while (1);
}
```

FIGURE 10.2   *(Continued)*

```
Enter LED Flash Rate (Seconds): 3
Flashing Rate Changed...
```

FIGURE 10.3 **Setting the flashing rate to 3 seconds.**

is initialized to operate at 9600 baud as in project 16. Then, the user is prompted to enter the required flashing rate and the following text is displayed on the PC screen

Enter LED Flash Rate (Seconds):

The program reads the flashing rate from the PC keyboard as numeric data and stores the total number in seconds in variable called Total. The user entry is terminated when the Enter key is pressed on the keyboard. Variable Total is then converted into milliseconds by multiplying by 1000. The value of this variable is then sent to the queue using the following statement. The parameter xTicksToWait is set to 10ms so that the task will be in Blocked state for 10ms if there is no space available in the queue:

xQueueSend(xQueue, &Total, pdMS_TO_TICKS(10));

The following text is then displayed on the PC screen to confirm that the flashing rate has changed:

Flashing Rate Changed...

Task 2
This task implements the LED flashing function. At the beginning of the task the queue handle is obtained from the task parameter. The flashing rate is stored in variable called FlashRateMs and this variable is set to 1000ms at the beginning by default. The LED keeps flashing as the user enters data from the keyboard. The flashing rate is read from the queue as follows. The data read from the queue is stored in variable FlashRateMs:

xQueueReceive(xQueue, &FlashRateMs, 0);

Parameter xTicksQueueWait is set to 0 so the function call will return immediately if there is no data in the queue. The value read by the queue function is used in function vTaskDelay() as the new flashing rate of the LED.

As you can see from Fig. 10.2, all the variables used in both tasks are local to their tasks and global variables are not used in the program. Although using global variables may seem to be an easier option in this case, it has the disadvantages outlined at the beginning of this Chapter in section 10.1.

Fig. 10.3 shows a typical run of the program where the flashing rate was set to 3 seconds.

10.5 Deleting a queue, name of a queue, resetting a queue

The API function xQueueDelete() deletes a queue that has been created earlier. A queue must not be deleted if there are any tasks currently blocked on it. The format of the function is:

vQueueDelete(TaskHandle_t pxQueueToDelete);

Parameters

pxQueueToDelete: This is the handle of the queue being deleted.

Return value

The function has no return value

The API function pcQueueGetName() returns the text formatted name of a queue. A queue will only have a text name if it has been added to the queue registry using function vQueueAddToregistry() described later. The format of this function is:

pcQueueGetName(QueueHandle_t xQueue);

Parameter

xQueue: This is the handle of the queue being queried.

Return value

Queue names are standard NULL terminated C strings. The value returned is a pointer to the name of the queue being queried.

The API function vQueueAddToRegistry() assigns a name to a queue and adds the name to the queue registry. The format of this function is:

vQueueAddToRegistry(QueueHandle_t xQueue, char *pcQueueName);

Parameters

xQueue: This is the handle of the queue that will be added to the queue registry.

pcQueueName: A descriptive name for the queue. Notice that queue names are not used by FreeRTOS in any way and they are intended as debugging aids since identifying a queue by its name is much easier than attempting to identify by its handle.

Return value

The function has no return values

The parameter configQUEUE_REGISTRY_SIZE defines the maximum number of queues and semaphores (we will see later) that can be registered at any one time. This parameter must be greater than 0 to and item to the queue registry.

The API function xQueueReset() resets a queue to its original state. Any data in the queue at the time of the function call is discarded. The format of the function is:

xQueueReset(QueueHandle_t xQueue);

Parameter

xQueue: This is the handle of the queue that is being reset.

Return values

pdPASS or pdFAIL is returned.

10.6 Project 22—using various queue functions

Description: This project shows how some of the queue functions described in Section 10.5 can be used in an application program. Only one task is used in this project. The following queue operations are performed by the program:

- Create a queue
- Give a name to the queue

- Display the queue name on PC screen
- Reset the queue
- Delete the queue

Aim: The aim of this project is to show how various queue functions can be used in a program.

Block diagram: The block diagram of this project is same as in Fig. 9.43. The USB UART Click board is plugged to mikroBUS 2 socket of the Clicker 2 for STM32 development board as in Project 16.

Program listing: Fig. 10.4 shows the program listing (program: **Queues.c**). The program consists of one task in addition to the Idle task. At the beginning of the program the queue length and queue size are defined, and UART is initialized to operate at 9600 baud. The message **Various queue operations** is then displayed on the PC screen. Following this, a queue is created and it is added to the queue registry with the name MyQueue. The program then gets the queue name by calling function pcQueueGetName() and stores in variable pointed to by QueueName. The queue name is then displayed on the PC screen by sending to the UART. Finally, the queue is reset and then deleted.

Fig. 10.5 shows the output from the program, displayed using the Putty terminal emulation program.

```
/*=============================================================================
                        USING VARIOUS QUEUE FUNCTIONS
                        =============================

This program shows how various queue functions can be used in a program. The
following queue operations are performed by the program:

Create a queue
Give name to the queue (e.g. MyQueue)
Display the queue name on PC screen
Reset the queue
Delete the queue

Only one task is used in this program for simplicity

Author: Dogan Ibrahim
Date  : September, 2019
File  : Queues.c
=============================================================================*/
#include "main.h"

//
// Define all your Task functions here
// ==================================
//

// Task 1 - Various Queue operations
void Task1(void *pvParameters)
{
    const char *QueueName;
    #define QueueLength 1                                    // Queue length
    #define QueueSizeBytes 2                                 // item size (bytes)

    QueueHandle_t xQueue;
```

FIGURE 10.4   Queues.c program listing.

```
        UART3_Init_Advanced(9600,_UART_8_BIT_DATA,_UART_NOPARITY,_UART_ONE_STOPBIT,
                    &_GPIO_MODULE_USART3_PD89);

        UART3_Write_Text("\n\rVarious Queue operations\n\r");
        xQueue = xQueueCreate(QueueLength, QueueSizeBytes);         // Create a Queue
        vQueueAddToRegistry(xQueue, "MyQueue");                     // Assign Queue name
        QueueName = pcQueueGetName(xQueue);                         // Get Queue name
        UART3_Write_Text("Queue name: ");
        UART3_Write_Text(QueueName);
        UART3_Write_Text("\n\r");                                   // New line
        xQueueReset(xQueue);                                        // Reset queue
        vQueueDelete(xQueue);                                       // Delete queue

        while (1)
        {
        }
}

//
// Start of MAIN program
// =====================
//
void main()
{
//
// Create all the TASKS here
// =========================
//
        // Create Task 1
        xTaskCreate(
            (TaskFunction_t)Task1,
            "QUEUE operations",
            configMINIMAL_STACK_SIZE,
            NULL,
            10,
            NULL
        );

//
// Start the RTOS scheduler
//
        vTaskStartScheduler();

//
// Will never reach here
//
        while (1);
}
```

FIGURE 10.4   (*Continued*)

```
                        Various Queue operations
                        Queue name: MyQueue
```

FIGURE 10.5   Output from the program.

10.7 Some other queue functions

The API function xQueueOverwrite() writes to the queue even if the queue is full. It is intended to be used for queues having lengths of one (the queue is empty or full). The format of the function is:

xQueueOverwrite(QueueHandle_t xQueue, const void *pvItemToQueue);

Parameters
xQueue: This the handle of the queue to which the data is to be sent.
pvItemToQueue: A pointer to the item that is to be placed in the queue.
Return value
xQueueOverwrite() is a macro that calls xQueueGenericSend(), and therefore has the same return values as xQueueSendToFront(). However, pdPASS is the only value that can be returned because xQueueOverwrite() will write to the queue even when the queue is already full.

The API function xQueuePeek() reads an item from the queue, it does not remove the item from the queue. The format of this function is:

xQueuePeek(QueueHandle_t xQueue, void *pvBuffer, TickType_t xTicksToWait);

Parameters
xQueue: This is the handle of the queue from which data is to be read.
pvBuffer: A pointer to the memory into which the data read from the queue will be copied to.
xTicksToWait: The maximum amount of time the task should remain in the Blocked state to wait for data to become available on the queue, should the queue already be empty. If xTicksToWait is zero,then xQueuePeek() will return immediately if the queue is already empty. The block time is specified in tick periods, the pdMS_TO_TICKS() macro can be used to convert a time specified in milliseconds to a time specified in ticks. Setting xTicksToWait to portMAX_DELAY will cause the task to wait indefinitely (without timing out) provided INCLUDE_vTaskSuspend is set to 1

Return values
pdPASS: Returned if data was successfully read from the queue.
errQUEUE_EMPTY: Returned if data cannot be read from the queue because the queue is already empty. If a block time was specified (xTicksToWait was not zero) then the calling task will have been placed into the Blocked state to wait for another task or interrupt to send data to the queue, but the block time expired before this happened.

The API function uxQueueSpacesAvailable() returns the number of free spaces available in the queue. The format of this function is:

uxQueueSpacesAvailable(const QueueHandle_txQueue);

Parameters
xQueue: This is the handle of the queue being queried
Return value
The number of free spaces that are available in the queue being queried at the time uxQueueSpacesAvailable() is called.

The API function uxQueueMessagesWaiting() returns the number of items that are currently in the queue. The format of this function is:

uxQueueMessagesWaiting(const QueueHandle_t xQueue);

Parameter
xQueue: This is the handle of the queue being queried.
Returned value
The number of items that are held in the queue at the time of the function call.

10.8 Project 23—ON-OFF temperature controller

Description: In this project we design an ON-OFF temperature control project based on a multitasking approach. An ON-OFF temperature controller, also known as a bang-bang controller, will turn OFF the heater whenever the temperature is above a pre-defined setpoint (i.e., the required value). Similarly, if the temperature is below the setpoint then the heater is turned ON. ON-OFF controllers are used for simplicity since there is no need to know the model of the plant to be controlled. The only parameter that need to be set is the setpoint value. ON-OFF control is suitable when the response delay of the plant to be controlled is short and the output rate of rise time is small. If precision temperature control is required, then it may be more appropriate to use professional PID (Proportional + Integral + Derivative) type controller algorithms with negative feedback, or to use an intelligent fuzzy-based controller. The problem with most professional controllers is that an accurate model of the plant to be controlled is normally required before a suitable control algorithm can be derived. ON-OFF type controller has the disadvantage that the relay used to turn the heater ON and OFF has to operate many times and this may shorten the life of the relay.

Aim: The aim of this project is to show how an ON-OFF type controller can be designed using a multitasking based approach.

Block diagram: The block diagram of this project is shown in Fig. 10.6. The following components are used in this project in addition to the Clicker 2 for STM32 development board:

- USB UART Click board
- Analog temperature sensor chip
- LCD
- 10K potentiometer for LCD contrast adjustment
- Buzzer
- Relay
- Heater
- Keyboard (with a PC)

In this project it is required to control the temperature of an oven using ON-OFF type controller. The setpoint temperature is entered using a keyboard connected to a PC. This setpoint value can be changed at any desired time while the oven is under control. i.e. there is no need to stop the controller in order to change the setpoint value (hence multitasking). A relay connected to the Clicker 2 for STM32 development board turns the heater ON or OFF under the control of software. An LCD connected to the development board displays the setpoint temperature as well as the actual measured oven temperature. The temperature of the oven is measured using an analog temperature sensor chip. A buzzer is used which becomes active if the temperature of the

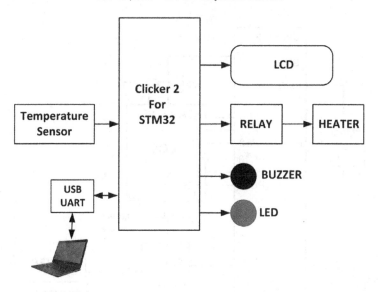

FIGURE 10.6   Block diagram of the project.

oven goes above a dangerous preset value to indicate an alarm condition. An LED displays the state of the oven at any time such that when the oven is ON then the LED is ON, and vice-versa.

Circuit diagram: A 16 × 2 character LCD is connected to the development board as described in previous projects in Chapter 9. The TMP36DZ type temperature sensor chip is used in this project. This is a small 3-pin chip that has the following basic specifications:

- 2.7–5.5 V operation
- 10 mV/°C output
- ±2°C accuracy
- ±0.5°C linearity
- −40°C to +125°C operation
- Less than 50 µA quiescent current

Fig. 10.7 shows the TMP36DZ chip pinout.

The relay used in the design is a standard relay that can operate with +3.3 V and it is assumed that the relay contacts can switch the mains supply ON or OFF with the heater connected to it. The buzzer is a standard low voltage (+3.3 V) active device that sounds when a logic 1 is

Bottom view

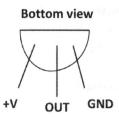

+V   OUT   GND

FIGURE 10.7   TMP36DZ temperature sensor pinout.

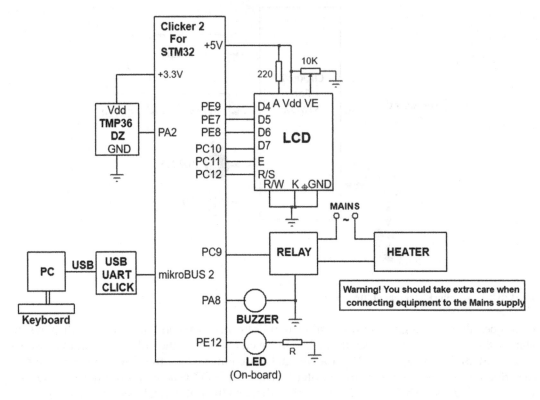

FIGURE 10.8   Circuit diagram of the project.

applied to its +V input. The on-board LED connected to port pin PE12 is used to indicate the status of the oven (an external LED can be connected to the development board if desired).

The circuit diagram of the project is shown in Fig. 10.8. The interface between the Clicker 2 for STM32 development board and the external components are as follows:

Clicker 2 for STM32 pin	External component pin	Mode
PE9	LCD pin D4	Digital output
PE7	LCD pin D5	Digital output
PE8	LCD pin D6	Digital output
PC10	LCD pin D7	Digital output
PC11	LCD pin E	Digital output
PC12	LCD pin R/S	Digital output
PC9	Relay	Digital output
PE12	LED (on-board)	Digital output
PA2	TMP36DZ	Analog input
PA8	Buzzer	Digital output

Program listing: The program consists of 4 tasks excluding the Idle task. All the tasks are configured to run at the same priority:

Task 1	Main task
Task 2	UART controller
Task 3	LCD controller
Task 4	Buzzer controller

At the beginning of the program, the interface between the LCD and the development board is defined. Three queues are used in this program with the following handles (these handles are defined as global in this program for simplicity):

Queue handle	Description	Used by Tasks
xUARTQueue	UART queue	Task 1, Task 2
xLCDQueue	LCD queue	Task 1, Task 3
xBuzzerQueue	Buzzer queue	Task 1, Task 4

The descriptions of the tasks are given below.

Task 1

This is the main task that controls the oven temperature. This task reads the analog temperature from the TMP36DZ temperature sensor chip which is connected to Channel 2 (port pin PA2) of the microcontroller. By default, at the beginning of this task the setpoint is set to 30°C and the alarm value is set to 50°C respectively. New setpoint values are received through the xUARTQueue from Task 2. The relay at port pin PC9 is configured as an output and also the LED at port pin PE12 is configured as an output. The temperature is read by calling the built-in ADC function ADC1_Read(2) where 2 is the channel number. The ADC on the microcontroller is 12-bits wide, thus having 4096 quantization levels. The reference voltage of the ADC is 3.3 V (3300 mV). The analog value read from Channel 2 is converted into physical millivolts by multiplying it by 3300 and dividing by 4096. The absolute temperature of the TMP36DZ is found by measuring its output voltage in millivolts, subtracting 500, and then dividing by 10, that is,

$$T = (Vo - 500)/10$$

where T is the absolute temperature in °C and Vo is the output voltage of the sensor chip in millivolts. If the measured temperature is less than the setpoint then the relay is activated to turn ON the heater. If on the other hand the measured temperature is greater than the setpoint then the relay is de-activated to turn OFF the heater. The measured temperature is compared with the pre-defined alarm value and if it is higher than the alarm value, then a 1 is sent to Task 4 (Buzzer Controller) using the xBuzzerQueue so that Task 4 activates the buzzer. If the measured temperature is less than the alarm value, then a 0 is sent to Task 4 to stop the buzzer. The measured and the setpoint temperature values are sent to the LCD via the xLCDQueue so that they can be displayed on the LCD. A structure is created to store the measured and the setpoint temperature values in character arrays Txt1 an Txt2 respectively. Both arrays have 4 cells since the built-in function ByteToStr() converts a byte into a string with 4 characters, including leading spaces.

```
Enter Temperature Setpoint (Degrees): 45
Temperature setpoint changed...
```

FIGURE 10.9   Message displayed by Task 2.

FIGURE 10.10   The LCD display.

Task 2

This is the UART Controller task. At the beginning of this task, UART is initialized to operate at 9600 baud. The message **Enter Temperature Setpoint (Degrees):** is displayed on the PC screen using the Putty terminal emulation software. The required setpoint value (in integer) is read from the keyboard and is sent to Task 1 through xUARTQueue. Then the message **Temperature setpoint changed…** is displayed on the PC screen. Fig. 10.9 shows the message displayed by this task where the setpoint temperature was set to 45°C.

Task 3

This is the LCD Controller task. At the beginning of this task the LCD is initialized, display is cleared, and the cursor is set to be OFF so that it is not visible. The task receives the measured and the setpoint temperature values through queue xLCDQueue in the form of a structure. Character arrays Txt1 and Txt2 store the measured and the setpoint temperature values respectively. The LCD display is refreshed every second. Fig. 10.10 shows the LCD display.

Task 4

This is the Buzzer Controller task. At the beginning of this task, port pin PA8 is configured as output. The task receives the buzzer state through the queue xBuzzerQueue. If 1 is received, then an alarm condition is assumed and the buzzer is activated. If on the other hand 0 is received, then the buzzer is de-activated.

Fig. 10.11 shows the program listing (program: **Temperature.c**).

The operation of the program is summarized in the Program Description Language (PDL) shown in Fig. 10.12.

Notice that the following items must be enabled in the Library Manager of mikroC Pro for ARM compiler before the program is compiled:

- ADC
- Conversions
- C_String
- C_Stdlib
- Lcd
- Lcd_Constants
- UART

```
/*==================================================================================
                    ON-OFF TEMPERATURE CONTROLLER
                    ==============================

This is a multitasking ON-OFF temperature controller program. The program
measures the temperature of an oven and uses ON-OFF algorithm to control the
temperature so that it is within the setpoint. The setpoint value is set using
a keyboard. An LCD displays both the setpoint value and the measured temperature.
A relay is used to turn a heater ON and OFF.  buzzer sounds if the temperature
is above a preset value. An LED indicates when the hester is ON. The temperature
of the oven si measured using an analog temperature sensor chip. Communication
with the PC is using a USB UART Click board, plugged to mikroBUS socket 2 of
the Clicker 2 for STM32 development board.

Author: Dogan Ibrahim
Date   : September, 2019
File   : Temperature.c
==================================================================================*/
#include "main.h"
// LCD module connections
sbit LCD_RS at GPIOC_ODR.B12;
sbit LCD_EN at GPIOC_ODR.B11;
sbit LCD_D4 at GPIOE_ODR.B9;
sbit LCD_D5 at GPIOE_ODR.B7;
sbit LCD_D6 at GPIOE_ODR.B8;
sbit LCD_D7 at GPIOC_ODR.B10;
// End LCD module connections

QueueHandle_t xUARTQueue;                              // UART Queue handle
QueueHandle_t xLCDQueue;                               // LCD Queue handle
QueueHandle_t xBuzzerQueue;                            // Buzzer Queue handle

//
// Define all your Task functions here
// ====================================
//

// Task 1 - MAIN Controller
void Task1(void *pvParameters)
{
    typedef struct Message
    {
       char Txt1[4];
       char Txt2[4];
    } AMessage;

    AMessage msg;

    #define HEATER GPIOC_ODR.B9
    #define LED GPIOE_ODR.B12
    #define ON 1
    #define OFF 0

    char *cpy;
    char *on;
    char off=0;
    unsigned char setpoint = 30;
    unsigned AdcValue;
    unsigned char Temperature;
    float mV;
```

FIGURE 10.11 Temperature.c program listing.

```
unsigned const char AlarmValue = 50;

GPIO_Config(&GPIOC_BASE, _GPIO_PINMASK_9, _GPIO_CFG_MODE_OUTPUT);
GPIO_Config(&GPIOE_BASE, _GPIO_PINMASK_12, _GPIO_CFG_MODE_OUTPUT);
ADC1_Init();
on = 1;
off = 0;

while (1)
{
    xQueueReceive(xUARTQueue, &setpoint, 0 );          // Receive data
    AdcValue = ADC1_Read(2);                           // Read ADC Channel 2
    mV = AdcValue*3300.0 / 4096.0;                     // in mV
    mV = (mV - 500.0)/ 10.0;                           // Temp in C
    Temperature = (int)mV;                             // Temp as integer
    if(Temperature < setpoint)                         // If cold
    {
        HEATER = ON;                                   // Heater ON
        LED = ON;                                      // LED ON
    }
    else                                               // If hot
    {
        HEATER = OFF;                                  // Heater OFF
        LED = OFF;                                      // LED OFF
    }

    ByteToStr(Temperature, msg.Txt1);                  // Measured value
    ByteToStr(setpoint, msg.Txt2);                     // setpoint
    xQueueSend(xLCDQueue, &msg, 0);                    // Send via Queue

    if(Temperature > AlarmValue)                       // Alarm?
        xQueueSend(xBuzzerQueue, &on, 0);             // Buzzer ON
    else
        xQueueSend(xBuzzerQueue, &off, 0);            // Buzzer OFF
}
}


// Task 2 - UART Controller
void Task2(void *pvParameters)
{
    unsigned N;
    unsigned AdcValue;
    unsigned char Total;

    UART3_Init_Advanced(9600,_UART_8_BIT_DATA,_UART_NOPARITY,_UART_ONE_STOPBIT,
                    &_GPIO_MODULE_USART3_PD89);

    while (1)
    {
        UART3_Write_Text("\n\r\n\rEnter Temperature Setpoint (Degrees): ");
        N = 0;
        Total = 0;

        while(1)
        {
            N = UART3_Read();                          // Read a number
            UART3_Write(N);                            // Echo the number
            if(N == '\r') break;                       // If Enter
            N = N - '0';                               // Pure number
```

FIGURE 10.11   (*Continued*)

```
                Total = 10*Total + N;                              // Total number
            }

        xQueueSend(xUARTQueue, &Total, pdMS_TO_TICKS(10));    // Send via Queue
        UART3_Write_Text("\n\rTemperature setpoint changed...");
    }
}

// Task 3 - LCD Controller
void Task3(void *pvParameters)
{
    typedef struct Message
    {
        char Txt1[4];
        char Txt2[4];
    } AMessage;

    AMessage msg;

    Lcd_Init();                                               // Initialize LCD
    Lcd_Cmd(_LCD_CLEAR);                                      // Clear LCD
    Lcd_Cmd(_LCD_CURSOR_OFF);                                 // Cursor OFF

    while (1)
    {
        xQueueReceive(xLCDQueue, &msg, 0 );                   // Receive data
        Lcd_Out(1, 1, "Measured:");                           // Heading
        Ltrim(msg.Txt1);                                      // Remove spaces
        Lcd_Out_CP(msg.Txt1);                                 // Display temp
        Lcd_Out(2, 1, "Setpoint:");                           // Heading
        Ltrim(msg.Txt2);                                      // Remove spaces
        Lcd_Out_CP(msg.Txt2);                                 // Display setpoint
        vTaskDelay(pdMS_TO_TICKS(1000));                      // Wait 1 second
        Lcd_Out(1, 10, "   ");                                // Clear numbers
        Lcd_Out(2, 10, "   ");                                // Clear numbers
    }
}


// Task 4 - Buzzer Controller
void Task4(void *pvParameters)
{
    #define BUZZER GPIOA_ODR.B8
    unsigned char BuzzerState;

    GPIO_Config(&GPIOA_BASE, _GPIO_PINMASK_8, _GPIO_CFG_MODE_OUTPUT);
    BuzzerState = 0;                                          // Default state

    while (1)
    {
        xQueueReceive(xBuzzerQueue, &BuzzerState, 0);         // Get data
        if(BuzzerState == 1)                                  // Alarm?
            BUZZER = 1;                                        // Buzzer ON
        else
            BUZZER = 0;                                        // Buzzer OFF
    }
}


//
```

FIGURE 10.11   (*Continued*)

```
// Start of MAIN program
// ====================
//
void main()
{
    xUARTQueue = xQueueCreate(1, 1);              // Create UART queue
    xLCDQueue = xQueueCreate(1,8);                // Create LCD queue
    xBuzzerQueue = xQueueCreate(1, 1);            // Create Buzzer queue


//
// Create all the TASKS here
// =========================
//
    // Create Task 1
    xTaskCreate(
        (TaskFunction_t)Task1,
        "MAIN Controller",
        configMINIMAL_STACK_SIZE,
        NULL,
        10,
        NULL
    );


    // Create Task 2
    xTaskCreate(
        (TaskFunction_t)Task2,
        "UART Controller",
        configMINIMAL_STACK_SIZE,
        NULL,
        10,
        NULL
    );


    // Create Task 3
    xTaskCreate(
        (TaskFunction_t)Task3,
        "LCD Controller",
        configMINIMAL_STACK_SIZE,
        NULL,
        10,
        NULL
    );


    // Create Task 4
    xTaskCreate(
        (TaskFunction_t)Task4,
        "BUZZER Controller",
        configMINIMAL_STACK_SIZE,
        NULL,
        10,
        NULL
    );
//
// Start the RTOS scheduler
//
    vTaskStartScheduler();
//
// Will never reach here
}
```

FIGURE 10.11   (*Continued*)

TASK 1 (Main Controller)

BEGIN
Configure buzzer as output
Configure LED as output
Initialize variables
Set the setpoint to 30
Set the AlarmValue to 50
DO FOREVER
Receive setpoint from UART Controller
Read Temperature from ADC Channel 2
Convert reading into millivolts
Convert reading into degrees centigrade
IF measured temperature < setpoint **THEN**
Turn ON heater
Turn ON LED
ELSE
Turn OFF heater
Turn OFF LED
ENDIF
Send the measured and setpoint temperatures to LCD Controller
IF measured temperature > AlarmValue **THEN**
Send 1 to Buzzer Controller
ELSE
Send 0 to Buzzer Controller
ENDIF
ENDDO
END

TASK 2 (UART Controller)

BEGIN
Initialize UART
DO FOREVER
Write heading on screen (Enter temperature setpoint)
Read a number (setpoint) from the keyboard
Send setpoint to Main Controller
Write heading on screen (Temperature setpoint changed)
ENDDO
END

TASK 3 (LCD Controller)

BEGIN
Initialize LCD
Clear LCD and turn OFF cursor
DO FOREVER
Receive measured and setpoint temperatures from Main Controller
Display measured and setpoint temperatures on LCD
Wait 1 second
ENDDO
END

FIGURE 10.12 Operation of the program.

TASK 4 (Buzzer Controller)

BEGIN
    Configure buzzer as output
    DO FOREVER
        Receive buzzer state from Main Controller
        IF buzzer state = 1 **THEN**
            Turn ON buzzer
        ELSE
            Turn OFF buzzer
        ENDIF
    ENDDO
END

FIGURE 10.12 *(Continued)*

10.9 Summary

Queues are used for inter-communication between tasks in a multitasking program. In this chapter, we have learned how to use the various FreeRTOS queue functions in application programs developed as multitasking projects.

In the next chapter, we shall be looking at the Semaphores and Mutexes and see how they can be used for synchronization purposes in application programs in multitasking projects.

Further readings

[1] R. Barry. Mastering the FreeRTOS Real Time Kernel: A Hands-On Tutorial Guide. Available from: https://www.freertos.org/wp-content/uploads/2018/07/161204_Mastering_the_FreeRTOS_Real_Time_Kernel-A_Hands-On_Tutorial_Guide.pdf.
[2] The FreeRTOS Reference Manual. Available from: https://www.freertos.org/wp-content/uploads/2018/07/FreeRTOS_Reference_Manual_V10.0.0.pdf.
[3] https://www.freertos.org/documentation.

Semapores and mutexes

11.1 Overview

In multitasking systems, it is very common for the tasks to cooperate and share the available resources. For example, various tasks may want to share the communications interfaces that can only be used by one task at a time. The readers may think that the resources can be shared using simple techniques (e.g., flags) as shown in the following example:

```
while (serial port is busy);       // Wait until serial port is free
Serial port busy flag = 1;         // Set busy flag
Send data to serial port;          // Send data
Serial port busy flag = 0;         // Clear busy flag
```

At first glance, it may look like that exclusive access is given to the serial port and that there are no problems. However, in a multitasking system, it is highly possible that another task jumps at the point between the first and the second lines and grabs the serial port before the first task is finished. The serial port can be thought of being in a critical section that needs to be protected so that only one task has access to it at any time.

Resource sharing such as above is handled in FreeRTOS using mutexes and semaphores.

Mutex: A mutex is also called a binary semaphore. Mutexes are used to protect critical sections of a code so that only one task has access to it at any time. The operation of a mutex is such that a mutex must be created before it can be used. A task then **takes** a mutex before entering a critical section. During this time, no other tasks can have access to the shared resource since the mutex controlling the critical section is not available. When the task finishes its processing within the critical section, it **gives** the mutex. At this point, the mutex is available for any other tasks who may want to use the critical section. A task that takes a mutex must always give it back; otherwise, no other task can access the critical region.

Semaphore: Semaphores can be binary or counting. A binary semaphore is similar to a mutex as it has two states. A counting semaphore contains a counter with an upper bound which is defined at the time the semaphore is created. The counter keeps track of limited access to the shared resource (i.e., critical section). When a task wants to use the critical section, it takes the semaphore and, as a result, the counter is decremented if it is not zero. Another task can also take the semaphore where the counter is decremented again. When the count value reaches zero, the resource is not available and furtherer attempts to take

ARM-Based Microcontroller Multitasking Projects. http://dx.doi.org/10.1016/B978-0-12-821227-1.00011-6

the semaphore will fail. When a task releases the semaphore (i.e., gives the semaphore), then the counter value is incremented. Semaphores that are created to manage resources should be created with an initial count value equal to the number of resource that are available.

Notice that although the mutexes and binary semaphores are very similar, there are some important differences between them. Mutexes include priority inheritance, binary semaphores do not. The priority of a task that holds a mutex is raised if another task of higher priority attempts to obtain the same mutex. The task that already holds the mutex is said to inherit the priority of the task attempting to take the same mutex. The inherited priority will be disinherited when the mutex is returned. A binary semaphore does not need to give back the semaphore after it has been taken. Creating a mutex or a semaphore returns a handle to the creator. This handle identifies the created mutex or the semaphore.

In this chapter, we are looking at the various FreeRTOS semaphore and mutex functions. An example project is given to show how a mutex can be used in a real-time multitasking project.

Further information on semaphores and mutexes can be obtained from the document at the following website:

https://www.freertos.org/wp-content/uploads/2018/07/FreeRTOS_Reference_Manual_V10.0.0.pdf

11.2 Creating binary semaphore and mutex

The application program interface (API) function xSemaphoreCreateBinary() creates a binary semaphore and returns its handle. The format of this function call is:

xSemaphoreCreateBinary(void);

The function has no parameters, but it returns the following values:
Return values
NULL: The semaphore could not be created because there is insufficient heap memory available for FreeRTOS to allocate the semaphore data structures.

Any other value: The semaphore was created successfully. The returned value is a handle by which the created semaphore can be referenced.

Binary semaphores are recommended for implementing synchronization between tasks or between an interrupt and a task. Mutexes ate recommended for implementing simple mutual exclusion.

The API function xSemaphoreCreateMutex() creates a mutex and returns its handle. The format of this function is:

xSemaphoreCreateMutex(void);

This function has no parameters and returns the handle as in creating a binary semaphore.

Parameter configSUPPORT_DYNAMIC_ALLOCATION must be set to 1 in file FreeRTOS Config.h, or simply left undefined, for this function to be available.

11.3 Creating a counting semaphore

The API function xSemaphoreCreateCounting() creates a counting semaphore and returns its handle. The format of the function is:

xSemaphoreCreateCounting(UBaseType_t uxMaxCount, UBaseType_t uxInitialCount);

Parameters
uxMaxCount: This is the maximum count value that can be reached. When the semaphore reaches this value, it can no longer be taken by a task.
uxInitialCount: The count value is assigned to the semaphore when it is created.
Return values
NULL: The semaphore cannot be created because there is insufficient heap memory available for FreeRTOS to allocate the semaphore data structures.
Any other value: The semaphore was created successfully. The returned value is a handle by which the created semaphore can be referenced.
Parameter configSUPPORT_DYNAMIC_ALLOCATION must be set to 1 in file FreeRTOS Config.h, or simply left undefined, for this function to be available.

11.4 Deleting a semaphore, getting the semaphore count

The API function call vSemaphoreDelete() deletes an existing semaphore. The format of the function is:

vSemaphoreDelete(SemaphoreHandle_t xSemaphore);

Parameter
xSemaphore: This is the handle of the semaphore being deleted.
Return value
The function has no return values.
Notice that a semaphore must not be deleted if there are any tasks currently blocked on it.
The API function uxSemaphoreGetCount() returns the semaphore count. The format of the function is:

uxSemaphoreGetCount(SemaphoreHandle_t xSemaphore);

Parameter
xSemaphore: This is the handle of the semaphore being queried.
Return value
The count of the semaphore referenced by the handle passed in the xSemaphore parameter.

11.5 Giving and taking the semaphores

The API function call xSemaphireGive() gives (or releases) a semaphore that has been created using a call to vSemaphoreCreateBinary(), xSemaphoreCreateCounting(), or xSemaphoreCreateMutex() and has also been successfully "taken." The format of the function is:

xSemaphoreGive(SemaphoreHandle_t xSemaphore);

Parameter

xSemaphore: The semaphore being "given." A semaphore is referenced by a variable of type SemaphoreHandle_t and must be explicitly created before being used.

Return values

pdPASS: The semaphore "give" operation was successful.

pdFAIL: The semaphore "give" operation was not successful because the task calling xSemaphoreGive() is not the semaphore holder. A task must successfully "take" a semaphore before it can successfully "give" it back.

The API function call xSemaphoreTake() takes (or obtains) a semaphore that has previously been created using a call to vSemaphoreCreateBinary(), xSemaphoreCreateCounting(), or xSemaphoreCreateMutex(). The format of the function is:

xSemaphoreTake(SemaphoreHandle_t xSemaphore, TickType_t xTicksToWait);

Parameters

xSemaphore: The semaphore being "taken." A semaphore is referenced by a variable of type SemaphoreHandle_t and must be explicitly created before being used.

xTicksToWait: The maximum amount of time the task should remain in the Blocked state to wait for the semaphore to become available, if the semaphore is not available immediately. If xTicksToWait is zero, then xSemaphoreTake() will return immediately if the semaphore is not available. The block time is specified in tick periods, so the absolute time it represents is dependent on the tick frequency. The pdMS_TO_TICKS() macro can be used to convert a time specified in milliseconds to a time specified in ticks. Setting xTicksToWait to portMAX_DELAY will cause the task to wait indefinitely (without timing out), provided the parameter INCLUDE_vTaskSuspend is set to 1 in file FreeRTOSConfig.h.

Return values

pdPASS: Returned only if the call to xSemaphoreTake() was successful in obtaining the semaphore. If a block time was specified (xTicksToWait was not zero), then it is possible that the calling task was placed into the Blocked state to wait for the semaphore if it was not immediately available, but the semaphore became available before the block time expired.

pdFAIL: Returned if the call to xSemaphoreTake() did not successfully obtain the semaphore. If a block time was specified (xTicksToWait was not zero), then the calling task will have been placed into the Blocked state to wait for the semaphore to become available, but the block time expired before this happened.

11.6 Project 24: sending internal and external temperature data to a PC

Description: In this project, two analog temperature sensor chips are used: a temperature sensor to measure the temperature inside an oven and another temperature sensor to measure the ambient temperature outside the oven. There are three tasks in the project in addition to the Idle task. The external and internal temperatures are read by the two tasks, and these data are sent to another task that displays the data on the PC screen. External temperature is displayed every 5 seconds and the internal one every 2 seconds. The display task is assumed to be in a critical section where the sending tasks must take/give a mutex in order to share the UART and send data to the PC.

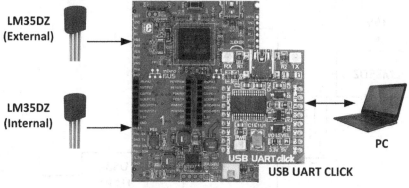

Clicker 2 for STM32

FIGURE 11.1 **Block diagram of the project.**

Aim: The aim of this project is to show how a mutex can be created and taken and given by tasks in a multitasking environment in order to access a shared critical region.

Block diagram: The block diagram of this project is shown in Fig. 11.1. The following components are used in this project in addition to the Clicker 2 for STM32 development board:

- USB UART Click board
- 2 × analog temperature sensor chips

Circuit diagram: Fig. 11.2 shows the circuit diagram of the project. In this project, two LM35DZ analog temperature sensor chips are used. The sensor called **External** is connected to analog input PA2 of the Clicker 2 for STM32 development board. Another LM35DZ, called **Internal,** is connected to analog input PA4. Both sensors are powered from +5 V supply derived from the development board. The USB UART Click board is connected to mikroBUS Socket 2 of the development board. Connection to the PC is through a mini USB cable connected between the USB UART Click board and any USB port of a PC.

Program listing: LM35DZ is a three-pin analog temperature sensor chip having the following specifications:

- 0°C to 100°C measurement range
- Operates from 4 to 20 V
- Less than 60 μA current
- ±4°C linearity

The output of the chip is an analog voltage directly proportional to the measured temperature. The relationship between the measured temperature and the output voltage is given by:

$T = 10 \, \text{mV}/°C$

For example, if the output voltage is 200 mV, then the measured temperature is 20°C; if the output voltage is 350 mV, the measured temperature is 35°C, and so on.

The program listing is shown in Fig. 11.3 (program: **mutex.c**). There are three tasks in the system, in addition to the Idle task. Inside the main program, a queue is created with

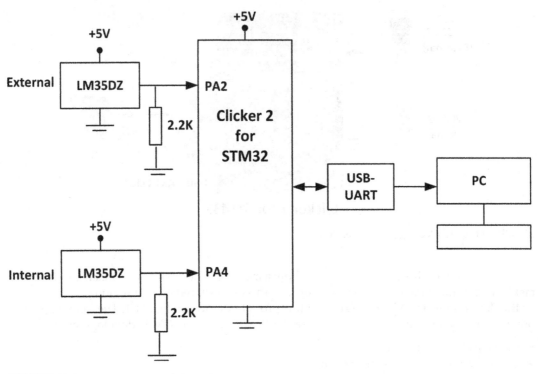

FIGURE 11.2   Circuit diagram of the project.

the handle xUARTQueue, having a size of 1 with 28 bytes. Also, a mutex is created with the handle xSemaphore. Each task performs the following:

Task 1

This is the External temperature task. The task reads the ambient analog temperature from LM35DZ, converts the reading into millivolts, and then converts it to °C by dividing with 10. In this task, analog input port PA2 of the Clicker 2 for STM32 development board is used. The reading is then converted into a string using the built-in function IntToStr(). The task then attempts to take the mutex. If the mutex is taken successfully (i.e., pdPASS is returned), then the temperature together with a heading is sent to the UART, as shown in the following code:

```
if(xSemaphoreTake(xSemaphore, pdMS_TO_TICKS(1000)) == pdTRUE)
    {
    xQueueSend(xUARTQueue, &msg, 0);
    xSemaphoreGive(xSemaphore);
    }
```

The task then gives the mutex and waits for 5 seconds.

Task 3

This task is similar to Task 1, but here the internal oven temperature is read and sent to UART. Analog port PA4 of the Clicker 2 for STM32 development board is used.

Task 2

This is the UART controller task. At the beginning of the task, the UART is initialized to operate at 9600 baud. The task then checks the queue and reads the message if there is 1.

```
/*==============================================================================
                              MUTEX EXAMPLE
                              =============

In this project two analog temperature sensors are used by two different tasks.
The tasks send the temperature to another task which displays the temperature via
the UART. Mutex is used to synchronize the access to the task handling the UART.

Author: Dogan Ibrahim
Date  : September, 2019
File  : mutex.c
==============================================================================*/
#include "main.h"
QueueHandle_t xUARTQueue;                              // UART Queue handle
SemaphoreHandle_t xSemaphore;                          // Semaphore handle

//
// Define all your Task functions here
// ====================================
//

// Task 1 - External sensor Controller
void Task1(void *pvParameters)
{
    typedef struct Message
    {
        char Head[21];
        char Temp[7];
    } AMessage;

    AMessage msg;

    unsigned AdcValue;
    unsigned int XTemperature;
    float mV;
    char Txt[14];

    ADC1_Init();
    strcpy(msg.Head, "External Temperature ");
    msg.Head[20]='\0';

    while (1)
    {
        AdcValue = ADC1_Read(2);                        // Read ADC Channel 2
        mV = AdcValue*3300.0 / 4096.0;                  // in mV
        mV = mV / 10.0;                                 // Temp in C
        XTemperature = (int)mV;                         // Temp as integer
        IntToStr(XTemperature, msg.Temp);               // Measured value

        if(xSemaphoreTake(xSemaphore, pdMS_TO_TICKS(1000)) == pdTRUE)
        {
            xQueueSend(xUARTQueue, &msg, 0);            // Send via Queue
            xSemaphoreGive(xSemaphore);                // Give mutex
        }
        vTaskDelay(pdMS_TO_TICKS(5000));               // Delay 5 secs
    }
}


// Task 2 - UART Controller
```

FIGURE 11.3 mutex.c program listing.

```
void Task2(void *pvParameters)
{
    typedef struct Message
    {
        char Head[21];
        char Temp[7];
    } AMessage;

    AMessage msg;

    UART3_Init_Advanced(9600,_UART_8_BIT_DATA,_UART_NOPARITY,_UART_ONE_STOPBIT,
                        &_GPIO_MODULE_USART3_PD89);
    UART3_Write_Text("\n\rExternal and Internal Temperature\n\r");

    while (1)
    {
        if(xQueueReceive(xUARTQueue, &msg, 0) == pdPASS)          // Receive queue
        {
            UART3_Write_Text(msg.Head);                          // Write heading
            UART_Write_Text(msg.Temp);                           // Write temp
            UART3_Write_Text("\n\r");                            // CR & LF
        }
    }
}

// Task 3 - Internal sensor Controller
void Task3(void *pvParameters)
{
    typedef struct Message
    {
        char Head[21];
        char Temp[7];
    } AMessage;

    AMessage msg;

    unsigned AdcValue;
    unsigned int ITemperature;
    float mV;

    ADC1_Init();
    strcpy(msg.Head, "Internal Temperature ");
    msg.Head[20]='\0';

    while (1)
    {
        AdcValue = ADC1_Read(4);                                 // Read ADC Channel 4
        mV = AdcValue*3300.0 / 4096.0;                           // in mV
        mV = mV / 10.0;                                          // Temp in C
        ITemperature = (int)mV;                                  // Temp as integer
        IntToStr(ITemperature, msg.Temp);                        // Measured value

        if(xSemaphoreTake(xSemaphore, pdMS_TO_TICKS(1000)) == pdTRUE)
        {
            xQueueSend(xUARTQueue, &msg, 0);                     // Send via Queue
            xSemaphoreGive(xSemaphore);                          // Give mutex
        }
        vTaskDelay(pdMS_TO_TICKS(2000));                         // Wait 2 secs
    }
}
```

FIGURE 11.3   (*Continued*)

```
//
// Start of MAIN program
// ======================
//
void main()
{
    xUARTQueue = xQueueCreate(1, 28);                    // Create UART queue
    xSemaphore = xSemaphoreCreateMutex();                // Create Mutex
//
// Create all the TASKS here
// =========================
//
    // Create Task 1
    xTaskCreate(
        (TaskFunction_t)Task1,
        "External sensor Controller",
        configMINIMAL_STACK_SIZE,
        NULL,
        10,
        NULL
    );


    // Create Task 2
    xTaskCreate(
        (TaskFunction_t)Task2,
        "UART Controller",
        configMINIMAL_STACK_SIZE,
        NULL,
        10,
        NULL
    );


    // Create Task 3
    xTaskCreate(
        (TaskFunction_t)Task3,
        "Internal sensor Controller",
        configMINIMAL_STACK_SIZE,
        NULL,
        10,
        NULL
    );
//
// Start the RTOS scheduler
//
    vTaskStartScheduler();

//
// Will never reach here
}
```

FIGURE 11.3   (*Continued*)

```
External and Internal Temperature
Internal Temperature      24
Internal Temperature      24
Internal Temperature      23
External Temperature      23
Internal Temperature      24
Internal Temperature      23
External Temperature      23
Internal Temperature      23
Internal Temperature      23
```

FIGURE 11.4 Output on the screen.

The message consists of two parts: a heading and the measured temperature. The message is sent to UART, which is displayed on the PC screen via a terminal emulation software.

Fig. 11.4 shows an output on the PC screen when the program is run.

11.7 Summary

In this chapter, we have learned the concepts of semaphores and mutexes. A project is given using the FreeRTOS to show how a mutex can be created and a critical region can be shared by two tasks by taking and giving the mutex.

In the next chapter, we shall be looking at the concept of Event Groups in multitasking systems and give examples of using them in multitasking projects.

Further reading

[1] R. Barry, Mastering the FreeRTOS real time kernel: a hands-on tutorial guide. https://www.freertos.org/wp-content/uploads/2018/07/161204_Mastering_the_FreeRTOS_Real_Time_Kernel-A_Hands-On_Tutorial_Guide.pdf.
[2] The FreeRTOS reference manual. https://www.freertos.org/wp-content/uploads/2018/07/FreeRTOS_Reference_Manual_V10.0.0.pdf https://www.freertos.org/documentation.

Event groups

12.1 Overview

Event groups allow events to be communicated to tasks and they allow a task to wait in the blocked state for a combination of one or more events to occur. Event groups unblock the tasks that is waiting for the same event, or combination of events, when the event occurs. Event groups therefore can be used to synchronize tasks, allowing a task to wait in blocked state for any one of a set of events to occur.

Event groups can be used in many applications to replace semaphores with a single event group, thus reducing the RAM usage. Notice that event groups are an optional part of FreeRTOS and source file FreeRTOS/source/event_groups.c must be compiled as part of your program. Also the header file event_groups.h must be included at the beginning of your program.

12.2 Event flags and event groups

An event flag, also called an event bit, is a one bit value (0 or 1) used to indicate if an event has occurred or not. Sets of event flags make an event group. An event group holds the state of all the event flags belonging to that group. The state of an event flag is represented by a variable of type EventBits_t. When an event bit is set, it is said that the event represented by that bit has occurred.

Event groups are stored in variables of type EventGroupHandle_t. Event groups can be accessed by any task in the system, and any number of tasks can set or read the bits in an event group. The number of bits (or flags) within an event group is 8 if parameter configUSE_16_BIT_TICKS is set to 1, or 24 if parameter configUSE_16_BIT_TICKS is set to 0 (the default setting) in the configuration file. An event flag inside an event group is identified by its bit position. For example, bit 0 is event flag 0, bit 20 is event flag 20, and so on. If for example an event group holds the hexadecimal value 0x92, then event flags 1, 4, and 7 are set (0x92 = "1001 0010" in binary). The programmer gives meanings to the event flags. For example, bit 0 may represent that the task is waiting for a message, bit 3 may mean that the LED has been turned ON and so on.

ARM-Based Microcontroller Multitasking Projects. http://dx.doi.org/10.1016/B978-0-12-821227-1.00012-8

In the remainder parts of this chapter, we shall be looking at some of the commonly used event group API functions of FreeRTOS, and also give a practical project to show how event groups can be used in a multitasking project.

Interested readers can find further information on event groups at the following web sites:

https://www.freertos.org/wp-content/uploads/2018/07/FreeRTOS_Reference_Manual_V10.0.0.pdf

and

https://www.freertos.org/wp-content/uploads/2018/07/161204_Mastering_the_FreeRTOS_Real_Time_Kernel-A_Hands-On_Tutorial_Guide.pdf

12.3 Creating and deleting an event group

The API function xEventGroupCreate() is used to create an event group. The handle of the created event group is returned to the calling program. The format of the function is:

xEventGroupCreate(void);

The function has no parameters.
Return values
Null: The event group could not be created because there was insufficient FreeRTOS heap available.

Any other value: The event group was created and the value returned is the handle of the created event group.

The API function vEventGroupDelete() is used to delete a previously created event group. Tasks that are blocked on the event group being deleted will be unblocked. The format of the function is:

vEventGroupDelete(EventGroupHandle_t xEventGroup);

Parameter
xEventGroupHandle_t: The handle of the event group to be deleted.
The function has no return value.

12.4 Setting, clearing, waiting For event group bits, and getting event group bits

The API function xEventGroupSetBits() is used to set the event flags within an event group. Setting an event flag will unblock a task that is waiting for that flag to be set. The format of the function is:

xEventGroupSetBits(EventGroupHandle_t xEventGroup, const EventBits_t uxBitsToSet);

Parameters
xEventGroup: The handle of the event group in which the bits are to be set. The event group must have previously been created.

uxBitsToSet: A bitwise value that indicates the bit or bits to set in the event group.
Return values
Any value: The value of the bits in the event group at the time the call to xEventGroupSet-
Bits() returned. There are two reasons why the returned value might have the bits specified
by the uxBitsToSet parameter cleared:

1. If setting a bit results in a task that was waiting for the bit leaving the blocked state,
   then it is possible the bit will have been cleared automatically (see the xClearBitsOnExit
   parameter of xEventGroupWaitBits()).
2. Any task that leaves the blocked state as a result of the bits being set (or otherwise any Ready
   state task) that has a priority above that of the task that called xEventGroupSetBits() will execute and may change the event group value before the call to xEventGroupSetBits() return

The API function xEventGroupClearBits() is used to clear event flags within an event
group. The format of the function is:

**xEventGroupClearBits(EventGroupHandle_t xEventGroup, const EventBits_t
uxBitsToClear);**

Parameters
xEventGroup: The event group in which the bits are to be cleared. The event group must
have previously been created using a call to xEventGroupCreate().
uxBitsToClear: A bitwise value that indicates the bit or bits to clear in the event group.
Return values
All values: The value of the bits in the event group before any bits were cleared
The API call xEventGroupWaitBits() is used to enter a blocked state (with a timeout) if the
specified event flag or flags are not set. The format of the function is:

**xEventGroupWaitBits(const EventGroupHandle_t xEventGroup, const EventBits_t
uxBitsToWaitFor, const BaseType_t xClearOnExit, const BaseType_t xWaitForAllBits,
TickType_t xTicksToWait);**

Parameters
xEventGroup: The event group in which the bits are being tested.
uxBitsToWaitFor: A bitwise value that indicates the bit or bits to test inside the event
group. For example, to wait for bit 0 and/or bit 2 set uxBitsToWaitFor to 0x05.
xClearOnExit: If xClearOnExit is set to pdTRUE then any bits set in the value passed as the
uxBitsToWaitFor parameter will be cleared in the event group before xEventGroupWaitBits()
returns if xEventGroupWaitBits() returns for any reason other than a timeout. The timeout
value is set by the xTicksToWait parameter. If xClearOnExit is set to pdFALSE then the bits set
in the event group are not altered when the call to xEventGroupWaitBits() returns.
xWaitAllBits: xWaitForAllBits is used to create either a logical AND test (where all bits
must be set) or a logical OR test (where one or more bits must be set) as follows:If xWait-
ForAllBits is set to pdTRUE then xEventGroupWaitBits() will return when either all the bits
set in the value passed as the uxBitsToWaitFor parameter are set in the event group or the
specified block time expires. If xWaitForAllBits is set to pdFALSE then xEventGroupWait-
Bits() will return when any of the bits set in the value passed as the uxBitsToWaitFor parameter are set in the event group or the specified block time expires.

xTicksToWait: The maximum amount of time to wait (in ticks) for one/all (depending on the xWaitForAllBits value) of the bits specified by uxBitsToWaitFor to become set.

Return values

Any value: The value of the event group at the time either the event bits being waited for became set, or the block time expired. The current value of the event bits in an event group will be different to the returned value if a higher priority task or interrupt changed the value of an event bit between the calling task leaving the blocked state and exiting the xEvent-GroupWaitBits() function. Test the return value to know which bits were set. If xEventGroup-WaitBits() returned because its timeout expired then not all the bits being waited for will be set. If xEventGroupWaitBits() returned because the bits it was waiting for were set then the returned value is the event group value before any bits were automatically cleared in the case that xClearOnExit parameter was set to pdTRUE.

The API function xEventGroupGetBits() is used to return the current values of the event flag bits in an event group. The format of the function is:

xEventGroupGetBits(EventGroupHandle_t xEventGroup);

Parameters

xEventGroup: The event group being queried. The event group must have previously been created using a call to xEventGroupCreate().Return ValuesAll values. The value of the event bits in the event group at the time xEventGroupGetBits() was called.

12.5 Project 25—sending internal and external temperature data to a PC

Description: This project is similar to Project 24 given in the previous chapter. In this project, two analog temperature sensor chips are used: a temperature sensor to measure the temperature inside an oven, and another temperature sensor to measure the ambient temperature outside the oven. There are three tasks in the project in addition to the Idle task. The external and internal temperatures and are read by the two tasks and this data is sent to another task which displays the data on the PC screen. In this project both the external and the internal temperatures are displayed every 2 seconds. In this program event flags are used instead of a mutex to synchronize the access to the UART. By setting, clearing, and waiting on event flags we make sure that only one task accesses the UART at any time.

Aim: The aim of this project is to show how event flags can be used to synchronize shared access to the UART.

Block diagram: The block diagram of this project is as in Fig. 11.1.

Circuit diagram: The circuit diagram of the project is as in Fig. 11.2, where, two LM35DZ analog temperature sensor chips are used to measure the temperature inside and outside an oven. Connection to the PC is through a mini USB cable connected between the USB UART Click board.

Program listing: The program listing is shown in Fig. 12.1 (program: **flags.c**). There are three tasks in the system, in addition to the Idle task. Inside the main program, an event group is created with the handle xEventGroup. Bits 1 and 2 of this event group are used in the program. The operation of the program is described in the following PDL where Task 1 and Task 3 send their temperature readings to the UART controller in Task 2 through a queue:

Main
Create Queue with handle xUARTQueue
Create event group with handle xEventGroup

```
/*=====================================================================
                         EVENT GROUPS EXAMPLE
                         ====================

In this project two analog temperature sensors are used by two different tasks.
The tasks send the temperature to another task which displays the temperature via
the UART. Two event flags are used (1 and 2) to synchronize the access to the
task handling the UART.

Author: Dogan Ibrahim
Date  : September, 2019
File  : flags.c
=====================================================================*/
#include "main.h"
#include "event_groups.h"

QueueHandle_t xUARTQueue;                                  // UART Queue handle
EventGroupHandle_t xEventGroup;                            // Event group handle

//
// Define all your Task functions here
// ====================================
//

// Task 1 - External sensor Controller
void Task1(void *pvParameters)
{
    #define BIT_2 (1 << 2)
    #define BIT_1 (1 << 1)

    typedef struct Message
    {
        char Head[21];
        char Temp[7];
    } AMessage;

    AMessage msg;

    EventBits_t uxBits;
    unsigned AdcValue;
    unsigned int XTemperature;
    float mV;

    ADC1_Init();
    strcpy(msg.Head, "External Temperature ");
    msg.Head[20]='\0';
    uxBits = xEventGroupSetBits(xEventGroup, BIT_2);         // Set flag 2

    while (1)                                                // DO FOREVER
    {
        uxBits = xEventGroupWaitBits(xEventGroup, BIT_2, pdFALSE, pdFALSE,
                 portMAX_DELAY);
        AdcValue = ADC1_Read(2);                             // Read ADC Channel 2
        mV = AdcValue*3300.0 / 4096.0;                       // in mV
        mV = mV / 10.0;                                      // Temp in C
        XTemperature = (int)mV;                              // Temp as integer
        IntToStr(XTemperature, msg.Temp);                    // Measured value
        xQueueSend(xUARTQueue, &msg, 0);                     // Send via Queue
        uxBits = xEventGroupSetBits(xEventGroup, BIT_1);     // Set flag 1
        uxBits = xEventGroupClearBits(xEventGroup, BIT_2 );  // Clear flag 2
```

FIGURE 12.1 flags.c program listing.

```
            vTaskDelay(pdMS_TO_TICKS(2000));                    // Delay 2 secs
    }
}


// Task 2 - UART Controller
void Task2(void *pvParameters)
{
    typedef struct Message
    {
        char Head[21];
        char Temp[7];
    } AMessage;

    AMessage msg;

    UART3_Init_Advanced(9600,_UART_8_BIT_DATA,_UART_NOPARITY,_UART_ONE_STOPBIT,
                        &_GPIO_MODULE_USART3_PD89);
    UART3_Write_Text("\n\rExternal and Internal Temperature\n\r");

    while (1)
    {
        if(xQueueReceive(xUARTQueue, &msg, 0) == pdPASS)        // Receive queue
        {
            UART3_Write_Text(msg.Head);                         // Write heading
            UART_Write_Text(msg.Temp);                          // Write temp
            UART3_Write_Text("\n\r");                           // CR & LF
        }
    }
}

// Task 3 - Internal sensor Controller
void Task3(void *pvParameters)
{
    #define BIT_2 (1 << 2)
    #define BIT_1 (1 << 1)

     typedef struct Message
    {
        char Head[21];
        char Temp[7];
    } AMessage;

    AMessage msg;

    EventBits_t uxBits;
    unsigned AdcValue;
    unsigned int ITemperature;
    float mV;

    ADC1_Init();
    strcpy(msg.Head, "Internal Temperature ");
    msg.Head[20]='\0';

    while (1)
    {
        uxBits = xEventGroupWaitBits(xEventGroup, BIT_1, pdFALSE, pdFALSE,
                portMAX_DELAY);
        AdcValue = ADC1_Read(4);                                // Read ADC Channel 4
        mV = AdcValue*3300.0 / 4096.0;                          // in mV
```

FIGURE 12.1   (Continued)

```
        mV = mV / 10.0;                                   // Temp in C
        ITemperature = (int)mV;                           // Temp as integer
        IntToStr(ITemperature, msg.Temp);                 // Measured value
        xQueueSend(xUARTQueue, &msg, 0);                  // Send via Queue
        uxBits = xEventGroupSetBits(xEventGroup, BIT_2);  // Set flag 2
        uxBits = xEventGroupClearBits(xEventGroup, BIT_1);// Clear flag 1
        vTaskDelay(pdMS_TO_TICKS(2000));                  // Wait 2 secs
    }
}

//
// Start of MAIN program
// =====================
//
void main()
{
    xUARTQueue = xQueueCreate(1, 28);                     // Create UART queue
    xEventGroup = xEventGroupCreate();                    // Create event group
//
// Create all the TASKS here
// =========================
//
    // Create Task 1
    xTaskCreate(
        (TaskFunction_t)Task1,
        "External sensor Controller",
        configMINIMAL_STACK_SIZE,
        NULL,
        10,
        NULL
    );


    // Create Task 2
    xTaskCreate(
        (TaskFunction_t)Task2,
        "UART Controller",
        configMINIMAL_STACK_SIZE,
        NULL,
        10,
        NULL
    );


    // Create Task 3
    xTaskCreate(
        (TaskFunction_t)Task3,
        "Internal sensor Controller",
        configMINIMAL_STACK_SIZE,
        NULL,
        10,
        NULL
    );

//
// Start the RTOS scheduler
//
    vTaskStartScheduler();

//
// Will never reach here
}
```

FIGURE 12.1 (*Continued*)

Task 1	Task 3	Task 2
Set event flag 2		
DO FOREVER	**DO FOREVER**	**DO FOREVER**
Wait for event flag 2	Wait for event flag 1	IF data in Queue **THEN**
Send Data via queue	Send data via queue	Send data to UART
Set event flag 1	Set event flag 2	ENDIF
Clear event flag 2	Clear event flag 1	**ENDDO**
ENDDO	**ENDDO**	

The details of each task are described in detail below.

Task 1

This is the External temperature task. The task reads the ambient analog temperature from sensor LM35DZ, converts the reading into millivolts, and then converts it to °C by dividing it with 10. In this task, analog input port PA2 of the Clicker 2 for STM32 development board is used. The reading is then converted into a string using the built-in function IntToStr() and sent to the UART. The task then sets event flag 1 and clears event flag 2 before exiting.

The following statement is used to set event flag 2:

uxBits = xEventGroupSetBits(xEventGroup, BIT_2);

Similarly, the following statement is used to clear event flag 2:

uxBits = xEventGroupClearBits(xEventGroup, BIT_2);

The task is blocked waiting for event flag 2 to be set with the following statement:

uxBits = xEventGroupWaitBits(xEventGroup, BIT_2, pdFALSE, pdFALSE,
        portMAX_DELAY);

Notice here that the task is blocked waiting forever until event flag 2 is set. Also, the xCLEAROnExit parameter is set to pdFALSE so that the flag is not cleared when function xEventGroupWaitBits() exits. We could have set this parameter to pdTRUE so that event flag 2 would be cleared automatically on exit from the function. This way, there would not be need to clear event flag 2 explicitly in Task 1.

Task 3

This task is similar to Task 1, but here the internal oven temperature is read and sent to UART. Analog port PA4 of the Clicker 2 for STM32 development board is used.

Task 2

This is the UART controller task. At the beginning of the task, the UART is initialized to operate at 9600 baud. The task then checks the queue and reads the message if there is one. The message consists of two parts: a heading and the measured temperature. The message is sent to UART which is displayed on the PC screen via a terminal emulation software.

12.6 Project 26—controlling the flashing of an LED

Description: This is a very simple project. In this project the LED on the Clicker 2 for STM32 development board at port PE12 is used. Two tasks are used in the project in addition to the Idle task. The LED is flashed in a task every second after receiving a command from the keyboard in another task. Entering command ON sets an event flag which starts the LED flashing. Similarly, entering OFF clears the event flag and this causes the LED to turn OFF.

A USB UART Click board is connected to mikroBUS 2 socket of the Clicker 2 for STM32 development board as in the previous project and the PC is connected to this board using a mini USB cable. A terminal emulation software is used on the PC to enter commands through the keyboard and to display the messages on the screen.

Aim: The aim of this project is to show how event groups (or event flags) can be used to synchronize shared access to a resource.

Program listing: The program listing is shown in Fig. 12.2 (program: **flashflag.c**). There are 2 tasks in the system, in addition to the Idle task. Inside the main program, an event group is created where event flag 1 is used. Task 2 prompts the user to enter a command from the keyboard. If command ON is entered then event flag 1 is set. If on the other hand command OFF is entered then event flag 1 is cleared. Task 1 flashes the LED every second whenever the event flag 1 is set. Clearing event flag 1 stops the LED flashing. At the beginning of the program the LED is configured to be OFF. The operation of the program is demonstrated by the following PDL:

Main

Create an event group

Clear event flag 1

Task 2	Task 1
DO FOREVER	Turn OFF LED
Read a command from the keyboard	**DO FOREVER**
IF command is ON **THEN**	**IF** event flag 1 is set **THEN**
Set event flag 1	Flash the LED
ELSE IF COMMAND is OFF **THEN**	**ELSE**
Clear event flag 1	Turn OFF the LED
ENDIF	**ENDIF**
ENDDO	**ENDDO**

Commands are received from the keyboard using the UART3_Read() statement as shown below. If UART is ready (i.e., it has received a character) then the character is read into character variable ch. The character read is then echoed on the screen so that the user can see the entered character. If the character is the Enter key then the program exits the loop. Otherwise, the received character is stored in Buffer and the buffer index is incremented:

```
j = 0;
while(1)
{
  if(UART3_Data_Ready)              // UART ready?
  {
    ch = UART3_Read();              // Read a character
    UART3_Write(ch);               // Echo the character
    if(ch == '\r')break;           // If CR, break
    Buffer[j] = ch;                // Save the character
    j + +;                         // Increment pointer
  }
}
```

A run of the program is shown in Fig. 12.3.

```
/*=====================================================================================
                              EVENT GROUPS EXAMPLE
                              ====================

In this project the on-board LEd at port PE12 is controlled from the keyboard.
Entering command ON sets an event flag which starts teh flashing. Entering
command OFF clears the event flag which turns OFF the LED.

Author: Dogan Ibrahim
Date   : September, 2019
File   : flashflag.c
=====================================================================================*/
#include "main.h"
#include "event_groups.h"

EventGroupHandle_t xEventGroup;                              // Event group handle

//
// Define all your Task functions here
// ====================================
//

// Task 1 - LED flashing Controller
void Task1(void *pvParameters)
{
    #define BIT_1 (1 << 1)
    #define LED GPIOE_ODR.B12                                // LED port
    #define ON 1
    #define OFF 0

    EventBits_t uxBits;
    uxBits = xEventGroupClearBits(xEventGroup, BIT_1);       // Set flag 2
    GPIO_Config(&GPIOE_BASE, _GPIO_PINMASK_12, _GPIO_CFG_MODE_OUTPUT);

    while (1)                                                // DO FOREVER
    {
        uxBits = xEventGroupWaitBits(xEventGroup, BIT_1, pdFALSE, pdFALSE,
                    portMAX_DELAY);
        LED = ON;                                            // LED ON
        vTaskDelay(pdMS_TO_TICKS(1000));                     // Wait 1 second
        LED = OFF;                                           // LED OFF
        vTaskDelay(pdMS_TO_TICKS(1000));                     // LED OFF
    }
}


// Task 2 - Keyboard Controller
void Task2(void *pvParameters)
{
    EventBits_t uxBits;
    char Buffer[10];
    char j, ch;

    uxBits = xEventGroupClearBits(xEventGroup, BIT_1);
    UART3_Init_Advanced(9600,_UART_8_BIT_DATA,_UART_NOPARITY,_UART_ONE_STOPBIT,
                    &_GPIO_MODULE_USART3_PD89);

    UART3_Write_Text("\n\rLED FLASHING CONTROLLER\n\r");
    UART3_Write_Text("========================\n\r");
```

FIGURE 12.2   flashflag.c program listing.

```
    while (1)
    {
        UART3_Write_Text("\n\rEnter a command (ON or OFF): ");
        j = 0;

        while(1)                                        // Get a command
        {
          if(UART3_Data_Ready)                          // UART raedy?
          {
            ch = UART3_Read();                          // Read a character
            UART3_Write(ch);                            // Echo the character
            if(ch == '\r')break;                        // If CR, break
            Buffer[j] = ch;                             // Save the character
            j++;                                        // Increment pointer
          }
        }

        if(Buffer[0] == 'O' && Buffer[1] == 'N')            // ON command?
        {
            uxBits = xEventGroupSetBits(xEventGroup, BIT_1);    // Set flag 1
            UART3_Write_Text("\n\rFlashing started...\n\r");
        }
        else
        {
            uxBits = xEventGroupClearBits(xEventGroup, BIT_1);  // Clear flag 1
            UART3_Write_Text("\n\rFlashing stopped...\n\r");
        }
    }
}


//
// Start of MAIN program
// =====================
//
void main()
{
    xEventGroup = xEventGroupCreate();                          // Create event group
//
// Create all the TASKS here
// =========================
//
    // Create Task 1
    xTaskCreate(
        (TaskFunction_t)Task1,
        "LED Controller",
        configMINIMAL_STACK_SIZE,
        NULL,
        10,
        NULL
    );


    // Create Task 2
    xTaskCreate(
        (TaskFunction_t)Task2,
        "Keyboard Controller",
        configMINIMAL_STACK_SIZE,
        NULL,
        10,
```

FIGURE 12.2   (Continued)

```
        NULL
    );

//
// Start the RTOS scheduler
//
    vTaskStartScheduler();

//
// Will never reach here
}
```

FIGURE 12.2   *(Continued)*

```
LED FLASHING CONTROLLER
=======================

Enter a command (ON or OFF): ON
Flashing started...

Enter a command (ON or OFF): OFF
Flashing stopped...

Enter a command (ON or OFF): _
```

FIGURE 12.3   Typical run of the program.

12.7 Project 27—GPS based project

Description: In this project a GPS receiver module is used to get the local latitude and longitude data from the GPS satellites. This data is read by a task every second and is sent to another task which controls a UART. The data is displayed on the PC screen. An LED is used to indicate whether or not the received data is valid (i.e., the GPS has received valid data from the satellites). The LED flashes if the received GPS data is valid, otherwise it is turned OFF.

Aim: The aim of this project is to show how event flags and queues can be used in a project. Also, it is shows how data can be received from a GPS receiver and how it can be decoded to extract the latitude and the longitude.

Block diagram: Fig. 12.4 shows the project block diagram. A GPS Click board (see www.mikroe.com) is connected to mikroBUS 1 socket of the Clicker 2 for STM32 development board. The GPS Click board is based on the u-blox LEA-6S GPS chip. The board is designed to run on a +3.3V power supply and communicates with the target microcontroller through UART or I2C interfaces. In this project, the UART interface is used for simplicity. The baud rate of the board is set to 9600 by default. GPS Click board can simultaneously track up to 16 satellites and has a TTFF (time to first fix) of less than one second. An external antenna is recommended if the GPS is used indoors as it may not be possible to receive signals from the GPS satellites. Additionally, a USB UART Click board is connected to mikroBUS 2 socket as in the previous project. A mini USB cable connects the USB UART Click board to the PC. The on-board LED connected to port pin PE12 is used to indicate the data validity.

When the USB UART Click board is plugged in to mikroBUS 2 socket, it connects to UART3 at port pins PD8 and PD9 of the development board. Similarly, when the GPS click board is

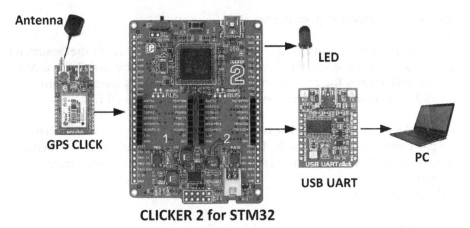

FIGURE 12.4 Block diagram of the project.

plugged in to microBUS 1 socket, it connects to UART2 at port pins PC5 and PC6 of the development board.

Program listing: There are three tasks in the system, in addition to the Idle task. Inside the main program, an event group and also a queue are created. Task 1 flashes the LED at a fast rate of 250 milliseconds if the received GPS data is valid. Task 2 receives the latitude and longitude from Task 3 and displays on the PC screen whenever valid data is received. The operation of the program is summarized with the following PDL statements:

Task 1
DO FOREVER
    Wait for event flag 1 to be set
    Flash the LED at a rate of 250ms
ENDDO
Task 2
DO FOREVER
    Wait for event flag 2 to be set
    Receive data from the queue
    Display Latitude/Longitude
ENDDO
Task 3
DO FOREVER
    Extract Latitude/Longitude from the GPS
    IF data is valid **THEN**
        Set event flags 1 and 2
        Send Latitude/Longitude to the queue
    ELSE
        Clear event flags 1 and 2
    ENDIF
ENDDO

The details of each task are given below.

Task 1

This is the simplest task in the program which controls the LED. At the beginning of the task loop the task waits for event flag 1 to be set. This flag is set by Task 3 if it receives valid GPS data. The task flashes the LED every 250 ms if valid data is received from the GPS by Task 3. If valid data is not received by the GPS then the LED stays OFF.

Task 2

This is the UART controller task. The task waits until event flag 2 is set which indicate that valid data has been received by Task 3. The latitude and longitude data are then read from the queue sent by Task 3. The data is received into a structure called msg which has the following format:

```
typedef struct Message
{
    char LatitudeString[11];
    char LatitudeDirection[2];
    char LongitudeString[12];
    char LongitudeDirection[2];
} AMessage;
```

UART3 is initialized to 9600 baud rate at port pins PD8 and PD9. The latitude and longitude are displayed starting from row 3, column 0 of the PC screen. The terminal emulation program is set to type VT100 where the cursor is controlled by various escape sequences. The following cursor control was used in this task:

```
char gotoscr[] = {0x1B, '[', '3', ';', '0', 'H', 0};
char clrscr[] = {0x1B, '[', '2', 'J', 0};
```

The above character array gotoscr positions the cursor at row 3, column 0. Similarly, character array clrscr clears the screen. In general, the cursor position can be set to row n, column m by the following escape sequence:

```
<esc>[n;mH
```

Task 3

This is the task which reads the GPS data from the GPS receiver and extracts the local latitude and longitude. LEA-6S type GPS receiver is used on the GPS Click board. This GPS receives data from the GPS satellites and sends out data in text form from its serial port. This data is also known as the NMEA sentences. LEA-6S sends out the NMEA sentences shown in Fig. 12.5. Each NMEA sentence starts with a $ character and the values in the sentence are

```
$GPGLL,5127.3917,N,00003.13141,E,10534.00,A,A*67
$GPRMC,05305.00,A,5127.35909,,0003.13148,E,0.030,,270919,,,A*7E
$GPVTG,,T,,M,0030,N,0.055,K,A*20
$GGGA,105305.00,5127.35909,N,00003.13148,E,1,09,1.18,46.5,M,45.4,M,,*66
$GPSA,A,3,01,32,08,28,18,03,22,14,11,,,,2.12,1.18,1.76*06
$GPGSV,4,1,13,01,7,304,40,03,40,224,31,08,38,165,32,10,05,054,*77
$GPGSV,4,2,13,11,83,217,3,14,39,094,24,17,17,314,22,18,73,091,41*76
$GPGSV,4,3,13,22,63,219,33,24,1,002,,27,05,150,,28,30,284,28*7F
$GPGSV,4,4,13,32,34,063,35*4E
```

FIGURE 12.5 NMEA sentences.

separated by commas. Some of the NMEA sentences returned by the GPS Click board are given below:

$GPGLL: This sentence returns the local geographical latitude and longitude

$GPRMC: This sentence returns the local geographical latitude and longitude, speed, track angle, date, time, and magnetic variation.

$GPVTG: This sentence true track, magnetic track, and the ground speed.

$GGGA: This sentence returns the local geographical latitude and longitude, time, fix quality, number of satellites being tracked, horizontal dilution of position, altitude, height of geoid, and DGPS data

$GPGSV: There are four sentences with this heading. These sentences return the number of satellites in view, satellite number, elevation, azimuth, and SNR.

In this task, $GPGLL sentence is used to get the geographical latitude and longitude. This sentence has the following fields:

$GPGLL,4916.45,N,12311.12,W,225444,A,*1D

Where:

GLL	Geographic position, Latitude and Longitude
4916.46,N	Latitude 49 deg. 16.45 min. North
12311.12,W	Longitude 123 deg. 11.12 min. West
225444	Fix taken at 22:54:44 UTC
A	Data Active or V (void)
*iD	checksum data

Notice that the fields are separated by commas. The validity of the data is shown by letters A or V in the data where A shows that the data is valid, and V indicates that the data is not valid.

The program uses the statement UART2_Read_Text(Buffer, "GPGLL", 255) to wait until the string GPGLL is received. The program waits until the starting character $ is received before waiting to receive GPGLL. This makes the task run faster so that it is not interrupted by the scheduler while reading the GPS data (i.e., not context switched). If we use the statement UART2_Read_Text(Buffer, "$GPGLL", 255) then the task may spend time waiting and thus may be interrupted by another task, causing part of the data not to be read properly. This may require the priority of the task to be higher than the priority of other tasks in the program.

The program looks for commas in the complete $GPGLL sentence and extracts the latitude, direction of latitude, longitude, direction of latitude, and the character indicating the validity of the data. If the received GPS data is valid then event flags 1 and 2 are set and the Latitude/ Longitude data are sent to the queue. If on the other hand the data is not valid then event flags 1 and 2 are cleared. The task waits for 10 seconds before it continues.

The program listing is shown in Fig. 12.6 (program: **gps.c**). Fig. 12.7 shows the Latitude and Longitude displayed at row 3, column 0 of the screen.

Fig. 12.8 shows the Clicker 2 for STM development board together with the USB UART Click board and the GPS Click board.

```
/*================================================================================
                        RECEIVE AND DISPLAY GPS DATA
                        ============================

In this project a GPC Click board is used to receive the geographical latitude
and longitude. The received data is displayed on the PC screen at a fixed
coordinate of the screen

Author: Dogan Ibrahim
Date   : September, 2019
File   : gps.c
================================================================================*/
#include "main.h"
#include "event_groups.h"

EventGroupHandle_t xEventGroup;                        // Event group handle
QueueHandle_t xUARTQueue;                              // UART Queue handle

//
// Define all your Task functions here
// ====================================
//

// Task 1 - LED flashing Controller
void Task1(void *pvParameters)
{
    #define BIT_1 (1 << 1)
    #define LED GPIOE_ODR.B12                          // LED port
    #define ON 1
    #define OFF 0

    EventBits_t uxBits;
    GPIO_Config(&GPIOE_BASE, _GPIO_PINMASK_12, _GPIO_CFG_MODE_OUTPUT);

    while (1)                                          // DO FOREVER
    {
        uxBits = xEventGroupWaitBits(xEventGroup, BIT_1, pdFALSE, pdFALSE,
                portMAX_DELAY);
        LED = ON;                                      // LED ON
        vTaskDelay(pdMS_TO_TICKS(250));                // Wait 250ms
        LED = OFF;                                     // LED OFF
        vTaskDelay(pdMS_TO_TICKS(250));                // Wait 250ms
    }
}


// Task 2 - UART Controller
void Task2(void *pvParameters)
{
    #define BIT_2 (1 << 2)

    typedef struct Message
    {
        char LatitudeString[11];
        char LatitudeDirection[2];
        char LongitudeString[12];
        char LongitudeDirection[2];
    } AMessage;

    AMessage msg;
```

FIGURE 12.6 gps.c program listing.

```
        EventBits_t uxBits;

        char gotoscr[] = {0x1B, '[', '3', ';', '0', 'H', 0};        // Goto position
        char clrscr[] = {0x1B, '[', '2', 'J', 0};                    // Clear screen

        UART3_Init_Advanced(9600,_UART_8_BIT_DATA,_UART_NOPARITY,_UART_ONE_STOPBIT,
                            &_GPIO_MODULE_USART3_PD89);

        UART3_Write_Text(clrscr);

        while (1)
        {
            uxBits = xEventGroupWaitBits(xEventGroup, BIT_2, pdTRUE, pdFALSE,
                    portMAX_DELAY);
            xQueueReceive(xUARTQueue, &msg, 0 );                    // Receive data
            UART3_Write_Text(gotoscr);
            UART3_Write_Text("\n\rLatitude : "); UART3_Write_Text(msg.LatitudeString);
            UART3_Write_Text(" ");
            UART3_Write_Text(msg.LatitudeDirection);
            UART3_Write_Text("\n\rLongitude: "); UART3_Write_Text(msg.LongitudeString);
            UART3_Write_Text(" ");
            UART3_Write_Text(msg.LongitudeDirection);
        }
}

// Task 3 - GPS Controller
void Task3(void *pvParameters)
{
        #define BIT_1 (1 << 1)
        #define BIT_2 (1 << 2)

        typedef struct Message
        {
            char LatitudeString[11];
            char LatitudeDirection[2];
            char LongitudeString[12];
            char LongitudeDirection[2];
        } AMessage;

        AMessage msg;

        char Buffer[1024];
        char j, k, ch;

        EventBits_t uxBits;

        UART2_Init_Advanced(9600,_UART_8_BIT_DATA,_UART_NOPARITY,_UART_ONE_STOPBIT,
                            &_GPIO_MODULE_USART2_PD56);

        while(1)
        {
                ch = ' ';
                while(ch != '$')                                    // Wait for $
                {
                    ch = UART2_Read();
                }
                UART2_Read_Text(Buffer, "GPGLL", 255);              // Wait for GPGLL
                UART2_Read_Text(Buffer, "*", 255);                  // Wait for *
```

FIGURE 12.6 (*Continued*)

```
                    j = 1;
                    k = 0;
                    while(Buffer[j] != ',')                   // Extract Latitude
                    {
                        msg.LatitudeString[k] = Buffer[j];
                        j++;
                        k++;
                    }
                    msg.LatitudeString[k]='\0';

                    j++;
                    msg.LatitudeDirection[0] = Buffer[j];      // Extract direction
                    msg.LatitudeDirection[1] = '\0';

                    j = j + 2;                                 // j points to longitude

                    k = 0;
                    while(Buffer[j] != ',')                    // Extract Longitude
                    {
                        msg.LongitudeString[k] = Buffer[j];
                        j++;
                        k++;
                    }
                    msg.LongitudeString[k] = '\0';

                    j++;
                    msg.LongitudeDirection[0] = Buffer[j];     // Extract direction
                    msg.LongitudeDirection[1] = '\0';

                    j = strchr(Buffer, 'A');                   // Extract validity
                    if(j != '\0')                              // If data is valid
                    {
                        uxBits = xEventGroupSetBits(xEventGroup, BIT_1 | BIT_2);
                        xQueueSend(xUARTQueue, &msg, pdMS_TO_TICKS(10));
                    }
                    else
                        uxBits = xEventGroupClearBits(xEventGroup, BIT_1 | BIT_2);

                    vTaskDelay(pdMS_TO_TICKS(10000));          // Wait 10 secs
            }
    }


//
// Start of MAIN program
// =====================
//
void main()
{
    xUARTQueue = xQueueCreate(1, 27);                 // Create UART queue
    xEventGroup = xEventGroupCreate();                // Create event group
//
// Create all the TASKS here
// =========================
//
    // Create Task 1
    xTaskCreate(
        (TaskFunction_t)Task1,
        "LED Controller",
        configMINIMAL_STACK_SIZE,
```

FIGURE 12.6   (*Continued*)

```
        NULL,
        10,
        NULL
    );


    // Create Task 2
    xTaskCreate(
        (TaskFunction_t)Task2,
        "UART Controller",
        configMINIMAL_STACK_SIZE,
        NULL,
        10,
        NULL
    );

      // Create Task 3
    xTaskCreate(
        (TaskFunction_t)Task3,
        "GPS Controller",
        configMINIMAL_STACK_SIZE,
        NULL,
        10,
        NULL
    );
//
// Start the RTOS scheduler
//
    vTaskStartScheduler();

//
// Will never reach here
}
```

FIGURE 12.6 (*Continued*)

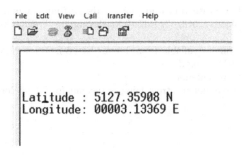

FIGURE 12.7   Displaying the latitude and longitude.

12.8 Summary

In this chapter, we have learned the concept of event groups and event flags. Two practical projects are given in the chapter to show how the event flags can be used in a multitasking project.

In the next chapter, we shall be looking at the FreeRTOS software timers and learn how the timers can be used in practical projects.

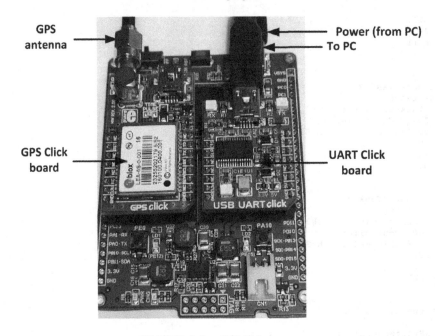

CLICKER 2 for STM32

FIGURE 12.8   Project components.

Further readings

[1] R. Barry. Mastering the FreeRTOS Real Time Kernel: A Hands-On Tutorial Guide. Available from: https://www.freertos.org/wp-content/uploads/2018/07/161204_Mastering_the_FreeRTOS_Real_Time_Kernel-A_Hands-On_Tutorial_Guide.pdf.

[2] The FreeRTOS Reference Manual. Available from: https://www.freertos.org/wp-content/uploads/2018/07/FreeRTOS_Reference_Manual_V10.0.0.pdf.

[3] https://www.freertos.org/documentation.

[4] D. Pham, E. Fattal, N. Tsapis, Pulmonary drug delivery systems for tuberculosis treatment, Int. J. Pharm. 478 (2015) 517–529.

CHAPTER

13

Software timers

13.1 Overview

Software timers are important parts of any real-time multitasking operating system. The timers are used in tasks to schedule the execution of a function at a time in the future, or periodically with a fixed frequency. Software timers under FreeRTOS do not require any hardware and are not related to hardware timers as they are implemented in software. When a timer expires, the program can be configured to call a function names as the timer's callback function.

Software timers are optional in FreeRTOS and the application programs must be built with the source file FreeRTOS/Source/timers.c included as part of the program. Parameter configUSE_TIMERS must be set to 1 in file FreeRTOSConfig.h before the software timers can be used.

Two types of software timers are supported by FreeRTOS: One-shot, and Auto-reload.

One-shot timers: These timers are started manually and do not re-start when they complete. The callback function is executed only one when the timer expires.

Auto-reload timers: These timers re-start each time they expire, thus resulting in repetitive execution of the callback function attached to the timer.

A software timer can be in one of two states: Dormant, and Running. A Dormat timer exists but it is not active. A Running timer is active and it will call its callback function when its period expires.

All software timer callback functions execute in the context of the same RTOS daemon (or "timer service") task. The daemon task is a standard FreeRTOS task that is created automatically when the scheduler is started. The priority and stack size are set at compile time by the two parameters in file FreeRTOSConfig.h: configTIMER_TASK_PRIORITY and config-TIMER_TASK_STACK_DEPTH. Callback functions must not call to functions that may cause the enter the Blocked state.

A timer must be created before it can be used. Creating a timer does not start it. Timers must be started, stopped, or reset manually by the user programs. Software timer API functions send commands from the calling task to the daemon task on a queue called the "timer command queue." The timer command queue is a standard FreeRTOS queue that is created automatically when the scheduler is started. The length of the timer command

ARM-Based Microcontroller Multitasking Projects. http://dx.doi.org/10.1016/B978-0-12-821227-1.00013-X
Copyright © 2020 Elsevier Ltd. All rights reserved.

queue is set by the configTIMER_QUEUE_LENGTH compile time configuration constant in FreeRTOSConfig.h.

The daemon task is scheduled like any other FreeRTOS task and it will process commands, or execute timer callback functions, when it is the highest priority task that is able to run. Parameter configTIMER_TASK_PRIORITY controls the timer task priority.

Some of the important software timer API functions are given below. Interested readers can get further detailed information on software timers from the following web sites:

https://www.freertos.org/wp-content/uploads/2018/07/161204_Mastering_the_ FreeRTOS_Real_Time_Kernel-A_Hands-On_Tutorial_Guide.pdf

and

https://www.freertos.org/wp-content/uploads/2018/07/FreeRTOS_Reference_Manual_ V10.0.0.pdf

13.2 Creating, deleting, starting, stopping, and resetting a timer

The API function xTimerCreate() creates a timer and returns a handle to identify the created timer. Notice that creating a timer does not start it. The format of the function is:

xTimerCreate(const char *pcTimerName, const TickType_t xTimerPeriod, const UBaseType_t uxAutoReload, void * const pv TimerID, TimerCallbackFunction_t pxCallbackFunction);

Parameters
pcTimerName: A plain text name that is assigned to the timer, purely to assist debugging.
xTimerPeriod: This is timer period, specified in multiples of tick periods. The pdMS_TO_TICKS() macro can be used to convert a time in milliseconds to a time in ticks. For example, if the timer must expire after 500ms, then the period can be set to pdMS_TO_TICKS(500), provided configTICK_RATE_HZ is less than or equal to 1000.
uxAutoReload: This parameter is set to pdTRUE to create an autoreload timer. When set to pdFALSE, a one-shot timer is created.
pvTimerID: An identifier that is assigned to the timer being created. The identifier can later be updated using the vTimerSetTimerID() API function. If the same callback function is assigned to multiple timers, then the timer identifier can be inspected inside the callback function to determine which timer actually expired.
pxCallbackFunction: This is the function to call when the timer expires. Callback functions must have the prototype defined by the TimerCallbackFunction_t typedef. An example prototype function is shown below:

void vCallbackFunctionExample(TimerHandle_t xTimer);

Return values
Null: The software timer could not be created because there was insufficient FreeRTOS heap memory available to successfully allocate the timer data structures.
Any other value: The software timer was created successfully.

Parameters configUSE_TIMERS and configSUPPORT_DYNAMIC_ALLOCATION must both be set to 1 in file FreeRTOSConfig.h before this function can be used. If left unspecified, configSUPPORT_DYNAMIC_ALLOCATION is set to 1 by default.

The API function xTimerDelete() is used to delete a timer. The format of the function is:

xTimerDelete(TimerHandle_t xTimer, TickType_t xTicksToWait);

xTimer: The handle of the timer being deleted.

xTicksToWait: Timer functionality is not provided by the core FreeRTOS code, but by a timer service (or daemon) task. The FreeRTOS timer API sends commands to the timer service task on a queue called the timer command queue. xTicksToWait specifies the maximum amount of time the task should remain in the Blocked state to wait for space to become available on the timer command queue, should the queue already be full. The block time is specified in tick periods, so the absolute time it represents is dependent on the tick frequency. The pdMS_TO_TICKS() macro can be used to convert a time specified in milliseconds to a time specified in ticks. Setting xTicksToWait to portMAX_DELAY will cause the task to wait indefinitely (without timing out), provided INCLUDE_vTaskSuspend is set to 1 in FreeRTOSConfig.h. xTicksToWait is ignored if xTimerDelete() is called before the scheduler is started.

Return values

pdPASS: The delete command was successfully sent to the timer command queue.

pdFAIL: The delete command was not sent to the timer command queue because the queue was already full.

The API function xTimerStart() starts a timer running. If the timer was already running, then xTimerStart() is functionally equivalent to resetting the timer.

xTimerStart(TimerHandle_t xTimer, TickType_t xTicksToWait);

Parameters

xTimer: The timer to be reset, started, or restarted.

xTicksToWait: Timer functionality is not provided by the core FreeRTOS code, but by a timer service (or daemon) task. The FreeRTOS timer API sends commands to the timer service task on a queue called the timer command queue. xTicksToWait specifies the maximum amount of time the task should remain in the Blocked state to wait for space to become available on the timer command queue, should the queue already be full.

Return values

pdPASS: The start command was successfully sent to the timer command queue. If a block time was specified (xTicksToWaitwas not zero), then it is possible that the calling task was placed into the Blocked state to wait for space to become available on the timer command queue before the function returned, but data was successfully written to the queue before the block time expired. When the command is actually processed will depend on the priority of the timer service task relative to other tasks in the system,

pdFAIL: The start command was not sent to the timer command queue because the queue was already full.

The API function xTimerStop() stops a timer running. The format of the function is:

xTimerStop(TimerHandle_t xTimer, TickType_t xTicksToWait);

Parameters

xTimer: The timer to be stopped.

xTicksToWait: Timer functionality is not provided by the core FreeRTOS code, but by a timer service (or daemon) task. The FreeRTOS timer API sends commands to the timer service task on a queue called the timer command queue. xTicksToWait specifies the maximum amount of time the task should remain in the Blocked state to wait for space to become available on the timer command queue, should the queue already be full.

Return values

pdPASS: The stop command was successfully sent to the timer command queue.

If a block time was specified (xTicksToWait was not zero), then it is possible that the calling task was placed into the Blocked state to wait for space to become available on the timer command queue before the function returned, but data was successfully written to the queue before the block time expired.

pdFAIL: The stop command was not sent to the timer command queue because the queue was already full. If a block time was specified (xTicksToWait was not zero) then the calling task will have been placed into the Blocked state to wait for the timer service task to make room in the queue, but the specified block time expired before that happened.

The API function xTimerReset() resets a timer. If the timer is already running, then the timer will recalculate its expiry time to be relative to when xTimerReset() was called. If the timer was not running, then the timer will calculate an expiry time relative to when xTimerReset() was called, and the timer will start running. In this case, xTimerReset() is functionally equivalent to xTimerStart(). Resetting a timer ensures the timer is running. The format of the function is:

xTimerReset(TimerHandle_t xTimer, TickType_t xTicksToWait);

Parameters

xTimer and xTicksToWait has the same functionality as in the function call xTimerStop().

Return values

The return values **pdPASS** and pdFAIL have the same functionality as in the call xTimerStop().

13.3 Change timer period, get timer period

This function changes the timer period. If the period of a timer that is already running is to be changed, then the timer will use the new period value to recalculate its expiry time. The recalculated expiry time will then be relative to when xTimerChangePeriod() was called, and not relative to when the timer was originally started. If xTimerChangePeriod() is used to change the period of a timer that is not already running, then the timer will use the new period value to calculate an expiry time, and the timer will start running. The format of this function is:

xTimerChangePeriod(TimerHandle_t xTimer, TickType_t xNewPeriod,TickType_t xTicksToWait);

Parameters

xTimer: The timer to which the new period is being assigned.

xNewPeriod: The new period for the timer. Timer periods are specified in multiples of tick periods. The pdMS_TO_TICKS() macro can be used to convert a time in milliseconds to a time in ticks.

xTicksToWait: This parameter has the same functionality as in the other timer functions.

Return values

The return values **pdPASS** and pdFAIL have the same functionality as in the call xTimerStop().

The API function xTimerGetPeriod() returns the period of a timer. The function has the format:

xTimerGetPeriod(TimerHandle_t xTimer);

Parameters

xTimer: The handle of the timer being queried.

Return values

The period of the timer, specified in ticks.

13.4 Timer name and ID

The function call pcTimerGetName() returns the name (in text format) assigned to the timer when the timer was created. The function has the following format:

pcTimerGetName(TimerHandle_t xTimer);

Parameters

xTimer: The timer being queried.

Return values

Timer names are standard NULL terminated C strings. The value returned is a pointer to the subject timer's name.

The function call pvTimerGetTimerID() returns the identifier (ID) assigned to the timer when the timer was created.

pvTimerGetTimerID(TimerHandle_t xTimer);

Parameters

xTimer: The timer being queried.

Return values

The identifier assigned to the timer being queried.

13.5 Project 28—reaction timer

Description: This is a reaction timer project which makes use of an LED and a push-button switch. The user is expected to press the push-button switch as soon as the LED is turned ON. The time between the LED being turned ON and the user pressing the button is measured and displayed on an LCD in milliseconds. The LED is turned ON again after a random delay, ready for the next measurement.

Aim: The aim of this project is to show how the elapsed time can be measured. In this program a FreRTOS software timer is not used, but instead the xTaskGetTickCount() API function is used. Additionally, the project shows how to use the random function generator in a program to generate random numbers.

Block diagram: Fig. 13.1 shows the block diagram of the project. The on-board LED at port pin PE12 and the push-button switch at the on-board port pin PE0 are used in this project.

Circuit diagram: The circuit diagram of the project is shown in Fig. 13.2. The LCD is connected to the Clicker 2 for STM32 development board as in the previous LCD based projects.

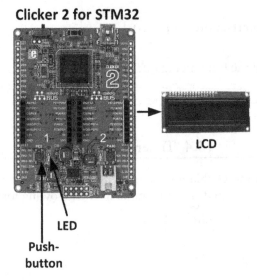

FIGURE 13.1   Block diagram of the project.

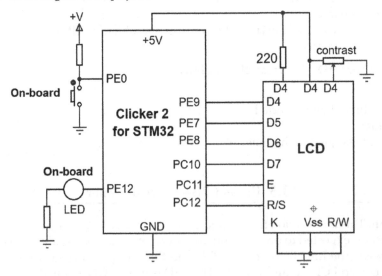

FIGURE 13.2   Circuit diagram of the project.

Program listing: The operation of the program is described by the following PDL:

BEGIN

    Configure the LCD

    DO FOREVER

        Wait 5 seconds

        Wait random time between 1 and 10 seconds

        Turn the LED ON

        Save the current tick count

        Wait until push-button switch is pressed

        Save the new tick count

        Calculate the elapsed time

        Turn LED OFF

        Display elapsed time in milliseconds on LCD

    ENDDO

END

The program listing (program: **reaction.c**) is shown in Fig. 13.3. The program consists of only one task in addition to the Idle task. At the beginning of the program the interface between the LCD and the Clicker 2 for STM2 development board is defined, the LCD is initialized, port pin PE12 is configured as output, and PE0 is configured as input. The remainder of the task is executed in an endless loop. Inside this loop, built-in function rand() is called. This function generates a random integer number between 0 and 32767. An integer variable called random is used to limit the generated random numbers between 1 and 10. This value is then used to create random delay in the program so that the user does not know when the LED will lit. As soon as the LED is turned ON, the current tick count is stored in variable StartTime. The program then waits until the button is pressed by the user, and then calculates the elapsed time by getting the new tick count and subtracting the old tick count from it. This value is the reaction time of the user in milliseconds, which is then displayed on the LCD.

```
/*=============================================================================
                            REACTION TIMER
                            ==============

In this project the onboard LED and the onboard push-button switch are used to
determine the reaction time of the user. The user presses the button as soon as
the LED is lit. The time between the LED being lit and the button pressed is
displayed on the LCD as the reaction time in milliseconds.

Author: Dogan Ibrahim
Date  : September, 2019
File  : reaction.c
=============================================================================*/
#include "main.h"

// LCD module connections
sbit LCD_RS at GPIOC_ODR.B12;
sbit LCD_EN at GPIOC_ODR.B11;
sbit LCD_D4 at GPIOE_ODR.B9;
sbit LCD_D5 at GPIOE_ODR.B7;
sbit LCD_D6 at GPIOE_ODR.B8;
sbit LCD_D7 at GPIOC_ODR.B10;
// End LCD module connections
```

FIGURE 13.3   reaction.c program listing.

```
//
// Define all your Task functions here
// ====================================
//

// Task 1 - Reaction Timer
void Task1(void *pvParameters)
{
    #define LED GPIOE_ODR.B12                                    // LED port
    #define BUTTON GPIOE_IDR.B0                                  // Button
    int random;
    unsigned long StartTime, ElapsedTime;
    unsigned char Txt[11];

    GPIO_Config(&GPIOE_BASE, _GPIO_PINMASK_12, _GPIO_CFG_MODE_OUTPUT);
    GPIO_Config(&GPIOE_BASE, _GPIO_PINMASK_0, _GPIO_CFG_MODE_INPUT);

    Lcd_Init();                                                 // Initialize LCD

    while (1)                                                   // DO FOREVER
    {
        vTaskDelay(pdMS_TO_TICKS(5000));                        // Wait 5 seconds
        Lcd_Cmd(_LCD_CLEAR);                                    // Clear LCD
        random = rand() % 10 + 1;                               // Between 1-10
        vTaskDelay(pdMS_TO_TICKS(random));                      // Wait 1-10 seconds
        LED = 1;                                                // LED ON
        StartTime = xTaskGetTickCount();                        // Get tick count
        while(BUTTON == 1);                                     // Wait for button
        LED = 0;                                                // LED OFF
        ElapsedTime = xTaskGetTickCount() - StartTime;          // Stop timer
        LongToStr(ElapsedTime, Txt);                            // Convert to string
        Ltrim(Txt);                                             // Remove spaces
        Lcd_Cmd(_LCD_CLEAR);                                    // Clear LCD
        Lcd_Out(1, 1, "Reaction Time");                         // Heading
        Lcd_Out(2, 1, Txt);                                     // Display reaction time
        Lcd_Out_CP(" ms");                                      // Display ms
    }
}

//
// Start of MAIN program
// ======================
//
void main()
{
//
// Create all the TASKS here
// =========================
//
    // Create Task 1
    xTaskCreate(
        (TaskFunction_t)Task1,
        "Reaction Timer",
        configMINIMAL_STACK_SIZE,
        NULL,
        10,
        NULL
    );

//
// Start the RTOS scheduler
//
    vTaskStartScheduler();

//
// Will never reach here
}
```

FIGURE 13.3 (*Continued*)

FIGURE 13.4   Reaction time displayed on the LCD.

Fig. 13.4 shows a typical display of the reaction time on the LCD.

13.6 Project 29—generate square waveform

Description: In this project an auto-reload FreeRTOS software timer is used to generate a positive square waveform signal with a frequency of 500 Hz, and equal ON and OFF times (i.e., 50% duty cycle). At 500 Hz, the ON and the OFF times of the waveform are 1ms each as shown in Fig. 13.5.

Aim: The aim of this project is to show how a FreeRTOS software can be used to generate a square waveform signal.

Circuit diagram: Fig. 13.6 shows the circuit diagram of the project. The waveform is generated at port pin PA2 of the Clicker 2 for STM32 development board. A digital oscilloscope is connected to this pin to display the generated waveform.

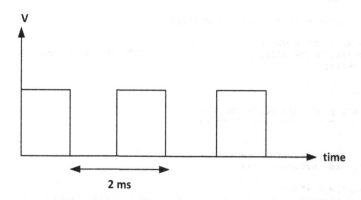

FIGURE 13.5   Positive square waveform at 500 Hz.

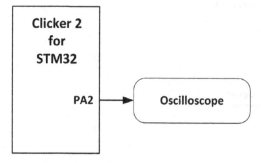

FIGURE 13.6   Circuit diagram of the project.

Program listing: The program listing (**squarewave.c**) is shown in Fig. 13.7. There is only one task in this program in addition to the Idle task. Variable Wave is assigned to port pin PA2. The program creates an auto-reload timer with a period of 1ms, using the following statement. The timer ID field is not used in this program:

xTimer = xTimerCreate("SquareWave", pdMS_TO_TICKS(1), pdTRUE, 0, vSquareWaveForm);

The callback function called vSquareWaveForm is executed at the end of each timer period. In this function port pin PA2 is toggled every time so that a square waveform is generated at this pin.

```
/*================================================================================
                        GENERATE SQUARE WAVEFORM
                        ========================

In this project a FreeRTOS software timer is usd in auto-reload mode in order
to generate a square waveform signal. The signal frequency is set to 500Hz (i.e.
period of 2ms) where the ON and the OFF times are 1ms.

Author: Dogan Ibrahim
Date  : September, 2019
File  : squarewave.c
================================================================================*/
#include "main.h"
#include "timers.h"

void vSquareWaveForm(TimerHandle_t xTimer)
{
    #define Wave GPIOA_ODR.B2
    GPIO_Config(&GPIOA_BASE, _GPIO_PINMASK_2, _GPIO_CFG_MODE_OUTPUT);
    Wave = ~Wave;
}

//
// Define all your Task functions here
// ====================================
//

// Task 1 - Square Waveform Generator
void Task1(void *pvParameters)
{
    TimerHandle_t xTimer;
    xTimer = xTimerCreate("SquareWave", pdMS_TO_TICKS(1), pdTRUE, 0,
                            vSquareWaveForm);
    xTimerStart(xTimer, 0);

    while (1)
    {
    }
}

//
// Start of MAIN program
// ======================
//
void main()
{
//
```

FIGURE 13.7 squarewave.c program listing.

```
// Create all the TASKS here
// =========================
//
    // Create Task 1
    xTaskCreate(
        (TaskFunction_t)Task1,
        "Square Waveform Generator",
        configMINIMAL_STACK_SIZE,
        NULL,
        10,
        NULL
    );
//
// Start the RTOS scheduler
//
    vTaskStartScheduler();

//
// Will never reach here
}
```

FIGURE 13.7 (*Continued*)

Fig. 13.8 shows the waveform on an oscilloscope. In this project the Velleman PCSGU250 is used to display the waveform on the PC screen. In this figure the horizontal axis is 1 ms/div and the vertical axis is 1 V/div. Clearly, the duration of the ON and OFF times are 1 ms each, corresponding to a period of 2 ms, that is, the frequency is 500 Hz.

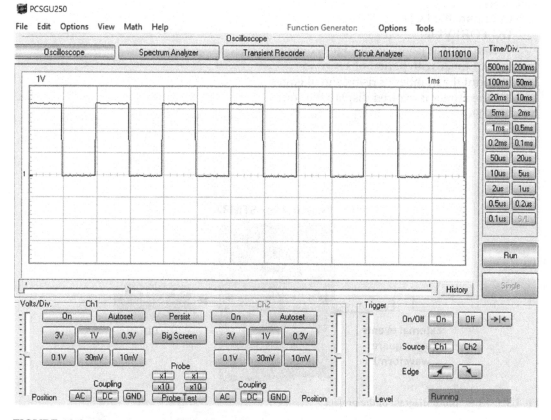

FIGURE 13.8 **Waveform generated by the program.**

13.7 Project 30—event counter (e.g., frequency counter)

Description: In this project an auto-reload FreeRTOS software timer is used. The project counts the number of events occurring in a second. For example, the project can be used as a frequency counter to measure and display the frequency of an analog waveform. It is assumed that the input signal is in the form of positive square waveform. If the signal is a sine wave, then it will be required to convert it to a positive square wave using for example a Schmitt trigger logic gate, or a transistor switch.

Aim: The aim of this project is to show how a FreeRTOS software can be used to create a frequency counter (or event counter) project.

Block diagram: Fig. 13.9 shows the block diagram of the project. The measured frequency is displayed on an LCD.

Circuit diagram: The circuit diagram of the project is similar to Fig. 13.2, but here the push-button and the LED are not used, but instead external events are applied to port pin PA2 of the development board. It is important to make sure that the input signal is positive and its magnitude is not greater than +3.3 V.

Program listing: The program listing (**freqcounter.c**) is shown in Fig. 13.10. There is only one task in this program in addition to the Idle task. The operation of the program is as follows:

BEGIN
    Configure the LCD
    DO FOREVER
        Wait until a rising signal edge is detected
        Start timer with period of 1 second
        Count the number of rising signal edges
        When timer is expired display the count
    ENDDO
END

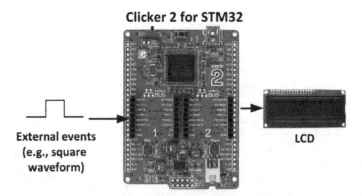

FIGURE 13.9   Block diagram of the project.

```
/*============================================================================
                    EVENT COUNTER (e.g. FREQUENCY COUNTER)
                    =====================================

In this project a FreeRTOS software timer is used in auto-reload mode to
measure the events applied to pin PA2 every second. The project can be used as
a frequency counter. It is important to make sure that the input signal
amplitude is not greater than +3.3V if used as a frequency counter.

Author: Dogan Ibrahim
Date  : September, 2019
File  : freqcounter.c
==============================================================================*/
#include "main.h"
#include "timers.h"

// LCD module connections
sbit LCD_RS at GPIOC_ODR.B12;
sbit LCD_EN at GPIOC_ODR.B11;
sbit LCD_D4 at GPIOE_ODR.B9;
sbit LCD_D5 at GPIOE_ODR.B7;
sbit LCD_D6 at GPIOE_ODR.B8;
sbit LCD_D7 at GPIOC_ODR.B10;
// End LCD module connections

unsigned int count = 0;

void vFrequencyCounter(TimerHandle_t xTimer)
{
   unsigned char Txt[14];
   unsigned long cnt;
   Lcd_Cmd(_LCD_CLEAR);                                // Clear LCD
   LongToStr(count, Txt);                              // Convert to string
   count = 0;                                          // Reset the counter
   Ltrim(Txt);                                         // Remove spaces
   Lcd_Out(2, 1, Txt);                                 // Display teh count
}

//
// Define all your Task functions here
// ====================================
//

// Task 1 - Frequency Counter
void Task1(void *pvParameters)
{
   #define FreqInput GPIOA_IDR.B2
   TimerHandle_t xTimer;

   Lcd_Init();
   GPIO_Config(&GPIOA_BASE, _GPIO_PINMASK_2, _GPIO_CFG_MODE_INPUT);
   xTimer = xTimerCreate("FreqCounter", pdMS_TO_TICKS(1000), pdTRUE, 0,
                         vFrequencyCounter);
   xTimerStart(xTimer, 0);

   while(1)                                            // Detect rising edge
   {
     while(FreqInput == 0);                            // If 0
     count++;                                          // Increment count
     while(FreqInput == 1);                            // If high
```

FIGURE 13.10 freqcounter.c program listing.

```
    }
}
//
// Start of MAIN program
// =====================
//
void main()
{
//
// Create all the TASKS here
// =========================
//
    // Create Task 1
    xTaskCreate(
        (TaskFunction_t)Task1,
        "Frequency counter",
        configMINIMAL_STACK_SIZE,
        NULL,
        10,
        NULL
    );

//
// Start the RTOS scheduler
//
    vTaskStartScheduler();

//
// Will never reach here
}
```

FIGURE 13.10 (*Continued*)

The following parameters must be defined and set in file FreeRTOSConfig.h before the program can be compiled:

configUSE_TIMERS
configTIMER_TASK_PRIORITY
configTIMER_QUEUE_LENGTH
configTIMER_TASK_STACK_DEPTH

At the beginning of the program the interface between the LCD and the development board is defined, the LCD is initialized, and port pin PA2 is configured as digital input. The program then creates an auto-load timer with a period of one second (1000 ms), specifying the callback function as vFrequencyCounter. The program detects the rising edge of the input signal and increment variable count when the rising edge is detected. The code to detect the rising edge and increment count is:

while(FreqInput == 0);
count++;
while(FreqInput == 1);

The callback function is called every second when the timer expires. This function clears the LCD, converts the count into a string variable in Txt and then displays the count. The count here is the number of events happening each second, or the frequency in the case if the input is a square wave signal. Tests showed that the frequency in the upper audio range up to 30 kHz can accurately be measured and displayed on the LCD by the project. Both the task priority and the timer priority were set to 10 in this project.

13.8 Summary

In this Chapter we have learned how to use the FreeRTOS software timers in projects. In the remaining Chapters of this book we will be developing additional projects using various functions of FreeRTOS.

Further readings

[1] R. Barry. Mastering the FreeRTOS Real Time Kernel: A Hands-On Tutorial Guide. Available from: https://www.freertos.org/wp-content/uploads/2018/07/161204_Mastering_the_FreeRTOS_Real_Time_Kernel-A_Hands-On_Tutorial_Guide.pdf.

[2] The FreeRTOS Reference Manual. Available from: https://www.freertos.org/wp-content/uploads/2018/07/FreeRTOS_Reference_Manual_V10.0.0.pdf

[3] https://www.freertos.org/documentation.

Some example projects

14.1 Overview

In this chapter, various example projects are given at different levels of complexity to make the readers familiar on how to develop microcontroller-based projects using the FreeRTOS application program interface (API) functions. The projects aim to use most of the functions that we have covered up to this point in the book.

14.2 Project 31: square wave generation with adjustable frequency

Description: In this project, a square waveform is generated as in Project 29, but here the period of the waveform can be changed from the keyboard while the program is running in a multitasking environment. The user enters the required ON time of the waveform in milliseconds as an integer value. The lowest value that can be entered is 1 ms. It is assumed that the waveform has 50% duty cycle. That is, it has equal ON and OFF times. The total period of the waveform is, therefore, 2 * ON time.

Aim: The aim of this project is to show how a FreeRTOS software can be used to generate square waveform signal where the frequency can be entered from the keyboard. An auto-reload timer is created where its frequency can be changed without stopping the program.

Circuit diagram: The circuit diagram of the project is shown in Fig. 14.1. This is similar to Fig. 13.6, but here the USB UART Click board is used to interface the development board to a PC.

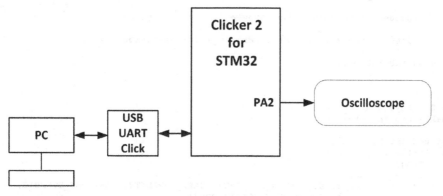

FIGURE 14.1   Circuit diagram of the project.

ARM-Based Microcontroller Multitasking Projects. http://dx.doi.org/10.1016/B978-0-12-821227-1.00014-1

Program listing: The program listing (**squarekey.c**) is shown in Fig. 14.2. The program consists of two tasks in addition to the Idle task. Task 1 creates the square waveform, while

```
/*=============================================================================
                 SQUARE WAVE GENERATOR WITH REQUIRED FERQUENCY
                 ============================================

In this project a square wave is genrated. The frequency of the waveform is
entered from the keyboard while the program is running (thus, multitasking). The
period of the waveform is initially set to 500Hz, but is changed depending on
the value entered from the keyboard. The period can be set as an integer starting
from 1ms and going up.

Author: Dogan Ibrahim
Date   : September, 2019
File   : squarekey.c
=============================================================================*/
#include "main.h"
#include "timers.h"
QueueHandle_t xUARTQueue;                                      // UART Queue handle

void vSquareWaveForm(TimerHandle_t xTimer)
{
    #define Wave GPIOA_ODR.B2                                  // Pin PA2 is used
    GPIO_Config(&GPIOA_BASE, _GPIO_PINMASK_2, _GPIO_CFG_MODE_OUTPUT);
    Wave = ~Wave;                                             // Generate square wave
}

//
// Define all your Task functions here
// ====================================
//

// Task 1 - Square Waveform Generator
void Task1(void *pvParameters)
{
    unsigned int NewPeriod;

    TimerHandle_t xTimer;
    xTimer = xTimerCreate("SquareWave", pdMS_TO_TICKS(1), pdTRUE, 0,
                          vSquareWaveForm);
    xTimerStart(xTimer, 0);

    while (1)
    {
        if(xQueueReceive(xUARTQueue, &NewPeriod, 0 ) == pdPASS)
        {
            xTimerChangePeriod(xTimer, pdMS_TO_TICKS(NewPeriod), 100);
        }
        else taskYIELD();
    }
}

// Task 2 - Keyboard Controller
void Task2(void *pvParameters)
{
    unsigned int N, Total;
    char Txt[14];
    float freq;
    QueueHandle_t xQueue;
    UART3_Init_Advanced(9600,_UART_8_BIT_DATA,_UART_NOPARITY,_UART_ONE_STOPBIT,
                        &_GPIO_MODULE_USART3_PD89);
```

FIGURE 14.2 squarekey.c program listing.

```
        while (1)
        {
            UART3_Write_Text("\n\r\n\rEnter ON time (ms): ");

            N = 0;
            Total = 0;

            while(1)
            {
                N = UART3_Read();                               // Read a number
                UART3_Write(N);                                 // Echo the number
                if(N == '\r') break;                            // If Enter
                N = N - '0';                                    // Pure number
                Total = 10*Total + N;                           // Total number
            }

            xQueueSend(xUARTQueue, &Total, pdMS_TO_TICKS(10));  // Send via Queue

            UART3_Write_Text("\n\rFrequency changed to: ");     // Display heading
            freq = 1000.0 / (2.0 * Total);                      // Calculate frequency
            FloatToStr(freq, Txt);                              // Convert to string
            Ltrim(Txt);                                         // Remove spaces
            UART3_Write_Text(Txt);                              // Frequency in Hz
            UART3_Write_Text(" Hz\n\r");                        // Display Hz
        }
}

//
// Start of MAIN program
// =====================
//
void main()
{
    xUARTQueue = xQueueCreate(1, 2);                            // Create a Queue
//
// Create all the TASKS here
// =========================
//
    // Create Task 1
    xTaskCreate(
        (TaskFunction_t)Task1,
        "Square Waveform Generator",
        configMINIMAL_STACK_SIZE,
        NULL,
        10,
        NULL
    );

    // Create Task 2
    xTaskCreate(
        (TaskFunction_t)Task2,
        "Keyboard Controller",
        configMINIMAL_STACK_SIZE,
        NULL,
        10,
        NULL
    );

//
// Start the RTOS scheduler
//
    vTaskStartScheduler();

//
// Will never reach here
}
```

FIGURE 14.2 (*Continued*)

Task 2 sets the required period. The operation of the program is as follows:

Task 1

Create a timer with period of 2 ms

Start the timer

DO FOREVER

   IF data are available in the queue **THEN**

      Get the data from the queue

      Change the period of the waveform

   ELSE

      Initiate task change (taskYIELD)

   ENDIF

ENDDO

Task 2

Initialize UART at 9600 baud

DO FOREVER

   Read the required period from the keyboard

   Send the period to the queue

   Calculate the frequency

   Display the frequency on the screen

ENDDO

Task 1 creates the timer with a period of 2 ms initially by calling the API function:

```
xTimer = xTimerCreate("SquareWave", pdMS_TO_TICKS(1), pdTRUE, 0,
    vSquareWaveForm);
```

The timer is then started with the function call:

```
xTimerStart(xTimer, 0);
```

The remainder of Task 1 runs in a loop and checks whether or not a message is available in the queue. If a message is available, then it is read and used to change the period of the waveform by the function call:

```
xTimerChangePeriod(xTimer, pdMS_TO_TICKS(NewPeriod), 100);
```

If there is no message in the queue, then function taskYIELD() is called to give up the CPU so that the keyboard can grab the CPU.

Task 2 prompts the user to enter the required ON time of the waveform. This is then sent to the queue so that the period of the waveform can be changed as required. This task then calculates the resulting frequency of the waveform and displays it on the screen.

Fig. 14.3 shows the screen when the required ON time of the waveform was 2 ms. The resulting was captured using an oscilloscope and is shown in Fig. 14.4.

```
Enter ON time (ms): 2
Frequency changed to: 250 Hz
```

FIGURE 14.3   Setting the ON time to 2 ms.

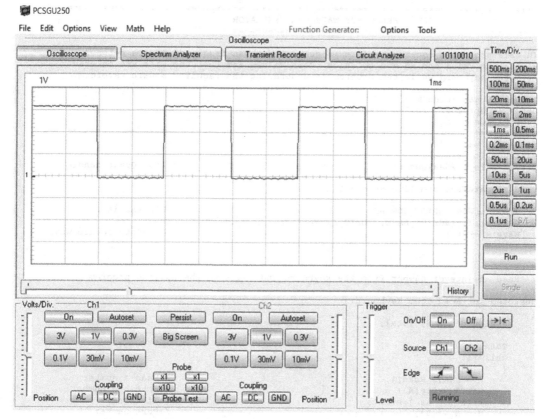

FIGURE 14.4 Waveform on the oscilloscope.

14.3 Project 32: frequency sweep waveform generator

Description: In this project, a square waveform is generated as in the previous project, but here the frequency of the generated waveform is changed from a given starting value to an end value with the steps specified by the user. For example, the user may require the frequency to change from 100 to 500 Hz in steps of 50 Hz where the waveform at each frequency should be output for 5 seconds. As in the previous project, it is assumed that the waveform will have equal ON and OFF times. Sweep frequency waveform generators are commonly used in radio frequency applications.

Aim: The aim of this project is to show how a FreeRTOS software can be used to generate square waveform signal where the frequency can be changed in required steps entered from the keyboard. Auto-reload timer is created where its frequency can be changed without stopping the program.

Circuit diagram: The circuit diagram of the project is as in Fig. 14.1.

Program listing: The program listing (**sweepfreq.c**) is shown in Fig. 14.5. The program consists of two tasks in addition to the Idle task. Task 1 creates a timer with the default period of 1 ms and then stats the timer. This task then enters a loop. Inside the loop, the program reads

```
/*=====================================================================
                  SWEEP FREQUENCY WAVEFORM GENERATOR
                  =================================

In this project a square waveform is generated whose frequency varies between
a starting value and an ending value. Both values and the step size are entered
from the keyboard while the program is generating the required square waveform.

Author: Dogan Ibrahim
Date   : September, 2019
File   : sweepfreq.c
=====================================================================*/
#include "main.h"
#include "timers.h"
QueueHandle_t xUARTQueue;                                    // UART Queue handle

void vSquareWaveForm(TimerHandle_t xTimer)
{
    #define Wave GPIOA_ODR.B2                                 // Pin PA2 is used
    GPIO_Config(&GPIOA_BASE, _GPIO_PINMASK_2, _GPIO_CFG_MODE_OUTPUT);
    Wave = ~Wave;                                            // Generate square wave
}

//
// Read an integer number from the keyboard and retun to the calling program
//
unsigned int Read_From_Keyboard()
{
    unsigned int N, Total;

    Total = 0;
    while(1)
    {
        N = UART3_Read();                                    // Read a number
        UART3_Write(N);                                      // Echo the number
        if(N == '\r') break;                                 // If Enter
        N = N - '0';                                         // Pure number
        Total = 10*Total + N;                                // Total number
    }
    return Total;
}

//
// Define all your Task functions here
// ===================================
//

// Task 1 - Square Waveform Generator
void Task1(void *pvParameters)
{
    typedef struct Message
    {
        unsigned int StartFrequency;
        unsigned int EndFrequency;
        unsigned int StepFrequency;
    } AMessage;

    AMessage msg;
    float FirstValue, EndValue, Strt,Flag;
    unsigned int freq;
```

FIGURE 14.5 sweepfreq.c program listing.

```
        TimerHandle_t xTimer;
        xTimer = xTimerCreate("SquareWave", pdMS_TO_TICKS(1), pdTRUE, 0,
                               vSquareWaveForm);
        xTimerStart(xTimer, 0);

        Flag = 0;

        while (1)
        {
            if((xQueueReceive(xUARTQueue, &msg, 0 ) == pdPASS) || Flag == 1)
            {
                if(Flag == 0)
                {
                    FirstValue = 1000.0 / (2.0 * msg.StartFrequency);
                    Strt = FirstValue;
                    freq = msg.StartFrequency;
                    EndValue = 1000.0 / (2.0 * msg.EndFrequency);
                }

                xTimerChangePeriod(xTimer, pdMS_TO_TICKS(FirstValue), 100);
                vTaskDelay(pdMS_TO_TICKS(5000));
                freq = freq + msg.StepFrequency;
                FirstValue = 1000.0 / (2.0 * freq);
                if(FirstValue <= EndValue)
                {
                    freq = msg.StartFrequency;
                    FirstValue = Strt;
                }
                Flag = 1;
            }
            else taskYIELD();
        }
    }

// Task 2 - Keyboard Controller
void Task2(void *pvParameters)
{
    typedef struct Message
    {
        unsigned int StartFrequency;
        unsigned int EndFrequency;
        unsigned int StepFrequency;
    } AMessage;

    AMessage msg;

    QueueHandle_t xQueue;
    UART3_Init_Advanced(9600,_UART_8_BIT_DATA,_UART_NOPARITY,_UART_ONE_STOPBIT,
                        &_GPIO_MODULE_USART3_PD89);

    while (1)
    {
        UART3_Write_Text("\n\r\n\rEnter Starting Frequency (Hz): ");
        msg.StartFrequency = Read_From_Keyboard();
        UART3_Write_Text("\n\rEnter Ending Frequency (Hz): ");
        msg.EndFrequency = Read_From_Keyboard();
        UART_Write_Text("\n\rEnter Frequency Step (Hz): ");
        msg.StepFrequency = Read_From_Keyboard();

        xQueueSend(xUARTQueue, &msg, pdMS_TO_TICKS(10));      // Send via Queue
```

FIGURE 14.5 (Continued)

```
            UART3_Write_Text("\n\rSweeping... ");              // Display heading
    }
}

//
// Start of MAIN program
// =====================
//
void main()
{
    xUARTQueue = xQueueCreate(1, 6);                           // Create a Queue
//
// Create all the TASKS here
// =========================
//
    // Create Task 1
    xTaskCreate(
        (TaskFunction_t)Task1,
        "Square Waveform Generator",
        configMINIMAL_STACK_SIZE,
        NULL,
        10,
        NULL
    );

    // Create Task 2
    xTaskCreate(
        (TaskFunction_t)Task2,
        "Keyboard Controller",
        configMINIMAL_STACK_SIZE,
        NULL,
        10,
        NULL
    );

//
// Start the RTOS scheduler
//
    vTaskStartScheduler();

//
// Will never reach here
}
```

FIGURE 14.5 (*Continued*)

the new user settings from the queue and then implements them. A structure is used to store the user settings, such as the starting frequency, ending frequency, and the step frequency:

```
    typedef struct Message
    {
      unsigned int StartFrequency;
      unsigned int EndFrequency;
      unsigned int StepFrequency;
    } AMessage;
```

The starting and the ending frequencies are converted into milliseconds and stored in variables FirstValue and EndValue, respectively. Inside the program loop, the frequency is incremented by the step value and the period of the generated waveform is set accordingly. When the period of the generated waveform reaches the required end period, then the process repeats again where the generated waveform is set to have the starting frequency and so on. The frequency of the generated waveform is changed every 5 seconds.

```
Enter Starting Frequency (Hz): 100
Enter Ending Frequency (Hz): 500
Enter Frequency Step (Hz): 100
Sweeping...

Enter Starting Frequency (Hz):
```

FIGURE 14.6   Example run of the program.

Task 2 calls function Read_From_Keyboard() to read the starting frequency, ending frequency, and the step frequency after prompting the user to enter the required data:

```
UART3_Write_Text("\n\r\n\rEnter Starting Frequency (Hz): ");
msg.StartFrequency = Read_From_Keyboard();
UART3_Write_Text("\n\rEnter Ending Frequency (Hz): ");
msg.EndFrequency = Read_From_Keyboard();
UART_Write_Text("\n\rEnter Frequency Step (Hz): ");
msg.StepFrequency = Read_From_Keyboard();
```

The user entered settings are then sent to a queue so that they can be received by Task 1:

```
xQueueSend(xUARTQueue, &msg, pdMS_TO_TICKS(10));
```

An example run of the program is shown in Fig. 14.6. When an oscilloscope is connected to port pin AP2, the frequency of the generated square waveform will be changed from 100 to 500 Hz in steps of 100 Hz every 5 seconds.

14.4 Project 33: RGB light controller

Description: In this project, an RGB (red + green + blue) LED is connected to one of the ports of the development board. The program flashes the three LEDs independently and randomly so that a nice visual effect is created.

Aim: The aim of this project is to show how an RGB LED can be controlled from FreeRTOS using a different task for each LED color.

Circuit diagram: In this project, the KY-016 type RGB LED module is used. As shown in Fig. 14.7, this module has four pins, one pin for each LED, and a common GND pin. 150 Ohm current-limiting resistors are provided on the module to limit the current; therefore, there is no need to use external resistors. Sending a logic 1 (+3.3 V or +5 V) to an LED pin turns ON that LED. By turning the LEDs ON and OFF randomly, we can have a nice visual effect.

The circuit diagram of the project is shown in Fig. 14.8. The connections between the Clicker 2 for STM32 development board and the RGB LED are as follows (some of the mikroBUS 2 socket pins are used):

RGB pin	Development board pin
Red (R)	PD12
Green (G)	PE14
Blue (B)	PD9
–	GND

FIGURE 14.7   KY-016 RGB LED.

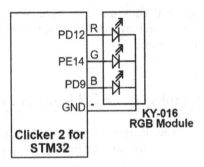

FIGURE 14.8   Circuit diagram of the project.

Program listing: The program listing (**rgb.c**) is shown in Fig. 14.9. The program consists of three tasks, called Red, Green, and Blue, in addition to the Idle task. The three tasks are similar to each other. At the beginning of each task, the LED port controlled by the task is configured as an output port. The remainder of the task codes execute forever in loops established by While statements. Independent random numbers are generated in each task between 101 and 600 ms, and these random numbers determine the flashing rates of each LED. All the three tasks run at the same priority. The net effect is that a nice visual effect is created on the RGB LED module. Built-in function rand() generates random numbers between 0 and 32767. These numbers are converted to be within the limits of 101 and 600 as illustrated below:

When rand() generates 0, the result of rand() %500 + 101 is 101
When rand() generates 499, the result of rand() %500 + 101 is 600
When rand() generates 32767, the result of rand() %500 + 101 is 166

14.5 Project 34: home alarm system with keyboard

Description: This is a simple home alarm system, designed for a two-storey house with upstairs and downstairs. A keyboard is used to control the various operations of the designed alarm system. The details of the system are given later in this section with the help of a block diagram (Fig. 14.10).

```
/*===============================================================================
                         RGB LED LIGHT FLASHING
                         ======================

In this project an RGB LED is conencted to the development board I/O pins. The
program consists of 3 tasks (in addition to the Idle task). A random number
is generated in each task and this is used to set the LED flashing rate. The net
effect is that the LED flashes with a nice visual effect.

Author: Dogan Ibrahim
Date   : September, 2019
File   : rgb.c
===============================================================================*/
#include "main.h"

//
// Define all your Task functions here
// ===================================
//

// Task 1 - RED LED
void Task1(void *pvParameters)
{
    #define RED GPIOD_ODR.B12                            // Pin PD12 is RED LED
    unsigned int random;
    GPIO_Config(&GPIOD_BASE, _GPIO_PINMASK_12, _GPIO_CFG_MODE_OUTPUT);

    while (1)
    {
        random = rand() % 500 + 101;                    // Generate random number
        RED = ~ RED;                                    // Toggle RED
        vTaskDelay(pdMS_TO_TICKS(random));              // Delay
    }
}

// Task 2 - GREEN LED
void Task2(void *pvParameters)
{
    #define GREEN GPIOE_ODR.B14                          // Pin PE14 is GREEN LED
    unsigned int random;
    GPIO_Config(&GPIOE_BASE, _GPIO_PINMASK_14, _GPIO_CFG_MODE_OUTPUT);

    while (1)
    {
        random = rand() % 500 + 101;                    // Generate random number
        GREEN = ~ GREEN;                                // Toggle GREEN
        vTaskDelay(pdMS_TO_TICKS(random));              // Delay
    }
}
```

FIGURE 14.9 rgb.c program listing.

```
// Task 3 - BLUE LED LED
void Task3(void *pvParameters)
{
    #define BLUE GPIOD_ODR.B9                                  // Pin PD9 is BLUE LED
    unsigned int random;
    GPIO_Config(&GPIOD_BASE, _GPIO_PINMASK_9, _GPIO_CFG_MODE_OUTPUT);

    while (1)
    {
        random = rand() % 500 + 101;                           // Generate random number
        BLUE = ~ BLUE;                                         // Toggle BLUE
        vTaskDelay(pdMS_TO_TICKS(random));                     // Delay
    }
}

//
// Start of MAIN program
// =====================
//
void main()
{
//
// Create all the TASKS here
// =========================
//
    // Create Task 1
    xTaskCreate(
        (TaskFunction_t)Task1,
        "RED LED",
        configMINIMAL_STACK_SIZE,
        NULL,
        10,
        NULL
    );

    // Create Task 2
    xTaskCreate(
        (TaskFunction_t)Task2,
        "GREEN LED",
        configMINIMAL_STACK_SIZE,
        NULL,
        10,
        NULL
    );

    // Create Task 3
    xTaskCreate(
        (TaskFunction_t)Task3,
        "BLUE LED",
        configMINIMAL_STACK_SIZE,
        NULL,
        10,
        NULL
    );

//
// Start the RTOS scheduler
//
    vTaskStartScheduler();

//
// Will never reach here
}
```

FIGURE 14.9   (*Continued*)

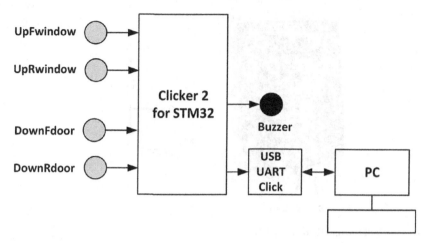

FIGURE 14.10   Block diagram of the system.

Aim: The aim of this project is to show how a simple home alarm system can be designed in a multitasking environment using FreeRTOS.

Block diagram: The block diagram of the system is shown in Fig. 14.10. There are four magnetic reed type sensors in the system (it is easy to expand the number of sensors in this system if desired). Two of the sensors are attached to two windows upstairs and are named as UpFwindow (Up Front window) and UpRwindow (Up Rear window). Two similar sensors are attached to the doors downstairs and are named as DownFdoor (Down Front door) and DownRdoor (Down Rear door). A buzzer is connected to the development board that is activated when the system is armed and one of the doors or windows is opened. The operation of the system is controlled from a PC keyboard for simplicity.

In this project, the KY-021 type mini reed switch module is used to detect when a window or a door is opened. This is a three-pin module with the connections GND, +V, and Signal. GND and +V pins are connected to the ground and power pins, respectively. The Signal pin can be connected to any general purpose input/output pin of the development board. An on-board 10 K resistor is connected between the +V and the S pins, as shown in Fig. 14.11. Reed switches are electrical switches operated by applied magnetic field. These switches consist of a pair of ferromagnetic flexible metal contacts in a sealed glass envelope (see Fig. 14.12). The contacts are normally open, closing when magnetic field (e.g., a magnet) is present near the contacts, and re-open, that is, return to their normal state when the magnetic field is removed. Reed switches are used in door and window mechanisms to detect when they are open or closed, and in many other security-based applications. In security applications, the reed switch and a magnet are mounted at either sides of an opening window or door as shown in Fig. 14.13. When the door or the window is closed, the magnet is close to the switch and the output state of the switch is at Logic 0. When the door or the window is opened, the magnet is separated from the switch and as a result the switch state goes to Logic 1.

A passive buzzer is used in this project so that when Logic 1 is sent to the buzzer, it generates sound at a fixed frequency. In a real alarm system, the buzzer may be replaced with a relay operated mains siren.

FIGURE 14.11   KY-021 magnetic reed switch.

FIGURE 14.12   A typical magnetic reed switch.

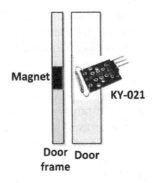

FIGURE 14.13   Reed switch and magnet.

Operation of the system is through a keyboard. Valid keyboard commands are as follows:

Full: set the alarm to scan all four sensors

Part: set the alar to scan only the downstairs sensors (DownFdoor and DownRdoor)

Reset: clear alarm settings

Entering **Full** followed by the Enter key will arm all the sensors so that the system scans all four sensors to check if there is any possible entry to the house. Entering **Part** followed by the Enter key arms only the downstairs sensors so that it is safe to walk upstairs without activating the alarm. When the system is armed, the user is given 30 seconds to leave the house. Similarly, when a switch is activated (e.g., the front door opened), the system gives 30 seconds for it to be disarmed before setting the alarm. Entering **Reset** followed by the Enter key cancels the alarm setting, that

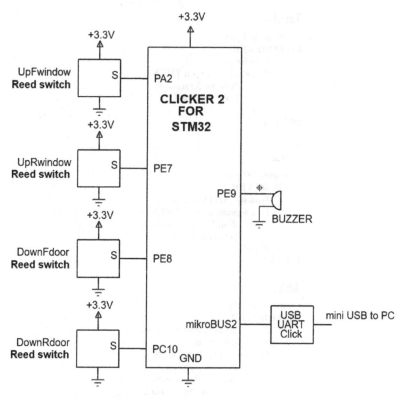

FIGURE 14.14   Circuit diagram of the project.

is, disarms the system. This command is only activated if the correct password is entered at the keyboard. For demonstration purposes, the password in this project is set to FreeRTOS.

Circuit diagram: Fig. 14.14 shows the circuit diagram of the project. The following connections were made between the Clicker 2 for STM32 development board and the external world (these pins are located on the connector of the mikroBUS Socket 1 of the development board):

Clicker 2 for STM32 pin	Connected to
PA2	UpFwindow sensor
PE7	UpRwindow sensor
PE8	DownFdoor
PC10	DownRdoor
PE9	Buzzer
mikroBUS 2	USB UART Click

A USB UART Click board is connected to mikroBUS Socket 2 of the development board. This board is connected to a PC using a mini USB cable. Commands can be entered on the PC using a terminal emulation software as in the previous PC-based projects.

The operation of the program is shown in the PDL in Fig. 14.15.

Task 1

Configure I/O ports
DO FOREVER
  Wait for event flag 1
  IF a window is open **THEN**
    Wait for 30 seconds
    Set event flag 3
  ENDIF
ENDDO

Task 2

Configure I/O ports
DO FOREVER
  Wait for event flag 1 or 2
  IF a window is open **THEN**
    Wait for 30 seconds
    Set event flag 3
  ENDIF
ENDDO

Task 3

Configure UART
DO FOREVER
  Read command from keyboard
  Echo the command
  IF command is Full **THEN**
    Display message
    Wait for 30 seconds
    Set event flags 1 and 2
  ELSE IF command is Part **THEN**
    Display message
    Wait for 30 seconds
    Set event flag 2
    Clear event flag 1
  ELSE IF command is Reset **THEN**
    Read password from keyboard
    IF correct password **THEN**
      Display message
      Clear event flags 1, 2, 3
    ENDIF
  ENDIF
ENDDO

Task 4

Configure I/O ports
DO FOREVER
  IF event flag 3 is set **THEN**
    Activate buzzer
  ELSE
    Deactivate buzzer
  ENDIF
ENDDO

FIGURE 14.15 Operation of the program.

Program listing: The program listing (program: **homealarm.c**) is shown in Fig. 14.16. The program consists of four tasks in addition to the Idle task. Resource synchronization between the tasks is done using event flags. The following event flags are used in the program:

Event flag 1	When set (1), it means that both upstairs and downstairs are armed
	When reset (0), it means that upstairs and downstairs are not armed
Event flag 2	When set (1), it means that downstairs only is armed.
	When reset (0), it means that downstairs is not armed
Event flag 3	When set (1), it forces the buzzer to be ON
	When reset (1), it forces the buzzer to be OFF

```
/*==============================================================================
                            HOME ALARM SYSTEM
                            =================

This is a simple home alarm system. The system has 4 reed switch type sensors,
2 upstairs (attached to windows) and 2 downstairs (attached to doors). The system
can be armed partially or fully. In partial arm the upstairs sensors are disabled.
In full arm all the sensors are active. A buzzer sounds if any door opens when
in armed mode. The system has 30 seconds exit delay and 30 seconds entry delay.
A password is required to reset the system.

Author: Dogan Ibrahim
Date  : September, 2019
File  : homealarm.c
==============================================================================*/
#include "main.h"
#include "event_groups.h"
EventGroupHandle_t xEventGroup;                         // Event group handle

//
// Define all your Task functions here
// ===================================
//

// Task 1 - UPSTAIRS CONTROLLER
void Task1(void *pvParameters)
{
    #define UpFwindow GPIOA_IDR.B2
    #define UpRwindow GPIOE_IDR.B7
    #define OPEN 1
    #define CLOSED 0

    #define BIT_1 (1 << 1)
    #define BIT_2 (1 << 2)
    #define BIT_3 (1 << 3)

    const TickType_t xEntryDelay = pdMS_TO_TICKS(30000);
    EventBits_t uxBits;

    GPIO_Config(&GPIOA_BASE, _GPIO_PINMASK_2, _GPIO_CFG_MODE_INPUT);
    GPIO_Config(&GPIOE_BASE, _GPIO_PINMASK_7, _GPIO_CFG_MODE_INPUT);

    while (1)
    {
        // If ALL is armed (i.e. if event flag 1 is set)
        uxBits = xEventGroupWaitBits(xEventGroup, BIT_1, pdFALSE, pdFALSE,
                portMAX_DELAY);
```

FIGURE 14.16 homealarm.c program listing.

```
        if(UpFwindow == OPEN || UpRwindow == OPEN)
        {
            vTaskDelay(xEntryDelay);
            // Set event flag 3 (activate buzzer)
            uxBits = xEventGroupSetBits(xEventGroup, BIT_3);
        }
        taskYIELD();
    }
}


// Task 2 - DOWNSTAIRS CONTROLLER
void Task2(void *pvParameters)
{
    #define DownFdoor GPIOE_IDR.B8
    #define DownRdoor GPIOC_IDR.B10
    #define OPEN 1
    #define CLOSED 0

    #define BIT_1 (1 << 1)
    #define BIT_2 (1 << 2)
    #define BIT_3 (1 << 3)

    const TickType_t xEntryDelay = pdMS_TO_TICKS(30000);
    EventBits_t uxBits;

    GPIO_Config(&GPIOE_BASE, _GPIO_PINMASK_8, _GPIO_CFG_MODE_INPUT);
    GPIO_Config(&GPIOC_BASE, _GPIO_PINMASK_10, _GPIO_CFG_MODE_INPUT);

    while (1)
    {
        // If all is armed (i.e. if event flag 1 or 2 is set)
        uxBits = xEventGroupWaitBits(xEventGroup, BIT_1 | BIT_2, pdFALSE, pdFALSE,
                portMAX_DELAY);

        if(DownFdoor == OPEN || DownRdoor == OPEN)
        {
            vTaskDelay(xEntryDelay);
            // Set event flag 3 (activate buzzer)
            uxBits = xEventGroupSetBits(xEventGroup, BIT_3);
        }
        taskYIELD();
    }
}



// Task 3 - UART Controller
void Task3(void *pvParameters)
{
    #define BIT_1 (1 << 1)
    #define BIT_2 (1 << 2)
    #define BIT_3 (1 << 3)

    const TickType_t xExitDelay = pdMS_TO_TICKS(30000);
    EventBits_t uxBits;

    unsigned char ch, j, Command[10], pwd[10];

    UART3_Init_Advanced(9600,_UART_8_BIT_DATA,_UART_NOPARITY,_UART_ONE_STOPBIT,
                    &_GPIO_MODULE_USART3_PD89);
```

FIGURE 14.16 (*Continued*)

```
while (1)
{
    UART3_Write_Text("\n\rEnter a command (Full, Part, Reset): ");
    // Get the command
    j = 0;
    while(1)
    {
        ch = UART3_Read();                          // Read a char
        UART3_Write(ch);                            // Echo the char
        if(ch == '\r') break;                       // If Enter
            Command[j] = ch;                            // Store the char
            j++;                                        // Increment pointer
        }
        Command[j] = '\0';                              // Terminator
        if(strstr(Command, "Full") > 0)
        {
            UART3_Write_Text("\n\rAlarm set for UPSTAIRS and DOWNSTAIRS. You have 30
            seconds to exit\n\r");
            vTaskDelay(xExitDelay);
            uxBits = xEventGroupSetBits(xEventGroup, BIT_1 | BIT_2);
        }
        else if(strstr(Command, "Part") > 0)
        {
            UART3_Write_Text("\n\rAlarm set for DOWNSTAIRS only. Go Upstairs now\n\r");
            vTaskDelay(xExitDelay);
            uxBits = xEventGroupSetBits(xEventGroup, BIT_2);
            uxBits = xEventGroupClearBits(xEventGroup, BIT_1);
        }
        else if(strstr(Command, "Reset") > 0)
        {
            UART3_Write_Text("\n\rEnter Password: ");
            // Get the password
            j = 0;
            while(1)
            {
                ch = UART3_Read();                          // Read a char
                UART3_Write(ch);                            // Echo the char
                if(ch == '\r') break;                       // If Enter
                pwd[j] = ch;                                // Store the char
                j++;                                        // Increment pointer
            }
            pwd[j] = '\0';                                  // Terminator
            if(strstr(pwd, "FreeRTOS") > 0)                 // Correct pwd?
            {
                UART3_Write_Text("\n\rPassword correct...");
                uxBits = xEventGroupClearBits(xEventGroup, BIT_1 | BIT_2); // Disarm
                uxBits = xEventGroupClearBits(xEventGroup, BIT_3);         // Buzzer OFF
            }
        }
    }
}


// Task 4 - Buzzer Controller
void Task4(void *pvParameters)
{
    #define BIT_1 (1 << 1)
    #define BIT_2 (1 << 2)
    #define BIT_3 (1 << 3)
    #define BUZZER GPIOE_ODR.B9

    EventBits_t uxBits;
```

FIGURE 14.16 (*Continued*)

```
GPIO_Config(&GPIOE_BASE, _GPIO_PINMASK_9, _GPIO_CFG_MODE_OUTPUT);

while (1)
{
     // Wait for efn 3
     uxBits = xEventGroupWaitBits(xEventGroup, BIT_3, pdFALSE, pdFALSE,
          pdMS_TO_TICKS(100));
          if((uxBits & (BIT_3)) == (BIT_3))          // If efn 3 set
              BUZZER = 1;                            // Buzzer ON
          else
              BUZZER = 0;                            // Buzzer OFF
   }
}


//
// Start of MAIN program
// =====================
//
void main()
{
    xEventGroup = xEventGroupCreate();              // Create event group
//
// Create all the TASKS here
// =========================
//
    // Create Task 1
    xTaskCreate(
         (TaskFunction_t)Task1,
         "UPSTAIRS Controller",
         configMINIMAL_STACK_SIZE,
         NULL,
         10,
         NULL
    );


    // Create Task 2
    xTaskCreate(
         (TaskFunction_t)Task2,
         "DOWNSTAIRS Controller",
         configMINIMAL_STACK_SIZE,
         NULL,
         10,
         NULL
    );


    // Create Task 3
    xTaskCreate(
         (TaskFunction_t)Task3,
         "UART Controller",
         configMINIMAL_STACK_SIZE,
         NULL,
         10,
         NULL
    );


    // Create Task 4
    xTaskCreate(
         (TaskFunction_t)Task4,
         "BUZZER Controller",
         configMINIMAL_STACK_SIZE,
         NULL,
         10,
         NULL
```

FIGURE 14.16 (*Continued*)

```
    );
//
// Start the RTOS scheduler
//
    vTaskStartScheduler();

//
// Will never reach here
}
```
FIGURE 14.16 (*Continued*)

Detailed operation of each task is summarized as follows:

Task 1

This is the upstairs controller task. At the beginning of this task, UpFwindow and UpRwindow are assigned to port pins PA2 and PE7, respectively, and these port pins are configured as outputs. The remainder of the task runs in an endless loop. Inside this loop the task waits until Event flag 1 is set. That is, until the system is armed. The task then checks the windows upstairs to make sure that they are closed. If a window is open, then either UpFwindow or UpRwindow sensor state will be OPEN. As a result of this, Event flag 3 will be set so that the alarm can be activated. Notice that 30 seconds of delay is inserted here as entry delay so that the user has enough time to enter the home and reset the system before the alarm activates.

Task 2

This is the downstairs controller task. Its operation is very similar to Task 1. Here, DownFdoor and DownRdoor reassigned to port pins PE8 and PC10, respectively, and these port pins are configured as outputs. This task waits for either Event flag 1 or 2 to be set before it checks the state of the door sensors. The remainder of the task operates as in Task 1, where the task checks whether the doors are closed or not and sets Event flag 3 to activate the buzzer if a door is open.

Task 3

This is the UART controller task. At the beginning of the task, UART is configured to operate at 9600 baud. The remainder of the task operates in an endless loop formed using a While statement. Inside this loop, the user is prompted to enter a command. Valid commands are Full, Part, and Reset. A command is received from the keyboard and is echoed back on the screen using the following code. The command is stored in character array Command and is terminated with a NULL character:

```
UART3_Write_Text("\n\rEnter a command (Full, Part, Reset): ");
j = 0;
while(1)
{
   ch = UART3_Read();   // Read a char
   UART3_Write(ch);   // Echo the char
   if(ch=='\r') break;   // If Enter
   Command[j] = ch;   // Store the char
   j + +;   // Increment pointer
}
Command[j] = '\0';
```

As described earlier, commands Full and Part arm either the complete system or the downstairs only. The entered command is checked using the built-in function strstr(), which

```
Enter a command (Full, Part, Reset): Full
Alarm set for UPSTAIRS and DOWNSTAIRS. You have 30 seconds to exit

Enter a command (Full, Part, Reset): Part
Alarm set for DOWNSTAIRS only. Go Upstairs now

Enter a command (Full, Part, Reset): Reset
Enter Password: FreeRTOS
Password correct...

Enter a command (Full, Part, Reset): _
```

FIGURE 14.17   User commands.

compares two strings and returns a NULL if the first string does not include the second string. If command **Full** is entered, a message is displayed and the task waits for 30 seconds as the exit delay so that the user can leave home without activating the alarm. After this delay, both Event flags 1 and 2 are set to arm the complete system. If command **Part** is entered, a message is displayed and the system again waits for 30 seconds as the exit delay and then sets Event flag 2, and at the same time clears Event flag 1. Command **Reset** is used to reset the system, that is, to disarm the system. This command should be entered when coming home so that the system can be disarmed. This command requires the user to enter the correct password before the system is reset. The password is hardcoded as FreeRTOS in this application. Event flags 1, 2, and 3 are cleared when the Reset command is entered so that the system is disarmed and at the same time the buzzer is deactivated.

Task 4
This is the buzzer controller task. This task waits for Event flag 3 to be set, and if it is set, it activates the buzzer, otherwise the buzzer is deactivated.

Fig. 14.17 shows the user commands entered on the keyboard.

14.6 Project 35: ultrasonic car parking with buzzer

Description: In this project, an ultrasonic sensor is used to measure the distance to objects while parking a vehicle. The sensor is assumed to be mounted at the rear of the vehicle. A buzzer sounds to indicate the distance to any object behind the vehicle such that the activation rate of the buzzer increases as the vehicle gets closer to an object. The measured distance is displayed in centimeters on the PC screen for convenience.

Aim: The aim of this project is to show how an ultrasonic sensor can be used in a multitasking environment.

Block diagram: Fig. 14.18 shows the block diagram of the project.

Circuit diagram: In this project, the HC-SR-04 type (Fig. 14.19) ultrasonic sensor pair is used. The output of this sensors is +5 V and, therefore, not compatible with the inputs of the Clicker 2 for STM32 development board. Resistive potential divider circuit is, therefore, used to lower the voltage to +3.3 V. The voltage at the output of the potential divider resistive circuit is:

$$V_o = 5 \text{ V} \times 2 \text{ K} / (2 \text{ K} + 1 \text{ K}) = 3.3 \text{ V}$$

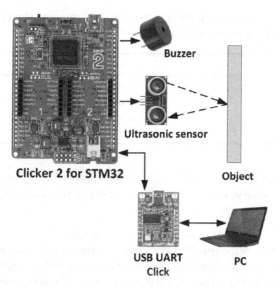

FIGURE 14.18   Block diagram of the project.

FIGURE 14.19   HC-SR-04 ultrasonic sensor module.

The HC-SR-04 ultrasonic sensor pair has the following specifications:

- Operating voltage (current): 5 V (2 mA) operation
- Detection distance: 2–450 cm
- Input trigger signal: 10 μs TTL
- Sensor angle: not more than 15 degrees

The sensor modules have the following pins:

Vcc	+V power
Trig	Trigger input
Echo	Echo output
Gnd	Power ground

An active piezoelectric buzzer module is used in this project. The connection between the development board and the external world is as follows:

Development board pin	External component pin
PA2	trig (ultrasonic sensor)
PE7	echo (ultrasonic sensor)
PC10	buzzer
mikroBUS 2 socket	USB UART Click

Ultrasonic sensor modules are mainly used in distance-measuring applications in mobile robotics, obstacle avoidance systems, and vehicle-parking applications. The principle of operation of the ultrasonic sensor module is as follows:

- A 10-μs high-level (+V) trigger pulse is sent to the module.
- The module then sends out eight 40-kHz square wave signals and automatically detects the returned (echoed) pulse signal (if the signal hit an object and returned by the object).
- If a high-level (+V) echo signal is returned, then the width of this echo signal is equal to the time taken by the ultrasonic pulse to leave and return to the sensor.
- The distance to the object is calculated as:

$$\text{Distance to object (in meters)} = \frac{\text{echo signal in seconds} \times \text{speed of sound}}{2}$$

The speed of sound is 340 m/s, or 0.034 cm/μs
Therefore,

$$\text{Distance to object (in cm)} = \frac{(\text{echo signal in μs}) \times 0.034}{2}$$

or,

$$\text{Distance to object (in cm)} = (\text{echo signal in μs}) \times 0.017$$

Fig. 14.20 shows the principle of operation of the ultrasonic sensor module. For example, if the width of the echo signal is 294 μs, then the distance to the object is calculated as:

Distance to object (cm) = 294 × 0.017 = 5 cm

The easiest way to determine the time is described in the following steps:

1. Send 10 μs TRIGGER pulse to ultrasonic module
2. Listen for Echo
3. Start Timer when ECHO HIGH is received
4. Stop Timer when ECHO goes LOW
5. Read Timer Value
6. Convert it to Distance
7. Process the data as required (e.g., display distance)

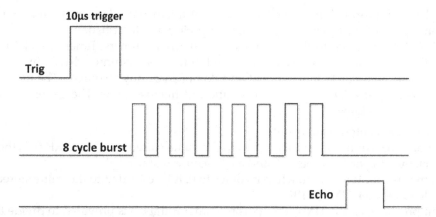

FIGURE 14.20   Operation of the ultrasonic sensor module.

Fig. 14.21 shows the circuit diagram of the project. The trig and echo pins of the ultrasonic sensor are connected to port pins PA2 and PE7 of the development board, respectively. Echo output of the ultrasonic sensor is connected to port pin PE7 through potential divider resistors to drop the voltage levels to +3.3 V. The buzzer is connected to port pin PC10.

Program listing: In this project, we need to generate a 10-μs pulse to trigger the ultrasonic sensor. Additionally, the width of the echo signal must be measured in microseconds. The timer and tick count of FreeRTOS do not provide the required timing resolution. The trigger pulse is generated using the built-in function Delay_us() of the mikroC for ARM compiler. This function creates a delay in microseconds for the duration specified in the function parameter. The width of the echo pulse is measured using one of the internal timers of the STM32F407 microcontroller (this is the ARM-based microcontroller used on the Clicker 2 for STM32 development board). The timer operation of the STM32F407 microcontroller is rather complex, and it is not the intention of this book to describe it in detail here. Interested readers

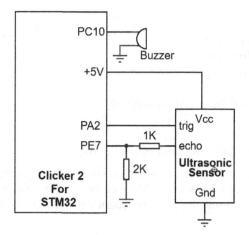

FIGURE 14.21   Circuit diagram of the project.

can find detailed information on the STM series of microcontrollers on the Internet. In this section, only parts of the timer necessary for our project are described.

The STM32F407 microcontroller provides many hardware timers. Timers 2–5 (TIM2–TIM5) are general purpose timers consisting of a 16-bit auto-reload counter, driven by a prescaler. These timers are completely independent and do not share any resources. The timers can be used to measure pulse lengths with a resolution of microseconds. The general features of these timers are as follows:

- 16-bit up/down auto-reload counters
- If the timer is counting up and it reaches to the value stored in TIMx_ARR (x is the timer number), then the timer resets to 0 and a new count is started.
- If the timer is counting down, when it comes to 0, it is re-loaded to the value stored in auto-reload register TIMx_ARR.
- A 16-bit prescaler, called TIMx_PSC (x is the timer number) is provided to divide the clock by any factor between 1 and 65535.

In this project, we shall be using a timer in what is known as the Time-Base mode, which can be used to measure the width of an event. In this mode, the counter can be configured to count up or down. By default, the counting is up. The following timer registers are used in Time-Base mode:

- Counter register, TIMx_CNT
- Prescaler register, TIMx_PSC
- Auto-reload register, TIMx_ARR

Additionally, the following timer register should be configured for the correct operation of a timer:

- Enable clock for the timer, RCC_APB1ENR.TIMxEN = 1
- Disable counting, TIMx_CR1.CEN = 0
- Enable counting, TIMx_CR1.CEN = 1

The steps to measure an external pulse width are as follows:

- Enable timer clock
- Disable counting
- Configure the prescaler register
- Configure the auto-reload register
- Wait until rising edge of the pulse is detected
- Start counting
- Wait until falling edge of the pulse is detected
- Stop counting
- Read the count value
- Convert the count value into required timing units

In this book, we will be using Timer 2 (TIM2). The clock frequency of the STM32F407 processor is set to 168 MHz (see Figure xx). TIM2 receives its clock from the APB1 bus. As shown in Figure xx, in our applications, the clock frequency of TIM2 is set to 84 MHz. The period of the timer clock is therefore:

Period = 1 /f = 1 /84 MHz

or, period = 0.0119047 μs

If we set the prescaler value to 1000, then the timer clock period will be:

Period = 1000 × 0.0119047, i.e., period = 11.9047 μs

We can load the timer register TIM2_CNT initially with 0 and then start the counter as soon as the rising edge of the echo pulse is detected. The counter is then stopped as soon as the falling edge of the echo pulse is detected. The value stored in register TIM2_CNT is then the duration of the pulse in terms of counter value. Multiplying this number with the clock period of 11.9047 will give us the pulse width in microseconds. Distance to the object in centimeters is then determined by multiplying the pulse width with 0.017, as shown earlier in this section. Auto-reload register can be loaded with its maximum value so that the timer does not reload.

Fig. 14.22 shows the program listing (program: **ultrasonic.c**). The program consists of two tasks in addition to the Idle task. Task 1 is the ultrasonic controller task, while Task 2 controls the buzzer. Communication between the two tasks is through a queue created in the main program. The operation of the program is described in the following PDL:

TASK 1
Configure trig as output and echo as input
Initialize UART
Configure TIM2 registers

DO FOREVER
Set trig = 0
Send a 10-μs pulse
Set trig = 0
Wait for rising edge of echo
Start counting
Wait for falling edge of echo
Stop counting
Read the timer count
Convert the count into microseconds
Calculate distance to the object
Send the distance to Task 2 through a queue
Display the distance in centimeters on screen
Wait 500 ms

ENDDO
TASK 2
DO FOREVER
  Receive the distance from the queue
  IF the distance < 100 cm **THEN**
    Call function BuzzerSound with different values to sound the buzzer
  ENDIF
ENDDO
Function BuzzerSound
Configure Buzzer port as output
Activate the Buzzer
Delay by the value specified by TASK 2
Deactivate the Buzzer
Delay by the value specified by TASK 2

```
/*==============================================================================
                        ULTRASONIC CAR PARKING
                        ======================

In this project an ultrasonic sensor module is used to aid in parking. An
ultrasnic sensor module is mounted at the rear panel of teh vehicle. A buzzer
makes sound when the sensor is near an obstacle. The sound frequency changes
depending on the distance of any objects from the sensor. The distance to an
object is displayed on the PC screen for convenience and for testing the program

Author: Dogan Ibrahim
Date  : September, 2019
File  : ultrasonic.c
==============================================================================*/
#include "main.h"
QueueHandle_t xQueue;                                       // Queue handle

//
// Define all your Task functions here
// ====================================
//

// Task 1 - ULTRASONIC CONTROLLER
void Task1(void *pvParameters)
{
    #define trig GPIOA_ODR.B2
    #define echo GPIOE_IDR.B7

    float Elapsed;
    unsigned int Present, IntDistance;
    char Txt[14];

    UART3_Init_Advanced(9600,_UART_8_BIT_DATA,_UART_NOPARITY,_UART_ONE_STOPBIT,
                    &_GPIO_MODULE_USART3_PD89);
    GPIO_Config(&GPIOA_BASE, _GPIO_PINMASK_2, _GPIO_CFG_MODE_OUTPUT);
    GPIO_Config(&GPIOE_BASE, _GPIO_PINMASK_7, _GPIO_CFG_MODE_INPUT);
    trig = 0;

    RCC_APB1ENR.TIM2EN = 1;                         // Enable clock to TIM2
    TIM2_CR1.CEN = 0;                               // Disable TIM2 count
    TIM2_PSC = 1000;                                // Set prescaler to 1000
    TIM2_ARR = 65535;                               // Set Auto-reload register

    while (1)
    {
        TIM2_CNT = 0;                               // Set counter to 0
        trig = 1;                                   // Send trig pulse
        Delay_us(10);                               // Wait 10 us
        trig = 0;                                   // Reset trig pulse

        vTaskPrioritySet(NULL, 11);                 // Increase priority
        while(echo == 0);                           // Wait for rising edge
        TIM2_CR1.CEN = 1;                           // Start counter
        while(echo == 1);                           // Wait for falling edge
        TIM2_CR1.CEN = 0;                           // Stop counter
        vTaskPrioritySet(NULL, 10);                 // Priority back to normal
        Present = TIM2_CNT;                         // Get counter value
        Elapsed = Present * 11.9047;                // Calculate pulse time
        Elapsed = 0.017 * Elapsed;                  // Distance in cm
        IntDistance = (int)Elapsed;                 // Distance as int
```

FIGURE 14.22   ultrasonic.c program listing.

```
            xQueueSend(xQueue, &IntDistance, pdMS_TO_TICKS(10));
            FloatToStr(Elapsed, Txt);
            Ltrim(Txt);                              // Remove spaces
            UART3_Write_Text(Txt);                   // Display distance
            UART3_Write_Text(" cm\n\r");             // In cm
            vTaskDelay(pdMS_TO_TICKS(500));          // Wait 500ms
    }
}

void BuzzerSound(int F)
{
    #define BUZZER GPIOC_ODR.B10

    GPIO_Config(&GPIOC_BASE, _GPIO_PINMASK_10, _GPIO_CFG_MODE_OUTPUT);

    BUZZER =1;                                       // Buzzer ON
    vTaskDelay(pdMS_TO_TICKS(F));                    // Wait F ms
    BUZZER = 0;                                       // Buzzer OFF
    vTaskDelay(pdMS_TO_TICKS(F));                    // Wait Fms
}

// Task 2 - Buzzer Controller
void Task2(void *pvParameters)
{
    unsigned int Distance;

    while (1)
    {
        if(xQueueReceive(xQueue, &Distance, 0 ) == pdPASS)    // If data in queue
        {
            if(Distance < 100)                                // If distance < 100
            {
                if(Distance < 10)
                    BuzzerSound(50);                          // Sound buzzer
                else if(Distance < 20)
                    BuzzerSound(150);                         // Sound buzzer
                else if(Distance < 30)
                    BuzzerSound(250);                         // Sound buzzer
                else if(Distance < 40)
                    BuzzerSound(350);                         // Sound buzzer
                else if(Distance < 50)
                    BuzzerSound(450);                         // Sound buzzer
                else if(Distance < 70)
                    BuzzerSound(700);                         // Sound buzzer
                else if(Distance < 90)
                    BuzzerSound(900);                         // Sound buzzer
            }

        }
    }
}


//
// Start of MAIN program
// =====================
//
void main()
{
    xQueue = xQueueCreate(1, 2);                     // Create queue
```

FIGURE 14.22   (Continued)

```
//
// Create all the TASKS here
// =========================
//
    // Create Task 1
    xTaskCreate(
        (TaskFunction_t)Task1,
        "Ultrasonic Controller",
        configMINIMAL_STACK_SIZE,
        NULL,
        10,
        NULL
    );


    // Create Task 2
    xTaskCreate(
        (TaskFunction_t)Task2,
        "Buzzer Controller",
        configMINIMAL_STACK_SIZE,
        NULL,
        10,
        NULL
    );

//
// Start the RTOS scheduler
//
    vTaskStartScheduler();

//
// Will never reach here
}
```

FIGURE 14.22   (*Continued*)

Notice that the priority of TASK 1 is increased (i.e., to 11) temporarily after sending the trigger pulse to the ultrasonic sensor so that the timing is not interrupted. As soon as the falling edge of the echo pulse is detected, the priority is lowered back to its normal value (i.e., to 10):

```
vTaskPrioritySet(NULL, 11);      // Increase the priority
while(echo == 0);        // Wait for rising edge of echo
TIM2_CR1.CEN = 1;        // Start timer
while(echo == 1);        // Wait for falling edge of echo
TIM2_CR1.CEN = 0;        // Stop the timer
vTaskPrioritySet(NULL, 10);      // Priority back to normal
```

Activation of the buzzer depends on the distance to the object. If this distance is greater than 100 cm, then no action is taken, that is, the buzzer is not activated. If, on the other hand, the distance to the object is less than 100 cm, then the buzzer sounds at different rates depending on the distance to the object. As this distance gets smaller, the frequency of the sound generated by the buzzer is increased to let the user know that the object is very close to the sensor. This is done in Task 2 as follows:

```
if(Distance < 100)
{
  if(Distance < 10)
    BuzzerSound(50);
```

```
    else if(Distance < 20)
      BuzzerSound(150);
    else if(Distance < 30)
      BuzzerSound(250);
    else if(Distance < 40)
      BuzzerSound(350);
    else if(Distance < 50)
      BuzzerSound(450);
    else if(Distance < 70)
      BuzzerSound(700);
    else if(Distance < 90)
      BuzzerSound(900);
  }
```

For example, if the distance to the object is less than 10 cm, the buzzer is turned ON and OFF every 50 ms. If this distance is less than 50 cm, then the buzzer is turned ON and OFF every 350 ms.

Fig. 14.23 shows the distance displayed on the PC screen.

As shown in Fig. 14.24, the project was constructed on a breadboard and connections were made to the development board using jumper wires.

```
24.89272 cm
26.91653 cm
25.49986 cm
24.28559 cm
21.85703 cm
25.0951 cm
31.77364 cm
42.2974 cm
37.44028 cm
36.42838 cm
38.04742 cm
40.47598 cm
```

FIGURE 14.23 Distance displayed on the PC screen.

FIGURE 14.24 The project was constructed on a breadboard.

14.7 Project 36: stepper motor project

Description: This project shows how to use a stepper motor in a multitasking environment. In this project, a small stepper motor is used and its operation is controlled from the keyboard by entering the following commands:

- **Direction of rotation**: This can be CW (clockwise) or CCW (counterclockwise).
- **Speed**: This is the number of revolutions per minute (RPM).
- **Turns**: Number of required to complete revolutions of the motor
- **Start**: Starts the motor rotating with the specified parameters.

Aim: The aim of this project is to show how a stepper motor can be used in a multitasking environment.

Block diagram: Fig. 14.25 shows the block diagram of the project.

Stepper motors

Stepper motors are DC motors that rotate in small steps. These motors have several coils that are energized in sequence, causing the motor to rotate one step at a time. Stepper motors have the advantages that very precise positioning or speed control of the motor shaft can be achieved. These motors are used in many precision motion control applications, robotic arms, and mobile robots to drive the wheels.

There are basically two types of stepper motors: unipolar and bipolar.

Unipolar stepper motors

Unipolar stepper motors have four windings with a common center tap on each pair of windings (see Fig. 14.26). Therefore, there are normally five or six leads depending on whether or not the common leads are joined.

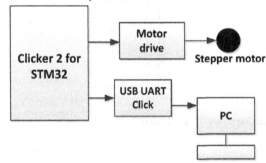

FIGURE 14.25 Block diagram of the project.

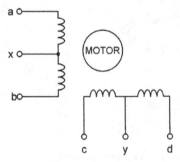

FIGURE 14.26 Unipolar stepper motor windings.

Unipolar motors can be rotated in reverse by reversing the sequence of applied pulses. Unipolar stepper motors can be driven in full stepping mode or in half stepping mode. Most popular drive modes are one-phase full-step, two-phase full-step, and two-phase half-step.

In one-phase full-step mode, as given in Table 14.1, each motor winding receives one pulse per step. This mode has the disadvantage that the available torque is low.

In two-phase full-step mode, as given in Table 14.2, two motor windings receive pulses per step. The advantage of this mode is that a higher torque is available from the motor.

In two-phase half-step mode, as given in Table 14.3, two motor windings sometimes receive pulses and sometimes only one winding receives a pulse. Because the motor is driven at half-step mode, eight steps are required to complete a cycle, instead of four. This mode gives higher precision, but at the expense of lower torque.

TABLE 14.1   One-phase full-step mode.

Step	a	c	b	d
1	1	0	0	0
2	0	1	0	0
3	0	0	1	0
4	0	0	0	1

TABLE 14.2   One-phase full-step mode.

Step	a	c	b	d
1	1	0	0	1
2	1	1	0	0
3	0	1	1	0
4	0	0	1	1

TABLE 14.3   Two-phase half-step mode.

Step	a	c	b	d
1	1	0	0	0
2	1	1	0	0
3	0	1	0	0
4	0	1	1	0
5	0	0	1	0
6	0	0	1	1
7	0	0	0	1
8	1	0	0	1

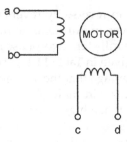

FIGURE 14.27 Bipolar stepper motor windings.

TABLE 14.4 Bipolar stepper motor driving sequence.

Step	a	c	b	d
1	+	−	−	−
2	−	+	−	−
3	−	−	+	−
4	−	−	−	+

Bipolar stepper motors

Bipolar stepper motors have one winding per phase as shown in Fig. 14.27. Bipolar motor driver circuits are more complicated since the current in the windings needs to be reversed in order to rotate them in the reverse direction.

Table 14.4 presents the steps required to drive a bipolar stepper motor. Here, +and − signs refer to the polarity of the voltages applied to the motor leads.

Speed of a stepper motor

The speed of a stepper motor depends on the time between the pulses given to its windings. For faster speeds, the pulses must be given with shorter delays between them. If T is the time between the pulses and β is the step constant of the motor, the motor rotates by β/T steps in 1 second. Since a complete revolution is 360°, the number of revolutions in a second is $\beta/360T$. The speed of a motor is normally quoted in RPM and therefore:

$$RPM = \frac{60\beta}{360T}$$

or, RPM = $\beta/6T$

where RPM is the number of revolutions per minute, β is the step constant of the motor in degrees, and T is the time between the steps in seconds.

As an example, assume that the step constant of a stepper motor is 10 degrees ($\beta = 10°$). If we want to rotate this motor at a speed of 1000 RPM (assuming that the motor is capable of rotating this fast), the time between the pulses is calculated as:

$$T = \frac{\beta}{6RPM} = \frac{10}{6 \times 1000} = 1.66 \text{ ms}$$

Therefore, the pulses between each step must be 1.66 ms.

Movement of the motor shaft

In some applications, we may want the motor shaft to rotate a specified amount and we need to know how many pulses to send to the motor. If β is the step constant of the motor and we want the shaft to rotate by v degrees, the required number of pulses is given by:

$$n = \frac{v}{\beta}$$

For example, assuming that the step constant is 5° ($\beta = 5$) and that we want the motor to rotate by 200 degrees, the required number of steps is:

$$n = \frac{200}{5} = 40$$

Motor rotation time

Sometimes we may want the motor to rotate for a given time and we want to know how many pulses to apply to the motor. If T is the time between the pulses and we send n pulses to the motor, the rotation time T_0 can be calculated as follows:

$T_0 = nT$

For example, assuming that the time between the pulses is 1 ms, if we want the motor to rotate for 5 seconds, the required number of pulses is given by:

$$N = \frac{T_0}{T} = \frac{5}{0.001} = 5000$$

Stepper motors can be driven by several ways, such as using bipolar transistors, MOSFET transistors, or integrated circuits such as L293, ULN2003, and so on. The Stepper Click boards manufactured by mikroElektronika can be plugged directly to the mikroBUS sockets of the Clicker 2 for STM development board and there are versions for driving both unipolar and bipolar stepper motors. An example unipolar stepper motor driver, called the Stepper 3 Click, is shown in Fig. 14.28.

Circuit diagram: In this project, a small 28BYJ-48 type unipolar stepper motor (see Fig. 14.29) is used. This motor has the following specifications:

Rated voltage	5 V
Number of phases	4
Gear ratio	64
Frequency	100 Hz
Step angle	11.25° / step
Maximum speed	18 RPM

In this project, the motor is driven using a ULN2003 IC-based motor driver module shown in Fig. 14.30 together with its circuit diagram. This module has four input connections labeled IN1, IN2, IN3, and IN4. The motor is plugged into the socket in the middle of the module. Four LEDs, labeled A, B, C, and D, are provided to see the status of the motor windings. Power to

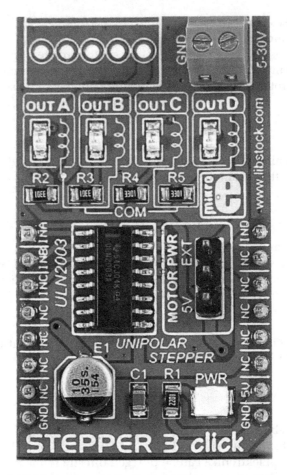

FIGURE 14.28   Stepper 3 Click board for unipolar stepper motors.

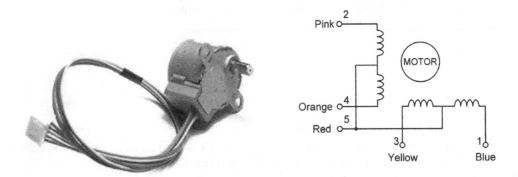

FIGURE 14.29   28BYJ-48 unipolar stepper motor.

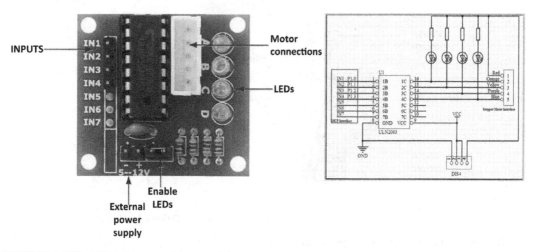

FIGURE 14.30   ULN2003 motor driver module.

the module is applied through the bottom two header pins at the right-hand side of the module. The LEDs can be enabled by shorting the two top header pins at the right-hand side of the module. In this project, the module was powered from an external +5 V DC power supply for the motor (it is recommended to use an external +5 V power supply and not use the Clicker 2 for STM32 +5 V power supply, as this may not provide enough current to drive the motor).

A USB UART Click board is connected to mikroBUS Socket 2 as in the previous projects that communicate with a PC.

Fig. 14.31 shows the circuit diagram of the project. Port pins PA2, PE7, PE8, and PC10 of the Clicker 2 for STM32 development board are connected to driver module inputs IN1, IN2, IN3, and IN4, respectively. The project with the stepper motor is shown in Fig. 14.32

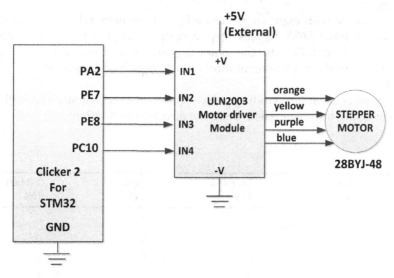

FIGURE 14.31   Circuit diagram of the project.

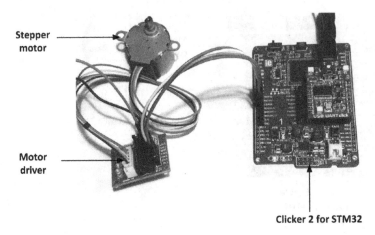

FIGURE 14.32   Project with the stepper motor.

Program listing:

The 28BYJ-48 stepper motor can either be operated in full-step or in half-step modes.

Full-step mode

In full-step mode, there are four steps per cycle and 11.25 degrees/step, corresponding to 32 steps per one revolution of the internal motor shaft. Because the motor is geared with a gear ratio of 64 (in fact, the gear ratio is 63.68395), the number steps for one external complete revolution is 2048 steps/revolution (512 cycles with four steps per cycle).

Table 14.5 presents the motor winding sequence for the full-step mode (this sequence is repeated. Reversing the sequence reverses the direction of rotation).

Half-step mode

The half-step mode with eight steps per cycle is recommended by the manufacturer. In half-step mode, we have 5.625 degrees/step, corresponding to 64 steps per one revolution of the internal motor shaft. Because the motor is geared with a gear ratio of 64, the number of steps for one external complete revolution is 4096 steps/revolution (512 cycles with eight steps per cycle).

Table 14.6 presents the motor winding pulse sequence for the half-step mode (this sequence is repeated. Reversing the sequence reverses the direction of rotation).

TABLE 14.5   Full-step mode.

Step	4 (orange) IN1	3 (yellow) IN2	2 (pink) IN3	1 (blue) IN4
1	1	1	0	0
2	0	1	1	0
3	0	0	1	1
4	1	0	0	1

TABLE 14.6 Half-step mode.

Step	4 (orange) IN1	3 (yellow) IN2	2 (pink) IN3	1 (blue) IN4
1	1	0	0	0
2	1	1	0	0
3	0	1	0	0
4	0	1	1	0
5	0	0	1	0
6	0	0	1	1
7	0	0	0	1
8	1	0	0	1

In this project, the stepper motor is controlled in Full-Step mode and Fig. 14.33 shows the program listing (program: **stepperfull.c**). The program consists of two tasks in addition to the Idle task.

TASK 1

Task 1 controls the stepper motor. Here, the motor is stopped by default when the program starts. As described earlier, the speed depends on the delay inserted between each step. In Full-step mode, there are 2048 steps in a complete revolution. The motor speed in RPM is given by the following equation:

$$RPM = \frac{60 \times 10^3}{2048 \times T}$$

or,

$$RPM = \frac{29.3}{T}$$

where RPM is the motor speed in revolutions per minute and T is the delay between each step in milliseconds. We usually want to know how much delay to insert between each step so that the required number of revolutions can be achieved. This is given in milliseconds by:

$$T = \frac{29.3}{RPM}$$

At the beginning of Task 1, motor driver pins IN1, IN2, IN3, and IN4 are assigned to port pins PA2, PE7, PE8, and PC10, respectively. Then, the motor speed is stopped, waiting to receive a command from the keyboard, sent by Task 2. The pulses to be sent to the motor in Full-mode clockwise direction are stored in character array **FullMode** in binary format, as indicates in Table 14.5. That is,

   int FullMode[4] = {0b01100, 0b00110, 0b00011, 0b01001};

```
/*=============================================================================
                         STEPPER MOTOR CONTROL
                         =====================

In this project a stepper motor is connected to the development board through a
driver module. Additionally, a USB UART Cick board is connected to mikroBUS socket
2 of the development board. The stepper motor is controlled by enering commands
from the keyboard.

Author: Dogan Ibrahim
Date  : September, 2019
File  : stepperfull.c
=============================================================================*/
#include "main.h"
#define StepsPerCycle 512
int FullMode[4] = {0b01100, 0b00110, 0b00011, 0b01001};     // Full Mode control
QueueHandle_t xQueue;                                       // Queue handle

//
// This function extract the bits of a variable
//
unsigned char BitRead(char i, char j)
{
    unsigned m;
    m = i & j;
    if(m != 0)
        return(1);
    else
        return(0);
}


//
// This function sends a bit to pins IN1,IN2,IN3,IN4 of the driver board
//
void SendPulse(int k)
{
    #define IN1 GPIOA_ODR.B2
    #define IN2 GPIOE_ODR.B7
    #define IN3 GPIOE_ODR.B8
    #define IN4 GPIOC_ODR.B10

    GPIO_Config(&GPIOA_BASE, _GPIO_PINMASK_2, _GPIO_CFG_MODE_OUTPUT);
    GPIO_Config(&GPIOE_BASE, _GPIO_PINMASK_7 | _GPIO_PINMASK_8, _GPIO_CFG_MODE_OUTPUT);
    GPIO_Config(&GPIOC_BASE, _GPIO_PINMASK_10, _GPIO_CFG_MODE_OUTPUT);

    IN1 = BitRead(FullMode[k], 1);
    IN2 = BitRead(FullMode[k], 2);
    IN3 = BitRead(FullMode[k], 4);
    IN4 = BitRead(FullMode[k], 8);
}


//
// This function rotates the stepper motor CLOCKWISE by count turns
//
void CLOCKWISE(int count, unsigned int StepDelay)
{
    unsigned int i, j, m, k;

    for(j = 0; j < count; j++)
    {
```

FIGURE 14.33   stepperfull.c program listing.

```
        for(m = 0; m < StepsPerCycle; m++)
        {
                for(i = 0; i < 4; i++)
                {
                  k = 3-i;
                  SendPulse(k);
                  VDelay_ms(StepDelay);
                }
        }
    }
}

//
// This function rotates the stepper motor ANTICLOCKWISE by count turns
//
void ANTICLOCKWISE(int count, float StepDelay)
{
    unsigned int i, j, m;

    for(j = 0; j < count; j++)
    {
        for(m = 0; m < StepsPerCycle; m++)
        {
                for(i = 0; i < 4; i++)
                {
                  SendPulse(i);
                  VDelay_ms(StepDelay);
                }
        }
    }
}

//
// Define all your Task functions here
// ====================================
//

// Task 1 - Stepper Motor CONTROLLER
void Task1(void *pvParameters)
{
    typedef struct Message
    {
      char Mode;
      int RPM;
      int Turns;
      char Strt;
    } AMessage;

    AMessage msg;
    float StpDelay;

    while (1)
    {
        if(xQueueReceive(xQueue, &msg, 0 ) == pdPASS)        // If data in queue
        {
          if(msg.Strt == 1)                                  // Start received
          {
            StpDelay = (29.3 / msg.RPM);                     // Step delay
            vTaskPrioritySet(NULL, 11);
            if(msg.Mode == 1)CLOCKWISE(msg.Turns, StpDelay);
```

FIGURE 14.33   (*Continued*)

```
                if(msg.Mode == 2)ANTICLOCKWISE(msg.Turns, StpDelay);
                vTaskPrioritySet(NULL,10);
            }
        }
    }
}


//
// Read an integer number from the keyboard and retun to the calling program
//
unsigned int Read_From_Keyboard()
{
    unsigned int N, Total;

    Total = 0;
    while(1)
    {
        N = UART3_Read();                            // Read a number
        UART3_Write(N);                              // Echo the number
        if(N == '\r') break;                         // If Enter
        N = N - '0';                                 // Pure number
        Total = 10*Total + N;                        // Total number
    }
    return Total;
}

// Task 2 - Keyboard Controller
void Task2(void *pvParameters)
{
    typedef struct Message
    {
      char Mode;
      int RPM;
      int Turns;
      char Strt;
    } AMessage;


    unsigned int RPM;
    char j, ch, Mode, Command[10];
    AMessage msg;
    UART3_Init_Advanced(9600,_UART_8_BIT_DATA,_UART_NOPARITY,_UART_ONE_STOPBIT,
                     &_GPIO_MODULE_USART3_PD89);

    while (1)
    {
        Mode = 0;
        UART3_Write_Text("\n\r\n\rSTEPPER MOTOR CONTROLLER");
        UART3_Write_Text("\n\r========================");
        UART3_Write_Text("\n\rEnter Direction (CW, CCW): ");
        j = 0;
        while(1)
        {
            ch = UART3_Read();                       // Read a char
            UART3_Write(ch);                         // Echo the char
            if(ch == '\r') break;                    // If Enter
            Command[j] = ch;                         // Store the char
            j++;                                     // Increment pointer
        }
```

FIGURE 14.33 (*Continued*)

```
        Command[j] = '\0';                                      // Terminator
        if(strstr(Command, "CW") > 0) msg.Mode = 1;
        if(strstr(Command, "CCW") > 0) msg.Mode = 2;

        UART3_Write_Text("\n\rEnter the speed (RPM): ");
        msg.RPM = Read_From_Keyboard();

        UART3_Write_Text("\n\rHow many turns?: ");
        msg.Turns = Read_From_Keyboard();

        msg.Strt = 0;
        UART3_Write_Text("\n\rStart (1=Yes, 0=No): ");
        msg.Strt = Read_From_Keyboard();

        if(msg.Strt == 1)
        {
            xQueueSend(xQueue, &msg, 0);                         // Send via Queue
        }
    }
}


//
// Start of MAIN program
// =====================
//
void main()
{
    xQueue = xQueueCreate(1, 8);                                // Create queue
//
// Create all the TASKS here
// =========================
//
    // Create Task 1
    xTaskCreate(
        (TaskFunction_t)Task1,
        "Stepper Motor Controller",
        configMINIMAL_STACK_SIZE,
        NULL,
        10,
        NULL
    );


    // Create Task 2
    xTaskCreate(
        (TaskFunction_t)Task2,
        "Keyboard Controller",
        configMINIMAL_STACK_SIZE,
        NULL,
        10,
        NULL
    );
//
// Start the RTOS scheduler
//
    vTaskStartScheduler();

//
// Will never reach here
}
```

FIGURE 14.33   (*Continued*)

Task 1 receives the required rotational parameters from Task 2 through a queue. The data in the queue are passed using a structure with the following items:

```
typedef struct Message
{
    char Mode;
    int RPM;
    int Turns;
    char Strt;
} AMessage;
```

The Mode specified the direction of rotation, where 1 corresponds to clockwise and 2 corresponds to anticlockwise. The step delay is calculated by dividing 29.3 by the required RPM as described earlier. Task 1 then calls function CLOCKWISE or ANTICLOCKWISE depending on the value of Mode.

Function CLOCKWISE sends four pulses to the motor with a delay of **StepDelay** milliseconds between each pulse. This ensures that the motor speed is as required. This is repeated **StepsPerRevolution** times so that the motor makes a complete revolution. This whole process is then repeated **count** times, which is the number of times we want the motor to rotate complete revolutions. Function ANTICLOCKWISE is similar to CLOCKWISE, but here the steps are sent in reverse order to the motor. The step delay is implemented by calling the built-in function vDelay_ms().

Both functions CLOCKWISE and ANTICLOCKWISE call function SendPulse() which configures the output pins and sends the required bit patterns to output pins IN1, IN2, IN3, and IN4. Function BitRead() extracts the bits from a variable. For example, if the input parameters to this function (i and j) are 0b00011 and 2, respectively, then the function will return 1, which is the bit at position 2 of the data.

TASK 2

This task receives commands from the keyboard and sends these commands to Task 1 so that the motor is controlled as required. At the beginning of this task, the UART is initialized to operate at 9600 baud. The user is prompted to enter responses to the following questions:

Enter Direction (CW, CCW):
Enter the speed (RPM):
How many turns?:
Start (1 = Yes, 0 = No):

After receiving the required rotational parameters, if the response to Start is 1, then these parameters are sent to Task 1 through a queue.

Notice that this is a real-time application where the correct control of the stepping motor requires precision microsecond timing of the pulses sent to the motor. Normally, this is not possible with the FreeRTOS since the task can be interrupted while sending pules to the motor. For this reason, it was necessary to increase the priority of Task 1 just before sending pulses to the motor via functions CLOCKWISE and ANTICLOCKWISE. The priority is lowered back to its normal value of 10 after the motor stops.

Fig. 14.34 shows a typical run of the motor with the motor rotational parameters entered from the keyboard.

```
STEPPER MOTOR CONTROLLER
==========================
Enter Direction (CW, CCW): CCW
Enter the speed (RPM): 10
How many turns?: 1
Start (1=Yes, 0=No): 1

STEPPER MOTOR CONTROLLER
==========================
Enter Direction (CW, CCW):
```

FIGURE 14.34   Entering the motor rotational parameters.

14.8 Project 37: communicating with the Arduino

Description: In this project, an Arduino computer reads the ambient temperature from an analog sensor and sends the readings to the Clicker 2 for STM32 development board over the serial link every second. An LCD is connected to the development board to display the temperature. The user determines the LCD data refreshing rate by entering a command from the keyboard.

Aim: The aim of this project is to show how the Clicker 2 for STM32 development board can receive data from its serial port and display these data on an LCD in a multitasking environment.

Block diagram: Fig. 14.35 shows the block diagram of the project. An L35DZ type analog temperature sensor is connected to one of the analog input ports of the Arduino. Software UART is used on the Arduino and a pin is configured as serial input/output. Serial output of the Arduino is connected to one of the serial inputs of the development board. Additionally, an LCD is connected to the development board to display the temperature. The display refresh rate is set initially to 1 second, but it can be changed from the keyboard.

Circuit diagram: The circuit diagram of the project is shown in Fig. 14.36. In this project, an Arduino Uno is used. The output pin of the LM35DZ temperature sensor is connected to analog input pin A0 of the Arduino. Pins 2 and 3 are configured as RX and TX pins of software serial port, respectively. Pin 3 (TX) is connected to pin PD6 (UART2 RX pin) of the

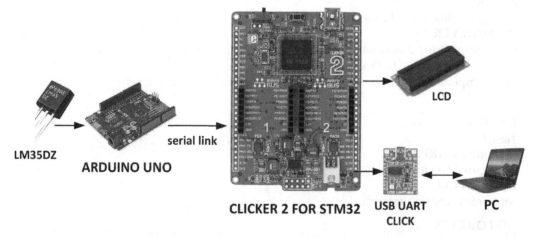

FIGURE 14.35   Block diagram of the project.

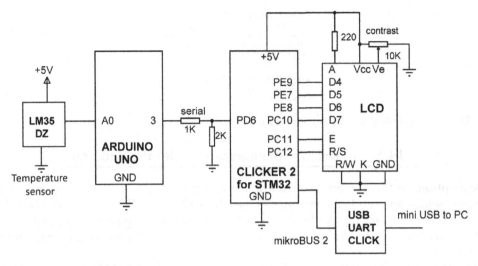

FIGURE 14.36 Circuit diagram of the project.

development board. This pin is easily accessible at the mikroBUS Socket 1 header. The LCD is connected to the development board as in the previous projects using an LCD. The USB UART Click board is connected to mikroBUS Socket 2 and is interfaced to the PC through a mini USB cable. A terminal emulation software (e.g., HyperTerm, Putty) is run on the PC to communicate over the serial link with the development board.

Notice that the output port signal levels of the Arduino Uno are +5 V and this is too high for the inputs of the Clicker 2 for STM32 development board. Therefore, a resistive potential divider circuit consisting of two resistors is used to lower the voltage to around +3.3 V before connecting to pin PD6 of the development board.

Programs
The operation of the programs is described below in PDL:
Arduino
Configure pins 3 and 4 as software UART
DO FOREVER
Read temperature from analog port A0
Convert temperature to Degrees Centigrade
Send temperature over the serial port
Wait 1 second

ENDDO
Task 1
Configure UART
Configure LCD interface
Initialize LCD
Set refresh-rate to 2 seconds

DO FOREVER
IF new refreshing rate is available **THEN**

Read refresh-rate from the queue

ENDIF

Wait refresh-rate seconds

Read temperature from serial port

Display temperature on LCD

ENDDO

Task 2

Configure UART

DO FOREVER

Read new refreshing-rate from the keyboard

Write the new refreshing rate to the queue

ENDDO

The details of each task are given as follows.

Arduino Uno program listing: The Arduino Uno program is very simple and its listing is shown in Fig. 14.37 (program: **arduinotemp**). At the beginning of the program, the software serial port is configured. Inside the main program loop, the temperature is received from the LM35DZ sensor chip and is converted into Degrees Centigrade. The measured temperature of the LM35DZ is directly proportional to the output voltage and is given by:

$$T = \frac{V_o}{10}$$

where T is the measured temperature and V_o is the output voltage in millivolts. The temperature readings are sent over the serial link to the Clicker 2 for STM32 development board every second. You should compile and then upload the code to your Arduino Uno.

Clicker 2 for STM32 program listing: This program consists of two tasks in addition to the Idle task. At the beginning of the program, the interface between the LCD and the

```
#include <SoftwareSerial.h>
SoftwareSerial MySerial(2, 3);        // RX, TX
int Tint;
float mV;

void setup()
{
  MySerial.begin(9600);
}

void loop()
{
  int sensor = analogRead(A0);        // Read sensor data
  mV = sensor * 5000.0 / 1024.0;      // in mV
  mV = mV / 10.0;                     // Temperature in Degrees C
  Tint = int(mV);                     // As integer
  MySerial.println(Tint);             // Send to serial port
  delay(1000);                        // Wait 1 sec
}
```

FIGURE 14.37 Arduino Uno program listing.

development board is defined. Task 1 is the Serial Port Controller which receives the temperature readings from the Arduino over the serial link and displays these readings on the LCD. Task 2 is the keyboard controller which receives the commands from the keyboard. The details of each task are described below:

TASK 1

At the beginning of this task, the UART2 baud rate is set to 9600 and port pins PD5 and PD6 are configured as the UART2 TX and RX pins, respectively. The LCD data refreshing rate is called RefreshRate and by default it is set to 1000 ms at the beginning of this task. The task receives new refreshing rates from Task 2 through a queue. The refreshing rate is displayed at the top row of the LCD. The program receives the temperature value from the Arduino through serial port UART2 and displays it at the second row of the LCD.

TASK 2

At the beginning of this task, the UART3 baud rate is set to 9600 and port pins PD8 and PD9 are configured as the UART3 TX and RX pins, respectively. The task then prompts the user to enter the required LCD data refresh rate and send the received value to Task 1 through the queue. Function Read_From_Keyboard() is used to read an integer number from the PC keyboard through UART 3 and the USB UART Click board.

Fig. 14.38 shows the program listing (program: **arduinostm.c**).

Fig. 14.39 shows the screen where the LCD data refreshing rate was set to 10000 ms (10 seconds) and then to 5000 ms. The data on the LCD are shown in Fig. 14.40.

```
/*=================================================================================
                        COMMUNICATING WITH AN ARDUINO
                        =============================

In this project an Arduino Uno computer is connected to the Clicker 2 for STM32
development board through a serial link. The Arduino reads the ambient temperature
using an analog sensor. The temperature readings are then sent to the development
board every second. The development board displays the temperature on an LCD. The
LCD data refresh rate is set by the user through the PC keyboard.

Author: Dogan Ibrahim
Date   : September, 2019
File   : arduinostm.c
=================================================================================*/
#include "main.h"

// LCD module connections
sbit LCD_RS at GPIOC_ODR.B12;
sbit LCD_EN at GPIOC_ODR.B11;
sbit LCD_D4 at GPIOE_ODR.B9;
sbit LCD_D5 at GPIOE_ODR.B7;
sbit LCD_D6 at GPIOE_ODR.B8;
sbit LCD_D7 at GPIOC_ODR.B10;
// End LCD module connections

QueueHandle_t xQueue;                                          // Queue handle

//
// Define all your Task functions here
// ====================================
//
```

FIGURE 14.38   arduinostm.c program listing.

```
// Task 1 - Serial Port CONTROLLER
void Task1(void *pvParameters)
{
    unsigned int RefreshRate, msg;
    char ch, Txt[4];
    UART2_Init_Advanced(9600,_UART_8_BIT_DATA,_UART_NOPARITY,_UART_ONE_STOPBIT,
                        &_GPIO_MODULE_USART2_PD56);
    Lcd_Init();
    RefreshRate = 1000;                            // Default refresh rate
    Lcd_Cmd(_LCD_CLEAR);                           // Clear LCD
    Lcd_Out(1, 1, "Refresh = ");                   // Display heading
    IntToStr(RefreshRate, Txt);                    // Convert to string
    Ltrim(Txt);                                    // Remove spaces
    Lcd_Out(1, 10, Txt);                           // Display refresh rate

    while (1)
    {
        if(xQueueReceive(xQueue, &msg, 0 ) == pdPASS)   // If data in queue
        {
            RefreshRate = msg;                     // Set new refresh rate
            Lcd_Cmd(_LCD_CLEAR);                   // Clear LCD
            Lcd_Out(1, 1, "Refresh = ");           // Display message
            IntToStr(RefreshRate, Txt);            // Convert to string
            Ltrim(Txt);                            // Remove spaces
            Lcd_Out(1, 10, Txt);                   // Display refresh rate
        }
        vTaskDelay(pdMS_TO_TICKS(RefreshRate));    // Wait refresh rate ms

        if(UART2_Data_Ready())                     // If data from Arduino
        {
            ch=UART2_Read();                       // Clear TX buffer
            ch = UART2_Read();                     // Read a number (MSD)
            Txt[0] = ch & 15 + '0';                // Convert to char
            ch = UART2_Read();                     // Read a number (LSD)
            Txt[1]=ch & 15 + '0';                  // Convert to char
            Txt[2]='\0';                           // NULL terminator
            Lcd_Out(2,2,Txt);                      // Display temperature
        }
    }
}


//
// Read an integer number from the keyboard and retun to the calling program
//
unsigned int Read_From_Keyboard()
{
    unsigned int N, Total;

    Total = 0;
    while(1)
    {
        N = UART3_Read();                          // Read a number
        UART3_Write(N);                            // Echo the number
        if(N == '\r') break;                       // If Enter
        N = N - '0';                               // Pure number
        Total = 10*Total + N;                      // Total number
    }
    return Total;                                  // Return the number
}
```

FIGURE 14.38 (*Continued*)

```
// Task 2 - Keyboard Controller
void Task2(void *pvParameters)
{
    int Refresh;
    UART3_Init_Advanced(9600,_UART_8_BIT_DATA,_UART_NOPARITY,_UART_ONE_STOPBIT,
                        &_GPIO_MODULE_USART3_PD89);

    while (1)
    {
        UART3_Write_Text("\n\rEnter LCD Refreshing Rate (ms): ");
        Refresh = Read_From_Keyboard();                        // New refresh rate
        xQueueSend(xQueue, &Refresh, 0);                       // Send via Queue
    }
}

//
// Start of MAIN program
// =====================
//
void main()
{
    xQueue = xQueueCreate(1, 4);                               // Create queue
//
// Create all the TASKS here
// =========================
//
    // Create Task 1

    xTaskCreate(
        (TaskFunction_t)Task1,
        "Serial Port Controller",
        configMINIMAL_STACK_SIZE,
        NULL,
        10,
        NULL
    );


    // Create Task 2
    xTaskCreate(
        (TaskFunction_t)Task2,
        "Keyboard Controller",
        configMINIMAL_STACK_SIZE,
        NULL,
        10,
        NULL
    );

//
// Start the RTOS scheduler
//
    vTaskStartScheduler();

//
// Will never reach here
}
```

FIGURE 14.38   (Continued)

```
Enter LCD Refreshing Rate (ms): 1000
Enter LCD Refreshing Rate (ms): 5000
```

FIGURE 14.39   Example display on the PC screen.

FIGURE 14.40   Data displayed on the LCD.

14.9 Summary

In this chapter, we have developed several projects to illustrate how to use the various FreeRTOS functions in multitasking projects.

In the next chapters, we shall be looking at some other important functions of FreeRTOS and see how they can be used in projects.

Further reading

[1] Clicker 2 for STM32 development board, www.mikroe.com.
[2] D. Ibrahim, Programming with STM32 Nucleo Boards, Elektor, 2014, ISBN: 978-1-907920-68-4.

15

The Idle task and the idle task hook

15.1 Overview

In the previous chapter, we have developed several projects using various application program interface (API) functions of the FreeRTOS. In this chapter, we are looking at some other important features of the FreeRTOS.

15.2 The Idle task

In FreeRTOS when all the tasks are in blocked state, there must be at least one task that can enter into the Running state at any time to keep the CPU busy, and this task is known as the *Idle* task. If there was no Idle task, then the list of the runnable tasks would be empty and the scheduler will probably crash. Apart from other useful benefits as we shall see shortly, the Idle task makes sure that the list of runnable tasks is never empty. The Idle task is automatically created when function vTaskStartScheduler() is called. The Idle task consists of a simple loop and it has the lowest priority of 0 so that it cannot prevent any other task in the system to run. The Idle task is forced out of the Running state as soon as a higher priority task (i.e., any other task with a priority higher than 0) enters the Ready state. The parameter configIDLE_SHOULD_YIELD in file FreeRTOSConfig.h can be used at compile time to prevent the Idle task from consuming processing time. The Idle task is responsible for cleaning up kernel resources after a task has been deleted. You can stop the Idle task, provided you do not delete any tasks at run time. Alternatively, you can create your own Idle task to run at the priority of 1. Then, the Idle task will never run as long as the task you created never blocks. That is, it is always in the Ready state.

15.3 Idle task hook functions

Idle callback (or idle hook) function is called automatically by the Idle task in every iteration of the Idle task loop. It is, therefore, possible to use the Idle task for the following reasons:

- Executing low priority background tasks
- Measuring the amount of free processing capacity available

ARM-Based Microcontroller Multitasking Projects. http://dx.doi.org/10.1016/B978-0-12-821227-1.00015-3

- Saving power by placing the processor into low power mode when there are no tasks running

An idle task hook function must never attempt to block or suspend, as blocking the Idle task will cause a situation where no tasks are able to enter the Running state. The idle hook function must always return to its caller within a reasonable time since the Idle task is responsible for cleaning up the kernel when function vTaskDelete() is used. If the idle hook function never returns, or it stays too long in its processing cycle, then this cleaning operation cannot be performed.

If parameter configUSE_IDLE_HOOK in file FreeRTOSConfig.h is set to 1, this ensures that the idle hook function will be called at every iteration of the Idle task. The application must then provide a hook function with the following format:

void vApplicationIdleHook(void);

An example project is given below, illustrating how an idle hook function can be used in a simple application.

15.4 Project 39: display the free processor time

Description: In this project, a task is used to flash an LED every 100 ms. An idle hook function is created which increments a counter every time it is called by the Idle task. The count is proportional to the available free processing time. The higher the count, the more free processing time there is.

Aim: The aim of this project is to show how the idle hook function can be used in an application.

Block diagram: In this project, the on-board LED at port pin PE12 of the Clicker 2 for STM32 development board is used for simplicity. A USB UART Click board is connected to mikroBUS 2 socket as in the previous projects using the USB UART Click board. This board is interfaced to a PC through a mini USB cable so that data can be sent to the PC and displayed on the PC screen using a terminal emulator program.

Program listing: Parameter configUSE_IDLE_HOOK must be set to 1 in file FreeRTOSConfig.h for the idle hook function to get called by the Idle task. The program listing is shown in Figure 15.1 (program: **hook.c**). There is only one task in the program in addition to the Idle task. At the beginning of the task, port pin PE12 is configured as an output where the on-board LED is attached to. Function vApplicationIdleHook() increments variable Count every time it is called. That is, every time there are no other tasks to run other than the Idle task. Task 1 flashes the LED every 100 ms and then displays the value of the Count on the screen. The count obtained depends on the type of hardware used and the clock speed. In this application, as shown in Figure 15.2, the count was around 1,099,600. The count is reset to 0 after being displayed.

Notice that Task 1 has two delay functions with 200 ms each, making a total of 400 ms. The Idle task is active when Task 1 is waiting for 400 ms. Therefore, one can assume that approximately, the count of 1,099,600 corresponds to a time of 400 ms. That is, the Idle time is approximately 2750 count/ms for the hardware and the clock rate used in this project. A more

```
/*=================================================================
                    THE IDLE HOOK FUNCTION
                    ======================

The aim of this project is to show how to use the idle hook function in a project.
Here,an LED is flashed every 100 ms and the idle hook function is incremented
every time it is called by the Idle function. The total Count is displayed.

Author: Dogan Ibrahim
Date   : October, 2019
File   : hook.c
=================================================================*/
#include "main.h"

unsigned long Count = 0;

//
// Thsi is the Idle Hook function, called from the IDle task
//
void vApplicationIdleHook(void)
{
  Count++;                                            // Increment Count
}

//
// Define all your Task functions here
// ===================================
//

// Task 1 - LED CONTROLLER
void Task1(void *pvParameters)
{
    #define LED GPIOE_ODR.B12
    char Txt[12];
    const TickType_t xDelay200ms = pdMS_TO_TICKS(200);

    GPIO_Config(&GPIOE_BASE, _GPIO_PINMASK_12, _GPIO_CFG_MODE_OUTPUT);
    UART3_Init_Advanced(9600,_UART_8_BIT_DATA,_UART_NOPARITY,_UART_ONE_STOPBIT,
                    &_GPIO_MODULE_USART3_PD89);

    while (1)
    {
       LED = 1;                                       // LED ON
       vTaskDelay(xDelay200ms);                       // Delay 200ms
       LED = 0;                                        // LED OFF
       vTaskDelay(xDelay200ms);                       // Delay 200ms
       LongToStr(Count, Txt);                         // Count to string
       Count=0;                                        // Reset Count
       Ltrim(Txt);                                     // Remove spaces
       UART3_Write_Text(Txt);                          // Display Count
       UART3_Write_Text("\n\r");                       // Carriage-return
    }
}

//
// Start of MAIN program
// ======================
//
void main()
{
```

FIGURE 15.1   hook.c program listing.

```
//
// Create all the TASKS here
// =========================
//
    // Create Task 1
    xTaskCreate(
        (TaskFunction_t)Task1,
        "LED Controller",
        configMINIMAL_STACK_SIZE,
        NULL,
        10,
        NULL
    );

//
// Start the RTOS scheduler
//
    vTaskStartScheduler();

//
// Will never reach here
//
    while (1);
}
```

FIGURE 15.1   *(Continued)*

accurate relationship between the count and Idle time can be obtained by modifying Task 1 as follows:

```
while (1)
{
    vTaskDelay(xDelay10 ms);
    LongToStr(Count, Txt);
    Count = 0;
    Ltrim(Txt);
    UART3_Write_Text(Txt);
    UART3_Write_Text("\n\r");
}
```

The delay time is approximately equal to the time that Task 1 is waiting, that is, the time that the Idle task is running. The delay can be varied and the count noted. The following values were obtained:

Delay time (ms)	Count
10	26,893
20	54,408
30	81,923
40	109,200
50	136,666

This gives an approximate straight line with the following equation:

$$Count = 2744 \times Delay - 547$$

where Delay is the Idle task processing time in milliseconds.

```
1099765
1099535
1099592
1099650
1099707
1099765
1099535
1099592
1099650
1099707
1099765
1099535
1099592
1099650
1099707
1099765
```

FIGURE 15.2   Displaying the count.

Notice that the above equation applies only to the Clicker 2 for STM32 development board with the STM32F407 processor running at 168 MHz. The same development board with different clock rates, or different development boards will give different readings. Although this is a very simple project, it illustrates the principles of using the idle task hook function.

15.5 Summary

In this chapter, we have seen how to use the idle hook function in a project to get an estimate of the processing time in a simple application.

In the next chapter, we shall be looking at the important topic of Task Notifications.

Further reading

[1] R. Barry, Mastering the FreeRTOS real time kernel: a hands-on tutorial guide. https://www.freertos.org/wp-content/uploads/2018/07/161204_Mastering_the_FreeRTOS_Real_Time_Kernel-A_Hands-On_Tutorial_Guide.pdf.

16

Task Notifications

16.1 Overview

In the previous chapter, we have developed several projects using various application program interface (API) functions of FreeRTOS. In this chapter, we are looking at how to use the "Task Notification" functions of FreeRTOS, which is one of the important features.

So far in this book, we have seen using mutexes, semaphores, queues, and event groups for task synchronization or communicating with other tasks. All of these methods are based on using communication objects where data are first sent to the communication object and from there to the receiving task. For example, for sending data to another task, we first place the data in a queue. The receiving task then gets these data from the queue.

Task Notifications allow us to send data directly to another task without the need to use a communication object. Using task notification has the advantage, in that significantly less RAM is required when compared with using queues, mutexes, semaphores, or event groups. Using a communication object has the disadvantage, in that the object must be created before it is used, whereas using task notification requires only 8 bytes of RAM per task and there is no need to create it before using. Additionally, using task notifications is 45% faster than using communication objects.

Each task has a 32-bit notification value as a 32-bit unsigned integer. When a task is created, its notification value is cleared automatically. When a task notification is sent to a blocked task, it unblocks the receiving task and optionally it can update the receiving task's notification value. By sending a notification to a task, the receiving task's notification value can be modified in one of four ways:

- The receiving task's notification value can be set without overwriting a previous value.
- The receiving task's notification value can be overwritten.
- One or more bits can be set in the receiving task's notification value.
- The receiving task's notification value can be incremented.

A notification is sent to a task using the API functions xTaskNotify() or xTaskNotifyGive(). When a notification is sent to a task, the notification is in Pending state until it is read by the receiving task in which case in becomes Not-Pending. The receiving task calls API function xTaskNotifyWait() or uITaskNotifyTake(). If the receiving task is Blocked waiting for a notification, it will be removed from the Blocked state and the notification will be cleared.

ARM-Based Microcontroller Multitasking Projects. http://dx.doi.org/10.1016/B978-0-12-821227-1.00016-5

To include task notification in our programs, we have to set parameter configUSE_TASK_
NOTIFICATIONS to 1 in file FreeRTOSConfig.h, which is the default value. We can set this
parameter to 0 to disable task notifications, which will save 8 bytes per task.

Task notifications have some limitations. They can only be used when there is only one
recipient task. A sending task cannot wait in the Blocked state if the send operation cannot
be completed immediately. Compared to queues, a task's notification value can hold one
value at a time, while a queue can hold more than one data item at a time. Compared to event
groups, event groups can be used to send an event to more than one task at a time, while task
notifications are sent only to a receiving task.

In the remainder sections of this chapter, we are looking at the various FreeRTOS task notification API functions and see how they can be used in practical projects. Interested readers
can get further information on task notifications from the following links:

https://www.freertos.org/wp-content/uploads/2018/07/161204_Mastering_the_
FreeRTOS_Real_Time_Kernel-A_Hands-On_Tutorial_Guide.pdf
or
https://www.freertos.org/RTOS-task-notifications.html
or
https://www.freertos.org/wp-content/uploads/2018/07/FreeRTOS_Reference_
Manual_V10.0.0.pdf
or
https://www.freertos.org/documentation

16.2 xTaskNotifyGive() and ulTaskNotifyTake()

xTaskNotifyGive() sends a notification directly to a task and increments the receiving
task's notification value. This function sets the receiving task's notification state to pending.
The receiving task should wait by calling function ulTaskNotifyTake(). When the call is made,
the state of the notification changes to Non-Pending. xTaskNotifyGive() and ulTaskNotify-
Take() are used as a faster alternative to binary and counting semaphores. The format of this
function is:

xTaskNotifyGive(TaskHandle_t xTaskToNotify);

Parameters
xTaskToNotify: This is the handle of the task being notified.
Return values
pdPASS is always returned.

Function ulTaskNotifyTake() returns when the task's notification value is not zero, decre-
menting the task's notification value before it returns. The notification value acts as a binary
semaphore or as a counting semaphore. As a binary semaphore, the notification value is
cleared to zero and the receiving task exits. As a counting semaphore, the receiving task's
notification value is decremented on exit. The format of this function is:

ulTaskNotifyTake(BaseType_t xClearCountOnExit, TickType_t xTicksToWait);

Parameters

xClearCountOnExit: If xClearCountOnExit is set to pdFALSE, then the task's notification value is decremented before ulTaskNotifyTake() exits (similar to a counting semaphore being decremented by a successful call to xSemaphoreTake()). If xClearCountOnExit is set to pdTRUE, then the task's notification value is reset to 0 before ulTaskNotifyTake() exits (similar to a binary semaphore left at zero after a call to xSemaphoreTake()).

xTicksToWait: The maximum time to wait in the Blocked state for a notification to be received if a notification is not already pending when ulTaskNotifyTake() is called.

Return values

The value of the task's notification value before it is decremented or cleared.

16.3 Project 40: start flashing an LED after receiving notification

Description: This is a very simple project. The on-board LED at port pin PE12 and the on-board push-button switch at port pin PE0 are used. There are two tasks in the program in addition to the Idle task. Task 1 is the LED controller where the LED is initially OFF, and the task waits for a notification before it starts flashing the LED. Task 2 is the button controller. Pressing the button gets the handle of Task 1 and then sends a notification to Task 1 which starts flashing the LED every second.

Aim: The aim of this project is to show how the API functions xTaskNotifyGive() and ulTaskNotifyTake() can be used in a simple project.

Block diagram: In this project, the on-board LED at port pin PE12 and the on-board push-button at port pin PE0 are used.

Program listing: Fig. 16.1 shows the program listing (program: **notify1.c**). In this program, Task 1 is in Blocked state until a notification is received from Task 2. Here, notification is used as a binary semaphore, which is cleared to zero on exit. The operation of the program is described by the following PDL:

TASK 1
Configure LED port as output
Wait to receive notification

DO FOREVER
   LED ON
   Wait 1 second
   LED OFF
   Wait 1 second
ENDDO
TASK 2
Configure BUTTON as input
Wait until the BUTTON is pressed
Get TASK 1's handle
Send notification to Task 1
Wait forever

```
/*==============================================================================
                        TASK NOTIFICATION
                        =================

The aim of this project is to show how task notification can be used in a very
simple application. Here the LED controller task waits for a notification. When
the button is pressed, a notifiation is sent to the LED controller, which starts
flashing the LED

Author: Dogan Ibrahim
Date  : October, 2019
File  : notify1.c
==============================================================================*/
#include "main.h"

//
// Define all your Task functions here
// ===================================
//

// Task 1 - LED CONTROLLER
void Task1(void *pvParameters)
{
    #define LED GPIOE_ODR.B12
    const TickType_t xDelay1000ms = pdMS_TO_TICKS(1000);

    GPIO_Config(&GPIOE_BASE, _GPIO_PINMASK_12, _GPIO_CFG_MODE_OUTPUT);
    //
    // Block indefinitely and wait for notification. Clear on exit. Here, the
    // notification is used as a binary semaphore which is cleared to zero on exit
    //
    ulTaskNotifyTake(pdTRUE, portMAX_DELAY);

    //
    // Now start flashing the LED
    //
    while (1)
    {
        LED = 1;                                    // LED ON
        vTaskDelay(xDelay1000ms);                   // Delay 1 second
        LED = 0;                                    // LED OFF
        vTaskDelay(xDelay1000ms);                   // Delay 1 second
    }
}

// Task 2 - BUTTON CONTROLLER
void Task2(void *pvParameters)
{
    #define BUTTON GPIOE_IDR.B0
    const char *pcNameToLookup = "LED Controller";
    TaskHandle_t xTaskToNotify;
    xTaskToNotify = xTaskGetHandle(pcNameToLookup);

    GPIO_Config(&GPIOE_BASE, _GPIO_PINMASK_0, _GPIO_CFG_MODE_INPUT);

    while(BUTTON == 1);                             // Wait for the button
    xTaskNotifyGive(xTaskToNotify);                 // Send notification

    while (1)
    {
    }
}
//
```

FIGURE 16.1 notify1.c program listing.

```
// Start of MAIN program
// =====================
//
void main()
{
//
// Create all the TASKS here
// =========================
//
    // Create Task 1
    xTaskCreate(
        (TaskFunction_t)Task1,
        "LED Controller",
        configMINIMAL_STACK_SIZE,
        NULL,
        10,
        NULL
    );

    // Create Task 2
    xTaskCreate(
        (TaskFunction_t)Task2,
        "BUTTON Controller",
        configMINIMAL_STACK_SIZE,
        NULL,
        10,
        NULL
    );
//
// Start the RTOS scheduler
//
    vTaskStartScheduler();

//
// Will never reach here
//
    while (1);
}
```
FIGURE 16.1 *(Continued)*.

16.4 xTaskNotify() and xTaskNotifyWait()

Function xTaskNotify() sends a notification to a task to unblock it and additionally it can update the following in the receiving task's notification value:

- Write a 32-bit number to the notification value
- Increment the notification value
- Set bits in the notification value
- Leave the notification value unchanged

The task has the following format:

xTaskNotify(TaskHandle_t xTaskToNotify, uint32_t ulValue, eNotifyAction eAction);

Parameters

xTaskToNotify: This is the handle of the task being notified.

ulValue: Used to update the notification value of the task being notified, depending on parameter eAction.

eAction; The action to perform when notifying the task's notification. eAction is an enumerated type and can take one of the following values:

- eNoAction: recipient task notified but its notification value is not changed (in which case parameter ulValue is not used)
- eSetBits: The task's notification value is bitwise ORed with ulValue. For example, if ulValue is set to 0×01, then bit 0 will be set within the task's notification value. If ulValue is 0×04, then bit 2 will be set in the task's notification value.
- eIncrement: Recipient task's notification value is incremented by 1 (in which case parameter ulValue is not used).
- eSetValueWithOverwrite: The task's notification value is unconditionally set to the value of ulValue, even if the task already had a notification pending when xTaskNotify() was called.
- eSetValueWithoutOverwrite: If the task already has a notification pending, then its notification value is not changed and xTaskNotify() returns pdFAIL. If the task did not already have a notification pending, then its notification value is set to ulValue.

Return values

If eAction is set to eSetValueWithoutOverwrite and the task's notification value is not updated, then pdFAIL is returned. In all other cases, pdPASS is returned.

Function xTaskNotifyWait() waits, with an optional timeout, for the calling task to receive a notification. The format of the function is:

xTaskNotifyWait(uint32_t ulBitsToClearOnEntry, uint32_t ulBitsToClearOnExit, uint32_t *pulNotificationValue, TickType_t xTicksToWait);

Parameters

ulBitsToClearOnEntry: Any bits set in ulBitsToClearOnEntry will be cleared in the calling task's notification value on entry to the xTaskNotifyWait() function (before the task waits for a new notification), provided a notification is not already pending when xTaskNotifyWait() is called. For example, if ulBitsToClearOnEntry is 0×1, then bit 0 of the task's notification value will be cleared on entry to the function. Setting ulBitsToClearOnEntry to 0xffffffff (ULONG_MAX) will clear all the bits in the task's notification value, effectively clearing the value to 0.

ulBitsToClearOnExit: Any bits set in ulBitsToClearOnExit will be cleared in the calling task's notification value before xTaskNotifyWait() function exits if a notification was received. The bits are cleared after the task's notification value has been saved in pulNotificationValue (see the description of pulNotificationValue below). For example, if ulBitsToClearOnExit is 0×03, then bit 0 and bit 1 of the task's notification value will be cleared before the function exits. Setting ulBitsToClearOnExit to 0xffffffff (ULONG_MAX) will clear all the bits in the task's notification value, effectively clearing the value to 0.

pulNotificationValue: Used to pass out the task's notification value. The value copied to *pulNotificationValue is the task's notification value as it was before any bits were cleared due to the ulBitsToClearOnExit setting. pulNotificationValue is an optional parameter and can be set to NULL if it is not required.

xTicksToWait: The maximum time to wait in the Blocked state for a notification to be received if a notification is not already pending when xTaskNotifyWait() is called.

Return values

pdTRUE: A notification was received, or a notification was already pending when xTaskNotifyWait() was called.

pdFALSE: Call to xTaskNotifyWait() timed out before a notification was received.

16.5 Project 41: flashing at different rates after receiving notifications

Description: This is a very simple project. The on-board LED at port pin PE12 and the on-board push-button switches at port pins PE0 and PA10 are used. There are two tasks in the program in addition to the Idle task. Task 1 is the LED controller where the LED is initially OFF and the task waits for a notification before starting to flash the LED. Task 2 is the button controller. Pressing button PE0 (called BUTTONFAST) gets the handle of Task 1 and then sends a notification to Task 1 so that the LED flashes every 200 ms. Pressing button PA10 (called BUTTONSLOW) sends a notification to Task 1 so that the LED flashes every second.

Aim: The aim of this project is to show how the API functions xTaskNotify() and xTaskNotifyWait() can be used in a simple project.

Block diagram: In this project, the on-board LED at port pin PE12 and the on-board push-buttons at port pins PE0 and PA10 are used.

Program listing: Fig. 16.2 shows the program listing (program: **notify2.c**). In this program, Task 2 checks the status of the two buttons. If the BUTTONFAST is pressed, then a notification is sent to Task 1 with bit 2 set. If, on the other hand, the BUTTONSLOW is pressed, then a notification is sent to Task1 with bit 4 set. Task 1 checks notifications. If there is notification and bit 2 is set, then the flashing rate is set to 200 ms. If, on the other hand, notification is received with bit 4 set, then the flashing rate is set to 1 second. Variable FirstTime controls whether or not the LED should flash. At the beginning of Task 1, this variable is set to 1, which disables flashing. When a flashing rate is set by the user by pressing either of the two buttons, then variable FirstTime is set to 0, which enables the flashing. Notice that this is a multitasking program where the flashing rate of the LED can be changed while the LED is flashing.

The operation of the program is described by the following PDL:

Task 1 (LED controller)
Configure port PE12 as digital output (LED port)
DO FOREVER
  Wait for notification
  IF bit 2 is set **THEN**
    Set flashing rate to fast (200 ms)
  ELSE IF bit 4 is set **THEN**
    Set flashing rate to slow (1 second)
  ENDIF
  Flash the LED at the chosen rate
ENDDO
Task 2 (button controller)
Configure port PE0 as digital input (button at PE0)
Configure port PA10 as digital input (button at PA10)

```
/*==============================================================================
                        TASK NOTIFICATION
                        ==================

The aim of this project is to show how task notification can be used in a very
simple application. Here the LED controller task waits for a notification. When
the button at PE0 is pressed, the LED flashes at a rate of 200 ms. When the
button at PA10 is pressed, the LED flashes every second. Notice that the flashing
rate can be changed while the LED is flashing

Author: Dogan Ibrahim
Date  : October, 2019
File  : notify2.c
==============================================================================*/
#include "main.h"

//
// Define all your Task functions here
// ====================================
//

// Task 1 - LED CONTROLLER
void Task1(void *pvParameters)
{
    #define LED GPIOE_ODR.B12
    #define ULONG_MAX 0xffffffff
    TickType_t xDelay;
    uint32_t ulNotificationValue;
    char FirstTime = 1;

    GPIO_Config(&GPIOE_BASE, _GPIO_PINMASK_12, _GPIO_CFG_MODE_OUTPUT);
    //
    // Do not Block. If notification is received, find out if slow or fast flashing
    // is required. Do not clear any notification bits on entry. Clear all
    // notification bits on exit. Store notified value in ulNotificationValue
    //
    while (1)
    {
        if(xTaskNotifyWait(0x00, ULONG_MAX, &ulNotificationValue, 0) == pdTRUE)
        {
            if((ulNotificationValue & 0x02) != 0)             // If bit 2 is set
            {
                xDelay = pdMS_TO_TICKS(200);                  // Fast flashing rate
            }

            if((ulNotificationValue & 0x04) != 0)             // If bit 4 is set
            {
                xDelay = pdMS_TO_TICKS(1000);                 // Slow flashing rate
            }
            FirstTime = 0;                                    // Set to start flashing
        }
        if(FirstTime == 0)
        {
            LED = 1;                                          // LED ON
            vTaskDelay(xDelay);                               // Delay of xDelay
            LED = 0;                                          // LED OFF
            vTaskDelay(xDelay);                               // Delay of xDelay
        }
    }
}
```

FIGURE 16.2   notify2.c program listing.

```
// Task 2 - BUTTON CONTROLLER
void Task2(void *pvParameters)
{
    #define BUTTONFAST GPIOE_IDR.B0
    #define BUTTONSLOW GPIOA_IDR.B10
    const char *pcNameToLookup = "LED Controller";
    TaskHandle_t xTaskToNotify;
    xTaskToNotify = xTaskGetHandle(pcNameToLookup);

    GPIO_Config(&GPIOE_BASE, _GPIO_PINMASK_0, _GPIO_CFG_MODE_INPUT);
    GPIO_Config(&GPIOA_BASE, _GPIO_PINMASK_10, _GPIO_CFG_MODE_INPUT);

    while (1)
    {
        if(BUTTONFAST == 0)                                 // Wait for button PE0
        {
            xTaskNotify(xTaskToNotify, 2 , eSetBits);     // Send notification, bit 2 set
        }
        if(BUTTONSLOW == 0)                                 // Wait for button PA10
        {
            xTaskNotify(xTaskToNotify, 4 , eSetBits);     // Send notification, bit 4 set
        }
    }
}


//
// Start of MAIN program
// =====================
//
void main()
{
//
// Create all the TASKS here
// =========================
//
    // Create Task 1
    xTaskCreate(
        (TaskFunction_t)Task1,
        "LED Controller",
        configMINIMAL_STACK_SIZE,
        NULL,
        10,
        NULL
    );

     // Create Task 2
    xTaskCreate(
        (TaskFunction_t)Task2,
        "BUTTON Controller",
        configMINIMAL_STACK_SIZE,
        NULL,
        10,
        NULL
    );

//
// Start the RTOS scheduler
//
    vTaskStartScheduler();
//
// Will never reach here
//
    while (1);
}
```

FIGURE 16.2 (*Continued*).

DO FOREVER
    IF button at port PE0 is pressed **THEN**
       Send notification, set bit 2
    ELSE IF button at port PA10 is pressed **THEN**
       Send notification, set bit 4
ENDIF
ENDDO

16.6 xTaskNotifyStateClear() and xTaskNotifyQuery()

Function xTaskNotifyStateClear() will clear a pending notification, but it does not change the notification value. If a task is not waiting for a notification when a notification arrives, then the notification will remain pending until either the receiving task reads its notification value or the receiving task is the subject task in a call to xTaskNotifyStateClear(). The format of this function is:

xTaskNotifyStateClear(TaskHandle_t xTask)

Parameters
xTask: This is the handle of the task that will have a pending notification cleared. Setting xTask to NULL will clear a pending notification in the task that called the function.
Return values
pdPASS: If the task referenced by xTask had a notification pending
pdFAIL: If the task referenced by xTask did not have a notification pending
Function xTaskNotifyAndQuery() is similar to xTaskNotify(), but includes an additional parameter in which the subject task's previous notification value is returned. Interested readers can get further information on this function from the links given at the beginning of this chapter.

16.7 Summary

In this chapter, we had a look at the important topic of FreeRTOS task notifications and gave examples of its use in applications.
In the next chapter, we shall be looking at the important topic of Critical Sections.

Further reading

[1] The FreeRTOS reference manual. https://www.freertos.org/wp-content/uploads/2018/07/FreeRTOS_Reference_Manual_V10.0.0.pdf.

Critical sections

17.1 Overview

In the previous chapter, we have developed several projects using the topic of Task Notifications. In this chapter, we are looking at another important topic, the Critical Sections.

Critical sections (also known as critical regions) are regions of code that are surrounded by two macros where entry to these sections of code is controlled so that the code is entered by only one task at any time. A critical section is entered by calling taskENTER_CRITICAL() and exited by calling taskEXIT_CRITICAL(). These calls do not have any parameters and also do not return any values. Critical sections can also be implemented using mutexes and semaphores, but it is quicker to use the entry and exit macros described in this chapters. Interrupts are disabled inside the critical sections, either globally, or up to a specific priority level. Interrupts whose priorities are above the value assigned to parameter configMAX_SYSCALL_INTERRUPT_PRIORITY are enabled and those interrupts whose priorities are at or below configMAX_SYSCALL_INTERRUPT_PRIORITY are disabled. It is also important that the critical sections must not be called from inside an interrupt service routine. More will be discussed in a later chapter on FreeRTOS and interrupt service routines.

Preemptive context switching cannot occur inside a critical section since interrupts are disabled inside these sections. As a result of this, when a task enters a critical section, it is guaranteed that it will run until it exits from the region. A task should not go into a Blocked state inside a critical section, or it should not yield to ask the scheduler to perform context switching.

The code inside a critical section must be short as long code may affect the scheduling of tasks in the program. Critical sections can be nested if required and it is safe to nest them. It is, however, important that all entries must be exited before a critical section is left by a task.

An example project is given in the next section to show how a critical section can be used in an application.

17.2 Project 42: critical sections – Sharing the UART

Description: This is a simple project. In this project, a task measures the outdoor temperature. Similarly, another task measures the indoor temperature. Both tasks share a UART and send their readings to the UART so that the measured values are displayed on a PC.

ARM-Based Microcontroller Multitasking Projects. http://dx.doi.org/10.1016/B978-0-12-821227-1.00017-7

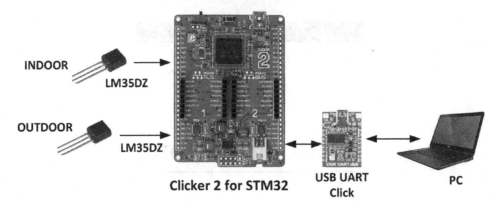

FIGURE 17.1   Block diagram of the project.

Aim: The aim of this project is to show how a critical section can be used in a project that shares the UART.

Block diagram: In this project, both the indoor temperature and the outdoor temperature are measured using the LM35DZ type analog temperature sensor chips as shown in Fig. 17.1.

Circuit diagram: The LM35DZ is a three-pin analog temperature sensor chip that was used in an earlier project, and therefore, its specifications are not repeated here again.

The following connections were made in this project between the Clicker 2 for STM32 development board and external components:

Development board pin	External component pin
PA2 (analog input)	LM35 output pin (for indoor temperature)
PA4	LM35 output pin (for outdoor temperature)
+5 V	LM35DZ Vcc pins
GND	LM35DZ GND pin
mikroBUS 2 socket	USB UART Click board

A USB UART Click board is plugged in to mikroBUS 2 socket of the development board. A mini USB cable is then connected between the USB UART Click board and the USB port of the PC. A terminal emulation software was used on the PC as described in earlier projects using the PC interface. Fig. 17.2 shows the circuit diagram of the project.

Program listing: As described in earlier projects, LM35DZ gives an output voltage directly proportional to the measured temperature. That is,

$$T = \frac{V_o}{10}$$

where T is the measured temperature in °C, and V_o is the sensor output voltage in millivolts. For example, at 20°C, the output voltage is 200 mV, at 30°C, the output voltage is 300 mV and so on. The following PDL shows the operation of the program:

TASK1
DO FOREVER
Read indoor temperature from LM35DZ

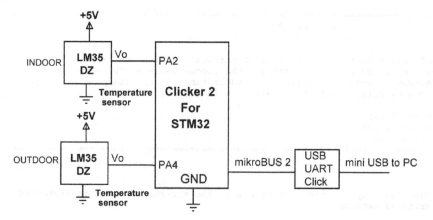

FIGURE 17.2   Circuit diagram of the project.

Convert to Degrees Centigrade
Call Display to display the data
Wait 1 second

ENDDO
TASK 2
DO FOREVER
Read outside temperature from LM35DZ
Convert to Degrees Centigrade
Call Display to display the data
Wait 1 second

ENDDO
Function display
Critical Section entry
   Receive data from UART
   Display data on PC screen
Critical Section exit

The program listing is shown in Fig. 17.3 (program: **critical.c**). The program consists of two tasks in addition to the Idle task. Task 1 reads the indoor temperature from the LM35DZ sensor chip. Task 2 reads the outdoor temperature using another LM35DZ sensor chip. Both tasks call a function named Display, which is protected by a critical section to display their readings on the PC screen.

The details of each task are given below:

TASK 1
Inside the main task loop, built-in function ADC1_Read(2) is called to read analog data from port PA2. The read value is then converted into Degrees Centigrade, converted into a string, leading spaces are removed and then function Display is called to display the temperature on the PC screen. The loop is repeated every second.

TASK 2
This task is similar to Task 1, but here function ADC1_Read(4) is called to read analog data from port PA4. The remainder code in this task is same as in Task 1.

```
/*==============================================================================
                        CRITICAL SECTION
                        ================

The aim of this project is to show how a critical section can be used in a program.
A temperature sensor is used to measure the indoor temperature. Additionally,
another sensor is used to measure the outdoor temperature. The program displays
temperatures by calling a function which is in a critical region.

Author: Dogan Ibrahim
Date  : October, 2019
File  : critical.c
==============================================================================*/
#include "main.h"

//
// This function displays the temperature on the screen. The code is protected
// as a critical section
//
void Display(unsigned char Temps[])
{
    taskENTER_CRITICAL();
    UART3_Write_Text(Temps);
    taskEXIT_CRITICAL();
}

//
// Define all your Task functions here
// ===================================
//

// Task 1 - Indoor Temperature CONTROLLER
void Task1(void *pvParameters)
{
    unsigned AdcValue;
    unsigned int Temperature;
    float mV;
    unsigned char j,Txt[7];
    unsigned char msg[15];
    unsigned char cr[] = "\n\r";
    ADC1_Init();                                    // Initialize ADC

    while (1)
    {
        for(j=0; j< 15; j++)msg[j]=0;
        AdcValue = ADC1_Read(2);                    // Read ADC Chan 2
        mV = AdcValue * 3300.0 / 4096.0;            // in mV
        mV = mV / 10.0;                             // Temp in C
        Temperature = (int)mV;                      // Temp as integer
        IntToStr(Temperature, Txt);                 // Convert to string
        Ltrim(Txt);                                 // Remove spaces
        strcpy(msg, "Indoor : ");                   // Copy to msg
        strcat(msg, Txt);                           // join with msg
        strcat(msg, cr);                            // carriage return
        Display(msg);                               // Display temp
        vTaskDelay(pdMS_TO_TICKS(1000));            // wait 1 second
    }
}
```

FIGURE 17.3   critical.c program listing.

```
// Task 2 - Outdoor temperature and Humidity CONTROLLER
void Task2(void *pvParameters)
{
    unsigned AdcValue;
    unsigned char Temperature;
    float mV;
    unsigned char j, Txt[7];
    unsigned char msg[20];
    unsigned char cr[] = "\n\r";
    ADC1_Init();                                        // Initialize ADC

    while (1)
    {
        for(j=0; j< 20; j++)msg[j]=0;
        AdcValue = ADC1_Read(4);                        // Read ADC Chan 4
        mV = AdcValue * 3300.0 / 4096.0;                // in mV
        mV = mV / 10.0;                                 // Temp in C
        Temperature = (int)mV;                          // Temp as integer
        IntToStr(Temperature, Txt);                     // Convert to string
        Ltrim(Txt);                                     // Remove spaces
        strcpy(msg, "Outdoor: ");                       // copy to msg
        strcat(msg, Txt);                               // Join to msg
        strcat(msg, cr);                                // Carriage return
        Display(msg);                                   // Display msg
        vTaskDelay(pdMS_TO_TICKS(1000));                // Wait 1 second
    }
}

//
// Start of MAIN program
// =====================
//
void main()
{
    UART3_Init_Advanced(9600,_UART_8_BIT_DATA,_UART_NOPARITY,_UART_ONE_STOPBIT,
                        &_GPIO_MODULE_USART3_PD89);
//
// Create all the TASKS here
// =========================
//
    // Create Task 1
    xTaskCreate(
        (TaskFunction_t)Task1,
        "Indoor Temperature Controller",
        configMINIMAL_STACK_SIZE,
        NULL,
        10,
        NULL
    );

    //Create Task 2
    xTaskCreate(
        (TaskFunction_t)Task2,
        "Outdoor Temperature Controller",
        configMINIMAL_STACK_SIZE,
        NULL,
        10,
        NULL
    );
```

FIGURE 17.3   (*Continued*)

```
//
// Start the RTOS scheduler
//
    vTaskStartScheduler();

//
// Will never reach here
//
    while (1);
}
```

FIGURE 17.3   (*Continued*)

```
Indoor  : 22
Outdoor: 27
Indoor  : 22
Outdoor: 27
Indoor  : 22
Outdoor: 28
Indoor  : 22
Outdoor: 28
Indoor  : 21
Outdoor: 28
```

FIGURE 17.4   **Displaying the temperatures.**

Function display

This task calls UART to display the indoor and outdoor temperatures on the PC screen. The UART is enclosed inside a critical section by calling taskENTER_CRITICAL() and taskEXIT_CRITICAL().

Fig. 17.4 shows the indoor and outdoor temperatures displayed on the PC screen.

17.3 Suspending the scheduler

Another method of creating a critical section is to suspend the scheduler temporarily. Again, it is very important that the code inside the critical section is short and not time-consuming. The critical section created by suspending the scheduler is protected and can only be accessed from only one task at any time. Notice that interrupts remain enabled when the scheduler is suspended, but they will not lead to a task switch (i.e., kernel swapping). If an interrupt requests a context switch while the scheduler is suspended, then the request is held pending and is performed when the scheduler is resumed. It is important that API functions that may cause task switching (e.g., task delay, queues, tasks that may block the task) must not be used inside the critical section.

A critical section is created by suspending the scheduler using the API call vTaskSuspendALL() at the entry and xTaskResumeAll() at the exit of the critical section:

```
vTaskSuspendAll();
{
    /* Critical section is here */
```

```
}
xTaskResumeAll();
```
It is possible to have nested suspending of the scheduler. The scheduler will return to normal operation when the nesting depth returns to zero.

17.4 Project 43: suspending the scheduler

Description: Project 42 can be modified so that the critical section is protected by suspending the scheduler before calling the UART function. The scheduler is resumed after the UART function. The only modification required to Project 42 is to modify function Display as follows:

```
void Display(unsigned char Temps[])
{
    vTaskSuspendAll();
    UART3_Write_Text(Temps);
    xTaskResumeAll();
}
```

17.5 Summary

In this chapter, we have learned about the critical sections and also about the FreeRTOS API functions used to suspend and resume the scheduler.

In the next chapter, we shall be looking at the basic theory of Cortex-M4-based external and internal (timer) interrupts and learn how to use them in projects.

Further reading

[1] The FreeRTOS reference manual. https://www.freertos.org/wp-content/uploads/2018/07/FreeRTOS_Reference_Manual_V10.0.0.pdf.

Interrupts in Cortex-M4 based microcontrollers

18.1 Overview

In the last chapter we have learned how to use critical sections and also how to suspend and resume the scheduler. In this chapter we shall be looking at both the theory and applications of the very important topic of interrupts. The STM32F407 microcontroller will be used as an example processor in this chapter since this is the processor used on our Clicker 2 for STM32 development board, and in addition this is a Cortex-M4 type processor.

18.2 Interrupts in general

An interrupt is an external or an internal (e.g., timer) event that requests the CPU to stop what it is currently executing, and immediately jump to execute a different code. The code that the CPU jumps to is known as the interrupt service routine (ISR). Interrupts are asynchronous events since the CPU does not know when the interrupt will occur in a program as it can occur at any time. The time between the generation of an interrupt request and the entry into the ISR is known as the "interrupt latency." The faster the interrupt latency (i.e., the lower the value) is always better as this shows that the system response is fast. When an interrupt occurs, the CPU remembers the location of the next instruction it was going to execute by storing the program counter in a register or memory location (usually called a stack). The CPU returns to this instruction and resumes normal operation after completing the ISR code and returning from the interrupt. In addition to saving the program counter, the CPU may also store the important register values, such as the CPU status register, flags, and other registers of importance. Interrupt request that triggered the interrupt may also be disabled so that further interrupts from the same source are not recognized until the present one returns.

In a microcontroller, the CPU may be designed to respond to large number of external and internal interrupts, for example in the region of 10 to over 100. Each interrupt source usually, but not necessarily has a dedicated are of memory where the ISR code is expected to be located at. In some processors, multiple interrupt sources share the same memory locations

ARM-Based Microcontroller Multitasking Projects. http://dx.doi.org/10.1016/B978-0-12-821227-1.00018-9

for their ISRs. It is then up to the user program to determine the actual source of the interrupt. Interrupts are always disabled when a processor is started. The following conditions must be met before an interrupts can be accepted by the CPU:

- Interrupt from the required source must be enabled.
- The source must generate an interrupt request.
- Processor global interrupts must be enabled.

External interrupts usually occur when a port pin is driven low (i.e., on the falling edge) or high (i.e., on the rising edge), or if there is change in the state of the port pin (low-to-high or high-to-low). Internal timer interrupts occur for example when a timer overflows or underflows.

Interrupt sources usually have priorities assigned to them. A higher priority interrupt can stop the execution of a lower priority interrupt and grab the CPU. When the higher priority ISR completes its processing, the lower priority ISR can resume.

It is important that the ISR code should consume as little processor time as possible. This is especially true when multiple interrupts are enabled in a program. If an ISR takes long time, then it may cause delayed response to other interrupts that may need fast response. Interrupts can be masked under software control so that requests from such sources cannot be accepted. Some processors also have nonmaskable interrupt (NMI) sources that cannot be masked (or disabled) under software control.

Various registers inside the CPU must be configured before an external or an internal interrupt can be accepted by the CPU. The next sections describe the STM32F407 interrupt features and show the bit mappings of the registers involved in configuring various interrupt sources.

18.3 STM32F407 interrupts

The STM32F407 processor supports up to 240 IRQs and 1 NMI. There are 16 levels of priority with level zero the highest and level 15 the lowest.

The following conditions must be met at the device and inside the CPU for an interrupt to be accepted:

At the device
- Each interrupt source has a separate enable bit. The bit must be set for the interrupt to be accepted.
- Each interrupt source has a separate flag bit. Hardware sets this bit when it makes an interrupt request. This bit must be cleared in ISR by software.

In the CPU
- Interrupt request is received via the Nested Vectored Interrupt Controller (NVIC). The highest priority interrupt request is sent to the CPU.
- Global interrupt enable bit must be enabled in the PRIMASK register.
- The priority level of the requesting source must be higher than the base priority BASEPRI.

The NVIC has the following features:

- 82 maskable interrupt channels.

- 16 programmable priority levels.
- Low-latency interrupt handling.

STM32F407 interrupt mechanism is designed for fast and efficient interrupt handling. The first line of a C code in the ISR is guaranteed to be executed after 12 cycles for a zero wait state memory system. In addition, the interrupt latency is fully deterministic so that the same interrupt latency is entered from any point in the code.

18.2.1 External Interrupts

The STM32F407 processor has 23 external interrupt sources, where 16 sources are available at the port pins, and the remaining ones are for events like RTC, Ethernet, USB, and so on. External interrupt/event controller (EXTI) consists of up to 23 edge detectors for generating event/interrupt requests. Each input line can be independently configured to select the type and the corresponding trigger event (rising or falling or both). Each line can also masked independently. A pending register maintains the status line of the interrupt requests.

Fig. 18.1 shows the EXTI block diagram. The edge of the external interrupt input is first detected. The interrupt source can be masked in software by configuring the interrupt mask register. After going through the pending request register, the interrupt is presented to the NVIC interrupt controller.

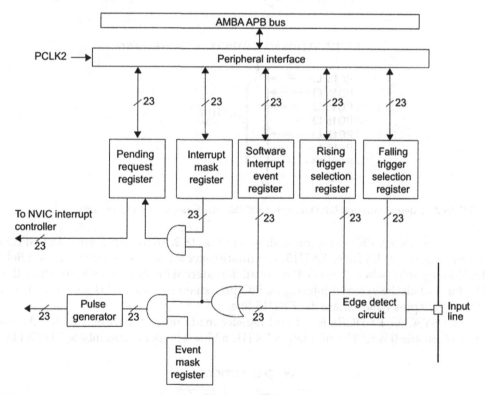

FIGURE 18.1   NVIC block diagram. ©STMiroelectronics. Used with permission.

EXTI0[3:0] bits in the SYSCFG_EXTICR1 register

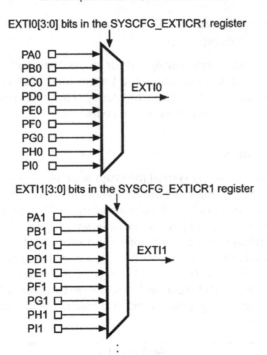

FIGURE 18.2   External interrupt GPIO mapping. ©STMiroelectronics. Used with permission.

External interrupt GPIO mapping is shown in Fig. 18.2. 16 multiplexers select GPIO pins as external interrupts EXTI0 to EXTI15. The multiplexer inputs are selected via 4-bit fields of EXTICR[k] registers, where k = 0–3. Pin 0 of all the external interrupt GPIO pins share the line EXTI0, Pin 1 of all the external interrupt GPIO pins share the line EXTI1 and so on up to pin 15 of the GPIO pins which share the EXTI15 line.

Register SYSCFG_EXTICRx is a 16-bit register made up of four 4-bit nibbles. As shown in Fig. 18.3, nibble 0 is EXTI0, nibble 1 is EXTI1, nibble 2 is EXTI2 and nibble 3 is EXTI3. The

SYSCFG_EXTICR1

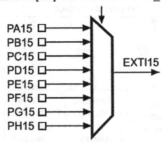

FIGURE 18.3   Register SYSCFG_EXTICR1.

interrupt lines are selected as follows: As an example, EXTIx = 0 selects PAx, 1 selects PBx, 2 selects PCx, etc. EXTICR1 selects EXTI3-EXTI0; EXTICR2 selects EXTI7-EXTI4, etc.

Tables 18.1–18.4 show the register SYSCFG_EXTICx and corresponding interrupt pin numbers.

The other EXTI lines are connected as follows:

- EXTI line 16 is connected to the PVD output.
- EXTI line 17 is connected to the RTC Alarm event.
- EXTI line 18 is connected to the USB OTG FS Wakeup event.

TABLE 18.1   SYSCFG_EXTICR1.

EXTI3 (bits 15..12)	EXTI2 (bits 11..8)	EXTI1 (bits 7..4)	EXTI0 (bits 3..0)
0: PA3	0: PA2	0: PA1	0: PA0
1: PB3	1: PB2	1: PB1	1: PB0
2: PC3	2: PC2	2: PC1	2: PC0
3: PD3	3: PD2	3: PD1	3: PD0
4: PE3	4: PE2	4: PE1	4: PE0
5: PF3	5: PF2	5: PF1	5: PF0

©STMiroelectronics. Used with permission.

TABLE 18.2   SYSCFG_EXTICR2.

EXTI7 (bits 15..12)	EXTI6 (bits 11..8)	EXTI5 (bits 7..4)	EXTI4 (bits 3..0)
0: PA7	0: PA6	0: PA5	0: PA4
1: PB7	1: PB6	1: PB5	1: PB4
2: PC7	2: PC6	2: PC5	2: PC4
3: PD7	3: PD6	3: PD5	3: PD4
4: PE7	4: PE6	4: PE5	4: PE4
5: PF7	5: PF6	5: PF5	5: PF4

©STMiroelectronics. Used with permission.

TABLE 18.3   SYSCFG_EXTICR3.

EXTI11 (bits 15..12)	EXTI10 (bits 11..8)	EXTI9 (bits 7..4)	EXTI8 (bits 3..0)
0: PA11	0: PA10	0: PA9	0: PA8
1: PB11	1: PB10	1: PB9	1: PB8
2: PC11	2: PC10	2: PC9	2: PC8
3: PD11	3: PD10	3: PD9	3: PD8
4: PE11	4: PE10	4: PE9	4: PE8
5: PF11	5: PF10	5: PF9	5: PF8

©STMiroelectronics. Used with permission.

TABLE 18.4 SYSCFG_EXTICR4.

EXTI15 (bits 15..12)	EXTI14 (bits 11..8)	EXTI3 (bits 7..4)	EXTI2 (bits 3..0)
0: PA15	0: PA14	0: PA13	0: PA12
1: PB15	1: PB14	1: PB13	1: PB12
2: PC15	2: PC14	2: PC13	2: PC12
3: PD15	3: PD14	3: PD13	3: PD12
4: PE15	4: PE14	4: PE13	4: PE12
5: PF15	5: PF14	5: PF13	5: PF12

©STMiroelectronics. Used with permission.

- EXTI line 19 is connected to the Ethernet Wakeup event.
- EXTI line 20 is connected to the USB OTG HS (configured in FS) Wakeup event.
- EXTI line 21 is connected to the RTC Tamper and TimeStamp events.
- EXTI line 22 is connected to the RTC Wakeup event.

EXTI registers

The following registers can be configured for external interrupts.

Interrupt mask register (EXTI_IMR): Used to mask an interrupt line. A 0 masks the interrupt, while a 1 unmasks the interrupt line. The register configuration is shown in Fig. 18.4.

Rising trigger selection register (EXTI_RTSR): Used to set the interrupt source as rising (low-to-high). A 1 sets the corresponding interrupt line as rising. The register configuration is shown in Fig. 18.5.

Falling trigger selection register (EXTI_FTSR): Used to set the interrupt source as falling (high-to-low). A 1 sets the corresponding interrupt line as falling. The register configuration is shown in Fig. 18.6.

Pending register (EXTI_PR): A bit in the register is set when the selected edge event arrives on an interrupt line. A 1 must be written by the ISR to clear the pending state of the interrupt (i.e., to cancel the IRQ request). The register configuration is shown in Fig. 18.7.

31	30	29	28	27	26	25	24	23	22	21	20	19	18	17	16
				Reserved					MR22	MR21	MR20	MR19	MR18	MR17	MR16
									rw	rw	rw	rw	rw	rw	rw

15	14	13	12	11	10	9	8	7	6	5	4	3	2	1	0
MR15	MR14	MR13	MR12	MR11	MR10	MR9	MR8	MR7	MR6	MR5	MR4	MR3	MR2	MR1	MR0
rw	rw	rw	rw	rw	rw	rw	rw	rw	rw	rw	rw	rw	rw	rw	rw

Bits 31:23   Reserved, must be kept at reset value.

Bits 22:0   **MRx:** Interrupt mask on line x
　　　　　　　0: Interrupt request from line x is masked
　　　　　　　1: Interrupt request from line x is not masked

FIGURE 18.4   EXTI_IMR register. *©STMiroelectronics. Used with permission.*

31	30	29	28	27	26	25	24	23	22	21	20	19	18	17	16
				Reserved					TR22	TR21	TR20	TR19	TR18	TR17	TR16
									rw	rw	rw	rw	rw	rw	rw
15	14	13	12	11	10	9	8	7	6	5	4	3	2	1	0
TR15	TR14	TR13	TR12	TR11	TR10	TR9	TR8	TR7	TR6	TR5	TR4	TR3	TR2	TR1	TR0
rw	rw	rw	rw	rw	rw	rw	rw	rw	rw	rw	rw	rw	rw	rw	rw

Bits 31:23 Reserved, must be kept at reset value.

Bits 22:0 **TRx:** Rising trigger event configuration bit of line x
0: Rising trigger disabled (for Event and Interrupt) for input line
1: Rising trigger enabled (for Event and Interrupt) for input line

FIGURE 18.5   **EXTI_RTSR register.** *©STMiroelectronics. Used with permission.*

31	30	29	28	27	26	25	24	23	22	21	20	19	18	17	16
				Reserved					TR22	TR21	TR20	TR19	TR18	TR17	TR16
									rw	rw	rw	rw	rw	rw	rw
15	14	13	12	11	10	9	8	7	6	5	4	3	2	1	0
TR15	TR14	TR13	TR12	TR11	TR10	TR9	TR8	TR7	TR6	TR5	TR4	TR3	TR2	TR1	TR0
rw	rw	rw	rw	rw	rw	rw	rw	rw	rw	rw	rw	rw	rw	rw	rw

Bits 31:23 Reserved, must be kept at reset value.

Bits 22:0 **TRx:** Falling trigger event configuration bit of line x
0: Falling trigger disabled (for Event and Interrupt) for input line
1: Falling trigger enabled (for Event and Interrupt) for input line.

FIGURE 18.6   **EXTI_FTSR register.** *©STMiroelectronics. Used with permission.*

31	30	29	28	27	26	25	24	23	22	21	20	19	18	17	16
				Reserved					PR22	PR21	PR20	PR19	PR18	PR17	PR16
									rc_w1	rc_w1	rc_w1	rc_w1	rc_w1	rc_w1	rc_w1
15	14	13	12	11	10	9	8	7	6	5	4	3	2	1	0
PR15	PR14	PR13	PR12	PR11	PR10	PR9	PR8	PR7	PR6	PR5	PR4	PR3	PR2	PR1	PR0
rc_w1	rc_w1	rc_w1	rc_w1	rc_w1	rc_w1	rc_w1	rc_w1	rc_w1	rc_w1	rc_w1	rc_w1	rc_w1	rc_w1	rc_w1	rc_w1

Bits 31:23 Reserved, must be kept at reset value.

Bits 22:0 **PRx:** Pending bit
0: No trigger request occurred
1: selected trigger request occurred
This bit is set when the selected edge event arrives on the external interrupt line.
This bit is cleared by programming it to '1'.

FIGURE 18.7   **EXTI_PR register.** *©STMiroelectronics. Used with permission*

TABLE 18.5 External interrupt positions and priorities.

IRQ no	Priority	Interrupt line	Description
6	13	EXTI0	EXTI Line0 interrupt
7	14	EXTI1	EXTI Line0 interrupt
8	15	EXTI2	EXTI Line0 interrupt
9	16	EXTI3	EXTI Line0 interrupt
10	17	EXTI4	EXTI Line0 interrupt
23	30	EXTI9_5	EXTI Line 9–5 interrupts
40	47	EXTI15_10	EXTI Line 15–10 interrupts

The positions and the priorities of external interrupt lines are shown in Table 18.5. All pins with same number are connected to line with same number. They are multiplexed to one line. You cannot use two pins on one line simultaneously. Notice that EXTI5_9 is shared and handles interrupts from pins 5 to 9. Similarly, EXTI10_15 is shared and handles interrupts from pins 10 to 15.

Interrupts in mikroC Pro for ARM compiler are enabled and disabled using the following statements (e.g., for line EXTI0):

```
NVIC_IntEnable(IVT_INT_EXTI0);      // Enable interrupts from line EXTI0
NVIC_IntDisable                     // Disable interrupts from line EXTI0
```

mikroC Pro for ARM compiler provides a tool called Interrupt Assistant that can be used to create the correct statements for enabling interrupts for the required source. This is shown in the next project.

An example project is given below that uses an external interrupt.

18.4 Project 44—External interrupt based event counter

Description: This is an external event counter example. A push-button switch is connected to the development board. Every time the button is pressed, an external interrupt is generated where inside the ISR, a counter is incremented by one. The count is displayed on the PC screen using a USB UART Click board.

Aim: The aim of this project is to show how an external interrupt program can be written using the mikro C Pro for ARM compiler. Additionally, the program shows how an external push-button switch can be used in an interrupt based project.

Block diagram: Fig. 18.8 shows the project block diagram. It is assumed that the occurrence of external events is simulated by pressing the button.

Circuit diagram: The circuit diagram of the project is shown in Fig. 18.9. A push-button switch is connected to port pin PA0. The switch state is held normally at logic LOW using a pull-down resistor connected to one of the switch contacts. Pressing the button changes its state to logic HIGH by connecting the button to +V supply voltage. The USB UART Click board is connected to mikroBUS 2 socket of the development board.

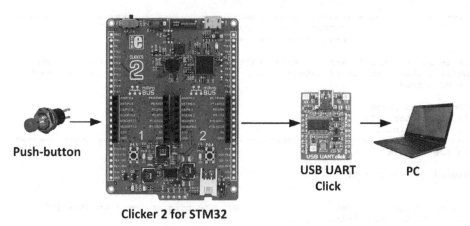

Push-button   **Clicker 2 for STM32**   **USB UART Click**   **PC**

FIGURE 18.8   Block diagram of the project.

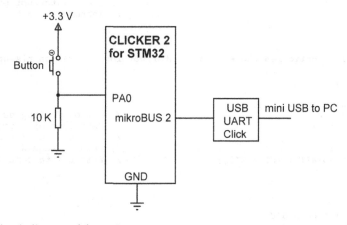

FIGURE 18.9   Circuit diagram of the project.

Program listing: This program does not use the FreeRTOS kernel, it is simply based on using the mikroC Pro for ARM compiler. The program listing is shown in Fig. 18.10 (program: **eventint.c**). At the beginning of the main program, port pin PA0 is configured as a digital input and the UART is initialized to 9600 baud. The main program calls function SetupInt to configure the external interrupt for port pin PA0. Interrupt is configured to be accepted on the rising edge of PA0 (i.e., on the low-to-high transition of the input pin). The following statements are used to configure the external interrupt:

```
SYSCFG_EXTICR1 = 0;
EXTI_FTSR = 0;                          // Not on falling edge
EXTI_RTSR = 1;                          // Interrupt on rising edge
EXTI_IMR = 1;                           // Unmask interrupt source
EXTI_PR = 1;                            // Pending request
NVIC_IntEnable(IVT_INT_EXTI0);          // Enable interrupt on line EXTI0
```

```
/*===============================================================================
                          EXTERNAL EVENT COUNTER
                          =======================

This is an external interrupt based event controller project. A push-button
simulates the occurence of external interrupts. The event count is displayed
on a PC screen

Author: Dogan Ibrahim
Date  : October, 2019
File  : eventint.c
=================================================================================*/
#include "main.h"

unsigned int Count = 0;

//
// External interrupt service routine (ISR). The program jumps to this ISR
// whenever the push-button is pressed
//
void Events() iv IVT_INT_EXTI0 ics ICS_AUTO
{
    EXTI_PR = 1;                               // Clear interrupt pending
    Count++;                                   // Increment Count
}

//
// This function configures the external interrupt for pin PA0 on rising edge
//
void SetupInt()
{
    SYSCFG_EXTICR1 = 0;
    EXTI_FTSR = 0;                             // Not on falling edge
    EXTI_RTSR = 1;                             // Interrupt on rising edge
    EXTI_IMR = 1;                              // Unmask interrupt source
    EXTI_PR = 1;                               // Pending request
    NVIC_IntEnable(IVT_INT_EXTI0);             // Enable interrupt on line EXTI0
}

void main()
{
    unsigned int CountOld;
    unsigned char Txt[7];

    GPIO_Config(&GPIOA_BASE, _GPIO_PINMASK_0, _GPIO_CFG_MODE_INPUT);
    UART3_Init_Advanced(9600,_UART_8_BIT_DATA,_UART_NOPARITY,_UART_ONE_STOPBIT,
                        &_GPIO_MODULE_USART3_PD89);
    UART3_Write_Text("EVENT COUNTER\n\r");      // Display heading
    SetupInt();                                 // Configure external interrupt
    CountOld = Count;

    while(1)
    {
        if(CountOld != Count)
        {
            IntToStr(Count, Txt);               // Convert to string
            UART3_Write_Text(Txt);              // Display event Count
            UART3_Write_Text("\n\r");
            CountOld = Count;
        }
    }
}
```

FIGURE 18.10 eventint.c program listing.

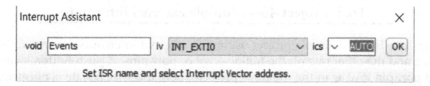

FIGURE 18.11   Generating the ISR function.

The main program runs in an endless loop where the variable Count is converted into string format and is displayed on the PC screen. Variable CountOld makes sure that the display is refreshed only when there is change in the value of Count.

The ISR is the function:

```
void Events() iv IVT_INT_EXTI0 ics ICS_AUTO
```

This function is created by using the Interrupt Assistant tool of the mikroC Pro for ARM compiler. The steps to use the Interrupt Assistant are:

- Click **Tools -> Interrupt Assistant** which should display the tool (see Fig. 18.11).
- Give a name to your ISR. In this program the ISR is called Events.
- Select the type of interrupt. In this program INT_EXTI0 is selected.
- Select whether or not context saving should be done when the interrupt occurs. In this program the auto option is selected.
- Click **OK** to generate the ISR function.
- Notice that **iv** is a reserved word that informs the compiler that it is an ISR. ics is the Interrupt Context Saving; Interrupt Context Saving can be performed in several ways:
  1. ICS_OFF—No context saving.
  2. ICS_AUTO—Compiler chooses whether the context saving will be performed or not.

If interrupt context saving is not explicitly declared, the compiler will set **ICS_AUTO** by default.

Inside the ISR, the pending interrupt flag is set and the counter is incremented by one to indicate that an event has occurred.

Notice that pressing the button may generate more than one count. The reason for this is the contact bouncing problem which is inherent with all types of mechanical switches. When the switch is pushed, its contacts make many movements before it settles down. As a result of this, more than one rising edge is sent to the processor which generates several interrupts. One can use flip-flop circuits, Schmitt trigger circuits, or simple resistor capacitor circuits to eliminate the contact bouncing problems. Interested readers can find many resources on the Internet on the topic of contact bouncing and how to eliminate it.

Fig. 18.12 shows a typical display on the PC screen where the total event count at the time of taking the picture was 4.

```
EVENT COUNTER
     1
     2
     3
     4
```

FIGURE 18.12   Display on the LCD.

18.5 Project 45—Multiple external interrupts

Description: This is a simple project using two external interrupts, one activating on the rising edge and the other one on the falling edge of port pins. A push-button switch is connected to port pin PA0 as in the previous project where the switch state is normally at logic LOW. Also, the on-board push-button switch at port pin PA10 is used to generate external interrupts when they are pressed. Additionally, the on-board LED at the port pin PE12 is used in the project. Pressing button at PA0 generates an interrupt which sets a flag to start the LED flashing. Pressing button at PA10 generates another external interrupt which resets the flag so that the LED stops flashing.

Aim: The aim of this project is to show how multiple external interrupts can be generated in a program.

Block diagram: Fig. 18.13 shows the project block diagram.

Circuit diagram: Fig. 18.14 shows the project circuit diagram. Push-button switch at port pin PA0 is normally at logic LOW and goes to HIGH when the switch is pressed. The on-board switch at port pin PA10 is normally at logic HIGH and goes to logic LOW when the button is pressed.

Program listing: Fig. 18.15 shows the program listing (program: **twoint.c**). The two interrupts are configured as follows:

Interrupt for button at port pin PA0

This interrupt configuration is same as in the previous project. But notice that in multiple interrupt applications it is important to set or reset only the bits relevant to the interrupt to be used. This is why the bit operator Bx is used in the program. The code to configure PA0 for rising external interrupts in a multi interrupt program is as follows. Notice here that the interrupt priority is set to Level 2 just to show the readers how the interrupt priority can be set using the mikroC Pro for ARM compiler:

```
SYSCFG_EXTICR1 = 0;                // For pin PA0
EXTI_FTSR.B0 = 0;                  // Interrupt on rising edge
```

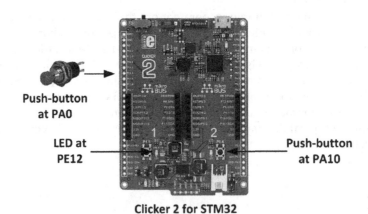

Push-button
at PA0

LED at
PE12

Push-button
at PA10

Clicker 2 for STM32

FIGURE 18.13 Block diagram of the project.

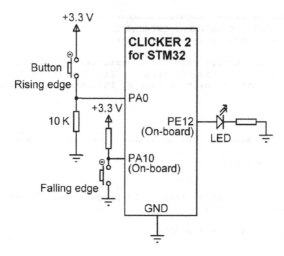

FIGURE 18.14   Circuit diagram of the project.

```
EXTI_RTSR.B0= 1;                        // Not on falling edge
EXTI_IMR.B0 = 1;                        // Unmask interrupt source
EXTI_PR.B0= 1;                          // Pending request
NVIC_SetIntPriority(IVT_INT_EXTI0, _NVIC_INT_PRIORITY_LVL2);
NVIC_IntEnable(IVT_INT_EXTI0);          // Enable interrupt on line EXTI0
```

When button at PA0 is pressed, the program jumps to the ISR named TurnON(). Here, pending interrupt flag is set to clear the interrupt, and variable Flag is set to 1 so that the LED starts flashing.

Interrupt for button at port pin PA10 (on-board button)

Interrupts on pin PA10 are handled by EXTICR3 (see Table 18.3). Bit 10 of FTSR register is set to 1 and bit 10 of RTSR is cleared so that interrupts are expected on the falling edge of the input. Bit 10 of the mask register is unmasked, and the pending request is set for bit 10. The interrupt priority is set to Level 1 for demonstration purposes, then the interrupt vector is enabled for line EXTI15_10 which includes interrupt on external pin PA10. The code that configures external interrupts on pin PA10 is as follows:

```
SYSCFG_EXTICR3 = 0;                     // For pin PA10
EXTI_FTSR.B10 = 1;                      // Interrupt on falling edge
EXTI_RTSR.B10 = 0;                      // Not on rising edge
EXTI_IMR.B10 = 1;                       // Unmask interrupt source
EXTI_PR.B10 = 1;                        // Pending request
NVIC_SetIntPriority(IVT_INT_EXTI15_10, _NVIC_INT_PRIORITY_LVL1);
NVIC_IntEnable(IVT_INT_EXTI15_10);      // Enable interrupt on line EXTI0
```

Inside the main program, port pins PA0 and PA10 are configured as inputs, and PE12 is configured as an output. The remainder of the program runs in a loop. Inside this loop the value of variable Flag is checked. If Flag is set then the LED starts flashing every second, otherwise the LED is turned OFF.

```
/*================================================================================
                         MULTIPLE EXTERNAL INTERRUPTS
                         ============================

In this project the on-board button PA10 and an external push-button at port pin
PA0 are used to generate two external interrupts. Pressing button at PA0 starts
the LED at port PE12 to flash. Pressing button at PA10 stops the flashing.

Author: Dogan Ibrahim
Date   : October, 2019
File   : twoint.c
================================================================================*/
#include "main.h"
volatile unsigned int Flag = 0;

//
// External interrupt service routine (ISR). The program jumps to this ISR
// whenever the push-button is pressed
//
void TurnON() iv IVT_INT_EXTI0 ics ICS_AUTO
{
    EXTI_PR.B0 = 1;
    Flag = 1;
}


void TurnOFF() iv IVT_INT_EXTI15_10 ics ICS_AUTO
{
    EXTI_PR.B10 = 1;
    Flag = 0;
}


//
// This function configures the external interrupt for pin PA0 on rising edge.
// The interrupt priority is set to 2
//
void SetupPA0()
{
    SYSCFG_EXTICR1 = 0;                           // For pin PA0
    EXTI_FTSR.B0 = 0;                             // Not on falling edge
    EXTI_RTSR.B0= 1;                              // Interrupt on rising edge
    EXTI_IMR.B0 = 1;                              // Unmask interrupt source
    EXTI_PR.B0= 1;                                // Pending request
    NVIC_SetIntPriority(IVT_INT_EXTI0, _NVIC_INT_PRIORITY_LVL2);
    NVIC_IntEnable(IVT_INT_EXTI0);                // Enable interrupt on line EXTI0
}


//
// This function configures the external interrupt for pin PA10 on falling edge.
// The interrupt priority is set to 1
//
void SetupPA10()
{
    SYSCFG_EXTICR3 = 0;                           // For pin PA10
    EXTI_FTSR.B10 = 1;                            // Interrupt on falling edge
    EXTI_RTSR.B10 = 0;                            // Not on rising edge
    EXTI_IMR.B10 = 1;                             // Unmask interrupt source
    EXTI_PR.B10 = 1;                              // Pending request
    NVIC_SetIntPriority(IVT_INT_EXTI15_10, _NVIC_INT_PRIORITY_LVL1);
    NVIC_IntEnable(IVT_INT_EXTI15_10);            // Enable interrupt on line EXTI15_10
```

FIGURE 18.15   twoint.c program listing.

```
    }

void main()
{
    #define LED GPIOE_ODR.B12

    GPIO_Config(&GPIOA_BASE, _GPIO_PINMASK_0, _GPIO_CFG_MODE_INPUT);
    GPIO_Config(&GPIOA_BASE, _GPIO_PINMASK_10, _GPIO_CFG_MODE_INPUT);
    GPIO_Config(&GPIOE_BASE, _GPIO_PINMASK_12, _GPIO_CFG_MODE_OUTPUT);

    SetupPA0();                                 // Configure PA0 interrupts
    SetupPA10();                                // Configure PA10 interrupts

    while(1)                                    // DO FOREVER
    {
        if(Flag == 1)                           // IF Flag is set
        {
            LED = 1;                            // LED ON
            Delay_ms(1000);                     // Wait 1 second
            LED = 0;                            // LED OFF
            Delay_ms(1000);                     // Wait 1 second
        }
        else                                    // Otherwise (Flag not set)
            LED = 0;                            // LED OFF
    }
}
```

FIGURE 18.15   (*Continued*)

18.6 Internal interrupts (timer interrupts)

Timers are important modules of all microcontrollers. They can be used for accurate timing operations, such as generating accurate delays, counting pulses occurring at an input in a given time period, and so on. In this section we shall be briefly looking at how the timer interrupts can be configured on the STM32F407 microcontroller. Interested readers can get further information on timers from various sources on the Internet and from the STM data sheets.

STM32F407 microcontroller includes 17 timers. 10 of these timers are general purpose timers, 2 are simple timers, 2 are advanced timers, 1 is independent watchdog type timer, 1 window watchdog timer, and 1 systemtick (system timing) type timer. The timers are:

TIM2, TIM5	—	32-bit general purpose timers
TIM6, TIM7	—	16-bit simple timers
TIM1, TIM8	—	16-bit advanced timers
TIM3, TIM4, TIM10–TIM14	—	16-bit general purpose timers

Timers TIM2, TIM3, TIM4, and TIM5 are up-down counting timers with auto re-load functions. Additionally, these timers include four capture/compare channels where PWM waveforms can easily be generated.

TIM1 and TIM8 are high speed timers that can count up or down and incorporate auto re-load functions and four capture/compare channels.

TIM9 and TIM12 can count only up and they incorporate auto re-load functions. They have only two channels of capture/compare channels.

TIM10 and TIM11 are high speed, while TIM13 and TIM14 are low speed timers. These timers can only count up and they incorporate auto re-load functions. They have only two channels of capture/compare channels.

TIM6 and TIM7 are called simple timers. They are low speed timers that can only count up. They incorporate auto re-load functions, but do not have capture/compare channels.

Perhaps the most important and most useful timers are TIM2 and TIM5 since they are 32-bit timers and they can count both up and down with auto re-load functions and have capture/compare channels.

Assuming that a timer is set to count up, the process is as follows: the timer counts from zero to its maximum value which is the auto re-load value. When the count reaches the auto-reload value, it is reset back to zero and the counting continues up. A prescaler is used to divide the clock frequency by the required amount so that higher timing values can be obtained with high frequency clocks. If configured, a timer interrupt is generated when the count rolls over from its maximum value to zero.

Timers can be configured as follows for timer based interrupt operations:

• Enable clock to the timer
• Disable the timer
• Load the required value to the prescaler register
• Load the required value to the auto re-load register
• Enable interrupts for the required timer
• Enable the timer

There are basically three registers that should be configured for timer operations. These are the counter register, prescaler register, and the auto reload register. Their functions are summarized below:

Counter register (TIMx_CNT): These are the counting registers. It counts up or down depending on the type of timer used. The frequency of counting depends on the clock applied to the timer. The clock frequency can be divided by the prescaler. For TIM3 and TIM4 timers this is a 16-bit register. For TIM2 and TIM5 these are 32-bit registers.

Prescaler register (TIMx_PSC): These registers divide the timer clock frequency. For Tim2, Tim3, TIM4, and Tim5 timers the prescaler is 16-bit wide, that is, the clock frequency can be divided from 1 to 65,535.

Auto reload register (TIMx_ARR): These registers hold the reload value. In up counting timers when the count reached this value it is reset back to zero. In down counting timers, when the count reaches to zero, it is reloaded with the value stored in the auto-reload register. For the TIM3 and TIM4 timers, this is a 16-bit register. For the TIM2 and TIM5 timers, this is a 32-bit register.

If for example, in an up counting timer, the basic timer clock frequency is 42 MHz and the prescaler register is set to 10 and the auto re-load register is set to 1000, then the timer will count up to 1000 and then reset back to 0. The counting frequency will be 42 MHz/10 = 4.2 MHz.

A software tool called TimerCalculator is provided on the PC by mikroElektronika (www.mikroe.com) that can be used to configure a STM32F407 microcontroller timer to generate interrupts at required intervals. The tool automatically calculates the requirements and gives a code that can be used to generate interrupts using a timer. The use of this tool is explained in the next project.

18.7 Project 46—Generating waveform using a timer interrupt

Description: This is a simple project using a timer interrupt. In this project TIM2 is used to generate interrupts at every 1 ms. The state of port pin PA2 is toggled every time an interrupt is generated. Therefore, a square waveform is generated at pin PA2 with a period of 2 ms, that is, frequency of 500 Hz.

Aim: The aim of this project is to show how a timer can be used to generate internal interrupts, and consequently generate a square waveform at the desired GPIO pin.

Block diagram: Fig. 18.16 shows the project block diagram. A digital oscilloscope is connected to pin PA2 of the development board to display the waveform.

Program listing: In this project the TimerCalculator **tool** is used to generate code for the timer. Fig. 18.17 shows the TimerCalculator tool startup screen.

The steps to generate the timer interrupt code are as follows:

- Select the Device as: **STM32F2xx/3xx/4xx**
- Select the MCU clock frequency as: **168 MHz, divided by 4 at APB1 prescaler (APB1 Bus clock is 42 MHz, but TIM2 runs at 42 × 2 = 84 MHz)**
- Choose timer as: **Timer2**
- Set the Interrupt time to: **1 ms**
- Click Calculate

Notice that we have to take the clock divide value at the APB1 bus divider (see Fig. 2.9). You should see the code generated at the right hand side of the screen as shown in Fig. 18.18.

Fig. 18.19 shows the generated code where both the timer configuration code and the timer ISR code template are given. You should enter your code in the ISR section. Notice that the prescaler value is set to 1, the auto re-load value is set to 41,999, timer clock is started with the statement: RCC_APB1ENR.TIM2EN = 1, Timer 2 interrupt vector is enabled by the statement: NVIC_IntEnable(IVT_INT_TIM2), Timer 2 is started with the statement: TIM2_CR1.CEN = 1. The timer ISR is by default called Timer2_interrupt(). The timer interrupt configuration code is by default inside the function called: InitTimer2().

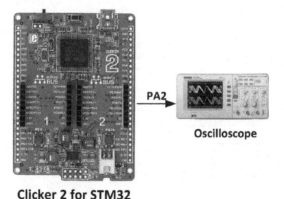

Clicker 2 for STM32

FIGURE 18.16   Block diagram of the project.

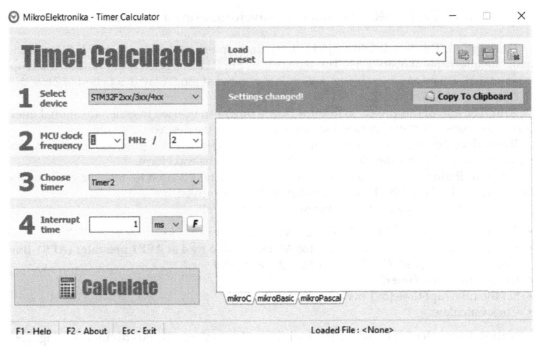

FIGURE 18.17   TimerCalculator tool startup screen.

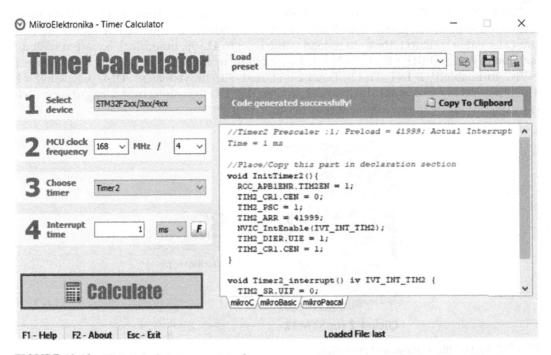

FIGURE 18.18   Click Calculate to generate code.

```
//Timer2 Prescaler :1; Preload = 41999; Actual Interrupt
Time = 1 ms

//Place/Copy this part in declaration section
void InitTimer2(){
  RCC_APB1ENR.TIM2EN = 1;
  TIM2_CR1.CEN = 0;
  TIM2_PSC = 1;
  TIM2_ARR = 41999;
  NVIC_IntEnable(IVT_INT_TIM2);
  TIM2_DIER.UIE = 1;
  TIM2_CR1.CEN = 1;
}

void Timer2_interrupt() iv IVT_INT_TIM2 {
  TIM2_SR.UIF = 0;
```

FIGURE 18.19   Generated code.

We can verify the correctness of the code generated by the TimerCalculator tool as follows:
At 84 MHz, the period is 0.011904 µs. With a prescaler of 1 and an auto re-load value of 41,499, the interrupt time will be:

$$0.011904 \times 1(+1) \times 41,499(+1) = 988 \ \mu s, \text{ or nearly 1 ms.}$$

Note that the prescaler and auto re-load register values will have to be incremented by 1.

Fig. 18.20 shows the program listing (program: **timerint.c**). At the beginning of the main program, port pin PA2 is configured as an output. The interrupt configuration code (function InitTimer) is called from the main program. The main program then waits in a loop for timer interrupts to occur. Port pin PA2 is assigned to name SQUARE and it is toggled inside the timer ISR.

The generated square waveform is shown in Fig. 18.21. The horizontal axis is 1 ms/division, and the vertical axis is 1 V/division. As can be seen from the display, the frequency of the waveform is 500 Hz. The waveform ON and OFF times are 1 ms each.

18.8 Project 47—External interrupt with timer interrupt

Description: This is another example where here both an external interrupt and an internal timer interrupt are used in a program. A push-button switch is connected to port pin PA0 as in Project 45. Timer 2 is configured to generate interrupts every second and then flash an LED inside the ISR. The on-board LED at port pin PE12 is used in this project. Push-button switch is connected as in Project 45 where the state of the button is normally at logic LOW and goes to HIGH when the button is pressed.

Aim: The aim of this project is to show how an external interrupt and a timer interrupt can be used in the same program.

```
/*===============================================================================
                          TIMER INTERRUPT - GENERATE WAVEFORM
                          ==================================

In this project a timer interrupt is configured using timer TIM2. The timer
interrupts every millisecond. Port pin PA2 is toggled in the ISR so that a square
waveform is generated at this pin with a frequency of 500Hz.

Author: Dogan Ibrahim
Date  : October, 2019
File  : timerint.c
===============================================================================*/
#include "main.h"
#define SQUARE GPIOA_ODR.B2

//
// Configure Timer 2 to generate an interrupt every 1ms
//
void InitTimer2()
{
  RCC_APB1ENR.TIM2EN = 1;                               // Set clock to Timer 2
  TIM2_CR1.CEN = 0;                                     // Disable Timer 2
  TIM2_PSC = 1;                                         // Set prescaler to 1
  TIM2_ARR = 41999;                                     // Set auto re-load to 41999
  NVIC_IntEnable(IVT_INT_TIM2);                         // Enable NVIC vector
  TIM2_DIER.UIE = 1;                                    // Set pending interrupt
  TIM2_CR1.CEN = 1;                                     // Enable timer
}


//
// This is the timer interrupt service routine. The program jumps here every 1ms
//
void Timer2_interrupt() iv IVT_INT_TIM2
{
  TIM2_SR.UIF = 0;
  SQUARE = ~SQUARE;                                     // Toggle pin PA2
}


//
// Main program configures PA2 as output, configures Timer 2 for 1ms interrupts
// and waits forever in a loop
//
void main()
{
    GPIO_Config(&GPIOA_BASE, _GPIO_PINMASK_2, _GPIO_CFG_MODE_OUTPUT);
    InitTimer2();

    while(1)                                            // Wait here
    {
    }
}
```

FIGURE 18.20   timerint.c program listing.

Program listing: In this program the TimerCalculator is used to generate code for 1 second interrupts. The required code is shown in Fig. 18.22.

Fig. 18.23 shows the program listing (program: **timerext.c**). External interrupts are configured as in Project 45. Pressing the button sets variable Flag to 1 which starts the LED flashing inside the timer ISR. The flashing is achieved by toggling the state of the LED. The LED flashes continuously such that it is ON for 1 s and then OFF for 1 s.

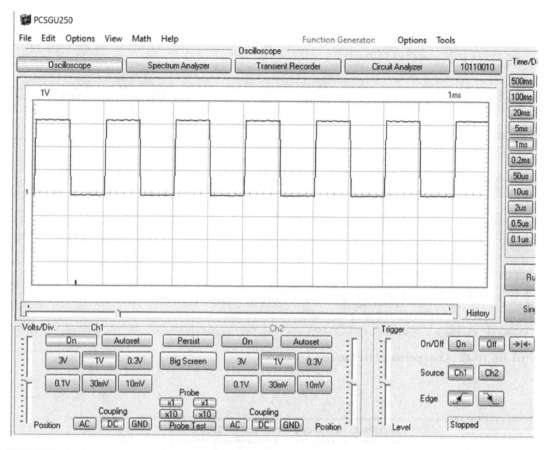

FIGURE 18.21   Waveform displayed on the screen.

We can verify the correctness of the code generated by the TimerCalculator tool as follows:
At 84 MHz, the period is 0.011904 µs. With a prescaler of 1343 and an auto re-load value of 62,499, the interrupt time will be:

$$0.011904 \times 1344 \times 41{,}500 = 1{,}000{,}000 \ \mu s, \text{ or } 1s$$

18.9 Summary

In this Chapter we have learned how to configure and use the STM32F407 microcontroller external and internal (timer) interrupts. Several example projects are given to show how interrupts can be generated in our programs.

In the next Chapter we shall be looking at how to use interrupts in FreeRTOS based programs.

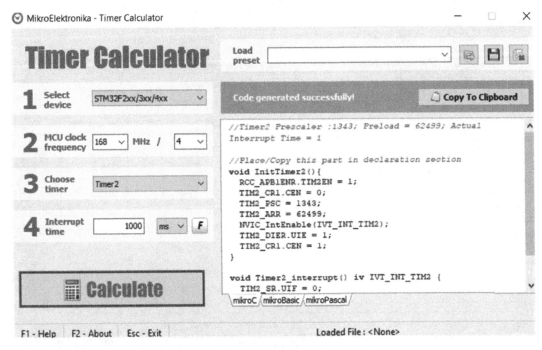

FIGURE 18.22   Code generated for 1 second interrupts.

```
/*===============================================================================
                    EXTERNAL INTERRUPT WITH TIMER INTERRUPT
                    =======================================

In this project a timer interrupt is configured using timer TIM2. The timer
interrupts every second. Port pin PA0 is configured as a rising edge external
interrupt source where a push-button switch is connected to this pin. Pressing the
button sets a Flag which starts the LED flashing inside the timer ISR

Author: Dogan Ibrahim
Date   : October, 2019
File   : timerext.c
===============================================================================*/
#include "main.h"
#define LED GPIOE_ODR.B12

volatile unsigned char Flag = 0;

//
// External interrupt ISR
//
void TurnON() iv IVT_INT_EXTI0 ics ICS_AUTO
{
    EXTI_PR.B0 = 1;
    Flag = 1;
}
```

FIGURE 18.23   timerext.c program listing.

```
//
// Configure external interrupt
//
void SetupPA0()
{
    SYSCFG_EXTICR1 = 0;                             // For pin PA0
    EXTI_FTSR.B0 = 0;                               // Not on falling edge
    EXTI_RTSR.B0= 1;                                // Interrupt on rising edge
    EXTI_IMR.B0 = 1;                                // Unmask interrupt source
    EXTI_PR.B0= 1;                                  // Pending request
    NVIC_IntEnable(IVT_INT_EXTI0);                  // Enable interrupt on line EXTI0
}

//
// Configure Timer 2 to generate an interrupt every second
//
void InitTimer2()
{
  RCC_APB1ENR.TIM2EN = 1;
  TIM2_CR1.CEN = 0;
  TIM2_PSC = 1343;
  TIM2_ARR = 62499;
  NVIC_IntEnable(IVT_INT_TIM2);
  TIM2_DIER.UIE = 1;
  TIM2_CR1.CEN = 1;
}


//
// This is the timer interrupt service routine. Toggle the LED
//
void Timer2_interrupt() iv IVT_INT_TIM2
{
  TIM2_SR.UIF = 0;
  if(Flag == 1) LED = ~LED;                         // Toggle the LED
}

//
// Main program configures PA0 as input, configures Timer 2 for 1s interrupts
// and waits forever in a loop
//
void main()
{
    GPIO_Config(&GPIOE_BASE, _GPIO_PINMASK_12, _GPIO_CFG_MODE_OUTPUT);
    GPIO_Config(&GPIOA_BASE, _GPIO_PINMASK_0, _GPIO_CFG_MODE_INPUT);
    SetupPA0();                                     // Configure external int
    InitTimer2();                                   // Configure timer int

    while(1)                                        // Wait here
    {
    }
}
```

FIGURE 18.23   (*Continued*)

Further readings

[1] R. Toulson, T. Wilmshurst, Fast and Effective Embedded Systems Design, Newnes, Oxon, UK, 2017. ISBN: 978-0-08-100880-5.
[2] P. Horowitz, W. Hill, The Art of Electronics, third ed., Cambridge University Press, Cambridge, UK, 2016.

USING the FreeRTOS API function calls from an ISR

19.1 Overview

In the last chapter we have learned how to use external and internal interrupts in our mikroC Pro for ARM based programs. In this chapter we shall learn how to call the FreeRTOS API functions from an ISR.

There are applications where we may want to call the FreeRTOS functions from inside an ISR. It is important to realize that most of the FreeRTOS functions are not valid inside an ISR. If a FreeRTOS function is called from an ISR, then it is not being called from a task. FreeRTOS provides two versions of some of the functions where one is for use from inside ISRs, and the other one for use outside ISRs. The functions that can be used inside an ISR have the word **FromISR** appended to their names and these are known as interrupt safe functions. It is recommended that a FreeRTOS function must not be called from an ISR unless its name is appended with the word **FromISR**.

As suggested by the FreeRTOS developers, there are some benefits of using separate interrupt safe functions. Firstly, using a separate function for use in interrupts makes both the task code and the ISR more efficient. There are also some disadvantages of using a separate interrupt safe function, usually when integrating third party code in our programs. Detailed explanations of the advantages and disadvantages of using separate FreeRTOS functions in ISRs is explained in the following references:

Mastering the FreeRTOS Real Time Kernel: A Hands on Tutorial Guide, by Richard Barry, link:

https://www.freertos.org/wp-content/uploads/2018/07/161204_Mastering_the_FreeRTOS_Real_Time_Kernel-A_Hands-On_Tutorial_Guide.pdf

And

The FreeRTOS Reference Manual: API Functions and Configuration Options, link:

https://www.freertos.org/wp-content/uploads/2018/07/FreeRTOS_Reference_Manual_V10.0.0.pdf

Also the FreeRTOS web site:

www.FreeRTOS.org

ARM-Based Microcontroller Multitasking Projects. http://dx.doi.org/10.1016/B978-0-12-821227-1.00019-0

19.2 The xHigherPriorityTaskWoken parameter

It is highly likely that if a context switching is done by an interrupt, then the task that runs after the interrupt exists may be different to the task that was running when the interrupt occurred. Consider the case where a task is in Blocked state. If this task gets unblocked by a FreeRTOS function call and if the priority of this task is higher that the task which is in the Running state, then the scheduler is expected to switch to the higher priority task. In fact, the algorithm to switch to the higher task is dependent whether the API function is called from a task or from an ISR.

If the API function was called from a task and if preemptive scheduling is enabled, then the scheduler automatically switched to the higher priority task, as this is the normal state of affairs with tasks running in FreeRTOS.

If on the other hand the API function was called from an ISR, switch to a higher priority task will not occur automatically inside the ISR. Instead, a variable called *pxHigherPriorityTask-Woken is set to pdTRUE by the interrupt safe API functions to indicate that a context switch should be performed. This variable must be initialized to pdFALSE before it is used so that its change can be detected. If the program developer does not want a context switch from the ISR then the higher priority task will remain in the Ready state until the scheduler runs on the next tick interrupt. As described in length in the above references, there are several reasons why context switching does not occur automatically inside an ISR. Some of the reasons are: avoiding unnecessary context switches, portability, efficiency, control of the execution sequence, etc.

The macros portEnd_SWITCHING (or portYIELD_FROM_ISR) are the interrupt safe versions of the taskYIELD() macro. The xHigherPriorityTaskWoken parameter is passed to these macros. If xHIGHERPriorityTaskWoken is pdFALSE then context switching does not occur. If on the other hand pdTRUE then a context switching is requested and the task in the Running state may change, even though the interrupt always returns to the task in the Running state.

19.3 Deferred interrupt processing

It is always advisable to keep an ISR as short as possible so that very little time is spent in the ISR. If the ISR is going to be long, then it is advisable to record the cause of the interrupt and do the main interrupt processing outside the ISR. This is called Deferred Interrupt and is a commonly used technique. For example, suppose that we have an event counter program where the occurrence of events causes an external interrupt to occur where a variable is incremented each time an interrupt occurs. We may then want to display the total count on an LCD. In such a case it is best only to increment the variable inside the ISR and then perform the display functions outside the ISR and inside a task. Deferring an interrupt processing makes the program more efficient also makes it easier to manage the priorities in a program. If the task where the interrupt is deferred has the highest priority in the system then it is guaranteed that it will run after returning from the interrupt. Additionally, by deferring an interrupt processing, we can use all of the FreeRTOS API functions safely inside a task.

In the next few sections of this chapter we shall be looking at some of the FreeRTOS API functions that can be called safely from ISRs. Further information on these functions can be obtained from the references given in the Overview section of this chapter.

19.4 Task related functions from ISR

Some task related functions are given in this section. Full details can be obtained from the references given in the Overview section of this chapter.

19.4.1 taskENTER_CRITICAL_FROM_ISR() and taskEXIT_CRITICAL_FROM_ISR()

These are the interrupt safe versions of the API functions taskENTER_CRITICAL() and taskEXIT_CRITICAL() that are used to implement critical sections. taskENTER_CRITICAL_FROM_ISR() returns The interrupt mask state at the time of the call. The return value must be saved so it can be passed into the matching call to taskEXIT_CRITICAL_FROM_ISR() which does not return any value.

19.4.2 xTaskNotifyFromISR()

This is the interrupt safe version of the function xTaskNotify(). The format of the function is:

xTaskNotifyFromISR(TaskHandle_t xTaskToNotify, uint32_t ulValue, eNotifyAction eActionBaseType_t *pxHigherPriorityTaskWoken);

The parameters are same as function xTaskNotify() except the last parameter which has the following definition:

pxHigherPriorityTaskWoken: This parameter must be initialized to pdFALSE before being used. It is set to pdTRUE if the task being notified has a priority above that of the currently running task. A context switching should be requested if the parameter is set to pdTRUE.

19.4.3 xTaskNotifyGiveFromISR()

This is the interrupt safe version of the function xTaskNotifyGive(). The format of the function is:

vTaskNotifyGiveFromISR(TaskHandle_t xTaskToNotify, BaseType_t *pxHigherPriorityTaskWoken);

The parameters are same as function xTaskNotify() except the *pxHigherPriorityTaskWoken which is described above.

19.4.4 xTaskResumeFromISR()

This is the interrupt safe version of the function xTaskResumeFromISR(). The format of the function is:

xTaskResumeFromISR(TaskHandle_t pxTaskToResume);

The function has only one parameter which is the handle of the task to be resumed. The function returns the following values:

pdTRUE: The task being resumed (unblocked) has a priority equal to or higher than the currently executing task (the task that was interrupted), therefore a context switch should be performed before exiting the interrupt.

pdFALSE: The task being resumed has a priority lower that the currently executing task, therefore there is no need to perform context switching

19.5 Project 48-Using function xTaskResumeFromISR()

Description: In this simple project two tasks are created. Task 1 flashes the LED connected to port pin PE12 of the clicker 2 for STM32 development board. Task 2 configures an external interrupt on port pin PA0. As soon as Task 1 runs it suspends itself (i.e., moves to Blocked state). When the button is pressed it creates an external interrupt. Inside the ISR Task 1 is resumed so that the LED starts flashing.

Aim: The aim of this project is to show how the interrupt safe function xTaskResumeFromISR() can be used in a program.

Block diagram: The block diagram of the project is shown in Fig. 19.1. The push-button switch is connected to port pin PA0 such that normally its state is at logic LOW and goes to logic HIGH when pressed.

Program listing: The program listing of the project (program: **isrresume.c**) is shown in Fig. 19.2. There are two tasks in the program in addition to the Idle task, and both tasks are configured to run at the same priority. The operation of the two tasks and the ISR are described by the following PDLs:

TASK 1
Configure the LED as an output
Suspend itself
DO FOREVER

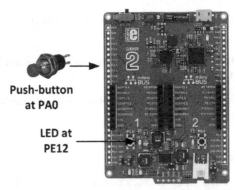

Push-button
at PA0

LED at
PE12

Clicker 2 for STM32

FIGURE 19.1   Block diagram of the project.

```
/*=====================================================================
                       INTERRUPT SAFE RESUME EXAMPLE
                       =============================

In this project a push-button switch is connected to port pin PA0 such that the
state of the button is logic LOW. There are two tasks in the program (in addition
to teh Idle task). Task 1 flsshes the on-board LED PE12 every second. But when
Task 1 starts it suspends itself. Task 1 is resumed by the ISR which is activated
when the button is pressed

Author: Dogan Ibrahim
Date   : October, 2019
File   : isrresume.c
=====================================================================*/
#include "main.h"
TaskHandle_t xHandle;

//
// External interrupt ISR. Resume Task 1 in the ISR
//
void TurnON() iv IVT_INT_EXTI0 ics ICS_AUTO
{
    BaseType_t xYieldRequired = pdFALSE;

    EXTI_PR.B0 = 1;

    if(xHandle != NULL)
    {
        xYieldRequired = xTaskResumeFromISR(xHandle);        // Resume Task 1
        if(xYieldRequired == pdTRUE)
        {
            portYIELD_FROM_ISR(xYieldRequired);
        }
    }
}

//
// Configure external interrupt
//
void SetupPA0()
{
    SYSCFG_EXTICR1 = 0;                                 // For pin PA0
    EXTI_FTSR.B0 = 0;                                   // Not on falling edge
    EXTI_RTSR.B0= 1;                                    // On rising edge
    EXTI_IMR.B0 = 1;                                    // Unmask interrupt source
    EXTI_PR.B0= 1;                                      // Pending request
    NVIC_IntEnable(IVT_INT_EXTI0);                      // Enable interrupt on line EXTI0
    NVIC_SetIntPriority(IVT_INT_EXTI0,_NVIC_INT_PRIORITY_LVL1);
}

// Task 1 - LED CONTROLLER
void Task1(void *pvParameters)
{
    #define LED GPIOE_ODR.B12
    GPIO_Config(&GPIOE_BASE, _GPIO_PINMASK_12, _GPIO_CFG_MODE_OUTPUT);
    vTaskSuspend(NULL);                                 // Suspend itself

    while (1)
    {
        LED = 1;                                        // LED ON
```

FIGURE 19.2   isrresume.c program listing.

```
            vTaskDelay(pdMS_TO_TICKS(1000));        // Wait 1 second
            LED = 0;                                 // LED OFF
            vTaskDelay(pdMS_TO_TICKS(1000));        // wait 1 second
        }
    }

    // Task 2 - BUTTON CONTROLLER
    void Task2(void *pvParameters)
    {
        const char *pcNameToLookup = "LED Controller";
        GPIO_Config(&GPIOA_BASE, _GPIO_PINMASK_0, _GPIO_CFG_MODE_INPUT);
        xHandle = xTaskGetHandle(pcNameToLookup);
        SetupPA0();                                  // Config ext interrupts

        while (1)                                    // Wait here forever
        {
        }
    }

    //
    // Start of MAIN program
    // =====================
    //
    void main()
    {
    //
    // Create all the TASKS here
    // =========================
    //
        // Create Task 1
        xTaskCreate(
            (TaskFunction_t)Task1,
            "LED Controller",
            configMINIMAL_STACK_SIZE,
            NULL,
            10,
            NULL
        );

        //Create Task 2
        xTaskCreate(
            (TaskFunction_t)Task2,
            "Button Controller",
            configMINIMAL_STACK_SIZE,
            NULL,
            10,
            NULL
        );

    //
    // Start the RTOS scheduler
    //
        vTaskStartScheduler();

    //
    // Will never reach here
    //
        while (1);
    }
```

FIGURE 19.2   (*Continued*)

Flash the LED
ENDDO
<u>**TASK 2**</u>
Configure pin PA0 to generate external interrupt
DO FOREVER
Wait
ENDDO
<u>**ISR**</u>
Resume Task 1
IF context switching is required **THEN**
Call portYIELD_FROM_ISR() to perform context switching
ENDIF

As soon as Task 1 runs it calls API function vTaskSuspend(NULL) to suspend itself at which point this task is blocked and cannot run. Task 2 gets the handle of Task 1 and when the button is pressed Task 1 is resumed from inside the ISR.

19.6 Project 49-Deferred interrupt processing

Description: In this project, Project 48 has been modified so that inside the ISR a flag is set to indicate that an interrupt has occurred. Then, the LED flashing task (TASK 1) is resumed outside the ISR and inside Task 2. This way we can use all of the FreeRTOS API functions outside the ISR.

Aim: The aim of this project is to show how the main processing can be moved to outside the ISR, that is, it shows the concept of deferred interrupt processing.

Block diagram: The block diagram of the project is as in Fig. 19.1.

Program listing: Fig. 19.3 shows the program listing (program: **deferred.c**). In this version of the program Task 1 suspends itself. When an interrupt occurs a flag is set inside the ISR. Task 2 checks the flag and when it is set resumes Task 1, which then starts the LED flashing.

19.7 Project 50-Using function xTaskNotifyFromISR( )

Description: In this project, Project 49 has been modified so that Task 1 waits for notification before starting to flash the LED. Inside the ISR, function xTaskNotifyFromISR() is called to send a notification to Task 1 so that the LED flashing can start.

Aim: The aim of this project is to show how the FreeRTOS API function xTaskNotifyFromISR() can be used in a project.

Block diagram: The block diagram of the project is as in Fig. 19.1.

Program listing: Fig. 19.4 shows the program listing (program: **isrnotify.c**). In this version of the program Task 1 waits for notification as soon as it runs. When an interrupt occurs a notification is sent to Task 1 from inside the ISR so that flashing can start. Notice that the macro portYIELD_FROM_ISR() is called to perform a context switching if the priority of the notified task is higher than the running task.

```
/*==============================================================================
                       DEFERRED INTERRUPT PROCESSING
                       =============================

In this project a push-button switch is connected to port pin PA0 such that the
state of the button is logic LOW. There are two tasks in the program (in addition
to the Idle task). Task 1 flashes the on-board LED PE12 every second. But when
Task 1 starts it suspends itself. Task 1 is resumed by the ISR which is activated
when the button is pressed

Author: Dogan Ibrahim
Date   : October, 2019
File   : deferred.c
==============================================================================*/
#include "main.h"
TaskHandle_t xHandle;
unsigned char Flag = 0;

//
// External interrupt ISR. Resume Task 1 in the ISR
//
void TurnON() iv IVT_INT_EXTI0 ics ICS_AUTO
{
    EXTI_PR.B0 = 1;
    Flag = 1;                                       // Set flag
}


//
// Configure external interrupt
//
void SetupPA0()
{
    SYSCFG_EXTICR1 = 0;                             // For pin PA0
    EXTI_FTSR.B0 = 0;                               // Not on falling edge
    EXTI_RTSR.B0= 1;                                // On rising edge
    EXTI_IMR.B0 = 1;                                // Unmask interrupt source
    EXTI_PR.B0= 1;                                  // Pending request
    NVIC_IntEnable(IVT_INT_EXTI0);                  // Enable interrupt on line EXTI0
    NVIC_SetIntPriority(IVT_INT_EXTI0,_NVIC_INT_PRIORITY_LVL1);
}

// Task 1 - LED CONTROLLER
void Task1(void *pvParameters)
{
    #define LED GPIOE_ODR.B12
    GPIO_Config(&GPIOE_BASE, _GPIO_PINMASK_12, _GPIO_CFG_MODE_OUTPUT);
    vTaskSuspend(NULL);                             // Suspend itself

    while (1)
    {
        LED = 1;                                    // LED ON
        vTaskDelay(pdMS_TO_TICKS(1000));            // Wait 1 second
        LED = 0;                                    // LED OFF
        vTaskDelay(pdMS_TO_TICKS(1000));            // wait 1 second
    }
}

// Task 2 - BUTTON CONTROLLER
void Task2(void *pvParameters)
{
```

FIGURE 19.3   deferred.c program listing.

```
        const char *pcNameToLookup = "LED Controller";
        GPIO_Config(&GPIOA_BASE, _GPIO_PINMASK_0, _GPIO_CFG_MODE_INPUT);
        xHandle = xTaskGetHandle(pcNameToLookup);
        SetupPA0();                                    // Config ext interrupts

        while (1)                                      // Wait here forever
        {   if(Flag == 1)
            {
                Flag = 0;
                vTaskResume(xHandle);                  // Resume Task 1
            }
        }
}


//
// Start of MAIN program
// =====================
//
void main()
{
//
// Create all the TASKS here
// =========================
//
        // Create Task 1
        xTaskCreate(
            (TaskFunction_t)Task1,
            "LED Controller",
            configMINIMAL_STACK_SIZE,
            NULL,
            10,
            NULL
        );

        //Create Task 2
        xTaskCreate(
            (TaskFunction_t)Task2,
            "Button Controller",
            configMINIMAL_STACK_SIZE,
            NULL,
            10,
            NULL
        );

//
// Start the RTOS scheduler
//
        vTaskStartScheduler();

//
// Will never reach here
//
        while (1);
}
```

FIGURE 19.3   (Continued)

```
/*===============================================================================
                        NOTIFY FROM INTERRUPT
                        =====================

In this project a push-button switch is connected to port pin PA0 such that the
state of the button is logic LOW. There are two tasks in the program (in addition
to the Idle task). Task 1 flashes the on-board LED PE12 every second. But when
Task 1 starts it waits for notification. When the button is pressed, a notification
is sent inside teh ISR so that the LED starts flashing.

Author: Dogan Ibrahim
Date   : October, 2019
File   : isrnotify.c
=================================================================================*/
#include "main.h"
TaskHandle_t xHandle;

//
// External interrupt ISR. Notify Task 1 in the ISR
//
void TurnON() iv IVT_INT_EXTI0 ics ICS_AUTO
{
    BaseType_t xHigherPriorityTaskWoken = pdFALSE;
    EXTI_PR.B0 = 1;
    xTaskNotifyFromISR(xHandle, 0x02, eSetValueWithOverwrite,&xHigherPriorityTaskWoken);
    portYIELD_FROM_ISR(xHigherPriorityTaskWoken);
}


//
// Configure external interrupt
//
void SetupPA0()
{
    SYSCFG_EXTICR1 = 0;                               // For pin PA0
    EXTI_FTSR.B0 = 0;                                 // Not on falling edge
    EXTI_RTSR.B0= 1;                                  // On rising edge
    EXTI_IMR.B0 = 1;                                  // Unmask interrupt source
    EXTI_PR.B0= 1;                                    // Pending request
    NVIC_IntEnable(IVT_INT_EXTI0);                    // Enable interrupt on line EXTI0
    NVIC_SetIntPriority(IVT_INT_EXTI0,_NVIC_INT_PRIORITY_LVL1);
}

// Task 1 - LED CONTROLLER
void Task1(void *pvParameters)
{
    #define LED GPIOE_ODR.B12
    #define ULONG_MAX 0xffffffff
    uint32_t ulNotifiedValue;
    GPIO_Config(&GPIOE_BASE, _GPIO_PINMASK_12, _GPIO_CFG_MODE_OUTPUT);
    xTaskNotifyWait(0, ULONG_MAX, &ulNotifiedValue, portMAX_DELAY);

    if((ulNotifiedValue & 0x02) != 0)
    {
        while (1)
        {
            LED = 1;                                  // LED ON
            vTaskDelay(pdMS_TO_TICKS(1000));          // Wait 1 second
            LED = 0;                                  // LED OFF
            vTaskDelay(pdMS_TO_TICKS(1000));          // wait 1 second
        }
```

FIGURE 19.4   isrnotify.c program listing.

```
        }
    }

    // Task 2 - BUTTON CONTROLLER
    void Task2(void *pvParameters)
    {
        const char *pcNameToLookup = "LED Controller";
        GPIO_Config(&GPIOA_BASE, _GPIO_PINMASK_0, _GPIO_CFG_MODE_INPUT);
        xHandle = xTaskGetHandle(pcNameToLookup);
        SetupPA0();                                    // Config ext interrupts

        while (1)                                      // Wait here forever
        {
        }
    }

    //
    // Start of MAIN program
    // =====================
    //
    void main()
    {
    //
    // Create all the TASKS here
    // =========================
    //
        // Create Task 1
        xTaskCreate(
            (TaskFunction_t)Task1,
            "LED Controller",
            configMINIMAL_STACK_SIZE,
            NULL,
            10,
            NULL
        );

        //Create Task 2
        xTaskCreate(
            (TaskFunction_t)Task2,
            "Button Controller",
            configMINIMAL_STACK_SIZE,
            NULL,
            10,
            NULL
        );

    //
    // Start the RTOS scheduler
    //
        vTaskStartScheduler();

    //
    // Will never reach here
    //
        while (1);
    }
```

FIGURE 19.4 *(Continued)*

As soon as Task 1 runs, it waits for notification by calling the following API function where the parameter portMAX_DELAY is used so that the task is blocked until a notification is received:

```
xTaskNotifyWait(0, ULONG_MAX, &ulNotifiedValue, portMAX_DELAY);
```

If the notification value is 0x02 then Task 1 starts flashing the LED every second.

The ISR notifies Task 1 by the following function call:

```
xTaskNotifyFromISR(xHandle, 0x02, eSetValueWithOverwrite,&xHigherPriority
TaskWoken);
```

where xHandle is the handle of Task 1, 0x02 is the notification value which is overwritten at the notified tasks notification value.

External interrupt at pin PA0 is configured and the interrupt priority is set to Level 1.

The handle of Task 1 is obtained by calling function xTaskGetHandle as follows:

```
const char *pcNameToLookup = "LED Controller";
xHandle = xTaskGetHandle(pcNameToLookup);
```

19.8 Event group related functions from ISR

Several event group related API functions are available that can be called from ISRs. Commonly used functions are described in the following sections. Interested readers can get further information on these functions from the references given in the Overview section of this chapter.

19.8.1 xEventGroupSetBitsFromISR()

This is the interrupt safe version of the API function xEventGroupSetBits(), where setting a bit unblocks a task that is waiting for that bit to be set. This task has the following format:

xEventGroupSetBitsFromISR(EventGroupHandle_t xEventGroup, const EventBits_t uxBitsToSet,BaseType_t *pxHigherPriorityTaskWoken);

where, xEventGroup is the handle of the event group in which the bits are to be set (the event group must be created before), uxBitsToSet is the bitwise value that indicates the bit (or bits) to be set in the event group, and pxHigherPriorityTaskWoken is the parameter as defined in the other interrupt safe API functions.

The function returns pdTRUE if the message to set the required event flags was sent to the RTOS deamon task.

19.8.2 xEventGroupClearBitsFrmISR()

This is the interrupt safe version of the API function xEventGroupClearBits(), where the specified event flag bits are cleared. The format of the function is:

xEventGroupClearBitsFromISR(EventGroupHandle_t xEventGroup, const EventBits_t uxBitsToClear);

where, xEventGroup is the handle of the event group, and uxBitsToClear is the bitwise value that indicates which bits to be cleared.

The function returns pdTRUE if the message to set the required event flags was sent to the RTOS deamon task.

An example project is given in the next section to illustrate how the function xEventGroupSetBitsFromISR() can be used in a practical application.

19.9 Project 51-Using function xEventGroupSetBitsFromISR()

Description: In this project, Project 49 has been modified so that Task 1 waits for an event flag to be set before starting to flash the LED. Inside the ISR, the API function xEventGroupSetBitsFromISR() is called to set the event flag that Task 1 is waiting for so that the LED flashing can start.

Aim: The aim of this project is to show how the FreeRTOS API function xEventGroupSetBitsFromISR() can be used in a project.

Block diagram: The block diagram of the project is as in Fig. 19.1.

Program listing: Fig. 19.5 shows the program listing (program: **isrflag.c**). In this version of the program Task 1 waits for event flag 2 to be set as soon as it runs. When an interrupt occurs, event flag 2 is set from inside the ISR so that flashing can start. Notice that the macro portYIELD_FROM_ISR() is called to perform a context switching if the priority of the notified task is higher than the running task.

An event flag group with the handle xEventGroup is created inside the main part of the program. When Task 1 runs it waits for event flag 2 to be set by calling the following API function:

```
uxBits = xEventGroupWaitBits(xEventGroup, BIT_2, pdTRUE, pdFALSE, portMAX_
DELAY);
```

This function blocks the task until the event flag is set. When the button is pressed an external interrupt occurs where the program jumps to the ISR named TurnON. Here, event flag 2 is set by calling the following API function:

```
xResult = xEventGroupSetBitsFromISR(xEventGroup, BIT_2, &xHigherPriority-
TaskWoken);
```

Notice that by setting the event flag Task 1 will be unblocked and it will start to flash the LED every second. The program checks to ensure that event flag 2 has actually been set before starting to flash the LED:

```
if((uxBits & BIT_2) !=0)              // Is event flag 2 set?
{
          while (1)
          {
          LED = 1;            // LED ON
          vTaskDelay(pdMS_TO_TICKS(1000));           // Wait 1 second
          LED = 0;// LED OFF
          vTaskDelay(pdMS_TO_TICKS(1000));           // wait 1 second
          }
          }
```

If a context switching is requested then the macro portYIELD_FROM_ISR() is called before returning from the ISR.

```
/*================================================================================
                            EVENT FLAG FROM INTERRUPT
                            =========================

In this project a push-button switch is connected to port pin PA0 such that the
state of the button is logic LOW. There are two tasks in the program (in addition
to the Idle task). Task 1 flashes the on-board LED PE12 every second. But when
Task 1 starts it waits for event flag 2 to be set. When the button is pressed,
event flag 2 is set inside the ISR so that the LED starts flashing.

Author: Dogan Ibrahim
Date  : October, 2019
File  : isrflag.c
================================================================================*/
#include "main.h"
#include "event_groups.h"
EventGroupHandle_t xEventGroup;

//
// External interrupt ISR. Set event flag 2 inside the ISR
//
void TurnON() iv IVT_INT_EXTI0 ics ICS_AUTO
{
    #define BIT_2 ( 1 << 2 )
    BaseType_t xResult, xHigherPriorityTaskWoken = pdFALSE;
    EXTI_PR.B0 = 1;
    xResult = xEventGroupSetBitsFromISR(xEventGroup, BIT_2, &xHigherPriorityTaskWoken);
    if(xResult != pdFAIL)
    {
        portYIELD_FROM_ISR(xHigherPriorityTaskWoken);
    }
}


//
// Configure external interrupt
//
void SetupPA0()
{
    SYSCFG_EXTICR1 = 0;                                // For pin PA0
    EXTI_FTSR.B0 = 0;                                  // Not on falling edge
    EXTI_RTSR.B0= 1;                                   // On rising edge
    EXTI_IMR.B0 = 1;                                   // Unmask interrupt source
    EXTI_PR.B0= 1;                                     // Pending request
    NVIC_IntEnable(IVT_INT_EXTI0);                     // Enable interrupt on line EXTI0
    NVIC_SetIntPriority(IVT_INT_EXTI0,_NVIC_INT_PRIORITY_LVL1);
}

// Task 1 - LED CONTROLLER
void Task1(void *pvParameters)
{
    #define LED GPIOE_ODR.B12
    #define BIT_2 ( 1 << 2)

    EventBits_t uxBits;
    GPIO_Config(&GPIOE_BASE, _GPIO_PINMASK_12, _GPIO_CFG_MODE_OUTPUT);
    uxBits = xEventGroupWaitBits(xEventGroup, BIT_2, pdTRUE, pdFALSE, portMAX_DELAY);

    if((uxBits & BIT_2) != 0)                          // Is event flag 2 set?
    {
       while (1)
```

FIGURE 19.5   isrflag.c program listing.

```
            {
                LED = 1;                              // LED ON
                vTaskDelay(pdMS_TO_TICKS(1000));      // Wait 1 second
                LED = 0;                              // LED OFF
                vTaskDelay(pdMS_TO_TICKS(1000));      // wait 1 second
            }
        }
}

// Task 2 - BUTTON CONTROLLER
void Task2(void *pvParameters)
{
    GPIO_Config(&GPIOA_BASE, _GPIO_PINMASK_0, _GPIO_CFG_MODE_INPUT);
    SetupPA0();                                       // Config ext interrupts

    while (1)                                         // Wait here forever
    {
    }
}

//
// Start of MAIN program
// =====================
//
void main()
{
  xEventGroup = xEventGroupCreate();                  // Create event group
//
// Create all the TASKS here
// =========================
//
    // Create Task 1
    xTaskCreate(
        (TaskFunction_t)Task1,
        "LED Controller",
        configMINIMAL_STACK_SIZE,
        NULL,
        10,
        NULL
    );

    //Create Task 2
    xTaskCreate(
        (TaskFunction_t)Task2,
        "Button Controller",
        configMINIMAL_STACK_SIZE,
        NULL,
        10,
        NULL
    );
//
// Start the RTOS scheduler
//
    vTaskStartScheduler();

//
// Will never reach here
//
    while (1);
}
```

FIGURE 19.5   (Continued)

The following parameters must be set and configured in file freeRTOSConfig.h before compiling the program:

```
#define configUSE_TIMERS              1
#define configTIMER_TASK_PRIORITY            10
#define configTIMER_QUEUE_LENGTH             10
#define configTIMER_TASK_STACK_DEPTH              configMINIMAL_STACK_SIZE
#define INCLUDE_xEventGroupSetBitsFromISR           1
#define INCLUDE_xTimerPendFunctionCall          1
```

19.10 Timer related functions from ISR

Several timer related API functions are available that can be called from inside ISRs. Commonly used functions are described in the following sections. Interested readers can get further information on these functions from the references given in the Overview section of this chapter.

19.10.1 xTimerStartFromISR()

This is the interrupt safe version of the API function xTimerStart(). The format of the function is:

xTimerStartFromISR(TimerHandle_t xTimer, BaseType_t *pxHigherPriorityTaskWoken);

where, parameter xTimer is the timer handle, and *pxHigherPriorityTaskWoken is as in the other interrupt safe functions. Function returns pdPASS of the command was successfully sent to the timer command queue.

19.10.2 xTimerStopFromISR()

This is the interrupt safe version of the API function xTimerStop(). This function has the same parameters and return values as the xTimerStartFromISR().

19.10.3 xTimerResetFromISR()

This is the interrupt safe version of the API function xTimerReset(). This function has the same parameters and return values as the xTimerStartFromISR().

19.10.4 xTimerChangePeriodFromISR()

This is the interrupt safe version of the API function xTimerChangePeriod(). The format of this function is:

xTimerChangePeriodFromISR(TimerHandle_t xTimer, TickType_t xNewPeriod, BaseType_t* pxHigherPriorityTaskWoken);

where, xNewPeriod is the new period of the timer and the other two parameters and the return values are same as function xTimerStartFromISR().

An example project is given in the next section to illustrate how the function xTimerStartFromISR() and xTimerChangePeriodFromISR() can be used in a practical application.

19.11 Project 52-Using functions xTimerStartFromISR() and xTimerChangePeriodFromISR()

Description: In this project two push-button switches and an LED are used. One of the buttons is connected to port pin PA0 and the other one is the on-board button at port pin PA10. The LED at port pin PE12 is used. Pressing PA0 generates an external interrupt which starts a timer from the ISR where the LED is flashed continuously every second at the of the timer period. Pressing button PA10 generates another external interrupt where the period of the flashing changes to every 250 ms.

Aim: The aim of this project is to show how the FreeRTOS API functions xTimerStartFromISR() and xTimerChangePeriodFromISR() can be used in a practical application.

Block diagram: The block diagram of the project is as in Fig. 18.14 where button at PA0 generates an interrupt on the rising edge when pressed, and button at PA10 generates an interrupt on the falling edge when pressed.

Program listing: Fig. 19.6 shows the program listing (program: **isrtimer.c**). The program consists of one task only in addition to the Idle task. Task 1 controls the buttons at port pins PA0 and PA10. The operation of the program is illustrated by the following PDLs:

TASK 1
Configure rising edge external interrupts at port pin PA0
Configure falling edge external interrupts at port pin PA10
Rising Edge ISR (StartTimer)
Start timer with 1 second period
Falling Edge ISR (ChangePeriod)
Change timer period to 250 ms
MAIN
Create a timer with period 1 second and running periodically
Set the callback function to FlashLED
A timer is created in the main program:

```
xTimer = xTimerCreate("Timer", (pdMS_TO_TICKS(1000)), pdTRUE, 0, vFlashLED);
```

Task 1 configures both external interrupts, where function SetupPA0() configures interrupts at port pin PA0, and function SetupPA10() configures interrupts at port pin PA10. Pressing button at PA0 starts the timer so that the callback function is called at the end of every second, thus causing the LED to flash every second:

```
xTimerStartFromISR(xTimer,&xHigherPriorityTaskWoken);
```

Pressing button at PA10 changes the timer period to 250 ms:

```
xTimerChangePeriodFromISR(xTimer,(pdMS_TO_TICKS(250)),   &xHigherPriority-
TaskWoken);
```

```
/*================================================================================
                            TIMER FROM INTERRUPT
                            ====================

In this project a push-button switch is connected to port pin PA0 such that the
state of the button is logic LOW. and goes to HIGH when the button is pressed.
Also, the on-board button at port pin PA10 is used in falling edge mode. When
PA0 is pressed a timer is started from the ISR with a period of 1 second and the
LED flashes at this rate. When PA10 is pressed, another external interrupt changes
the period of the timer to 250ms.

Author: Dogan Ibrahim
Date  : October, 2019
File  : isrtimer.c
================================================================================*/
#include "main.h"
#include "timers.h"
TimerHandle_t xTimer;

//
// External interrupt service routine (ISR). The program jumps to this ISR
// whenever the push-button PA0 is pressed. This ISR starts the timer
//
void StartTimer() iv IVT_INT_EXTI0 ics ICS_AUTO
{
    BaseType_t xHigherPriorityTaskWoken = pdFALSE;
    EXTI_PR.B0 = 1;
    xTimerStartFromISR(xTimer,&xHigherPriorityTaskWoken);
    if(xHigherPriorityTaskWoken != pdFALSE)
    {
        portYIELD_FROM_ISR(xHigherPriorityTaskWoken);
    }
}


//
// External interrupt service routine (ISR). The program jumps to this ISR
// whenever the push-button PA10 is pressed. This ISR changes the timer period
//
void ChangePeriod() iv IVT_INT_EXTI15_10 ics ICS_AUTO
{
    BaseType_t xHigherPriorityTaskWoken = pdFALSE;
    EXTI_PR.B10 = 1;
    xTimerChangePeriodFromISR(xTimer,(pdMS_TO_TICKS(250)), &xHigherPriorityTaskWoken);
    if(xHigherPriorityTaskWoken != pdFALSE)
    {
        portYIELD_FROM_ISR(xHigherPriorityTaskWoken);
    }
}


//
// This function configures the external interrupt for pin PA0 on rising edge.
// The interrupt priority is set to 1
//
void SetupPA0()
{
    SYSCFG_EXTICR1 = 0;                          // For pin PA0
    EXTI_FTSR.B0 = 0;                            // Not on falling edge
    EXTI_RTSR.B0= 1;                             // Interrupt on rising edge
    EXTI_IMR.B0 = 1;                             // Unmask interrupt source
    EXTI_PR.B0= 1;                               // Pending request
```

FIGURE 19.6   isrtimer.c program listing.

```
    NVIC_IntEnable(IVT_INT_EXTI0);                        // Enable interrupt on line EXTI0
    NVIC_SetIntPriority(IVT_INT_EXTI0,_NVIC_INT_PRIORITY_LVL1);
}

//
// This function configures the external interrupt for pin PA10 on falling edge.
// The interrupt priority is set to 1
//
void SetupPA10()
{
    SYSCFG_EXTICR3 = 0;                                   // For pin PA10
    EXTI_FTSR.B10 = 1;                                    // Interrupt on falling edge
    EXTI_RTSR.B10 = 0;                                    // Not on rising edge
    EXTI_IMR.B10 = 1;                                     // Unmask interrupt source
    EXTI_PR.B10 = 1;                                      // Pending request
    NVIC_IntEnable(IVT_INT_EXTI15_10);                    // Enable interrupt on line EXTI5_10
    NVIC_SetIntPriority(IVT_INT_EXTI0,_NVIC_INT_PRIORITY_LVL1);
}

//
// Thsi is the timer callback function which is called periodically when the
// timer expires. Initially the period is 1 second , but when button PA10 is
// pressed, the period changes to 250ms
//
void vFlashLED(TimerHandle_t xTimer)
{
    #define LED GPIOE_ODR.B12
    GPIO_Config(&GPIOE_BASE, _GPIO_PINMASK_12, _GPIO_CFG_MODE_OUTPUT);

    LED = ~LED;                                           // Toggle the LED
}


// Task 1 - BUTTON CONTROLLER
void Task1(void *pvParameters)
{
    GPIO_Config(&GPIOA_BASE, _GPIO_PINMASK_0, _GPIO_CFG_MODE_INPUT);
    GPIO_Config(&GPIOA_BASE, _GPIO_PINMASK_10, _GPIO_CFG_MODE_INPUT);
    SetupPA0();                                           // Configura PA0 interrupts
    SetupPA10();                                          // Configure PA10 interrupts

    while (1)
    {
    }
}

//
// Start of MAIN program
// =====================
//
void main()
{
  xTimer = xTimerCreate("Timer", (pdMS_TO_TICKS(1000)), pdTRUE, 0, vFlashLED);
//
// Create all the TASKS here
// =========================
//
    // Create Task 1
    xTaskCreate(
```

FIGURE 19.6   (*Continued*)

```
            (TaskFunction_t)Task1,
            "Button PA0 Controller",
            configMINIMAL_STACK_SIZE,
            NULL,
            10,
            NULL
    );

//
// Start the RTOS scheduler
//
    vTaskStartScheduler();

//
// Will never reach here
//
    while (1);
}
```

FIGURE 19.6   *(Continued)*

The following parameters must be set and configured in file freeRTOSConfig.h before compiling the program:

```
    #define configUSE_TIMERS                    1
    #define configTIMER_TASK_PRIORITY                10
    #define configTIMER_QUEUE_LENGTH                 10
    #define configTIMER_TASK_STACK_DEPTH               configMINIMAL_STACK_SIZE
    #define INCLUDE_xEventGroupSetBitsFromISR           1
    #define INCLUDE_xTimerPendFunctionCall             1
```

19.12 Semaphore related functions from ISR

A few semaphore related API functions are available that can be called from inside ISRs. Commonly used functions are described in the following sections. Interested readers can get further information on these functions from the references given in the Overview section of this chapter.

19.12.1 xSemaphoreGiveFromISR()

This is the interrupt safe version of the API function xSemaphoreGive(). This function has two parameters: the semaphore handle, and parameter *pxHigherPriorityTaskWoken which has already been described in earlier interrupt safe functions.

19.12.2 xSemaphoreTakeFromISR()

This is the interrupt safe version of the API function xSemaphoreTake(). This function has two parameters: the semaphore handle, and parameter *pxHigherPriorityTaskWoken which has already been described in earlier interrupt safe functions.

An example project is given in the next section to illustrate how the function xSemaphore-GiveFromISR() and xSemaphoreTakeFromISR() can be used in a practical application.

19.13 Project 53-Using functions xSemaphoreTakeFromISR() and xSemaphoreGive()

Description: This project shows how a task and the ISR can be synchronized. There is only one task in the program. A push-button switch is connected to port pin PA0 as in the previous projects and the on-board LED at port pin PE12 is used. The task and ISR are synchronized such that each time the button is pressed an interrupt is created to take the semaphore and then the state of the LED is toggled.

Aim: The aim of this project is to show how the FreeRTOS API functions xSemaphoreTakeFromISR() and xSemaphoreGive() can be used in a practical application.

Program listing: Fig. 19.7 shows the program listing (program: **isrsemaphore.c**). The program consists of one task only in addition to the Idle task. When the program runs Task 1 configures the LED as output and the button as input. Then, external interrupt is configured on the rising edge of the button. Task 1 then gives the semaphore and the LED is ON. Pressing the button creates an interrupt where the semaphore is taken and therefore the LED is toggled.

The binary semaphore is created using the following function call in the main program:xSemaphore = xSemaphoreCreateBinary();

The semaphore is taken using the following function call:xSemaphoreTakeFromISR(xSemaphore, &xHigherPriorityTaskWoken);

The semaphore is given and the LED is toggled using the following function call:

```
if(xSemaphoreGive(xSemaphore) == pdTRUE)
    {
    LED = ~LED;
    }
```

19.14 Queue related functions from ISR

There are several queue related API functions are available that can be called from ISRs. Commonly used functions are described in the following sections. Interested readers can get further information on these functions from the references given in the Overview section of this chapter.

19.14.1 xQueueReceiveFromISR()

This is the interrupt safe version of the API function xQueueReceive(). This function has three parameters: the semaphore handle, a pointer in memory into which the received data will be written, and parameter *pxHigherPriorityTaskWoken which has already been described in earlier interrupt safe functions.

19.14.2 xQueueSendFromISR()

This is the interrupt safe version of the API function xQueueSend(). This function has three parameters as in function xQueueReceiveFromISR(). Notice that there are other interrupt safe

```
/*==============================================================================
                        SEMAPHORE FROM INTERRUPT
                        ========================

In this project a push-button switch is connected to port pin PA0 such that the
state of the button is logic LOW, and goes to HIGH when the button is pressed.
Also, the on-board LED at port pin PE12 is used. When the program runs the LED
is turned ON. The task then waits for semaphore to be given. The semaphore is
taken when the button is pressed. Therefore, each time the button is pressed, the
state of the LED will toggle (ON to OFF and OFF to ON).

Author: Dogan Ibrahim
Date  : October, 2019
File  : isrsemaphore.c
==============================================================================*/
#include "main.h"
SemaphoreHandle_t xSemaphore;

//
// External interrupt service routine (ISR). The program jumps to this ISR
// whenever the push-button PA0 is pressed. Here, use the semaphore to unblock
// the task every time the button is pressed
//
void StartTimer() iv IVT_INT_EXTI0 ics ICS_AUTO
{
    BaseType_t xHigherPriorityTaskWoken = pdFALSE;
    EXTI_PR.B0 = 1;
    xSemaphoreTakeFromISR(xSemaphore, &xHigherPriorityTaskWoken);
    if(xHigherPriorityTaskWoken != pdFALSE)
    {
        portYIELD_FROM_ISR(xHigherPriorityTaskWoken);
    }
}


//
// This function configures the external interrupt for pin PA0 on rising edge.
// The interrupt priority is set to 1
//
void SetupPA0()
{
    SYSCFG_EXTICR1 = 0;                          // For pin PA0
    EXTI_FTSR.B0 = 0;                            // Not on falling edge
    EXTI_RTSR.B0= 1;                             // Interrupt on rising edge
    EXTI_IMR.B0 = 1;                             // Unmask interrupt source
    EXTI_PR.B0= 1;                               // Pending request
    NVIC_IntEnable(IVT_INT_EXTI0);               // Enable interrupt on line EXTI0
    NVIC_SetIntPriority(IVT_INT_EXTI0,_NVIC_INT_PRIORITY_LVL1);
}

// Task 1 - LED CONTROLLER
void Task1(void *pvParameters)
{
    #define LED GPIOE_ODR.B12
    GPIO_Config(&GPIOE_BASE, _GPIO_PINMASK_12, _GPIO_CFG_MODE_OUTPUT);
    GPIO_Config(&GPIOA_BASE, _GPIO_PINMASK_0, _GPIO_CFG_MODE_INPUT);
    SetupPA0();                                  // Configura PA0 interrupts

    while (1)
    {
        if(xSemaphoreGive(xSemaphore) == pdTRUE)     // Give the semaphore
```

FIGURE 19.7   isrsemaphore.c program listing.

```
    {
        LED = ~LED;                                    // Toggle the LED
    }
    }
}

//
// Start of MAIN program
// =====================
//
void main()
{
xSemaphore = xSemaphoreCreateBinary();             // Create binary semaphore

//
// Create all the TASKS here
// =========================
//
    // Create Task 1
    xTaskCreate(
        (TaskFunction_t)Task1,
        "LED Controller",
        configMINIMAL_STACK_SIZE,
        NULL,
        10,
        NULL
    );

//
// Start the RTOS scheduler
//
    vTaskStartScheduler();

//
// Will never reach here
//
    while (1);
}
```

FIGURE 19.7   (*Continued*)

queue send operations such as: xQueueSendToBackFromISR (same as xQueueSendFromISR) and xQueueSendToFrontFromISR.

19.15 Project 54-Using functions xQueueSendFromISR() and xQueueReceive()

Description: This project shows how a queue can be setup to send data to a task from inside the ISR. There is only one task in the program. A push-button switch is connected to port pin PA0 as in the previous projects and the on-board LED at port pin PE12 is used. When the button is pressed the external interrupt occurs which sends the flashing rate (250ms) to the task so that the task starts to flash at this rate.

Aim: The aim of this project is to show how the FreeRTOS API functions xQueueSendFromISR() and xQueueReceive() can be used in a practical application.

Program listing: Fig. 19.8 shows the program listing (program: **isrqueue.c**). The program consists of one task only in addition to the Idle task. When the program runs Task 1 configures

```
/*================================================================================
                          QUEUE FROM INTERRUPT
                          ====================

In this project a push-button switch is connected to port pin PA0 such that the
state of the button is logic LOW, and goes to HIGH when the button is pressed.
Also, the on-board LED at port pin PE12 is used. When the button is pressed, the
LED flashing rate (250ms) is sent to the LED Controller task (TASK 1) in a queue
and the LED starts to flash at this rate.

Author: Dogan Ibrahim
Date  : October, 2019
File  : isrqueue.c
================================================================================*/
#include "main.h"
QueueHandle_t xQueue;

//
// External interrupt service routine (ISR). The program jumps to this ISR
// whenever the push-button PA0 is pressed. Here, the LED flashing rate is
// sent to the task in a queue
//
void StartTimer() iv IVT_INT_EXTI0 ics ICS_AUTO
{
    int delay = 250;
    BaseType_t xHigherPriorityTaskWoken = pdFALSE;
    EXTI_PR.B0 = 1;
    xQueueSendFromISR(xQueue, &delay, &xHigherPriorityTaskWoken);
    if(xHigherPriorityTaskWoken != pdFALSE)
    {
        portYIELD_FROM_ISR(xHigherPriorityTaskWoken);
    }
}


//
// This function configures the external interrupt for pin PA0 on rising edge.
// The interrupt priority is set to 1
//
void SetupPA0()
{
    SYSCFG_EXTICR1 = 0;                                    // For pin PA0
    EXTI_FTSR.B0 = 0;                                      // Not on falling edge
    EXTI_RTSR.B0= 1;                                       // Interrupt on rising edge
    EXTI_IMR.B0 = 1;                                       // Unmask interrupt source
    EXTI_PR.B0= 1;                                         // Pending request
    NVIC_IntEnable(IVT_INT_EXTI0);                         // Enable interrupt on line EXTI0
    NVIC_SetIntPriority(IVT_INT_EXTI0,_NVIC_INT_PRIORITY_LVL1);
}

// Task 1 - LED CONTROLLER
void Task1(void *pvParameters)
{
    #define LED GPIOE_ODR.B12
    int dly;
    GPIO_Config(&GPIOE_BASE, _GPIO_PINMASK_12, _GPIO_CFG_MODE_OUTPUT);
    GPIO_Config(&GPIOA_BASE, _GPIO_PINMASK_0, _GPIO_CFG_MODE_INPUT);
```

FIGURE 19.8   isrqueue.c program listing.

```
    SetupPA0();                                        // Configura PA0 interrupts
    if(xQueueReceive(xQueue, &dly, portMAX_DELAY) == pdPASS)
    {
      while (1)
      {
        {
            LED = 1;                                    // LED ON
            vTaskDelay(pdMS_TO_TICKS(dly));             // Wait dly ms
            LED = 0;                                    // LED OFF
            vTaskDelay(pdMS_TO_TICKS(dly));             // Wait dly ms
        }
      }
    }
}

//
// Start of MAIN program
// =====================
//
void main()
{
#define QUEUE_LENGTH 1
#define QUEUE_ITEM_SIZE 2
xQueue = xQueueCreate(QUEUE_LENGTH, QUEUE_ITEM_SIZE);
//
// Create all the TASKS here
// =========================
//
    // Create Task 1
    xTaskCreate(
        (TaskFunction_t)Task1,
        "LED Controller",
        configMINIMAL_STACK_SIZE,
        NULL,
        10,
        NULL
    );

//
// Start the RTOS scheduler
//
    vTaskStartScheduler();

//
// Will never reach here
//
    while (1);
}
```

FIGURE 19.8   (*Continued*)

the LED as output and the button as input. Then, external interrupt is configured on the rising edge of the button. Task 1 then waits to receive the LED flashing rate from the queue. When the button is pressed the flashing rate is sent to Task 1 which starts the flashing.

The queue is created as follows:

```
#define QUEUE_LENGTH 1
#define QUEUE_ITEM_SIZE 2
xQueue = xQueueCreate(QUEUE_LENGTH, QUEUE_ITEM_SIZE);
```

The flashing rate is sent to Task 1 using the following function:

```
xQueueSendFromISR(xQueue, &delay, &xHigherPriorityTaskWoken);
```

The flashing rate is received by Task 1 and the LED is flashed using the following statements:

```
if(xQueueReceive(xQueue, &dly, portMAX_DELAY) == pdPASS)
{
            while (1)
            {
            {
            LED = 1;
            vTaskDelay(pdMS_TO_TICKS(dly));
            LED = 0;
            vTaskDelay(pdMS_TO_TICKS(dly));
            }
            }
}
```

19.16 Summary

In this chapter we have learned how to call the FreeRTOS API functions from inside ISRs. It is important to take care that only the functions ending with FromISR must be used inside the ISRs.

In the next chapters we shall be developing more complex multitasking projects using the FreeRTOS API functions.

Further reading

[1] R. Barry, Mastering the FreeRTOS Real Time Kernel: A Hands-On Tutorial Guide. Available from: https://www.freertos.org/wp-content/uploads/2018/07/161204_Mastering_the_FreeRTOS_Real_Time_Kernel-A_Hands-On_Tutorial_Guide.pdf.

Car park management system

20.1 Overview

In the previous chapters, we have covered most features and application program interface (API) functions of the FreeRTOS kernel. We have also developed many simple projects to show how different functions and features can be used in practical applications.

In this chapter, we develop a more complex multitasking project as a car park management system, using several sensors and a servo motor in a multitasking environment with the FreeRTOS kernel and the Clicker 2 for STM32 microcontroller development board.

20.2 Project 55: car park control

Description: This is a car park management system where the idea is to control the operation of a car park. It is assumed that the car park has one level with a capacity of 100 cars. An LCD display close to the car park shows the number of free spaces available in the car park. Only members of the car park are allowed to use the car park where each member is given an RFID (Radio Frequency IDentification) card for identification. A barrier is placed at the entrance to the car park that is operated (i.e., lifted up) with a stepper motor. If there are spaces in the car park and when a member customer places an authorized RFID card close to the card reader near the entrance to the car park, then the barrier is lifted up automatically to let the driver into the car park. Unauthorized RFID cards are rejected and the barrier is not lifted up. There is no barrier at the exit from the car park, but a passive pressure switch is placed under the exit route that detects the vehicles as they leave the car park. The number of spaces available inside the car park is calculated as the cars enter and leave the car park and this is displayed on the LCD continuously. The barrier is not lifted up if there are no spaces inside the car park. A Red and a Green light (e.g., LED in this project) are mounted at the entrance to the car park. When the Red LED is ON, the driver is required to wait until the Green LED comes ON. The Green LED comes ON when the barrier is lifted up so that a car can enter the car park. When the barrier is down, the Red LED comes ON and the Green LED is turned OFF. The car park is managed from a PC, where the person in charge can set the capacity of the car park. Although the default capacity is 100, this can be changed from the keyboard, for example, when part of the car park is not available for parking. All of the

ARM-Based Microcontroller Multitasking Projects. http://dx.doi.org/10.1016/B978-0-12-821227-1.00020-7

operations of the car park are controlled using a Clicker 2 for STM32 microcontroller development board together with the mikroC Pro for ARM compiler and FreeRTOS kernel as in the previous projects in this book.

Aim: The aim of this project is to show how some of the FreeRTOS API functions we have covered in the earlier chapters can be used in a practical application.

Block diagram: Fig. 20.1 shows the block diagram of the car park. Interface to the microcontroller development board is not shown in this figure.

The stepper motor

Stepper motors are rotary actuators that allow for precise control of the angular position of an object connected to the shaft of the motor. As was described in Chapter 14, stepper motors can be driven by several ways, such as using bipolar transistors, MOSFET transistors, or integrated circuits such as L293, ULN2003, and so on. In this project, the 28BYJ-48 unipolar stepper motor is used (see Fig. 14.29) with the ULN2003 IC-based motor driver module (see Fig. 14.30) to control the barrier at the entry to the car park. The stepper motor rotates anti-clockwise by 90 degrees to lift the barrier up to let a car into the car park. Similarly, it is rotated by 90 degrees clockwise to close the barrier after the vehicle is entered the car park.

The pressure switch

A pressure switch is placed under the road in the path of the exit route that detects when a car is leaving the car park. The state of this switch is at logic 0 and goes to logic 1 when a car is over the switch. This is detected by the system and is used in calculating the available free spaces in the car park.

The RFID reader

RFID systems consists of RFID devices (or readers) and RFID tags (or cards). RFID devices use electromagnetic fields to automatically identify and track compatible RFID tags. The

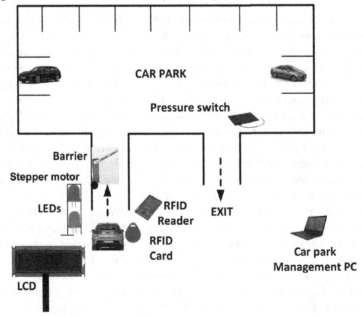

FIGURE 20.1   Block diagram of the car park.

tags contain unique electronically stored information, which is read by the RFID readers. RFID tags are used in many industries and commonly in security applications. For example, the reader-tag pairs can be used to unlock doors, they can be attached to possessions or implanted in animals and people so that they can be tracked. RFIDs are similar to barcodes used in supermarkets to identify products, but unlike the barcodes, the tags do not need to be within the line of sight of the readers. Additionally, tags can contain much more information than the simple barcodes.

RFID tags can be either passive or active (battery operated). Passive tags are cheaper and smaller and are used more commonly. Passive tags must be placed very close to the RFID readers (e.g., at 5 cm) so that their contents can be read. These tags can be read-only or read-write type. Read-only tags are pre-programmed in factory with unique numbers and these numbers can be read using compatible RFID readers. Active RFID tags have the advantages, in that they can be read from longer distances, but they are much more expensive than the passive tags.

In this project, a passive RFID tag system is used. The RFID reader used in this project is the RDM6300 type UART-based reader (see Fig. 20.2). This reader is EM4100 protocol compatible and operates with the 125-kHz RFID tags (see Fig. 20.3). The basic features of the RDM6300 readers are as follows:

- Operating frequency: 25 kHz
- Working voltage: +5 V

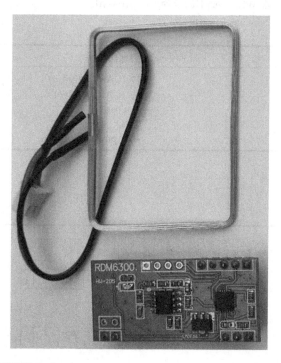

FIGURE 20.2   RDM6300 RFID reader.

FIGURE 20.3 125-kHz RFID tags.

- Current consumption: <50 mA
- Receive distance: <5cm
- Working temperature: −10°C to +70°C

The RDM6300 is sold with a coil antenna that communicates with the RFID cards. This antenna must be connected to the reader board. Fig. 20.4 shows the pin configuration of the RDM6300 reader.

There are three headers on the board with the following functions. Notice that Header 3 is for testing where an optional external LED can be connected to this header. The LED goes from logic HIGH to LOW when an RFID tag is present:

Header P1

Pin number	Description
1	TX (UART transmit)
2	RX (UART receive)
3	Not used
4	GND
5	+5 V power supply

Header P2

1 Antenna
2 Antenna

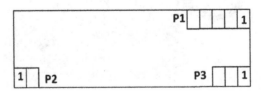

FIGURE 20.4 RDM6300 pin configuration.

Header 3

1 External LED
2 +5 V power supply
3 GND

The RDM6300 reader operates at 9600 Baud, eight data bits, one stop bit, and no parity bit. At 9600 baud, the bit time is 104 μs. The interface protocols available for this reader are the Weigang26 and TTL level RS232. In this project, the TTL level RS232 interface and protocol is used. Normally, the standard RS232 signal voltage levels are ±12 V. TTL-based RS232 signal voltage levels are 0 or +5 V (or 0 to +3.3 V) where the line is normally at +5 V and goes to 0 V at the beginning of data transmission (i.e., the start bit is at logic 0 V). The reader output consists of 14 bytes as follows:

- 1 byte start flag (0×02)
- 10 ASCII data characters
- 2 byte checksum
- 1 byte end flag (0×03)

The start and end flags are always 0×02 and 0×03, respectively. The checksum is calculated by exclusive Or'ing all the data bytes.

Notice that the card numbers marked on the RFID cards is a 10-digit decimal number. For example, if the decimal number on the card is 007564912, this corresponds to hexadecimal number 00736E70.

Circuit diagram: The circuit diagram of the project is shown in Fig. 20.5. The LCD is connected to the Clicker 2 for STM32 development board as in the previous projects using LCDs. The stepper motor is attached to the motor driver board and the board pins IN1, IN2, IN3, and IN4 are connected to port pins PC0, PC1, PC2, and PC3, respectively. The motor driver board is powered from an external +5 V power supply. The pressure switch is connected to port pin PA4. The output of this switch is at logic 0 and goes to logic 1 when a car is present on the switch. The RFID reader module is connected to UART pins PD5 (TX) and PD6 (RX). Power to the RFID reader module is supplied from the development board. The two LEDs on the development board are used: LED at port pin PE12 is assumed to be the Red LED, and the LED at port pin PE15 is assumed to be the Green LED.

The interface between the development board and the various peripheral devices is summarized as follows:

External device	Clicker 2 for STM32 pin
Pressure switch	PA4
RFID reader	PD5 (TX), PD6 (RX)
Stepper motor	PC0, PC1, PC2, PC3
Red LED	PE12
Green LED	PE15
LCD	PE7, PE8, PE9, PC10, PC11, PC12
USB UART Click board	mikroBUS 2

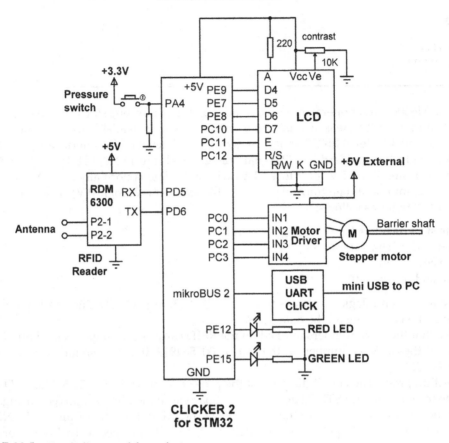

FIGURE 20.5   Circuit diagram of the project.

The antenna of the RFID reader module is connected to header pins P2. The LED interface of the RFID reader module is not used in this project.

Program listing: Fig. 20.6 shows the program listing (program: **carprk.c**). The program consists of five tasks in addition to the Idle task. The tasks are:

TASK1: Stepper motor controller
TASK2: LCD controller
TASK3: UART controller
TASK4: RFID controller
TASK5: Pressure switch controller

The operation of each task is described using PDL statements:
TASK1 (stepper motor controller)
DO FOREVER
Wait for event flag 0 to be set
Increase task priority
Lift up the barrier

```
/*===============================================================================
                         CAR PARK
                         ========

This is a single level car park project. Members enter the car park using their
RFID tags. A barrier opens at the entrance to the car park for authorized users
when they place their RFID tags near the RFID reader module. An LCD is used to
show how many spaces are available in the car park (it is assumed that the car
park capacity is 100 cars). A pressure switch at the exit of the car park is
activated when a car leaves the car park. An USB UART Click board is used to
interface the system to a PC so that the car park can be managed from a PC.

Author: Dogan Ibrahim
Date  : December, 2019
File  : carprk.c
================================================================================*/
#include "main.h"
#include "event_groups.h"

// LCD module connections
sbit LCD_RS at GPIOC_ODR.B12;
sbit LCD_EN at GPIOC_ODR.B11;
sbit LCD_D4 at GPIOE_ODR.B9;
sbit LCD_D5 at GPIOE_ODR.B7;
sbit LCD_D6 at GPIOE_ODR.B8;
sbit LCD_D7 at GPIOC_ODR.B10;
// End LCD module connections

// Stepper motor connections
#define IN1 GPIOC_ODR.B0
#define IN2 GPIOC_ODR.B1
#define IN3 GPIOC_ODR.B2
#define IN4 GPIOC_ODR.B3
// End of stepper motor connections

float StepsPerCycle = 512.0;
int FullMode[4] = {0b01100, 0b00110, 0b00011, 0b01001};        // Full Mode control
unsigned int TotalCapacity, capacity = 100;
EventGroupHandle_t xBarrierEventGroup;                          // Event group

//
// This function extract the bits of a variable
//
unsigned char BitRead(char i, char j)
{
    unsigned m;
    m = i & j;
    if(m != 0)
        return(1);
    else
        return(0);
}

//
// This function stops the motor
//
void StopMotor()
{
```

FIGURE 20.6   carprk.c program listing.

```
      IN1 = 0;
      IN2 = 0;
      IN3 = 0;
      IN4 = 0;
}

//
// This function sends a bit to pins IN1,IN2,IN3,IN4 of the motor driver board
//
void SendPulse(int k)
{
    GPIO_Config(&GPIOC_BASE, _GPIO_PINMASK_0 | _GPIO_PINMASK_1 | _GPIO_PINMASK_2
                | _GPIO_PINMASK_3, _GPIO_CFG_MODE_OUTPUT);

    IN1 = BitRead(FullMode[k], 1);
    IN2 = BitRead(FullMode[k], 2);
    IN3 = BitRead(FullMode[k], 4);
    IN4 = BitRead(FullMode[k], 8);
}


//
// This function rotates the stepper motor by specified degrees
//
void BarrierDown(int degrees, float StepDelay)
{
    unsigned int i, m, k, d;
    float DegreeTurn;
    DegreeTurn = StepsPerCycle * degrees / 360.0;
    d=(int)DegreeTurn;

    for(m = 0; m < d; m++)
    {
        for(i = 0; i < 4; i++)
        {
            k = 3-i;
            SendPulse(k);
            VDelay_ms(StepDelay);
        }
    }
}


//
// This function rotates the stepper motor by specified degrees
//
void BarrierUp(int degrees, float StepDelay)
{
    unsigned int i, m, d;
    float DegreeTurn;
    DegreeTurn = StepsPerCycle * degrees / 360.0;
    d=(int)DegreeTurn;

    for(m = 0; m < d; m++)
    {
        for(i = 0; i < 4; i++)
        {
            SendPulse(i);
            VDelay_ms(StepDelay);
        }
}
```

FIGURE 20.6   (*Continued*)

```
        }
    }


//
// Define all your Task functions here
// ====================================
//

// Task 1 - Stepper Motor Controller
void Task1(void *pvParameters)
{
    #define BIT_0 ( 1 << 0 )                        // Bit 0
    float StpDelay;
    int RPM = 10;                                   // Motor RPM
    EventBits_t uxBits;
    StpDelay = (29.3 / RPM);                        // Step delay

    while (1)
    {
        uxBits = xEventGroupWaitBits(               // Wait for event flag
                xBarrierEventGroup,                 // Handle
                BIT_0,                              // Wait for bit 0
                pdTRUE,                             // Clear before returning
                pdFALSE,                            // Wait for bit 0
                portMAX_DELAY);                     // Block until set

        vTaskPrioritySet(NULL, 11);                 // Increase priority
        BarrierUp(90, StpDelay);                    // Barrier up
        vTaskPrioritySet(NULL, 10);                 // Priority back to default
        StopMotor();                                // Stop motor
        vTaskDelay(pdMS_TO_TICKS(10000));           // Wait for 10 secs
        vTaskPrioritySet(NULL, 11);                 // Increase priority
        BarrierDown(90, StpDelay);                  // Barrier down
        vTaskPrioritySet(NULL, 10);                 // Priority back to default
        StopMotor();                                // Stop motor
    }
}


//
// Read an integer number from the keyboard and retun to the calling program
//
unsigned int Read_From_Keyboard()
{
    unsigned int Total;
    unsigned char N;
    Total = 0;
    while(1)
    {
        if(UART3_Data_Ready())
        {
        N = UART3_Read();                           // Read a number
        UART3_Write(N);                             // Echo the number
        if(N == '\r') break;                        // If Enter
        N = N - '0';                                // Pure number
        Total = 10*Total + N;                       // Total number
        }
```

FIGURE 20.6   (*Continued*)

```
      }
      return Total;                                   // Return the number
}

// Task 2 - LCD Controller
void Task2(void *pvParameters)
{
    unsigned char Txt[4];
    Lcd_Init();                                        // Initialize LCD
    Lcd_Cmd(_LCD_CLEAR);                                // Clear LCD
    Lcd_Out(1, 1, "Free Spaces:");                     // Heading

    while(1)
    {
      ByteToStr(capacity, Txt);                        // Convert to string
      Ltrim(Txt);                                      // Remove spaces
      Lcd_Out(2, 1, "    ");
      Lcd_Out(2, 1, Txt);                              // Display free spaces
      vTaskDelay(pdMS_TO_TICKS(1000));
    }                                                  // Wait 1 second
}


// Task 3 - UART Controller
void Task3(void *pvParameters)
{
    int N;
    UART3_Init_Advanced(9600,_UART_8_BIT_DATA,_UART_NOPARITY,_UART_ONE_STOPBIT,
                      &_GPIO_MODULE_USART3_PD89);

    while(1)
    {
        UART3_Write_Text("\n\rCAR PARK MANAGEMENT SYSTEM");
        UART3_Write_Text("\n\r============================");
        UART3_Write_Text("\n\rEnter the Car Park Capacity: ");
        N = Read_From_Keyboard();
        TotalCapacity = N;
        capacity = TotalCapacity;                       // Car prk capacity
    }
}

// Task 4 - RFID Controller
void Task4(void *pvParameters)
{
    unsigned char k, j,flag, Buffer[20];
    #define RedLED GPIOE_ODR.B12
    #define GreenLED GPIOE_ODR.B15
    #define BIT_0 ( 1 << 0 )
    char ValidTags[3][20] = {"00736E70", "00739BC2", "00E38F26"};
    EventBits_t uxBits;

    GPIO_Config(&GPIOE_BASE, _GPIO_PINMASK_12 | _GPIO_PINMASK_15, _GPIO_CFG_MODE_OUTPUT);
    UART2_Init_Advanced(9600,_UART_8_BIT_DATA,_UART_NOPARITY,_UART_ONE_STOPBIT,
                      &_GPIO_MODULE_USART2_PD56);
    RedLED = 1;                                          // RED LED ON
    GreenLED = 0;                                        // GREEN LED OFF
```

FIGURE 20.6   (*Continued*)

```
    while(1)
    {
        while (1)
        {                                                    // IF data from RFID tag
            if(UART2_Data_Ready())
            {
                vTaskPrioritySet(NULL,11);                   // Increae priority
                for(k=0; k < 14; k++)Buffer[k] = UART2_Read();  // Read tag data
                vTaskPrioritySet(NULL,10);                   // Priority to default
                break;
            }
        }

        for(k=0; k < 8; k++)Buffer[k] = Buffer[k+4];         // Extract the tag data
        Buffer[k] = '\0';                                    // Add NULL terminator

        flag = 0;
        for(k = 0; k < 3; k++)
        {
            if(strcmp(Buffer, ValidTags[k]) == 0 )flag = 1;  // Valid tag?
        }
        if(flag == 1 && capacity > 0)                        // Yes, lift the barrier
        {
            capacity--;                                      // Decrease the capacity
            uxBits = xEventGroupSetBits(xBarrierEventGroup,BIT_0);
            RedLED = 0;
            GreenLED = 1;
            vTaskDelay(pdMS_TO_TICKS(15000));                // wait 15 seconds
            RedLED = 1;                                      // RED LED ON
            GreenLED = 0;                                    // GREEN LED OFF
            while(UART2_Data_Ready())
            {
                Buffer[k] = UART2_Read();                    // Flash the serial buffer
            }
        }
    }
}

// Task 5 - Pressure Switch Controller
void Task5(void *pvParameters)
{
    #define PressureSwitch GPIOA_IDR.B4
    GPIO_Config(&GPIOA_BASE, _GPIO_PINMASK_4, _GPIO_CFG_MODE_INPUT);

    while(1)
    {
        while(PressureSwitch == 0);                          // Pressure switch is OFF
        capacity++;                                          // Increase capacity
        if(capacity > TotalCapacity)capacity = TotalCapacity; // Adjust capacity
        while(PressureSwitch == 1);                          // Wait until switch os OFF
    }
}


//
// Start of MAIN program
// =====================
```

FIGURE 20.6 *(Continued)*

```
//
void main()
{

xBarrierEventGroup = xEventGroupCreate();

//
// Create all the TASKS here
// =========================
//
    // Create Task 1
    xTaskCreate(
        (TaskFunction_t)Task1,
        "Stepper Motor Controller",
        configMINIMAL_STACK_SIZE,
        NULL,
        10,
        NULL
    );

    // Create Task 2
    xTaskCreate(
        (TaskFunction_t)Task2,
        "LCD Controller",
        configMINIMAL_STACK_SIZE,
        NULL,
        10,
        NULL
    );

    // Create Task 3
    xTaskCreate(
        (TaskFunction_t)Task3,
        "UART Controller",
        configMINIMAL_STACK_SIZE,
        NULL,
        10,
        NULL
    );

    // Create Task 4
    xTaskCreate(
        (TaskFunction_t)Task4,
        "RFID Controller",
        configMINIMAL_STACK_SIZE,
        NULL,
        10,
        NULL
    );

    // Create Task 5
    xTaskCreate(
        (TaskFunction_t)Task5,
        "Pressure Switch Controller",
        configMINIMAL_STACK_SIZE,
        NULL,
        10,
        NULL
```

FIGURE 20.6   (*Continued*)

```
    );
//
// Start the RTOS scheduler
//
    vTaskStartScheduler();

//
// Will never reach here
}
```

FIGURE 20.6   *(Continued)*

    Task priority back to default
    Wait for 10 seconds for a car to enter
    Increase task priority
    Lower the barrier
    Task priority back to default

ENDDO
TASK2 (LCD controller)
Initialize the LCD
Display heading "Free Spaces:" at row 1
DO FOREVER
    Display free spaces at row 2
ENDDO
TASK3 (UART controller)
Set the UART baud rate
DO FOREVER
Display heading "CAR PARK MANAGEMENT SYSTEM"
Display "Enter the Car Park Capacity:"
Read the car park capacity

ENDDO
TASK4 (RFID controller)
Set the UART baud rate
Turn ON Red LED
Turn OFF Green LED

DO FOREVER
    Read RFID tag number
    IF this is a valid tag and there are free spaces in the car park **THEN**
        Decrement free space count by one
        Turn ON Green LED
        Turn OFF Red LED
        Set event flag 0 so that the barrier is lifted up
        Wait 15 seconds for the barrier
        Turn OFF Green LED
        Turn ON Red LED
    ENDIF

ENDDO
TASK5 (pressure switch controller)
DO FOREVER
    IF a car is present on the switch **THEN**
        Increment free space count by one
        Wait until the car is not on the switch
    ENDIF
ENDDO

A typical operation cycle of the car park is as follows:

On entry:
- Car park capacity is displayed on the LCD.
- Red LED is ON, Green LED is OFF.
- A car approaches the car park.
- Member places the RFID tag close to the tag reader.
- The card is accepted.
- Car park free space count is decremented by 1.
- Barrier is lifted up.
- Green LED is ON, Red Led is OFF.
- Car enters the car park.

On exit:
- Car is on the pressure switch at the exit.
- Increment the free space count by 1.
- Wait until the car leaves.

Management:
- Car park manger is prompted to enter the car park capacity.
- New car park capacity is accepted.

At the beginning of the program, the interface between the LCD and the development board is defined. Also, the interface between the stepper motor and the development board is defined. The program then defines some of the variables, such as the StepsPerCycle, FullMode, and default capacity.

The motor RPM is set to 10 in Task 1. This task waits until event flag 0 is set. When this flag is set, function BarrierUP is called to lift the barrier up. The stepper motor is requested to turn by 90 degrees anticlockwise to open the barrier. This is done after the priority of the task is increased so that the task cannot be interrupted by other tasks in the system. A complete turn of the stepper motor requires StepsPerCycle steps, where each step consists of 4 pulses. Since a complete turn is 360 degrees, 90 degrees of rotation is achieved by sending DegreeTurn steps to the motor where:

$$\text{DegreeTurn} = \frac{\text{StepsPerCycle} \times \text{degrees}}{360.0}$$

After the barrier is lifted up, the task priority is lowered to its default value and the task waits for 10 seconds so that the car is entered the car park. The priority of the task is increased again, and the barrier is lowered.

The LCD controller task gets the free space count from variable capacity and then displays the free spaces in the second row of the LCD.

New capacity is entered through the PC keyboard. UART3 of the development board is used to interface to the PC. As soon as the capacity is changed, the new capacity is displayed on the LCD. Notice that variable capacity is the number of free spaces at any time and variable TotalCapacity is the actual capacity of the car park.

In this program, three valid RFID tags are used for demonstration purposes. Notice that the card reader returns 14 bytes, but only the bytes that represent the number on the cards are extracted and used in the program. These valid tags had the following identities:

Number on the tag	Number returned by the tag reader
0014913318	00E38F26
0007564912	00736E70
0007576514	00739BC2

The valid tags are stored in a two-dimensional character array called ValidTags:

char ValidTags[3][20] = {"00736E70", "00739BC2", "00E38F26"};

UART2 of the development board is interfaced to the RFID tag reader. If a character is available at the UART buffer, then the priority of Task 4 is increased so that the UART is not interrupted by other tasks, and the tag data are read and stored in character array called Buffer. The priority is then lowered back to its default value. The tag number is then checked against the valid tags:

```
flag = 0;
for(k = 0; k < 3; k++)
{
    if(strcmp(Buffer, ValidTags[k]) == 0)flag = 1;
}
```

Variable flag is set to 1 if the tag read is a valid tag. Event flag 0 is then set if the car park has free spaces available. Red LED is turned OFF and Green LED is turned ON so that the car is given permission to enter the car park.

The output state of the pressure switch is at logic 0. When a car is present on this switch, the switch state goes to logic 1. This change of state is detected by the program and the free space count is increased by 1 as a car is leaving the car park.

Fig. 20.7 shows an example display on the PC screen prompting the user to enter the car park capacity.

```
CAR PARK MANAGEMENT SYSTEM
============================
Enter the Car Park Capacity: 100
CAR PARK MANAGEMENT SYSTEM
============================
Enter the Car Park Capacity: _
```

FIGURE 20.7 Display on the PC screen.

FIGURE 20.8   Example display on the LCD.

The LCD displays the free space available at the cark park and an example display is shown in Fig. 20.8.

Further reading

[1] Clicker 2 for STM32 development board, www.mikroe.comwww.mikroe.com.
[2] RDM6300. https://www.itead.cc/rdm6300.html.

Time in different cities

21.1 Overview

In this chapter, we develop a multitasking clock project where the current time in one of 10 cities in different countries can be selected from the PC keyboard. The time in the selected city is then displayed on the LCD together with the name of the city. The user selects the city where the time is to be displayed from a menu displayed on the PC screen.

21.2 Project 56: time project

Description: When the program is started, the user by default is prompted to enter the time in London and this is displayed by default on the LCD and updated automatically every second. A menu is displayed on the PC that enables the user to select the city where the current time is to be displayed. The city name is displayed on the first row of the LCD, while the current time is displayed on the second row of the LCD.

Aim: The aim of this project is to show how multitasking can be used in a practical and useful clock project.

Block diagram: Fig. 21.1 shows the block diagram of the project.

Circuit diagram: The circuit diagram of the project is shown in Fig. 21.2. The LCD is connected to the Clicker 2 for STM32 development board as in the previous projects using an LCD. The PC is connected to the development board using the USB UART Click board, plugged in to mikroBUS 2 socket as in the previous projects using this click board.

Program listing: The program consists of three tasks in addition to the Idle task. The city names and their time differences from London are stored in two dimensional character arrays called **cities** and **timediff,** respectively. Ten cities are defined with the following names and time differences from London:

char cities[][10] = {"London", Paris", "Madrid", "Rome", "Athens", "Ankara", "Istanbul", "Cairo", "Moscow", "Tehran"};

char timediff[] = {0, 1, 1, 1, 2, 2, 2, 2, 3, 4};

For example, the time in Paris is 1 hour ahead of the time in London. Similarly, the time in Istanbul is 2 hours of the time in London and so on. Current time in London is entered by

ARM-Based Microcontroller Multitasking Projects. http://dx.doi.org/10.1016/B978-0-12-821227-1.00021-9

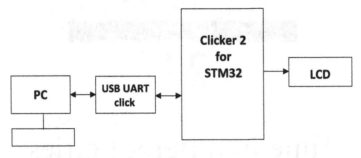

FIGURE 21.1　Block diagram of the project.

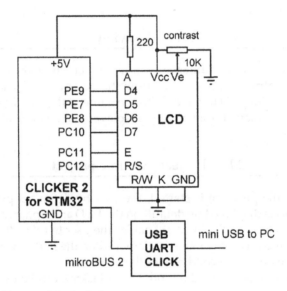

FIGURE 21.2　Circuit diagram of the project.

default into the program when the program is started and this is stored in a structure called **AMessage** in the following format:

```
typedef struct Message
{
    unsigned char hours;
    unsigned char minutes;
    unsigned char seconds;
} AMessage;
AMessage Tim;
```

Current time in London is received by calling to function Read_Time() in the following format: hh:mm:ss where the time is entered in 24 hours format. The function returns the entered time to the calling program after the ENTER key is pressed. The time is then sent to Task 2 via xQueue1 so that it can be updated and displayed every second on the LCD:

Variables Tim.hours, Tim.minutes, and Tim.seconds are the current hours, minutes, and seconds, respectively. Task 1 increments variable Tim.seconds every second by calling to FreeRTOS application program interface (API) function vTaskDelay(). When the count reaches to 60, it is reset to 0 and variable Tim.minutes is incremented by 1. When Tim.minutes reaches to 60, it is reset to 0 and variable Tim.hours is incremented by 1. When Tim.hours reaches to 24, it is reset to 0.

Task 2 displays the city name and the current time in that city on the LCD, which is updated every second. The city name is displayed on the top row, while the time in that city is displayed in the second row of the LCD. The time difference from London is added to the current time for the selected city before it is displayed. If the total hours is greater than 23, then it is adjusted by subtracting 24 from it so that it is never greater than 23.

Task 3 controls the keyboard entries. At the beginning of Task 3, the user is initially prompted to enter the current time in London. The hours, minutes, and seconds are converted into numbers and are stored in structure called **Tim**. The program then displays a menu with the city names on the PC screen and prompts the user to select the desired city, where the time in that city should be displayed on the LCD. The user selects the required city by entering the number next to the required city name. The menu is displayed using a for loop which displays the contents of character array **cities** with numbers on the left-hand side of each city name so that the user can make a selection easily.

Two queues are created in the main program, each having only one item with a size of 8 bytes:

```
xQueue1 = xQueueCreate(1, 8);
xQueue2 = xQueueCreate(1, 8);
```

All the user created tasks run at the same priority of 10. The operation of the program is described by the following PDL:

TASK 1
Get current time from Task 3
DO FOREVER
  Wait one second
  Increment seconds counter
  IF seconds counter = 60 **THEN**
    Set seconds counter to 0
    Increment minutes counter
    IF minutes counter = 60 **THEN**
      Set minutes counter to 0
      Increment hours counter
      IF hours counter = 24 **THEN**
        Set hours counter to 0
      ENDIF
    ENDIF
  ENDIF
  Send time to Task 2 via xQueue1
ENDDO
TASK 2
Define the LCD interface
DO FOREVER
  Wait until new time is received
  Extract the required city name (global)

Extract the time difference (global)
Get the current time from Task 1 via xQueue1
Find the time in the required city
Display the city name at row 1
Display current time at row 2
ENDDO
<u>**TASK 3**</u>
Configure UART at 9600 baud
Read current time in London
Send current time to Task 1 via xQueue2
DO FOREVER
Display the city names
Select the required city
ENDDO

Fig. 21.3 shows the program listing (program: **citytimes.c**). The code that updates the time every second is as follows. The code runs in an endless loop every second and updates the seconds, then the minutes, and finally the hours. Notice that the API function vTasKDelay() is very accurate and as a result of this, the timing of the clock is highly accurate in this project:

```
while (1)
{
  vTaskDelay(pdMS_TO_TICKS(1000));     // Wait for 1 second
  Tim.seconds + +;    // Increment seconds
  if(Tim.seconds == 60)    // If 60
  {
    Tim.seconds = 0;    // Reset to 0
    Tim.minutes + +;    // Increment minutes
    if(Tim.minutes == 60)    // If 60
    {
      Tim.minutes = 0;    // Reset to 0
      Tim.hours + +;    // Increment hours
      if(Tim.hours == 24)    // If 24
      {
        Tim.hours = 0;    // Reset to 0
      }
    }
  }
}
```

An example run of the program is shown in Fig. 21.4 where the menu on the PC screen displays the city names and prompts the user to select the required city where the time should be displayed. In this example, current time in London was entered as 10:00:00 at the beginning of the program, and it was then required to display the time in Istanbul. Fig. 21.5 shows the LCD displaying the time in Istanbul after a short while which is 2 hours ahead of the time in London.

The clock in this project is very accurate as it is based on the accurate timing of the FreeRTOS API function vTaskDelay(). The aim here has been to show the development of the multitasking application where the clock runs continuously as one task, and other tasks handle the

```
/*=====================================================================
                    TIME IN DIFFERENT CITIES
                    ========================

In this project, an LCD and a USB UART click board are connected to the Clicker 2
for STM32 development board. This is a clock project where by default the time
in London is displayed on the LCD. The user can select a different city via the
keyboard and the time in the selected city is displayed every second.

Author: Dogan Ibrahim
Date  : November, 2019
File  : citytimes.c
=====================================================================*/
#include "main.h"

// LCD module connections
sbit LCD_RS at GPIOC_ODR.B12;
sbit LCD_EN at GPIOC_ODR.B11;
sbit LCD_D4 at GPIOE_ODR.B9;
sbit LCD_D5 at GPIOE_ODR.B7;
sbit LCD_D6 at GPIOE_ODR.B8;
sbit LCD_D7 at GPIOC_ODR.B10;
// End LCD module connections

//
// Cities and their time differences from London
//
char cities[][10]   = {"London", "Paris", "Madrid", "Rome", "Athens", "Ankara", "Istanbul",
                       "Cairo", "Moscow", "Tehran"};
char timediff[] = {0, 1, 1, 1, 2, 2, 2, 2, 3, 4};

unsigned int selection;
QueueHandle_t xQueue1;                                    // Queue1 handle
QueueHandle_t xQueue2;                                    // Queue2 handle

//
// Define all your Task functions here
// ===================================
//

// Task 1 - Time Controller
void Task1(void *pvParameters)
{
    typedef struct Message
    {
        unsigned char hours;
        unsigned char minutes;
        unsigned char seconds;
    } AMessage;

    AMessage Tim;

    xQueueReceive(xQueue2, &Tim, portMAX_DELAY);          // Receive initial time

    while (1)
    {
        vTaskDelay(pdMS_TO_TICKS(1000));                  // Wait for 1 second
        Tim.seconds++;                                    // Increment seconds
```

FIGURE 21.3   citytimes.c program listing.

```
            if(Tim.seconds == 60)                    // If 60
            {
               Tim.seconds = 0;                      // Reset to 0
               Tim.minutes++;                        // Increment minutes
               if(Tim.minutes == 60)                 // If 60
               {
                  Tim.minutes = 0;                   // Reset to 0
                  Tim.hours++;                       // Increment hours
                  if(Tim.hours == 24)                // If 24
                  {
                     Tim.hours = 0;                  // Reset to  0
                  }
               }
            }
            xQueueSend(xQueue1, &Tim, 0);            // Send to Task 2
         }
    }


//
// Read an integer number from the keyboard and retun to the calling program
//
unsigned int Read_From_Keyboard()
{
     unsigned int Total;
     unsigned char N;
     Total = 0;
     while(1)
     {
         if(UART3_Data_Ready())
         {
           N = UART3_Read();                         // Read a number
           UART3_Write(N);                           // Echo the number
           if(N == '\r') break;                      // If Enter
           N = N - '0';                              // Pure number
           Total = 10*Total + N;                     // Total number
         }
     }
     return Total;                                   // Return the number
}


//
// Read time from the keyboard. The time is entered as hh:mm:ss
//
void Read_Time(char buf[])
{
     unsigned char c, k = 0;

     while(1)
     {
         c = UART3_Read();                           // Read a char
         UART3_Write(c);                             // Echo the char
         if(c == '\r') break;                        // If Enter
         buf[k] = c;                                 // Save char
         k++;                                        // Increment pointer
     }
     buf[k] = '\0';                                  // NULL terminator
}
```

FIGURE 21.3 (*Continued*)

```
// Task 2 - LCD Controller
void Task2(void *pvParameters)
{
    char Txt[7];
    typedef struct Message
    {
        unsigned char hours;
        unsigned char minutes;
        unsigned char seconds;
    } AMessage;

    AMessage Tim;
    Lcd_Init();                                          // Initialize LCD
    Lcd_Cmd(_LCD_CLEAR);                                 // Clear LCD
    selection = 0;                                       // Clear selection

    while(1)
    {
        xQueueReceive(xQueue1, &Tim, portMAX_DELAY);     // Get time
        Lcd_Out(1, 1, cities[selection]);                // Display city

        Tim.hours = Tim.hours + timediff[selection];     // Hour adjustment
        if(Tim.hours > 23)Tim.hours = Tim.hours - 24;    // If > 24
        ByteToStr(Tim.hours, Txt);                       // Convert to string
        Ltrim(Txt);                                      // Remove spaces
        if(Tim.hours < 10)                               // If < 10
        {
          Txt[1] = Txt[0];                               //Insert leading 0
          Txt[0] = '0';
          Txt[2] = '\0';                                 // NULL terminator
        }
        Lcd_Out(2, 0, Txt);                              // Display hours
        Lcd_Out_CP(":");                                 // Colon

        ByteToStr(Tim.minutes, Txt);                     // To string
        Ltrim(Txt);                                      // Remove spaces
        if(Tim.minutes < 10)                             // If < 10
        {
          Txt[1] = Txt[0];                               // Insert leading 0
          Txt[0] = '0';
          Txt[2] = '\0';                                 // NULL terminator
        }
        Lcd_Out_CP(Txt);                                 // Display minutes
        Lcd_Out_CP(":");                                 // Colon

        ByteToStr(Tim.seconds, Txt);                     // To string
        Ltrim(Txt);                                      // Remove spaces
        if(Tim.seconds < 10)                             // If < 10
        {
          Txt[1] = Txt[0];                               // Insert leading 0
          Txt[0] = '0';
          Txt[2] = '\0';                                 // NULL terminator
        }
        Lcd_Out_CP(Txt);                                 // Display seconds
    }
}


// Task 3 - UART Controller
void Task3(void *pvParameters)
```

FIGURE 21.3 (*Continued*)

```
{
    char k, Buffer[10];
    typedef struct Message
    {
        unsigned char hh;
        unsigned char mm;
        unsigned char ss;
    } AMessage;

    AMessage Tim;

    UART3_Init_Advanced(9600,_UART_8_BIT_DATA,_UART_NOPARITY,_UART_ONE_STOPBIT,
                        &_GPIO_MODULE_USART3_PD89);

    UART3_Write_Text("\n\rTime in Different Countries");
    UART3_Write_Text("\n\r=============================");
    UART3_Write_Text("\n\rEnter the time in London (hh:mm:ss): ");
    Read_Time(Buffer);
    Tim.hh = 10*(Buffer[0] - '0') + Buffer[1] - '0';      // Convert to nmbr
    Tim.mm = 10*(Buffer[3] - '0') + Buffer[4] - '0';      // Convert to nmbr
    Tim.ss = 10*(Buffer[6] - '0') + Buffer[7] - '0';      // Convert to nmbr

    xQueueSend(xQueue2, &Tim, 0);                         // Send to Task 1

    while (1)
    {
        UART3_Write_Text("\n\r\n\rSelect a City:");       // Heading
        for(k = 0; k < 10; k++)                           // Display cities
        {
            UART3_Write_Text("\n\r");                     // New line
            UART3_Write(k+'0');
            UART3_Write_Text(". ");
            UART3_Write_Text(cities[k]);                  // City names
        }
        UART3_Write_Text("\n\rSelection: ");              // Selection prompt
        selection = Read_From_Keyboard();                 // Read selection
    }
}

//
// Start of MAIN program
// =====================
//
void main()
{
    xQueue1 = xQueueCreate(1, 8);                         // Create queue
    xQueue2 = xQueueCreate(1, 8);                         // Create queue
//
// Create all the TASKS here
// =========================
//
    // Create Task 1
    xTaskCreate(
        (TaskFunction_t)Task1,
        "Time Controller",
        configMINIMAL_STACK_SIZE,
```

FIGURE 21.3 (*Continued*)

```
            NULL,
            10,
            NULL
        );

        // Create Task 2
        xTaskCreate(
            (TaskFunction_t)Task2,
            "LCD Controller",
            configMINIMAL_STACK_SIZE,
            NULL,
            10,
            NULL
        );

        // Create Task 3
        xTaskCreate(
            (TaskFunction_t)Task3,
            "UART Controller",
            configMINIMAL_STACK_SIZE,
            NULL,
            10,
            NULL
        );

//
// Start the RTOS scheduler
//
    vTaskStartScheduler();

//
// Will never reach here
}
```

FIGURE 21.3   (*Continued*)

```
Time in Different Countries
============================
Enter the time in London (hh:mm:ss): 10:00:00

Select a City:
0. London
1. Paris
2. Madrid
3. Rome
4. Athens
5. Ankara
6. Istanbul
7. Cairo
8. Moscow
9. Tehran
Selection: _
```

FIGURE 21.4   Example run of the program.

FIGURE 21.5   Displaying the time in Istanbul.

LCD and keyboard entry. Interested readers can use dedicated RTC chips such as the DS1307, DS3231, and MCP79410 for highly accurate clock-based applications.

Further reading

[1] USB UART user guide. www.mikroe.com.
[2] Clicker 2 for STM32 development board. www.mikroe.com.

Mobile robot project: the Buggy

22.1 Overview

In this chapter, we develop some other multitasking projects based on using a four-wheel mobile robot, that is, a Buggy using the Clicker 2 for STM32 development board and the FreeRTOS application program interface (API) functions. The Buggy chosen for this project is the one manufactured by miktoElektronika. Full details of this buggy are given in the next sections of this chapter.

22.2 The Buggy

The Buggy used in the projects in this chapter is a four-wheel mobile robot manufactured by mikroElektronika (www.mikroe.com). Fig. 22.1 shows a picture of the Buggy in assembled form (the buggy is sold in parts and needs to be assembled before it can be used).

Basically, the Buggy consists of a four-wheel mobile robot with a Clicker 2 type microcontroller development board (see mikroElektronika website) plugged-in inside the Buggy. In this project, a Clicker 2 for STM32 type development board is plugged-in inside the Buggy. Additionally, the Buggy contains four motors to drive the wheels and includes associated electronics to control these motors. Several mikroBUS sockets are provided on the buggy so that the user can simply plug-in Click boards for various sensor- and actuator-based applications. Lights in the form of LEDs are provided at the front and rear of the Buggy that can be controlled from software. The operation of the Buggy is programmed by programming the Clicker 2 for STM32 development board using the mikroC Pro for ARM compiler and the IDE.

Fig. 22.2 shows the basic parts of the Buggy. Parts of the buggy in unassembled form as sold by the distributors are shown in Fig. 22.3.

Before controlling the Buggy, it is necessary to know in detail all the parts mounted on it. The front of the Buggy is equipped with the following components (see Fig. 22.4):

- Two microBUS socket plates
- 2× Front signal lights (Yellow)
- 2× front headlights (White)

ARM-Based Microcontroller Multitasking Projects. http://dx.doi.org/10.1016/B978-0-12-821227-1.00022-0

FIGURE 22.1   The Buggy.

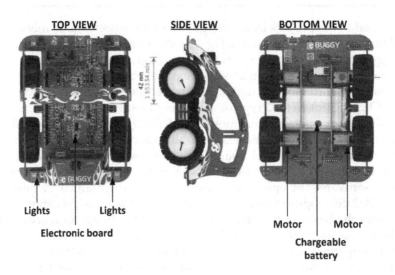

FIGURE 22.2   Basic parts of the Buggy.

FIGURE 22.3   **Buggy in unassembled form.**

The rear of the Buggy is equipped with the following components (see Fig. 22.5):

- Analog input (screw terminal)
- Power (screw terminal)
- 2× stop lights (Red)
- 2× signal lights (Yellow)
- ON/OFF switch
- miniUSB connector (for charging the battery)
- Power ON LED (Green)
- Battery charging LED (Red)
- mikroBUS socket plate

The main Buggy PCB contains the motors for the four wheels, battery charger circuitry, screw terminals for power and analog input, ON/OFF switch, signal lights, headlights, stop lights, connector to plug-in a Clicker 2 development board (in this project the Clicker 2 for STM32 development board is used), and mikroBUS socket plates.

Multiple slots for
soldering the top bar

Top bar with mounting
holes for antennas

Two mikroBUS™ socket
plates on the front

Front signal light

Front (main
beam) headlight

Removable wheels

FIGURE 22.4   Front of the Buggy.

Analog input screw
terminals (shared with
mikroBUS™ sockets 2 & 3)

Power screw terminal
(5 and 3.3V)

Rear and stop light

Rear signal light

ON/OFF switch

Mini USB connector for
charging the battery

Rear mikroBUS™
socket plate

FIGURE 22.5   Rear of the Buggy.

22.3 Wheel motors

The Buggy has a differential motor drives, controlled by two DRV833RTY type motor drivers (U6 and U7), one for each side of the Buggy. DRV833RTY is a dual H-bridge type motor driver chip that can be used for bi-directional control of a motor. Steering is achieved when the relative rate of rotation between the left and right sides are varied. When one pair of wheels is put in reverse while the other is in normal mode, the Buggy will start to spin. To prevent the motors from drawing too much current from the battery, a few resistors are placed to limit the current draw. Each motor can draw a maximum of 400 mA, for a total of 1.6 A when all four motors are running. Fig. 22.6 shows the motors assembly.

With the Clicker 2 for STM32 development board plugged-in to the Buggy, the following port pins control the wheel motors:

Motor pin	Description	Clicker 2 for STM32 pin
PWM-A	Left-side motor	PB9
PWM-B	Left-side motor	PB8
PWM-C	Right-side motor	PE5
PWM-D	Right-side motor	PB0

The motor direction, and hence the direction of the Buggy, is controlled by activating the correct pins of the motor driver chip. Fig. 22.7 shows how an H-bridge type motor driver operates. The inputs of the driver are connected together and the motor is connected as shown in the figure. When, for example, pin PWM-A is at logic 1 and pin PWM-B is at logic 0, then the motor rotates in one direction. When pin PWM-A is at logic 0 and pin PWM-B is at logic 1, then the motor rotates in the opposite direction. The two left motors are connected

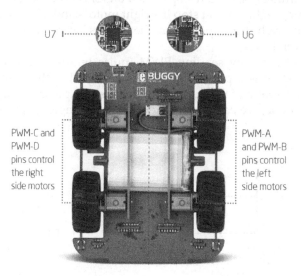

FIGURE 22.6   The motor assembly.

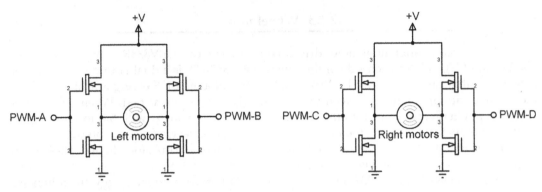

FIGURE 22.7   H-bridge motor direction control.

to pins PWM-A and PWM-B. Similarly, the two right motors are connected to pins PWM-C and PWM-D of the development board. By activating the pins in the correct sequence, we can control the movements of the Buggy as given in the following table.

Buggy movement	Pin configuration
Forward	PWM-A = 0, PWM-B = active, PWM-C = 0, PWM-D = active
Backward	PWM-A = active, PWM-B = 0, PWM-C = active, PWM-D = 0
Spin	PWM-A = active, PWM-B = 0, PWM-C = 0, PWM-D = active
Turn left	PWM-A = 0, PWM-B = 0, PWM-C = 0, PWM-D = active
Turn right	PWM-A = 0, PWM-B = active, PWM-C = 0, PWM-D = 0

In the forward and backward directions, both left and right motors are activated at the same speed. When turning left, we can stop the left motors and only activate the right motors. Similarly, when turning right, we can stop the right motors and activate only the left motors. Notice that in left and right turn operations, the motors can be activated at reduced speed (e.g., half speed or even lower).

The motors are activated by sending PWM (pulse width modulated) signals to them (Fig. 22.8). A PWM signal is a positive square wave signal with a fixed period. The Duty Cycle of the signal is the ratio of the duration of the positive pulse to the period of the signal. By varying the duty cycle, we can effectively vary the average voltage supplied to the mo-

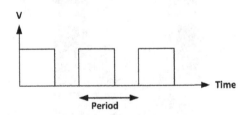

FIGURE 22.8   PWM waveform.

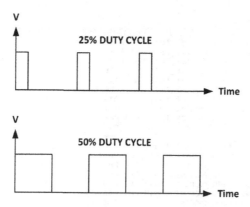

FIGURE 22.9   PWM waveform with different duty cycles.

tors, and this is how the speed of the Buggy can be changed. Fig. 22.9 shows example PWM waveforms with 25% and 50% duty cycles.

Most microcontrollers have built-in PWM generator modules. The STM32F407 microcontroller used in this book supports a large number of PWM modules. Using the mikroC Pro for ARM compiler, the PWM channels on the STM32F407 microcontroller are configured using the following built-in library functions:

PWM_TIMn_Init()
PWM_TIMn_Set_Duty()
PWM_TIMn_Start()
PWM_TIMn_Stop()

PWM_TIMn_Init(): This function is used to initialize a timer module for PWM operation, where n is the chosen timer module number. The frequency of the required PWM signal must be supplied to the function. The function returns an integer which is equal to the calculated maximum period of the PWM waveform. A timer between 0 and 17 can be selected, but it is important to make sure that the chosen output pin supports PWM operation with the chosen timer. Some of the available timers and output pin names supported by STM32F407 microcontroller are shown in Fig. 22.10 (complete list can be obtained by typing _GPIO_MODULE_TIM inside the compiler and pressing keys Cntrl + Space).

The example library function call below shows how the PWM frequency can be set to 1000 Hz for timer 11. The maximum period is returned and saved in variable called PWMA:

PWMA = PWM_TIM11_Init(1000);

PWM_TIMn_Set_Duty(): This function changes the duty cycle of the PWM waveform. The required duty cycle, its mode, and the channel number must be supplied to the function. The duty cycle can be expressed as a percentage of the maximum value returned by call to function PWM_TIMn_Init(). The mode can be _PWM_INVERTED or _PWM_NON_INVERTED. The PWM channel number can be selected from the list given in Fig. 22.10. The example below sets the duty cycle to 50% (PWMA / 2) with non-inverted waveform for channel 1, using timer 11:

PWM_TIM11_Set_Duty(PWMA/2, _PWM_NON_INVERTED, _PWM_CHANNEL1);

Code Assistant

variable	signed int	GPIO_MODULE_TIM
struct	struct	_GPIO_MODULE_TIM1_CH1_PA8
struct	struct	_GPIO_MODULE_TIM1_CH1_PE9
struct	struct	_GPIO_MODULE_TIM1_CH2_PA9
struct	struct	_GPIO_MODULE_TIM1_CH2_PE11
struct	struct	_GPIO_MODULE_TIM1_CH3_PA10
struct	struct	_GPIO_MODULE_TIM1_CH3_PE13
struct	struct	_GPIO_MODULE_TIM1_CH4_PA11
struct	struct	_GPIO_MODULE_TIM1_CH4_PE14
struct	struct	_GPIO_MODULE_TIM10_CH1_PB8
struct	struct	_GPIO_MODULE_TIM10_CH1_PF6
struct	struct	_GPIO_MODULE_TIM11_CH1_PB9
struct	struct	_GPIO_MODULE_TIM11_CH1_PF7
struct	struct	_GPIO_MODULE_TIM12_CH1_PB14
struct	struct	_GPIO_MODULE_TIM12_CH1_PH6
struct	struct	_GPIO_MODULE_TIM12_CH2_PB15
struct	struct	_GPIO_MODULE_TIM12_CH2_PH9
struct	struct	_GPIO_MODULE_TIM13_CH1_PA6
struct	struct	_GPIO_MODULE_TIM13_CH1_PF8
struct	struct	_GPIO_MODULE_TIM14_CH1_PA7
struct	struct	_GPIO_MODULE_TIM14_CH1_PF9
struct	struct	_GPIO_MODULE_TIM2_CH1_PA0
struct	struct	_GPIO_MODULE_TIM2_CH1_PA15
struct	struct	_GPIO_MODULE_TIM2_CH1_PA5
struct	struct	_GPIO_MODULE_TIM2_CH2_PA1
struct	struct	_GPIO_MODULE_TIM2_CH2_PB3
struct	struct	_GPIO_MODULE_TIM2_CH3_PA2
struct	struct	_GPIO_MODULE_TIM2_CH3_PB10
struct	struct	_GPIO_MODULE_TIM2_CH4_PA3
struct	struct	_GPIO_MODULE_TIM2_CH4_PB11
struct	struct	_GPIO_MODULE_TIM3_CH1_PA6
struct	struct	_GPIO_MODULE_TIM3_CH1_PB4
struct	struct	_GPIO_MODULE_TIM3_CH1_PC6
struct	struct	_GPIO_MODULE_TIM3_CH2_PA7
struct	struct	_GPIO_MODULE_TIM3_CH2_PB5
struct	struct	_GPIO_MODULE_TIM3_CH2_PC7
struct	struct	_GPIO_MODULE_TIM3_CH3_PB0
struct	struct	_GPIO_MODULE_TIM3_CH3_PC8
struct	struct	_GPIO_MODULE_TIM3_CH4_PB1
struct	struct	_GPIO_MODULE_TIM3_CH4_PC9
struct	struct	_GPIO_MODULE_TIM4_CH1_PB6
struct	struct	_GPIO_MODULE_TIM4_CH1_PD12
struct	struct	_GPIO_MODULE_TIM4_CH2_PB7
struct	struct	_GPIO_MODULE_TIM4_CH2_PD13
struct	struct	_GPIO_MODULE_TIM4_CH3_PB8
struct	struct	_GPIO_MODULE_TIM4_CH3_PD14
struct	struct	_GPIO_MODULE_TIM4_CH4_PB9
struct	struct	_GPIO_MODULE_TIM4_CH4_PD15
struct	struct	_GPIO_MODULE_TIM5_CH1_PA0
struct	struct	_GPIO_MODULE_TIM5_CH1_PH10
struct	struct	_GPIO_MODULE_TIM5_CH2_PA1

FIGURE 22.10   Some supported timers and output pin names.

PWM_TIMn_Start(): This function starts generating PWM waveform on the selected output pin, channel, and the timer. The channel number and the output pin names must be supplied to the function. The example below starts PWM on output pin PB9, using timer 11 with channel 1 (see Fig. 22.10 on how to select an output pin, timer, and channel number):

PWM_TIM11_Start(_PWM_CHANNEL1, &_GPIO_MODULE_TIM11_CH1_PB9);

PWM_TIMn_Stop(): This function stops the PWM. The channel number must be supplied to the function. The example below shows how PWM on channel 1 can be stopped:

PWM_TIM11_Stop(_PWM_CHANNEL1);

We will be seeing in a later project how to configure the wheel motors to move the Buggy forward, backward, and turning left and right.

22.4 Lights (LEDs)

Just like a real car, the Buggy has a set of front and rear lights for signaling and lighting the way. All of these lights are programmable from software. The lights are grouped as follows:

- The pair of white LEDs on the front are headlights with two modes of brightness.
- The Red LEDs at the rear are brake lights, having two modes of brightness.
- The two pair of Yellow LEDs at the front and rear are the signal lights.

With the Clicker 2 for STM32 development board plugged-in to the Buggy, the following port pins control the lights:

Light	Description	Clicker 2 for STM32 pin
Brake	Rear	PE1
Signal	Right	PE2
Signal	Left	PC4
Head lights	Front (main beam)	PB6
Head lights	Front (low intensity)	PE3

Head lights and brake lights have two brightness levels as shown by the following combinations:

Main beam + low intensity: gives bright head lights and normal brightness brake lights
Low intensity only: gives low-intensity head lights and normal intensity brake lights
Break light + low intensity: gives bright brake lights and normal intensity head lights

Further details and the complete circuit diagram of the Buggy can be obtained from the Buggy manual available at the following website:

https://download.mikroe.com/documents/specials/educational/buggy/buggy-development-platform-manual-v102.pdf

22.5 Project 57: controlling the Buggy lights

Description: This project shows how the Buggy lights can be controlled using functions. In this project, the Buggy lights are controlled as follows:

- Flash left signal lights 10 times at a rate of 250 ms
- Flash right signal lights 10 times at a rate of 250 ms
- Turn ON brake lights
- Wait 1 second
- Turn OFF brake lights
- Turn ON head lights

- Wait 1 second
- Turn OFF head lights

Aim: The aim of this project is to make the user familiar with controlling the Buggy lights.

Program listing: Fig. 22.11 shows the program listing (**lights.c**). The program uses the following functions to control the lights:

LeftSignalFlash(int ratems, int count): This function flashes the left signal lights count times at a rate of ratems milliseconds.

RightSignalFlash(int ratems, int count): This function flashes the right signal lights count times at a rate of ratems milliseconds.

BrakeLights(int mode): This function turns ON (mode = 1) or OFF (mode = 0) the brake lights.

HeadLights(int mode): This function turns ON (mode = 1) or OFF (mode = 0) the head lights.

22.6 Project 58: controlling the Buggy motors

Description: This project shows how the Buggy motors can be controlled using functions to move the Buggy forward, backward, and to turn left and right. In this project, the Buggy movement is controlled as follows:

- Move the Buggy forwards for 1 second at half speed
- Stop and wait 5 seconds
- Turn the Buggy left
- Stop and wait 5 seconds
- Move the Buggy backward for 1 second at half speed
- Stop and wait for 5 seconds
- Move the Buggy right
- Stop and wait 5 seconds
- Move the Buggy forward for 1 second at half speed
- Stop

Aim: The aim of this project is to make the user familiar with controlling the Buggy movements.

Program listing: Fig. 22.12 shows the program listing (**motors.c**). The program uses the following functions to control the Buggy movements:

MoveForward(int n, int mode): This function moves the Buggy forward for n seconds and then stops it. Mode specifies the speed of the Buggy as follows:

Mode	Speed
1	Full speed
2	Half speed
3	Quarter speed, etc.

MoveBackward(int n, int mode): This function moves the Buggy backward for n seconds and then stops it. Mode specifies the speed of the Buggy as above.

TurnLeft(): This function turns the Buggy left and then stops it.

```
/*===========================================================================
                            BUGGY LIGHTS
                            ============

This is program shows how the Buggy lights can be controlled by using various
functions.

Author: Dogan Ibrahim
Date  : December, 2019
File  : lights.c
=============================================================================*/
#include "main.h"

//
// Flash the left signal lights "count" times at the given "rate (in ms)"
//
void LeftSignalFlash(int ratems, int count)
{
    #define LeftSignalLights GPIOC_ODR.B4
    int k;
    GPIO_Config(&GPIOC_BASE, _GPIO_PINMASK_4, _GPIO_CFG_MODE_OUTPUT);

    for(k = 0; k < count; k++)
    {
        LeftSignalLights = 1;                       // Lights ON
        vTaskDelay(pdMS_TO_TICKS(ratems));          // Wait rate ms
        LeftSignalLights = 0;                       // Lights OFF
        vTaskDelay(pdMS_TO_TICKS(ratems));          // Wait rate ms
    }
}


//
// Flash the right signal lights "count" times at the given "rate (in ms)"
//
void RightSignalFlash(int ratems, int count)
{
    #define RightSignalLights GPIOE_ODR.B2
    int k;
    GPIO_Config(&GPIOE_BASE, _GPIO_PINMASK_2, _GPIO_CFG_MODE_OUTPUT);

    for(k = 0; k < count; k++)
    {
        RightSignalLights = 1;                      // Lights ON
        vTaskDelay(pdMS_TO_TICKS(ratems));          // Wait rate ms
        RightSignalLights = 0;                      // Lights OFF
        vTaskDelay(pdMS_TO_TICKS(ratems));          // Wait rate ms
    }
}


//
// Turn ON (1), OFF(0) brake lights
//
void BrakeLights(int mode)
{
    #define BrakeLight GPIOE_ODR.B1
    GPIO_Config(&GPIOE_BASE, _GPIO_PINMASK_1, _GPIO_CFG_MODE_OUTPUT);
    BrakeLight = mode;
}

//
```

FIGURE 22.11   lights.c program listing.

```
// Turn ON(1), OFF(0) head lights
//
void HeadLights(int mode)
{
    #define HeadLight GPIOB_ODR.B6
    GPIO_Config(&GPIOB_BASE, _GPIO_PINMASK_6, _GPIO_CFG_MODE_OUTPUT);
    HeadLight = mode;
}


//
// Define all your Task functions here
// ====================================
//

// Task 1 - Lights Controller
void Task1(void *pvParameters)
{
  while(1)
  {
    LeftSignalFlash(250, 10);                  // Flash left signal 10 times
    RightSignalFlash(250, 10);                 // Flash right signal 10 times
    BrakeLights(1);                            // Brake lights ON
    vTaskDelay(pdMS_TO_TICKS(1000));           // Wait 1 second
    BrakeLights(0);                            // Brake lights OFF
    HeadLights(1);                             // Head lights ON
    vTaskDelay(pdMS_TO_TICKS(1000));           // Wait 1 second
    HeadLights(0);                             // Head lights OFF
    while(1);                                  // Stop
  }
}


//
// Start of MAIN program
// =====================
//
void main()
{
//
// Create all the TASKS here
// =========================
//
    // Create Task 1
    xTaskCreate(
        (TaskFunction_t)Task1,
        "Lights Controller",
        configMINIMAL_STACK_SIZE,
        NULL,
        10,
        NULL
    );

//
// Start the RTOS scheduler
//
    vTaskStartScheduler();

//
// Will never reach here
}
```

FIGURE 22.11   (*Continued*)

```
/*===============================================================================
                        BUGGY MOTORS
                        ============

This is program shows how the Buggy motors can be controlled by using various
functions to move the Buggy forward, backward, turning left, and right.

Author: Dogan Ibrahim
Date  : December, 2019
File  : motors.c
===============================================================================*/
#include "main.h"

unsigned int PWMA, PWMB, PWMC, PWMD;

//
// Stop the Buggy by setting all the Duty Cycles to 0
//
void Stop()
{
  PWM_TIM11_Set_Duty(0, _PWM_NON_INVERTED, _PWM_CHANNEL1);
  PWM_TIM10_Set_Duty(0, _PWM_NON_INVERTED, _PWM_CHANNEL1);
  PWM_TIM9_Set_Duty(0, _PWM_NON_INVERTED, _PWM_CHANNEL1);
  PWM_TIM3_Set_Duty(0, _PWM_NON_INVERTED, _PWM_CHANNEL3);
}


//
// Move Buggy Forward n seconds. mode=0 (Half Speed), mode=1 (Full speed)
//
void MoveForward(int n, int mode)
{
    int secs;
    secs = n * 1000;

    PWM_TIM11_Set_Duty(0, _PWM_NON_INVERTED, _PWM_CHANNEL1);
    PWM_TIM9_Set_Duty(0, _PWM_NON_INVERTED, _PWM_CHANNEL1);
    PWM_TIM3_Set_Duty(PWMD/mode, _PWM_NON_INVERTED, _PWM_CHANNEL3);
    PWM_TIM10_Set_Duty(PWMB/mode, _PWM_NON_INVERTED, _PWM_CHANNEL1);
    vTaskDelay(pdMS_TO_TICKS(secs));
    Stop();
}


//
// Move Buggy Backwards n seconds. mode=0 (Half Speed), mode=1 (Full speed)
//
void MoveBackward(int n, int mode)
{
  int secs;
  secs = n * 1000;

  PWM_TIM3_Set_Duty(0, _PWM_NON_INVERTED, _PWM_CHANNEL3);
  PWM_TIM10_Set_Duty(0, _PWM_NON_INVERTED, _PWM_CHANNEL1);
  PWM_TIM11_Set_Duty(PWMA/mode, _PWM_NON_INVERTED, _PWM_CHANNEL1);
  PWM_TIM9_Set_Duty(PWMC/mode, _PWM_NON_INVERTED, _PWM_CHANNEL1);
  vTaskDelay(pdMS_TO_TICKS(secs));
  Stop();
}

//
// Turn Left 90 degrees at half speed and Stop
```

FIGURE 22.12   motors.c program listing.

```
//
void TurnLeft()
{
  PWM_TIM11_Set_Duty(0, _PWM_NON_INVERTED, _PWM_CHANNEL1);
  PWM_TIM10_Set_Duty(0, _PWM_NON_INVERTED, _PWM_CHANNEL1);
  PWM_TIM9_Set_Duty(0, _PWM_NON_INVERTED, _PWM_CHANNEL1);
  PWM_TIM3_Set_Duty(PWMD, _PWM_NON_INVERTED, _PWM_CHANNEL3);
  vTaskDelay(pdMS_TO_TICKS(200));
  Stop();
}

//
// Turn Right 90 degrees at half speed and Stop
//
void TurnRight()
{
  PWM_TIM11_Set_Duty(0, _PWM_NON_INVERTED, _PWM_CHANNEL1);
  PWM_TIM10_Set_Duty(PWMB, _PWM_NON_INVERTED, _PWM_CHANNEL1);
  PWM_TIM9_Set_Duty(0, _PWM_NON_INVERTED, _PWM_CHANNEL1);
  PWM_TIM3_Set_Duty(0, _PWM_NON_INVERTED, _PWM_CHANNEL3);
  vTaskDelay(pdMS_TO_TICKS(200));
  Stop();
}

//
// Define all your Task functions here
// ====================================
//

// Task 1 - Buggy Movement Controller
void Task1(void *pvParameters)
{
  while(1)
  {
    MoveForward(1, 2);                              // Move at half speed
    vTaskDelay(pdMS_TO_TICKS(5000));                // Wait 5 seconds
    TurnLeft();                                     // Turn left
    vTaskDelay(pdMS_TO_TICKS(5000));                // Wait 5 seconds
    MoveBackward(1, 2);                             // Move at half speed
    vTaskDelay(pdMS_TO_TICKS(5000));                // Wait 5 seconds
    TurnRight();                                    // Turn right
    vTaskDelay(pdMS_TO_TICKS(5000));                // Wait 5 seconds
    MoveForward(1, 2);                              // Move at half speed
    vTaskDelay(pdMS_TO_TICKS(5000));                // Wait 5 seconds
    while(1);                                       // Stop
  }
}

//
// Start of MAIN program
// ======================
//
void main()
{
//
// Create PWM channels
//
  PWMA = PWM_TIM11_Init(1000);                      // For pin PB9
  PWMB = PWM_TIM10_Init(1000);                      // For pin PB8
  PWMC = PWM_TIM9_Init(1000);                       // For pin PE5
```

FIGURE 22.12   (*Continued*)

```
    PWMD = PWM_TIM3_Init(1000);                              // For pin PB0

//
// Start all PWM channels
//
    PWM_TIM11_Start(_PWM_CHANNEL1, &_GPIO_MODULE_TIM11_CH1_PB9);
    PWM_TIM10_Start(_PWM_CHANNEL1, &_GPIO_MODULE_TIM10_CH1_PB8);
    PWM_TIM9_Start(_PWM_CHANNEL1, &_GPIO_MODULE_TIM9_CH1_PE5);
    PWM_TIM3_Start(_PWM_CHANNEL3, &_GPIO_MODULE_TIM3_CH3_PB0);
//
// Set Duty Cycles to all 0s (i.e. Stop the Buggy)
//
    Stop();


//
// Create all the TASKS here
// ==========================
//
    // Create Task 1
    xTaskCreate(
        (TaskFunction_t)Task1,
        "Buggy Movement Controller",
        configMINIMAL_STACK_SIZE,
        NULL,
        10,
        NULL
    );

//
// Start the RTOS scheduler
//
    vTaskStartScheduler();

//
// Will never reach here
}
```

FIGURE 22.12   (*Continued*)

TurnRight(): This function turns the Buggy right and then stops it.

Stop(): This function sets all the duty cycles to 0, thus stopping all the motors.

Inside the main program, the PWM channels are initialized as follows (check with Fig. 22.10 for pin numbers and channels):

PWMA = PWM_TIM11_Init(1000);   // For pin PB9
PWMB = PWM_TIM10_Init(1000);   // For pin PB8
PWMC = PWM_TIM9_Init(1000);   // For pin PE5
PWMD = PWM_TIM3_Init(1000);   // For pin PB0

According to Fig. 22.10, the PWM channel and timer assignments for the motor pins are as follows:

Pin	Pin name	Channel	Timer	Description
PB9	PWM-A	1	11	Left-side motor
PB8	PWM-B	1	10	Left-side motor
PE5	PWM-C	1	9	Right-side motor
PB0	PWM-D	3	3	Right-side motor

The PWM signals were then started on each channel using the following functions:

PWM_TIM11_Start(_PWM_CHANNEL1, &_GPIO_MODULE_TIM11_CH1_PB9);
PWM_TIM10_Start(_PWM_CHANNEL1, &_GPIO_MODULE_TIM10_CH1_PB8);
PWM_TIM9_Start(_PWM_CHANNEL1, &_GPIO_MODULE_TIM9_CH1_PE5);
PWM_TIM3_Start(_PWM_CHANNEL3, &_GPIO_MODULE_TIM3_CH3_PB0);

The MoveForward function moves the Buggy forward for the specified number of seconds. In this function, the duty cycles of PWM-A (PWM_TIM11) and PWM-C (PWM_TIM9) are set to 0. The duty cycles of PWB-B (PEM_TIM10) and PWM-D (PWM_TIM3) can be set by argument mode of the function as described earlier.

The MoveBackward function is similar to MoveForward, but here, the duty cycles of PWM-B (PWM_TIM10) and PWM-D (PWM_TIM3) are set to 0. The duty cycles of PWM-A (PWM_TIM11) and PWM-C (PWM_TIM9) can be set by argument mode of the function as described earlier.

The TurnLeft function turns the Buggy 90 degrees to its left. Here, the duty cycles of PWM-A, PWM-B, and PWM-C are set to 0, and the duty cycle of PWM-D is set to full mode, that is, PWMD. It was found by experimenting that 200 ms turning action results in 90 degrees turning of the Buggy. Using a longer delay will turn the Buggy further. Similarly, using a smaller delay will turn the Buggy less than 90 degrees.

The TurnRight function is similar to TurnLeft, but here the duty cycles of PWM-A, PWM-C, and PWM-D are set to 0, and the duty cycle of PWM-B is set to full mode.

It is important to notice that PWM must be enabled in the Library Manager before the program can be compiled.

22.7 Project 59: obstacle avoiding Buggy

Description: This is a multitasking obstacle avoiding Buggy project. An infrared (IR) distance sensor is mounted in-front of the Buggy. The Buggy moves forward, and if it detects an obstacle on its way, it turns left by 90 degrees with the hope of avoiding the obstacle. A buzzer is connected to the Buggy which sounds when an obstacle is on its way. The left signal lights are flashed to indicate when the Buggy is about to turn left. Additionally, a light sensor (ambient click) is mounted on the Buggy which detects when it is dark and turns ON the head lights automatically. A sound sensor module detects ambient sounds, and when the sound level is above a threshold level (e.g., when the user claps hands near the buggy), the Buggy is stopped on emergency. The brake lights are activated when the Buggy stops. The LED at port pin PE12 on the Clicker 2 for STM32 development board flashes rapidly to indicate that the Buggy is active.

Aim: The aim of this project is to develop a multitasking system using the FreeRTOS API functions to control the motors and lights of the Buggy.

Block diagram: Fig. 22.13 shows the block diagram. The Buggy with all the components mounted on it is shown in Fig. 22.14. A number of sensor click boards, a buzzer click board, and a sound sensor module are used in the system (see www.mikroe.com for a list and details of all the click boards).

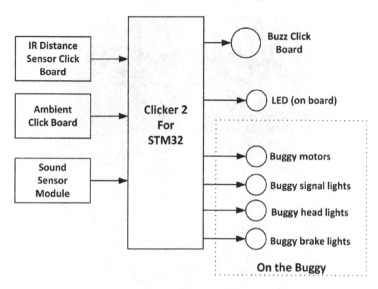

FIGURE 22.13   Block diagram of the project.

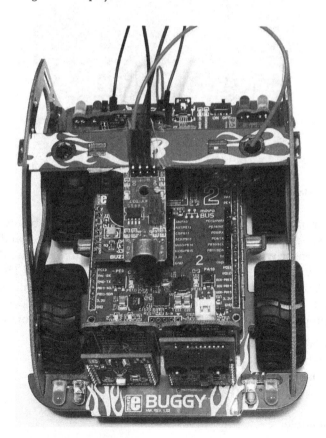

FIGURE 22.14   The Buggy with the components.

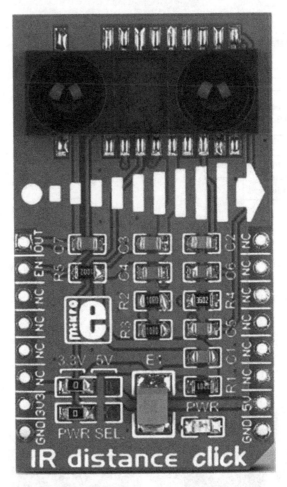

FIGURE 22.15   IR Distance Sensor Click Board.

Details of the various sensor boards used in the project are given below.

IR distance sensor click board: This click board (Fig. 22.15) is based on the GP2Y0A60SZ0F distance measuring sensor, which comprises an integrated position-sensitive detector, an IR LED, and a signal processing circuit. The measuring range is between 10 and 150 cm, which is well suited to mobile robotic applications. The sensor on the board is not influenced by variations caused by the reflectivity of the object whose distance is measured. The board outputs an analog voltage inversely proportional to the distance of the object. Key features of this sensor board are:

- +3.3 and +5 V operation, selectable with a jumper
- +3.3 V operation by default
- 10 to 150 cm measurement range
- Analog output
- Enable pin
- mikroBUS compatible

Fig. 22.16 shows the typical output of the sensor when operated with +3.3 V. It is clear from this figure that the output voltage goes down from about 2 V when the distance to the object is very close, to about 0.3 V when the object is about 150 cm away from the sensor.

This click board is used to detect the distance to an object so that the Buggy can avoid collision with the object.

Ambient click board: This click board (Fig. 22.17) is based on the MLX75305 integrated optical sensor chip which consists of a photodiode, a transimpedance amplifier, and an output transistor. The chip converts ambient light intensity into a voltage and can operate from either +3 V or +5 V, and is configured for +3.3 V operation by default. The analog output voltage is directly proportional to the light intensity ($\mu W/cm^2$) and is 0 when the sensor is dark. The voltage increases linearly as the ambient light intensity is increased. This click board is used to detect when it is dark to turn ON the head lights.

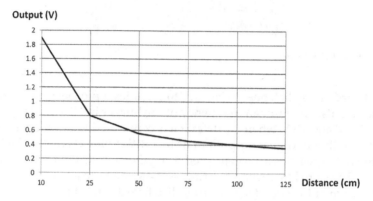

FIGURE 22.16   Output response of the sensor.

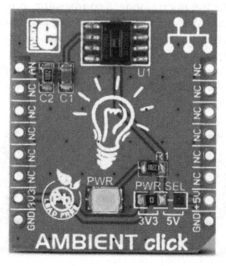

FIGURE 22.17   Ambient Click Board.

FIGURE 22.18   Buzz Click Board.

Buzz click board: This click board (Fig. 22.18) includes a piezoelectric buzzer capable of emitting audio signals. The resonant frequency of the buzzer is 3.8 kHz. The board can operate with both +3.3 V and +5 V, where by default it is configured for +5 V operation. The board can be connected either to digital output pin or to a PWM line. Using the PWM line enables sounds at different frequencies to be generated using the mikroC Pro for ARM compiler built-in sound library. The signal frequency determines the sound pitch, while the duty cycle determines the amplitude of the sound signal. This click board is used to generate audible sound when the Buggy detects an obstacle on its way.

Sound sensor board: The KY-038 sound sensor board was used in the project (Fig. 22.19). This board consists of an electret microphone, a comparator chip, a potentiometer, and a few resistors. The board is operated from +3.3 V power supply, obtained from the click board socket mikroBUS 3 mounted at the rear of the Buggy. The sound sensor board provides both a digital and an analog output. In this project, the digital output (D0) is used only. In digital mode, the board detects sounds, and when the sound level is above a threshold level, the output goes from logic 0 to 1 as long as the sound is present, otherwise the output is at logic 0.

FIGURE 22.19   Sound sensor board.

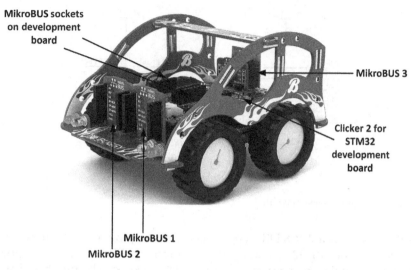

FIGURE 22.20   mikroBUS sockets on the Buggy.

This click board is used to detect sound (e.g., clapping hands) and then stops the Buggy as an emergency.

Circuit diagram: There are three mikroBUS sockets on the Buggy in the form of vertical plates. As shown in Fig. 22.20, two sockets (mikroBUS 1 and mikroBUS 2) are in front of the Buggy, and one socket (mikroBUS 3) is at the rear of the Buggy. Additionally, the Clicker 2 for STM32 development board has two mikroBUS sockets mounted on it. Therefore, in total, there are five mikroBUS sockets available for the use of Clicker boards.

The click boards are connected to the mikroBUS sockets on the Buggy as follows (see Fig. 22.14):

Click board	mikroBUS socket	Place of the mikroBUS socket
IR distance sensor	mikroBUS 1	Front of the Buggy
Ambient	mikroBUS 2	Front of the Buggy
Buzz	mikroBUS 1	Clicker 2 for STM32

The Sound sensor board (KY-038) was connected as follows:

KY-038 pin	Clicker 2 for STM32 pin
GND	GND on mikroBUS 3 socket
+3.3 V	+3.3 V on mikroBUS 3 socket
D0	pin 1 (AN) on mikroBUS 3 socket

Notice that pin 1 (AN) on mikroBUS 3 socket is internally connected to port pin PC2 of the Clicker 2 for STM32 development board.

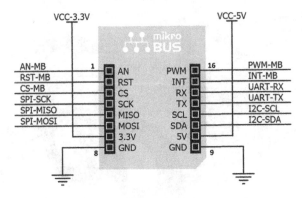

FIGURE 22.21   **mikroBUS socket layout.**

A mikroBUS socket is a 2 × 8 DIL type socket with the pin names as shown in Fig. 22.21, providing interface for SPI, I2C, analog, UART, interrupt, PWM, reset, and power supply pins. As shown in the figure, the pins of a mikroBUS socket can be numbered such that the pin at the top left position is pin 1.

The interface between the click boards used in this project and the corresponding Clicker 2 for STM32 pin names is as follows (see the Buggy user manual at:

https://download.mikroe.com/documents/specials/educational/buggy/buggy-development-platform-manual-v102.pdf).

Click board	Pin number	Description	Clicker 2 for STM32 pin name
IR distance sensor	1	In (analog)	PC0
	2	Enable (digital)	PD11
Ambient	1	In (analog)	PC1
Buzz	3	Out (digital)	PE9

Program listing: Fig. 22.22 shows the program listing (program: **obstacle.c**). The program consists of four tasks excluding the Idle task. The operation of each task is described below:

Task 1 (IR sensor controller)
Define the IR Distance Threshold
Initialize the ADC
DO FOREVER
   Read distance to obstacle
   IF distance to obstacle < IR Distance Threshold **THEN**
     Move Forward
   ELSE
     Stop the Buggy
     Turn ON Brake lights
     Activate buzzer

```
/*===============================================================================
                          OBSTACLE AVOIDING BUGGY
                          =======================

This is the obstacle avoiding Buggy. An IR distance sensor is mounted in-front of
teh Buggy to measure teh distance to obtacles. If an obstacle is within a preset
range then the Buggy is forced to turn left to avoid the obstacle. A light sensor
mounted in-front of the Buggy detects when it is dark and turns ON the head lights.
The signal lights are activated when the Buggy makes a turn. The brake lights are
activated when the Buggy stops. A buzzer sounds when an obstacle is detected in-front
of the Buggy. The Buggy can be stopped on emergency when hands are clapped near it.

Author: Dogan Ibrahim
Date   : December, 2019
File   : obstacle.c
===============================================================================*/
#include "main.h"

unsigned int PWMA, PWMB, PWMC, PWMD;

//
// Stop the Buggy by setting all the Duty Cycles to 0
//
void StopBuggy()
{
  PWM_TIM11_Set_Duty(0, _PWM_NON_INVERTED, _PWM_CHANNEL1);
  PWM_TIM10_Set_Duty(0, _PWM_NON_INVERTED, _PWM_CHANNEL1);
  PWM_TIM9_Set_Duty(0, _PWM_NON_INVERTED, _PWM_CHANNEL1);
  PWM_TIM3_Set_Duty(0, _PWM_NON_INVERTED, _PWM_CHANNEL3);
}


//
// Move Buggy Forward, mode specifies the speed
//
void MoveForward(int mode)
{
    PWM_TIM11_Set_Duty(0, _PWM_NON_INVERTED, _PWM_CHANNEL1);
    PWM_TIM9_Set_Duty(0, _PWM_NON_INVERTED, _PWM_CHANNEL1);
    PWM_TIM3_Set_Duty(PWMD/mode, _PWM_NON_INVERTED, _PWM_CHANNEL3);
    PWM_TIM10_Set_Duty(PWMB/mode, _PWM_NON_INVERTED, _PWM_CHANNEL1);
}


//
// Turn Left 90 degrees
//
void TurnLeft()
{
  PWM_TIM11_Set_Duty(0, _PWM_NON_INVERTED, _PWM_CHANNEL1);
  PWM_TIM10_Set_Duty(0, _PWM_NON_INVERTED, _PWM_CHANNEL1);
  PWM_TIM9_Set_Duty(0, _PWM_NON_INVERTED, _PWM_CHANNEL1);
  PWM_TIM3_Set_Duty(PWMD, _PWM_NON_INVERTED, _PWM_CHANNEL3);
  vTaskDelay(pdMS_TO_TICKS(250));
  StopBuggy();
}


//
// Turn ON(1), OFF(0) head lights
//
void HeadLights(int mode)
{
```

FIGURE 22.22   obstacle.c program listing.

```
        #define HeadLight GPIOB_ODR.B6
        GPIO_Config(&GPIOB_BASE, _GPIO_PINMASK_6, _GPIO_CFG_MODE_OUTPUT);
        HeadLight = mode;
}


//
// Flash the left signal lights "count" times at the given "rate (in ms)"
//
void LeftSignalFlash(int ratems, int count)
{
    #define LeftSignalLights GPIOC_ODR.B4
    int k;
    GPIO_Config(&GPIOC_BASE, _GPIO_PINMASK_4, _GPIO_CFG_MODE_OUTPUT);

    for(k = 0; k < count; k++)
    {
      LeftSignalLights = 1;                          // Lights ON
      vTaskDelay(pdMS_TO_TICKS(ratems));             // Wait rate ms
      LeftSignalLights = 0;                          // Lights OFF
      vTaskDelay(pdMS_TO_TICKS(ratems));             // Wait rate ms
    }
}


//
// Turn ON (1), OFF(0) brake lights
//
void BrakeLights(int mode)
{
    #define BrakeLight GPIOE_ODR.B1
    GPIO_Config(&GPIOE_BASE, _GPIO_PINMASK_1, _GPIO_CFG_MODE_OUTPUT);
    BrakeLight = mode;
}


//
// Activate the buzzer at 1000Hz for 100ms
//
void ActivateBuzzer()
{
    Sound_Init(&GPIOE_ODR, 9);
    Sound_Play(1000,100);
}


//
// Define all your Task functions here
// =====================================
//

// Task 1 - IR Sensor Controller
void Task1(void *pvParameters)
{
    #define IREnable GPIOD_ODR.B11

    unsigned IRSensorValue;
    float mV;
    float DistanceThreshold = 980.0;                     // 30cm distance

    GPIO_Config(&GPIOD_BASE, _GPIO_PINMASK_11, _GPIO_CFG_MODE_OUTPUT);
    ADC1_Init();
    IREnable = 1;                                        // Initialzie ADC
```

FIGURE 22.22   (*Continued*)

```
    while (1)                                          // DO FOREVER
    {
        IRSensorValue = ADC1_Read(10);                 // Read ADC Channel 10
        mV = IRSensorValue*3300.0 / 4096.0;            // In mV

        if(mV < DistanceThreshold)                     // If no obstacle
        {
            MoveForward(5);                            // Go forward
        }
        else                                           // Obstacle
        {
            StopBuggy();                               // Stop
            BrakeLights(1);                            // Brake lights ON
            ActivateBuzzer();                          // Buzzer ON
            LeftSignalFlash(250, 3);                   // Flash signal lights
            BrakeLights(0);                            // Brake lights OFF
            TurnLeft();                                // Turn left
        }
    }
}

// Task 2 - Head Light Controller
void Task2(void *pvParameters)
{
    unsigned AmbientSensorValue;
    float mV;
    float DarkThreshold = 105.0;                       // Dark threshold
    ADC1_Init();                                       // Initialzie ADC

    while(1)                                           // DO FOREVER
    {
        AmbientSensorValue = ADC1_Read(11);            // Read ADC Channel 11
        mV = AmbientSensorValue*3300.0 / 4096.0;       // In mV
        if(mV < DarkThreshold)                         // If dark
            HeadLights(1);                             // Head lights ON
        else
            HeadLights(0);                             // Head lights OFF
    }
}

// Task 3 - Buggy Active Light Controller
void Task3(void *pvParameters)
{
    #define BuggyActiveLED GPIOE_ODR.B12
    GPIO_Config(&GPIOE_BASE, _GPIO_PINMASK_12, _GPIO_CFG_MODE_OUTPUT);
    while(1)
    {
        BuggyActiveLED = 1;                            // LED ON
        vTaskDelay(pdMS_TO_TICKS(200));                // Wait 200ms
        BuggyActiveLED = 0;                            // LED OFF
        vTaskDelay(pdMS_TO_TICKS(200));                // Wait 200ms
    }
}

// Task 4 - Emergency Stop Controller
void Task4(void *pvParameters)
{
    #define AmbientSound GPIOC_IDR.B2
    GPIO_Config(&GPIOC_BASE, _GPIO_PINMASK_2, _GPIO_CFG_MODE_INPUT);
```

FIGURE 22.22   (*Continued*)

```
    while(1)
    {
        if(AmbientSound == 1)                               // Ambient sound detected
        {
          StopBuggy();                                      // Stop Buggy
          HeadLights(0);                                    // Headlights OFF
          BrakeLights(0);                                   // Brake lights OFF
          vTaskSuspendAll();                                // Suspend scheduler
        }
    }
}

//
// Start of MAIN program
// =====================
//
void main()
{
//
// Create PWM channels
//
  PWMA = PWM_TIM11_Init(1000);                              // For pin PB9
  PWMB = PWM_TIM10_Init(1000);                              // For pin PB8
  PWMC = PWM_TIM9_Init(1000);                               // For pin PE5
  PWMD = PWM_TIM3_Init(1000);                               // For pin PB0

//
// Start all PWM channels
//
  PWM_TIM11_Start(_PWM_CHANNEL1, &_GPIO_MODULE_TIM11_CH1_PB9);
  PWM_TIM10_Start(_PWM_CHANNEL1, &_GPIO_MODULE_TIM10_CH1_PB8);
  PWM_TIM9_Start(_PWM_CHANNEL1, &_GPIO_MODULE_TIM9_CH1_PE5);
  PWM_TIM3_Start(_PWM_CHANNEL3, &_GPIO_MODULE_TIM3_CH3_PB0);
//
// Set Duty Cycles to all 0s (i.e. Stop the Buggy)
//
  StopBuggy();

//
// Create all the TASKS here
// =========================
//
    // Create Task 1
    xTaskCreate(
        (TaskFunction_t)Task1,
        "IR Sensor Controller",
        configMINIMAL_STACK_SIZE,
        NULL,
        10,
        NULL
    );


    // Create Task 2
    xTaskCreate(
        (TaskFunction_t)Task2,
        "Head Light Controller",
        configMINIMAL_STACK_SIZE,
        NULL,
        10,
```

FIGURE 22.22   (*Continued*)

```
        NULL
    );


    // Create Task 3
    xTaskCreate(
        (TaskFunction_t)Task3,
        "Buggy Active Light Controller",
        configMINIMAL_STACK_SIZE,
        NULL,
        10,
        NULL
    );

    // Create Task 4
    xTaskCreate(
        (TaskFunction_t)Task4,
        "Emetgency Stop Controller",
        configMINIMAL_STACK_SIZE,
        NULL,
        10,
        NULL
    );
//
// Start the RTOS scheduler
//
    vTaskStartScheduler();

//
// Will never reach here
}
```

FIGURE 22.22   (*Continued*)

      Flash the left signal lights
      Turn OFF Brake lights
      Turn left
   ENDIF
ENDDO

Task 2 (head lights controller)
Define the Dark Threshold
Initialize the ADC
DO FOREVER
   Read light level
   IF light level < Dark Threshold **THEN**
      Turn ON the head lights
   ELSE
      Turn OFF the head lights
   ENDIF
ENDDO

Task 3 (active light controller)
DO FOREVER
   Turn ON on-board LED at port PE12

        Wait 200 ms
        Turn OFF on-board LED at port PE12
        Wait 200 ms
    ENDDO
    <u>**Task 4 (emergency stop controller)**</u>
    DO FOREVER
        IF ambient sound detected **THEN**
        Stop the Buggy
            Turn OFF the head lights
            Turn OFF the Brake lights
            Suspend the scheduler
        ENDIF
    ENDDO

The analog output of the IR distance sensor board is connected to port pin PC0, which corresponds to channel 10 of the ADC on the development board. It was determined by experimentation that when the distance in-front of the Buggy is about 30 cm, then the value returned by the IR Distance Sensor Click board was about 980 mV. This value was, therefore, used to determine when an object was in-front of the Buggy. If the returned value is less than 980 mV, then it is assumed that the obstacle is about 30 cm away from the Buggy. When this happens, the Buggy is stopped to avoid collision with the obstacle. The brake lights are turned ON, the buzzer is activated for a short time and the left signal lights are flashed 3 times. Then, the brake lights are turned OFF and the Buggy makes a 90-degree left turn with the hope to avoid the obstacle. The Buggy then moves forward if there are no more obstacles within 30 cm. The speed of the Buggy is set to 1/5th of its full-scale value to make the Buggy move slowly. Notice that because there are no encoders on the wheel motors, it is not possible to turn the Buggy exactly by 90 degrees. The functions to control the motors and lights are similar to the ones given in the previous project. The buzzer is activated using the built-in Sound Library (this library must be enabled in the Library Manager before the program is compiled) where a 1-kHz signal is sent to the buzzer for the duration of 100 ms.

The analog output of the Ambient Click is connected to port pin PC1 which corresponds to channel 11 of the ADC on the development board. This board measures the ambient light level in-front of the Buggy. It was determined by experimentation that the value of about 105 mV corresponds to a dark level threshold below which the head lights of the Buggy are turned ON, and above this value the head lights are turned OFF using the following code:

```
    while(1)
    {
      AmbientSensorValue = ADC1_Read(11);
      mV = AmbientSensorValue*3300.0 / 4096.0;
      if(mV < DarkThreshold)
         HeadLights(1);
      else
         HeadLights(0);
    }
```

The on-board LED connected to port pin PE12 of the development board flashes rapidly (every 200 ms) to indicate that the Buggy is active.

The Buggy can be stopped on emergency by clapping hands near the microphone of the sound sensor board. The potentiometer of this sensor board should be adjusted carefully so that the output of the board is normally at logic 0 when the Buggy is operating. The output should go to logic 1 when hands are clapped close to the sound sensor. When the output of the sound sensor board goes to logic 1, the wheel motors are stopped, head lights and the brake lights are turned OFF (if they are ON), and finally the FreeRTOS scheduler is suspended so that all the tasks stop.

22.8 Project 60: controlling the Buggy remotely

Description: In the previous project, we have learned how to control the Buggy in a multitasking environment and developed an obstacle avoiding mobile robot using the Buggy together with a number of sensors. In this project, we will be controlling the Buggy remotely using radiofrequency (RF) transmitter and receiver modules. An RF receiver module is mounted on the Buggy which receives commands from an RF transmitter module interfaced to a PC via the USB socket. In addition, an IR distance sensor click board is mounted in-front of the Buggy and a Buzz click board is plugged-in to mikroBUS 1 socket on the development board as in the previous project. The movements, signal lights, head lights, and brake lights of the Buggy are controlled by sending commands from the PC. The following are the valid commands:

F:	go forward
L:	turn left
R:	turn right
S:	stop
H:	turn ON the head lights
h:	turn OFF the head lights
B:	turn ON the brake lights
b:	turn OFF the brake lights
P:	flash the left signal lights 3 times
Q:	flash the right signal lights 3 times

Command F moves the Buggy forward at a reduced speed. As in the previous project, if there is an obstacle in-front of the Buggy as it is moving forward, then it stops and activates the buzzer for a short time. Commands L and R turn the Buggy left and right, respectively. Since there are no encoders on the wheel motors, it is not possible to turn exactly by 90 degrees. Command S stops the Buggy. Commands H and h turn ON and OFF the head lights, respectively. Similarly, commands B and b turn ON and OFF the brake lights, respectively. Commands P and Q flash the left and the right signal lights 3 times, respectively, at a rate of 100 ms.

Block diagram: Fig. 22.23 shows the block diagram of the project. The Buggy with all the components mounted on it is shown in Fig. 22.24. The IR distance sensor click board and

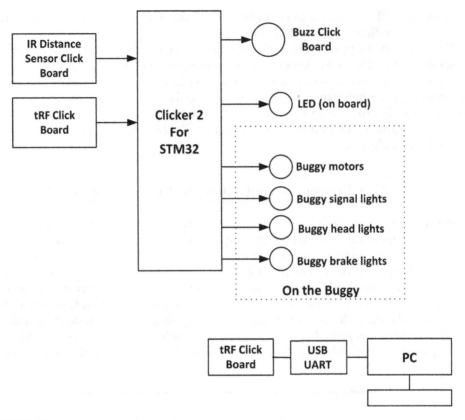

FIGURE 22.23 **Block diagram of the project.**

the Buzz click board were used in the previous project and their details are not repeated again.

Communication between the PC and the Buggy is via a pair of RF transmitter/receiver modules known as the tRF click boards. tRF click board (Fig. 22.25) is based on the LE70-868 RF module from Telit. tRF click is a complete short-range RF communication solution, operating in the 868 MHz ISM license-free frequency band. It features the complete RF, software stack, and packet handling onboard, exposing just a simple UART interface, offering familiar Hayes AT command set. It can be used in PTP (Point to Point) or Star topology wireless networks, using the Telit proprietary protocol. This module is also capable operating as the smart repeater, greatly improving the network range.

tRF includes both an RF transmitter and a receiver, and it is interfaced to a host computer through its UART ports. The operating voltage of the device is +3.3 V. A suitable 868-MHz antenna must be connected to the device before it is used (Fig. 22.26). tRF has an output power of 500 mW, which is within the acceptable license limits. Manufacturer's data sheet quotes that the device has a range of around 10 km in PTP applications, where the transmitter and the receiver antennas are in sight of each other (the range can be increased by directional antennas).

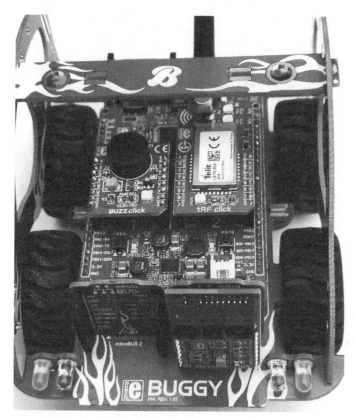

FIGURE 22.24 The Buggy with the components.

Circuit diagram: The click boards are connected to the mikroBUS sockets on the Buggy as follows (see Fig. 22.24):

Click board	mikroBUS socket	Place of the mikroBUS socket
IR distance sensor	mikroBUS 1	Front of the Buggy
Buzz	mikroBUS 1	Clicker 2 for STM32
tRF click	mikroBUS 2	Clicker 2 for STM32

When connected to mikroBUS 2 socket on the development board, the tRF UART pins are by default connected to UART pins PD8 and PD9 of the development board. The interface between the click boards used in this project and the corresponding Clicker 2 for STM32 pin names is as follows (see the Buggy user manual at:

https://download.mikroe.com/documents/specials/educational/buggy/buggy-development-platform-manual-v102.pdf).

FIGURE 22.25   tRF Click board.

FIGURE 22.26   tRF antenna (a 90-degree antenna is also available).

Click board	Pin number	Description	Clicker 2 for STM32 pin name
IR distance sensor	1	In (analog)	PC0
	2	Enable (digital)	PD11
Buzz	3	Out (digital)	PE9
tRF click	13, 14	UART	PD8, PD9

The Buggy communicates with the PC wirelessly by connecting a tRF click board to the PC via the USB port of the PC. A USB UART board is used to interface the PC to the tRF click board. UAB UART board (Fig. 22.27) consists of a mini USB socket, a UART chip, and a jumper used to select the output voltage between +3.3 and +5 V. Because the tRF click board operates at +3.3 V, the jumper on the USB UART board must be set to +3.3 V (see Fig. 22.27).

The connections between the USB UART board and the tRF click board are as follows (see Fig. 22.28):

USB UART board	tRF click board
VCC	+3.3 V
GND	GND
TX	TXD
RX	RXD

FIGURE 22.27   USB UART board.

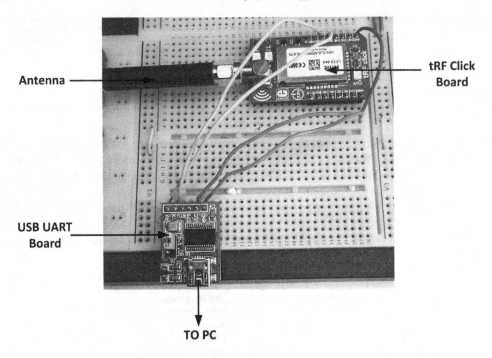

FIGURE 22.28   Connecting USB UART board to tRF click board.

Program listing: Fig. 22.29 shows the complete program listing (program: **remote.c**). The program consists of three tasks in addition to the Idle task. The tasks perform the following operations:

<u>**Task 1 (IR distance sensor click)**</u>
Define distance threshold
Initialize ADC
Enable IR distance sensor click
DO FOREVER
   Check event flag 1
   IF event flag 1 is set **THEN**
     Read distance to obstacle
     IF distance to obstacle < distance threshold **THEN**
       Move forward
     ELSE
       Stop Buggy
       Activate buzzer
     ENDIF
   ENDIF
ENDDO
<u>**Task 2 (command controller)**</u>
Set tRF port baud rate to 19200

```
/*=================================================================
                    REMOTE CONTROL OF THE BUGGY
                    ===========================

In this program the lights and the movemsnts of the Buggy is controlled remotely.
An IR distance sensor is mounted in-front of the Buggy as in the previous project
in order to measure the distance to obtacles. If an obstacle is within a preset
range then the Buggy is stopped. The Buggy is controlled from a PC where the
communication is established using a pair of tRF 868MHz RF transmitter/receiver
click boards. Full details of the interface and list of valid commands are given
in the text.

Author: Dogan Ibrahim
Date  : December, 2019
File  : remote.c
=================================================================*/
#include "main.h"
#include "event_groups.h"

EventGroupHandle_t xEventGroup;

unsigned int PWMA, PWMB, PWMC, PWMD;

//
// Stop the Buggy by setting all the Duty Cycles to 0
//
void StopBuggy()
{
  #define BIT_1 ( 1 << 1 )
  EventBits_t uxBits;

  uxBits = xEventGroupClearBits(xEventGroup, BIT_1);            // Clear efn 1
  PWM_TIM11_Set_Duty(0, _PWM_NON_INVERTED, _PWM_CHANNEL1);
  PWM_TIM10_Set_Duty(0, _PWM_NON_INVERTED, _PWM_CHANNEL1);
  PWM_TIM9_Set_Duty(0, _PWM_NON_INVERTED, _PWM_CHANNEL1);
  PWM_TIM3_Set_Duty(0, _PWM_NON_INVERTED, _PWM_CHANNEL3);
}

//
// Move Buggy Forward, mode specifies the speed
//
void MoveForward(int mode)
{
    PWM_TIM11_Set_Duty(0, _PWM_NON_INVERTED, _PWM_CHANNEL1);
    PWM_TIM9_Set_Duty(0, _PWM_NON_INVERTED, _PWM_CHANNEL1);
    PWM_TIM3_Set_Duty(PWMD/mode, _PWM_NON_INVERTED, _PWM_CHANNEL3);
    PWM_TIM10_Set_Duty(PWMB/mode, _PWM_NON_INVERTED, _PWM_CHANNEL1);
}

//
// Turn Left
//
void TurnLeft()
{
  EventBits_t uxBits;
  PWM_TIM11_Set_Duty(0, _PWM_NON_INVERTED, _PWM_CHANNEL1);
  PWM_TIM10_Set_Duty(0, _PWM_NON_INVERTED, _PWM_CHANNEL1);
  PWM_TIM9_Set_Duty(0, _PWM_NON_INVERTED, _PWM_CHANNEL1);
  PWM_TIM3_Set_Duty(PWMD, _PWM_NON_INVERTED, _PWM_CHANNEL3);
  vTaskDelay(pdMS_TO_TICKS(180));
```

FIGURE 22.29   remote.c program listing.

```
      uxBits = xEventGroupSetBits(xEventGroup, BIT_1);                    // Set efn 1
  }

  //
  // Turn Right
  //
  void TurnRight()
  {
    EventBits_t uxBits;
    PWM_TIM11_Set_Duty(0, _PWM_NON_INVERTED, _PWM_CHANNEL1);
    PWM_TIM10_Set_Duty(PWMB, _PWM_NON_INVERTED, _PWM_CHANNEL1);
    PWM_TIM9_Set_Duty(0, _PWM_NON_INVERTED, _PWM_CHANNEL1);
    PWM_TIM3_Set_Duty(0, _PWM_NON_INVERTED, _PWM_CHANNEL3);
    vTaskDelay(pdMS_TO_TICKS(180));
    uxBits = xEventGroupSetBits(xEventGroup, BIT_1);                      // Set efn 1
  }

  //
  // Turn ON(1), OFF(0) head lights
  //
  void HeadLights(int mode)
  {
      #define HeadLight GPIOB_ODR.B6
      GPIO_Config(&GPIOB_BASE, _GPIO_PINMASK_6, _GPIO_CFG_MODE_OUTPUT);
      HeadLight = mode;
  }

  //
  // Flash the left signal lights "count" times at the given "rate (in ms)"
  //
  void LeftSignalFlash(int ratems, int count)
  {
      #define LeftSignalLights GPIOC_ODR.B4
      int k;
      GPIO_Config(&GPIOC_BASE, _GPIO_PINMASK_4, _GPIO_CFG_MODE_OUTPUT);

      for(k = 0; k < count; k++)
      {
         LeftSignalLights = 1;                                 // Lights ON
         vTaskDelay(pdMS_TO_TICKS(ratems));                    // Wait rate ms
         LeftSignalLights = 0;                                 // Lights OFF
         vTaskDelay(pdMS_TO_TICKS(ratems));                    // Wait rate ms
      }
  }

  //
  // Flash the right signal lights "count" times at the given "rate (in ms)"
  //
  void RightSignalFlash(int ratems, int count)
  {
      #define RightSignalLights GPIOE_ODR.B2
      int k;
      GPIO_Config(&GPIOE_BASE, _GPIO_PINMASK_2, _GPIO_CFG_MODE_OUTPUT);

      for(k = 0; k < count; k++)
      {
         RightSignalLights = 1;                                // Lights ON
         vTaskDelay(pdMS_TO_TICKS(ratems));                    // Wait rate ms
         RightSignalLights = 0;                                // Lights OFF
         vTaskDelay(pdMS_TO_TICKS(ratems));                    // Wait rate ms
```

FIGURE 22.29   (*Continued*)

```
        }
    }

    //
    // Turn ON (1), OFF(0) brake lights
    //
    void BrakeLights(int mode)
    {
        #define BrakeLight GPIOE_ODR.B1
        GPIO_Config(&GPIOE_BASE, _GPIO_PINMASK_1, _GPIO_CFG_MODE_OUTPUT);
        BrakeLight = mode;
    }

    //
    // Activate the buzzer at 1000Hz for 100ms
    //
    void ActivateBuzzer()
    {
        Sound_Init(&GPIOE_ODR, 9);                          // Buzzer port
        Sound_Play(1000,100);                               // Activate buzzer
    }

    //
    // Define all your Task functions here
    // ====================================
    //

    // Task 1 - IR Sensor Controller
    void Task1(void *pvParameters)
    {
        #define IREnable GPIOD_ODR.B11
        #define LED GPIOE_ODR.B15
        #define BIT_1 ( 1 << 1 )

        unsigned IRSensorValue;
        float mV;
        float DistanceThreshold = 980.0;                    // 30cm distance

        EventBits_t uxBits;
        GPIO_Config(&GPIOD_BASE, _GPIO_PINMASK_11, _GPIO_CFG_MODE_OUTPUT);
        ADC1_Init();                                        // Initialize ADC
        IREnable = 1;                                       // Enable IR

        while (1)                                           // DO FOREVER
        {   uxBits = xEventGroupWaitBits(xEventGroup, BIT_1, pdFALSE, pdFALSE, 0);
            if((uxBits & BIT_1 ) != 0)
            {
                IRSensorValue = ADC1_Read(10);              // Read ADC Chan 10
                mV = IRSensorValue*3300.0 / 4096.0;         // In mV

                if(mV < DistanceThreshold)                  // If no obstacle
                {
                    MoveForward(5);                         // Go forward
                }
                else                                        // Obstacle
                {
                    StopBuggy();                            // Stop
                    ActivateBuzzer();                       // Buzzer ON
                }
            }
        }
```

FIGURE 22.29   (*Continued*)

```
                vTaskDelay(pdMS_TO_TICKS(350));                    // Small delay
        }
    }


    // Task 2 - Command Controller
    void Task2(void *pvParameters)
    {
        #define BIT_1 ( 1 << 1 )
        char c;
        EventBits_t uxBits;

        UART3_Init_Advanced(19200,_UART_8_BIT_DATA,_UART_NOPARITY,_UART_ONE_STOPBIT,
                            &_GPIO_MODULE_USART3_PD89);

        while(1)
        {
          if(UART3_Data_Ready())                               // Command?
          {
            c = UART3_Read();                                  // Get command
            switch(c)
            {
              case 'S':                                        // IS it S?
                  StopBuggy();                                 // Stop Buggy
                  break;
              case 'L':                                        // Is it L?
                  TurnLeft();                                  // Turn left
                  break;
              case 'R':                                        // Is it R?
                  TurnRight();                                 // Turn right
                  break;
              case 'F':                                        // Is it F?
                  uxBits = xEventGroupSetBits(xEventGroup, BIT_1);  // Set efn 1
                  break;
              case 'H':                                        // Is it H?
                  HeadLights(1);                               // Head lights ON
                  break;
              case 'h':                                        // Is it h?
                  HeadLights(0);                               // Head lights OFF
                  break;
              case 'B':                                        // Is it B?
                  BrakeLights(1);                              // Brake lights ON
                  break;
              case 'b':                                        // Is it b?
                  BrakeLights(0);                              // Brake lights OFF
                  break;
              case 'P':                                        // IS it P?
                  LeftSignalFlash(100, 3);                     // Left signal
                  break;
              case 'Q':                                        // Is it Q?
                  RightSignalFlash(100, 3);                    // Right flash
                  break;
            }
          }
        }
    }

    // Task 3 - Buggy Active Light Controller
    void Task3(void *pvParameters)
    {
```

FIGURE 22.29 (*Continued*)

```
    #define BuggyActiveLED GPIOE_ODR.B12
    GPIO_Config(&GPIOE_BASE, _GPIO_PINMASK_12, _GPIO_CFG_MODE_OUTPUT);
    while(1)
    {
        BuggyActiveLED = 1;                                      // LED ON
        vTaskDelay(pdMS_TO_TICKS(200));                          // Wait 200ms
        BuggyActiveLED = 0;                                      // LED OFF
        vTaskDelay(pdMS_TO_TICKS(200));                          // Wait 200ms
    }
}


//
// Start of MAIN program
// =====================
//
void main()
{
  xEventGroup = xEventGroupCreate();                            // Create event group

//
// Create PWM channels
//
  PWMA = PWM_TIM11_Init(1000);                                  // For pin PB9
  PWMB = PWM_TIM10_Init(1000);                                  // For pin PB8
  PWMC = PWM_TIM9_Init(1000);                                   // For pin PE5
  PWMD = PWM_TIM3_Init(1000);                                   // For pin PB0

//
// Start all PWM channels
//
  PWM_TIM11_Start(_PWM_CHANNEL1, &_GPIO_MODULE_TIM11_CH1_PB9);
  PWM_TIM10_Start(_PWM_CHANNEL1, &_GPIO_MODULE_TIM10_CH1_PB8);
  PWM_TIM9_Start(_PWM_CHANNEL1, &_GPIO_MODULE_TIM9_CH1_PE5);
  PWM_TIM3_Start(_PWM_CHANNEL3, &_GPIO_MODULE_TIM3_CH3_PB0);
//
// Set Duty Cycles to all 0s (i.e. Stop the Buggy)
//
  StopBuggy();

//
// Create all the TASKS here
// =========================
//
    // Create Task 1
    xTaskCreate(
        (TaskFunction_t)Task1,
        "IR Sensor Controller",
        configMINIMAL_STACK_SIZE,
        NULL,
        10,
        NULL
    );

    // Create Task 2
    xTaskCreate(
        (TaskFunction_t)Task2,
        "Command Controller",
        configMINIMAL_STACK_SIZE,
        NULL,
```

FIGURE 22.29   (*Continued*)

```
        10,
        NULL
    );

    // Create Task 3
    xTaskCreate(
        (TaskFunction_t)Task3,
        "Buggy Active Light Controller",
        configMINIMAL_STACK_SIZE,
        NULL,
        10,
        NULL
    );

//
// Start the RTOS scheduler
//
    vTaskStartScheduler();

//
// Will never reach here
}
```

FIGURE 22.29   *(Continued)*

DO FOREVER
   IF a command is entered **THEN**
      IF command is S **THEN**
        Stop the Buggy
      ELSE IF command is L **THEN**
        Turn left
      ELSE IF command is R **THEN**
        Turn right
      ELSE IF command is F **THEN**
        Set vent flag 1
      ELSE IF command is H **THEN**
        Turn head lights ON
      ELSE IF command is h **THEN**
        Turn head lights OFF
      ELSE IF command is B **THEN**
        Turn brake lights ON
        ELSE IF command is b **THEN**
        Turn brake lights OFF
      ELSE IF command is P **THEN**
        Flash left signal light 3 times
      ELSE IF command is Q **THEN**
        Flash right signal light 3 times
      ENDIF
   ENDIF
ENDDO
<u>Task 3 (active light controller)</u>

Turn the on-board LED ON
Wait 200 ms
Turn the on-board LED OFF
Wait 200 ms

When a command is entered at the PC keyboard, this command is transmitted to the tRF module mounted on the Buggy which is then read by the UART of the Clicker 2 for STM32 development board. Commands are received using the standard UART data receive commands. Command F sets event flag 1 which then enables Task 1 to call function MoveForward to move the Buggy forward. If the Buggy detects an obstacle in-front of it within the pre-specified distance, then it stops and activates the buzzer for a short time. Event flag 1 is cleared when the Buggy stops. Commands L and R turn the Buggy left and right respectively. The Buggy can be turned wither after it is stopped, or while it is moving forward. Event flag 1 is set inside the left and right turn functions so that the Buggy starts moving if it was stopped either by the S command or after encountering an obstacle.

Testing the program: The steps to test the program are given below:

- Compile the program and upload it to the development board
- Connect a USB cable between the PC USB port and the USB UART board (see Fig. 22.28)
- Start a terminal emulation program on the PC (e.g., Hyperterm or Putty) and set the baud rate to 19200 (default baud rate of the tRF module)
- Put the Buggy on the floor
- Enter command H on the PC keyboard. The head lights should come ON. Entering command h should turn OFF the head lights
- Enter commands B and b to turn the brake lights ON or OFF, respectively
- Test the signal lights by entering commands P and Q
- Enter command F on the PC keyboard. The Buggy should start moving forward and it will stop when an obstacle is within the pre-specified threshold distance from the Buggy.
- Turn L or R to turn the Buggy as required
- Test the S command to make sure that the Buggy stops when this command is entered

Further reading

[1] Buggy user guide, www.mikroe.com/buggy.
[2] Electronza, https://electronza.com/mikroe-buggy-assembly-first-impressions/

APPENDIX

A

Number systems

A.1 Overview

The efficient use of a microprocessor or microcontroller requires a working knowledge of binary, decimal, and hexadecimal numbering systems. This section provides a background for those who are unfamiliar with these numbering systems and who do not know how to convert from one number system to another one.

Number systems are classified according to their bases. The numbering system used in everyday life is base 10 or the decimal number system. The most commonly used numbering system in microprocessor and microcontroller applications is base 16, or hexadecimal. In addition, base 2 (binary) or base 8 (or octal) number systems are also used.

A.2 Decimal number system

As you all know the numbers in this system are 0, 1, 2, 3, 4, 5, 6, 7, 8, 9. We can use the subscript 10 to indicate that a number is in decimal format. For example, we can show decimal number 235 as 235_{10}.

In general, a decimal number is represented as follows:

$$a_n \times 10^n + a_{n-1} \times 10^{n-1} + a_{n-2} \times 10^{n-2} + \cdots + a_0 \times 10^0$$

For example, decimal number 825_{10} can be shown as follows:

$$825_{10} = 8 \times 10^2 + 2 \times 10^1 + 5 \times 10^0$$

Similarly, decimal number 26_{10} can be shown as:

$$26_{10} = 2 \times 10^1 + 6 \times 10^0$$

or,

$$3359_{10} = 3 \times 10^3 + 3 \times 10^2 + 5 \times 10^1 + 9 \times 10^0$$

ARM-Based Microcontroller Multitasking Projects. http://dx.doi.org/10.1016/B978-0-12-821227-1.00023-2

A.3 Binary number system

In binary number system, there are two numbers: 0 and 1. We can use the subscript 2 to indicate that a number is in binary format. For example, we can show binary number 1011 as 1011_2.

In general, a decimal number is represented as follows:

$$a_n \times 2^n + a_{n-1} \times 2^{n-1} + a_{n-2} \times 2^{n-2} + \cdots + a_0 \times 2^0$$

For example, binary number 1110_2 can be given as follows:

$$1110_2 = 1 \times 2^3 + 1 \times 2^2 + 1 \times 2^1 + 0 \times 2^0$$

Similarly, binary number 10001110_2 can be shown as:

$$10001110_2 = 1 \times 2^7 + 0 \times 2^6 + 0 \times 2^5 + 0 \times 2^4 + 1 \times 2^3 + 1 \times 2^2 + 1 \times 2^1 + 0 \times 2^0$$

A.4 Octal number system

In octal number system, the valid numbers are 0, 1, 2, 3, 4, 5, 6, 7. We can use the subscript 8 to indicate that a number is in octal format. For example, we can show octal number 23 as 23_8.

In general, an octal number is represented as:

$$a_n \times 8^n + a_{n-1} \times 8^{n-1} + a_{n-2} \times 8^{n-2} + \cdots + a_0 \times 8^0$$

For example, octal number 237_8 can be given as:

$$237_8 = 2 \times 8^2 + 3 \times 8^1 + 7 \times 8^0$$

Similarly, octal number 1777_8 can be given as:

$$1777_8 = 1 \times 8^3 + 7 \times 8^2 + 7 \times 8^1 + 7 \times 8^0$$

A.5 Hexadecimal number system

In hexadecimal number system, the valid numbers are 0, 1, 2, 3, 4, 5, 6, 7, 8, 9, A, B, C, D, E, F. We can use the subscript 16 of H to indicate that a number is in hexadecimal format. For example, we can show hexadecimal number 1F as $1F_{16}$ or as $1F_H$.

In general, a hexadecimal number is represented as:

$$a_n \times 16^n + a_{n-1} \times 16^{n-1} + a_{n-2} \times 16^{n-2} + \cdots + a_0 \times 16^0$$

For example, hexadecimal number $2AC_{16}$ can be given as:

$$2AC_{16} = 2 \times 16^2 + 10 \times 16^1 + 12 \times 16^0$$

Similarly, hexadecimal number $3FFE_{16}$ can be represented as:

$$3FFE_{16} = 3 \times 16^3 + 15 \times 16^2 + 15 \times 16^1 + 14 \times 16^0$$

A.6 Converting binary numbers into decimal

To convert a binary number into decimal, write the number as the sum of the powers of 2.

Example A.1

Convert binary number 1011_2 into decimal.

Solution A.1

Write the number as the sum of the powers of 2:

$$1011_2 = 1 \times 2^3 + 0 \times 2^2 + 1 \times 2^1 + 1 \times 2^0$$
$$= 8 + 0 + 2 + 1$$
$$= 11$$

or, $1011_2 = 11_{10}$

Example A.2

Convert binary number 11001110_2 into decimal.

Solution A.2

Write the number as the sum of the powers of 2:

$$11001110_2 = 1 \times 2^7 + 1 \times 2^6 + 0 \times 2^5 + 0 \times 2^4 + 1 \times 2^3 + 1 \times 2^2 + 1 \times 2^1 + 0 \times 2^0$$
$$= 128 + 64 + 0 + 0 + 8 + 4 + 2 + 0$$
$$= 206$$

or, $11001110_2 = 206_{10}$

Table A.1 presents the decimal equivalent of numbers from 0 to 31.

TABLE A.1   Decimal equivalent of binary numbers.

Binary	Decimal	Binary	Decimal
00000000	0	00010000	16
00000001	1	00010001	17
00000010	2	00010010	18
00000011	3	00010011	19
00000100	4	00010100	20
00000101	5	00010101	21
00000110	6	00010110	22
00000111	7	00010111	23
00001000	8	00011000	24
00001001	9	00011001	25
00001010	10	00011010	26
00001011	11	00011011	27
00001100	12	00011100	28
00001101	13	00011101	29
00001110	14	00011110	30
00001111	15	00011111	31

A.7 Converting decimal numbers into binary

To convert a decimal number into binary, divide the number repeatedly by 2 and take the remainders. The first remainder is the least significant digit (LSD), and the last remainder is the most significant digit (MSD).

Example A.3

Convert decimal number 28_{10} into binary.

Solution A.3

Divide the number into 2 repeatedly and take the remainders:

28/2	→	14	Remainder 0	(LSD)
14/2	→	7	Remainder 0	
7/2	→	3	Remainder 1	
3/2	→	1	Remainder 1	
½	→	0	Remainder 1	(MSD)

The required binary number is 11100_2.

Example A.4

Convert decimal number 65_{10} into binary.

Solution A.4

Divide the number into 2 repeatedly and take the remainders:

65/2	→	32	Remainder 1	(LSD)
32/2	→	16	Remainder 0	
16/2	→	8	Remainder 0	
8/2	→	4	Remainder 0	
4/2	→	2	Remainder 0	
2/2	→	1	Remainder 0	
½	→	0	Remainder 1	(MSD)

The required binary number is 1000001_2.

Example A.5

Convert decimal number 122_{10} into binary.

Solution A.5

Divide the number into 2 repeatedly and take the remainders:

122/2	→	61	Remainder 0	(LSD)
61/2	→	30	Remainder 1	
30/2	→	15	Remainder 0	
15/2	→	7	Remainder 1	
7/2	→	3	Remainder 1	
3/2	→	1	Remainder 1	
½	→	0	Remainder 1	(MSD)

The required binary number is 1111010_2.

A.8 Converting binary numbers into hexadecimal

To convert a binary number into hexadecimal, arrange the number in groups of 4 and find the hexadecimal equivalent of each group. If the number cannot be divided exactly into groups of 4, insert zeroes to the left-hand side of the number.

Example A.6

Convert binary number 10011111_2 into hexadecimal.

Solution A.6

First, divide the number into groups of 4 and then find the hexadecimal equivalent of each group:

$$10011111 = 1001 \quad 1111$$
$$9 \quad\quad F$$

The required hexadecimal number is $9F_{16}$.

Example A.7

Convert binary number 1110111100001110_2 into hexadecimal.

Solution A.7

First, divide the number into groups of 4 and then find the equivalent of each group:

$$1110111100001110 = 1110 \quad 1111 \quad 0000 \quad 1110$$
$$E \quad\quad F \quad\quad 0 \quad\quad E$$

The required hexadecimal number is $EF0E_{16}$

Example A.8

Convert binary number 111110_2 into hexadecimal.

Solution A.8

Since the number cannot be divided exactly into groups of 4, we have to insert zeroes to the left-hand side of the number:

$$111110 = 0011 \quad 1110$$
$$3 \quad\quad E$$

The required hexadecimal number is $3E_{16}$.

Table A.2 presents the hexadecimal equivalent of numbers 0 to 31.

A.9 Converting hexadecimal numbers into binary

To convert a hexadecimal number into binary, write the 4-bit binary equivalent of each hexadecimal digit.

Example A.9

Convert hexadecimal number $A9_{16}$ into binary.

Solution A.9

Writing the binary equivalent of each hexadecimal digit:

$$A = 1010_2 \quad\quad 9 = 1001_2$$

The required binary number is 10101001_2.

TABLE A.2   Hexadecimal equivalent of decimal numbers.

Decimal	Hexadecimal	Decimal	Hexadecimal
0	0	16	10
1	1	17	11
2	2	18	12
3	3	19	13
4	4	20	14
5	5	21	15
6	6	22	16
7	7	23	17
8	8	24	18
9	9	25	19
10	A	26	1A
11	B	27	1B
12	C	28	1C
13	D	29	1D
14	E	30	1E
15	F	31	1F

Example A.10
Convert hexadecimal number $FE3C_{16}$ into binary.
Solution A.10
Writing the binary equivalent of each hexadecimal digit:

$$F = 1111_2 \quad E = 1110_2 \quad 3 = 0011_2 \quad C = 1100_2$$

The required binary number is 1111111000111100_2.

A.10 Converting hexadecimal numbers into decimal

To convert a hexadecimal number into decimal, we have to calculate the sum of the powers of 16 of the number.

Example A.11
Convert hexadecimal number $2AC_{16}$ into decimal.
Solution A.11
Calculating the sum of the powers of 16 of the number:

$$2AC_{16} = 2 \times 16^2 + 10 \times 16^1 + 12 \times 16^0$$
$$= 512 + 160 + 12$$
$$= 684$$

The required decimal number is 684_{10}.

Example A.12
Convert hexadecimal number EE_{16} into decimal.
Solution A.12
Calculating the sum of the powers of 16 of the number:

$$EE_{16} = 14 \times 16^1 + 14 \times 16^0$$
$$= 224 + 14$$
$$= 238$$

The required decimal number is 238_{10}.

A.11 Converting decimal numbers into hexadecimal

To convert a decimal number into hexadecimal, divide the number repeatedly into 16 and take the remainders. The first remainder is the LSD, and the last remainder is the MSD.

Example A.13
Convert decimal number 238_{10} into hexadecimal.
Solution A.13
Dividing the number repeatedly into 16:

238/16	→	14	Remainder 14 (E)	(LSD)
14/16	→	0	Remainder 14 (E)	(MSD)

The required hexadecimal number is EE_{16}.
Example A.14
Convert decimal number 684_{10} into hexadecimal.
Solution A.14
Dividing the number repeatedly into 16:

684/16	→	42	Remainder 12 (C)	(LSD)
42/16	→	2	Remainder 10 (A)	
2/16	→	0	Remainder 2	(MSD)

The required hexadecimal number is $2AC_{16}$.

A.12 Converting octal numbers into decimal

To convert an octal number into decimal, calculate the sum of the powers of 8 of the number.
Example A.15
Convert octal number 15_8 into decimal.
Solution A.15
Calculating the sum of the powers of 8 of the number:

$$15_8 = 1 \times 8^1 + 5 \times 8^0$$
$$= 8 + 5$$
$$= 13$$

The required decimal number is 13_{10}.

Example A.16
Convert octal number 237_8 into decimal.
Solution A.16
Calculating the sum of the powers of 8 of the number:

$$237_8 = 2 \times 8^2 + 3 \times 8^1 + 7 \times 8^0$$
$$= 128 + 24 + 7$$
$$= 159$$

The required decimal number is 159_{10}.

A.13 Converting decimal numbers into octal

To convert a decimal number into octal, divide the number repeatedly into 8 and take the remainders. The first remainder is the LSD, and the last remainder is the MSD.

Example A.17
Convert decimal number 159_{10} into octal.
Solution A.17
Dividing the number repeatedly into 8:

159/8	→	19	Remainder 7	(LSD)
19/8	→	2	Remainder 3	
2/8	→	0	Remainder 2	(MSD)

The required octal number is 237_8.
Example A.18
Convert decimal number 460_{10} into octal.
Solution A.18
Dividing the number repeatedly into 8:

460/8	→	57	Remainder 4	(LSD)
57/8	→	7	Remainder 1	
7/8	→	0	Remainder 7	(MSD)

The required octal number is 714_8.
Table A.3 presents the octal equivalent of decimal numbers 0 to 31.

A.14 Converting octal numbers into binary

To convert an octal number into binary, write the 3-bit binary equivalent of each octal digit.
Example A.19
Convert octal number 177_8 into binary.
Solution A.19
Write the binary equivalent of each octal digit:

$$1 = 001_2 \qquad 7 = 111_2 \qquad 7 = 111_2$$

TABLE A.3   Octal equivalent of decimal numbers.

Decimal	Octal	Decimal	Octal
0	0	16	20
1	1	17	21
2	2	18	22
3	3	19	23
4	4	20	24
5	5	21	25
6	6	22	26
7	7	23	27
8	10	24	30
9	11	25	31
10	12	26	32
11	13	27	33
12	14	28	34
13	15	29	35
14	16	30	36
15	17	31	37

The required binary number is 001111111_2.
Solution A.20
Convert octal number 75_8 into binary.
Solution A.20
Write the binary equivalent of each octal digit:

$$7 = 111_2 \qquad 5 = 101_2$$

The required binary number is 111101_2.

A.15 Converting binary numbers into octal

To convert a binary number into octal, arrange the number in groups of 3 and write the octal equivalent of each digit.
Example A.21
Convert binary number 110111001_2 into octal.
Solution A.21
Arranging in groups of 3:

$$110111001 = 110 \quad 111 \quad 001$$
$$\qquad\qquad\qquad\quad 6 \qquad 7 \qquad 1$$

The required octal number is 671_8.

A.16 Negative numbers

The most significant bit of a binary number is usually used as the sign bit. By convention, for positive numbers this bit is 0, and for negative numbers this bit is 1. Fig. A.1 shows the 4-bit positive and negative numbers. The largest positive and negative numbers are +7 and −8, respectively.

To convert a positive number into negative, take the complement of the number and add 1. This process is also called the 2's complement of the number.

Example A.22

Write decimal number −6 as a 4-bit number.

Solution A.22

First, write the number as a positive number, then find the complement and add 1:

0110	**+6**
1001	compliment
1	add 1

1010	which is **−6**

Example A.23

Write decimal number −25 as a 8-bit number.

Solution A.23

First, write the number as a positive number, then find the complement and add 1:

00011001	**+25**
11100110	compliment
1	add 1

11100111	which is **−25**

Binary number	Decimal equivalent
0111	+7
0110	+6
0101	+5
0100	+4
0011	+3
0010	+2
0001	+1
0000	0
1111	−1
1110	−2
1101	−3
1100	−4
1011	−5
1010	−6
1001	−7
1000	−8

FIGURE A.1 4-bit positive and negative numbers.

A.17 Adding binary numbers

The addition of binary numbers is similar to the addition of decimal numbers. Numbers in each column are added together with a possible carry from a previous column. The primitive addition operations are:

$0 + 0 = 0$	
$0 + 1 = 1$	
$1 + 0 = 1$	
$1 + 1 = 10$	generate a carry bit
$1 + 1 + 1 = 11$	generate a carry bit

Some examples are given below.

Example A.24

Find the sum of binary numbers 011 and 110.

Solution A.24

We can add these numbers as in the addition of decimal numbers:

011	First column	$1 + 0 = 1$
+ 110	Second column	$1 + 1 = 0$ and a carry bit
--------	Third column	$1 + 1 = 10$
1001		

Example A.25

Find the sum of binary numbers 01000011 and 00100010.

Solution A.25

We can add these numbers as in the addition of decimal numbers:

01000011	First column	$1 + 0 = 1$
+ 00100010	Second column	$1 + 1 = 10$
----------------	Third column	$0 + carry = 1$
01100101	Fourth column:	$0 + 0 = 0$
	Fifth column:	$0 + 0 = 0$
	Sixth column:	$0 + 1 = 1$
	Seventh column:	$1 + 0 = 1$
	Eighth column:	$0 + 0 = 0$

A.18 Subtracting binary numbers

To subtract two numbers, convert the number to be subtracted into negative and then add the two numbers.

Example A.26

Subtract binary number 0010 from 0110.

Solution A.26

First, let's convert the number to be subtracted into negative:

0010	number to be subtracted
1101	compliment
1	add 1

1110	

Now, add the two numbers:

```
  0110
+ 1110
----------
  0100
```

Since we are using 4-bits only, we cannot show the carry bit.

A.19 Multiplication of binary numbers

Multiplication of two binary numbers is same as the multiplication of decimal numbers. The four possibilities are:

$$0 \times 0 = 0$$
$$0 \times 1 = 0$$
$$1 \times 0 = 0$$
$$1 \times 1 = 1$$

Some examples are given below.

Example A.27

Multiply the two binary numbers 0110 and 0010.

Solution A.27

Multiplying the numbers:

```
0110
0010
-------
0000
0110
0000
0000
-------
001100 or 1100
```

In this example, 4-bits are needed to show the final result.

Example A.28
Multiply binary numbers 1001 and 1010.
Solution A.28
Multiplying the numbers:

```
1001
1010
-------
0000
1001
0000
1001
-----------
1011010
```

In this example, 7-bits are required to show the final result.

A.20 Division of binary numbers

The division of binary numbers is similar to the division of decimal numbers. An example is given below.
Example A.29
Divide binary number 1110 into binary number 10.
Solution A.29
Dividing the numbers:

```
        111
     ---------
10 | 1110
     ----------
     10
     ---
     11
     10
     ---
     10
     10
     ---
     00
```

giving the result 111_2.

A.21 Floating point numbers

Floating point numbers are used to represent non-integer fractional numbers. For example: 3.256, 2.1, 0.0036, and so forth. Floating point numbers are used in most engineering and technical calculations. The most commonly used floating point standard is the IEEE standard.

According to this standard, floating point numbers are represented with 32-bit (single precision) or 64-bit (double precision).

In this section, we are looking at the format of 32-bit floating point numbers only and see how mathematical operations can be performed with such numbers.

According to the IEEE standard, 32-bit floating point numbers are represented as:

31	30	23	22	0
X	XXXXXXXX		XXXXXXXXXXXXXXXXXXXXXXX	
↑	↑		↑	
sign	exponent		mantissa	

The most significant bit indicates sign of the number, where 0 indicates positive and 1 indicates that the number is negative.

The 8-bit exponent shows the power of the number. To make the calculations easy, the sign of the exponent is not shown, but instead excess 128 numbering system is used. Thus, to find the real exponent, we have to subtract 127 from the given exponent. For example, if the mantissa is "10000000", the real value of the mantissa is $128 - 127 = 1$.

The mantissa is 23-bits wide and represents the increasing negative powers of 2. For example, if we assume that the mantissa is: "11100000000000000000000", the value of this mantissa is calculated as: $2^{-1} + 2^{-2} + 2^{-3} = 7/8$.

The decimal equivalent of a floating point number can be calculated using the formula:

$$\text{Number} = (-1)^s \, 2^{e-127} \, 1.f$$

where

$s = 0$ for positive numbers, 1 for negative numbers
$e = $ exponent (between 0 and 255)
$f = $ mantissa

As shown in the above formula, there is a hidden "1" in-front of the mantissa. That is, mantissa is shown as "$1.f$."

The largest and the smallest numbers in 32-bit floating point format are:

The largest number

0 11111110 11111111111111111111111

This number is: $(2 - 2^{-23}) \, 2^{127}$ or decimal 3.403×10^{38}. The numbers keep their precision up to 6 digits after the decimal point.

The smallest number

0 00000001 00000000000000000000000

This number is: 2^{-126} or decimal 1.175×10^{-38}.

A.22 Converting a floating point number into decimal

To convert a given floating point number into decimal, we have to find the mantissa and the exponent of the number and then convert into decimal as shown above.

Some examples are given here.

Example A.30

Find the decimal equivalent of the floating point number given below:

$$0\ 10000001\ 10000000000000000000000$$

Solution A.30

Here,

sign = positive
exponent = $129 - 127 = 2$
mantissa = $2^{-1} = 0.5$

The decimal equivalent of these number is $+1.5 \times 2^2 = +6.0$

Example A.31

Find the decimal equivalent of the floating point number given below:

$$0\ 10000010\ 11000000000000000000000$$

Solution A.31

In this example,

sign = positive
exponent = $130 - 127 = 3$
mantissa = $2^{-1} + 2^{-2} = 0.75$

The decimal equivalent of the number is $+1.75 \times 2^3 = 14.0$

A.22.1 Normalizing the floating point numbers

Floating point numbers are usually shown in normalized form. A normalized number has only one digit before the decimal point (A hidden number 1 is assumed before the decimal point).

To normalize a given floating point number, we have to move the decimal point repetitively one digit to the left and then increase the exponent after each move.

Some examples are given below.

Example A.32

Normalize the floating point number 123.56

Solution A.32

If we write the number with a single digit before the decimal point, we get:

$$1.2356 \times 10^2$$

Example A.33

Normalize the binary number 1011.1_2

Solution A.33

If we write the number with a single digit before the decimal point, we get:

$$1.111^3$$

A.22.2 Converting a decimal number into floating point

To convert a given decimal number into floating point, we have to carry out the following steps:

- Write the number in binary
- Normalize the number
- Find the mantissa and the exponent
- Write the number as a floating point number

Some examples are given below:
Example A.34
Convert decimal number 2.25_{10} into floating point.
Solution A.34
Writing the number in binary:

$$2.25_{10} = 10.01_2$$

Normalizing the number,

$$10.01_2 = 1.001_2 \times 2^1$$

Here, $s = 0, e - 127 = 1$ or $e = 128$, and $f = 00100000000000000000000$
(Remember that a number 1 is assumed on the left-hand side, even though it is not shown in the calculation). We can now write the required floating point number as:

s	e	f
0	10000000	(1)001 0000 0000 0000 0000 0000

or, the required 32-bit floating point number is:

$$01000000001000000000000000000000$$

Example A.35
Convert the decimal number 134.0625_{10} into floating point.
Solution A.35
Writing the number in binary:

$$134.0625_{10} = 10000110.0001$$

Normalizing the number,

$$10000110.0001 = 1.00001100001 \times 2^7$$

Here, $s = 0, e - 127 = 7$ or $e = 134$, and $f = 00001100001000000000000$
We can now write the required floating point number as:

s	e	f
0	10000110	(1)00001100001000000000000

or, the required 32-bit floating point number is:

$$01000011000001100001000000000000$$

A.22.3 Multiplication and division of floating point numbers

The multiplication and division of floating point numbers is rather easy and the steps are given below:

- Add (or subtract) the exponents of the numbers
- Multiply (or divide) the mantissa of the numbers
- Correct the exponent
- Normalize the number
- The sign of the result is the EXOR of the signs of the two numbers

Since the exponent is processed twice in the calculations, we have to subtract 127 from the exponent.

An example is given below to show the multiplication of two floating point numbers.

Example A.36

Show the decimal numbers 0.5_{10} and 0.75_{10} in floating point and then calculate the multiplication of these numbers.

Solution A.36

We can convert the numbers into floating point as:

$$0.5_{10} = 1.0000 \times 2^{-1}$$

Here, $s = 0$, $e - 127 = -1$ or $e = 126$, and $f = 0000$
or,

$$0.5_{10} = 0\ 01110110\ (1)000\ 0000\ 0000\ 0000\ 0000\ 0000$$

Similarly,

$$0.75_{10} = 1.1000 \times 2^{-1}$$

Here, $s = 0$, $e = 126$, and $f = 1000$
or,

$$0.75_{10} = 0\ 01110110\ (1)100\ 0000\ 0000\ 0000\ 0000\ 0000$$

Multiplying the mantissas, we get "(1)100 0000 0000 0000 0000 0000." The sum of the exponents is $126 + 126 = 252$. Subtracting 127 from the mantissa, we obtain, $252 - 127 = 125$. The EXOR of the signs of the numbers is 0. Thus, the result can be shown in floating point as:

$$0\ 01111101\ (1)100\ 0000\ 0000\ 0000\ 0000\ 0000$$

The above number is equivalent to decimal 0.375 ($0.5 \times 0.75 = 0.375$), which is the correct result.

A.22.4 Addition and subtraction of floating point numbers

The exponents of floating point numbers must be the same before they can be added or subtracted. The steps to add or subtract floating point numbers are:

- Shift the smaller number to the right until the exponents of both numbers are the same. Increment the exponent of the smaller number after each shift.
- Add (or subtract) the mantissa of each number as an integer calculation, without considering the decimal points.
- Normalize the obtained result.

An example is given below.

Example A.37

Show decimal numbers 0.5_{10} and 0.75_{10} in floating point and then calculate the sum of these numbers.

Solution A.37

As shown in Example A.36, we can convert the numbers into floating point as:

$$0.5_{10} = 0\ 01110110\ (1)000\ 0000\ 0000\ 0000\ 0000\ 0000$$

Similarly,

$$0.75_{10} = 0\ 01110110\ (1)100\ 0000\ 0000\ 0000\ 0000\ 0000$$

Since the exponents of both numbers are the same, there is no need to shift the smaller number. If we add the mantissa of the numbers without considering the decimal points, we get:

$$
\begin{array}{r}
(1)000\ 0000\ 0000\ 0000\ 0000\ 0000 \\
(1)100\ 0000\ 0000\ 0000\ 0000\ 0000 \\
\hline
+ \\
\hline
(10)100\ 0000\ 0000\ 0000\ 0000\ 0000
\end{array}
$$

To normalize the number, we can shift it right by one digit and then increment its exponent. The resulting number is:

$$0\ 01111111\ (1)010\ 0000\ 0000\ 0000\ 0000\ 0000$$

The above floating point number is equal to decimal number 1.25, which is the sum of decimal numbers 0.5 and 0.75.

To convert floating point numbers into decimal, and decimal numbers into floating point, the freely available program given in the following website can be used:

http://babbage.cs.qc.edu/courses/cs341/IEEE-754.html

A.23 BCD numbers

BCD (Binary Coded Decimal) numbers are usually used in display systems such as LCDs and 7-segment displays to show numeric values. In BCD, each digit is a 4-bit number from 0 to 9. As an example, Table A.4 presents the BCD numbers between 0 and 20.

TABLE A.4 BCD numbers between 0 and 20.

Decimal	BCD	Binary
0	0000	0000
1	0001	0001
2	0010	0010
3	0011	0011
4	0100	0100
5	0101	0101
6	0110	0110
7	0111	0111
8	1000	1000
9	1001	1001
10	0001 0000	1010
11	0001 0001	1011
12	0001 0010	1100
13	0001 0011	1101
14	0001 0100	1110
15	0001 0101	1111
16	0001 0110	1 0000
17	0001 0111	1 0001
18	0001 1000	1 0010
19	0001 1001	1 0011
20	0010 0000	1 0100

Example A.38
Write the decimal number 295 as a BCD number
Solution A.38
Writing the 4-bit binary equivalent of each digit,

$$2 = 0010_2 \qquad 9 = 1001_2 \qquad 5 = 0101_2$$

The required BCD number is: 0010 1001 0101_2
Example A.39
Write the decimal equivalent of BCD number 1001 1001 0110 0001_2
Solution A.39
Writing the decimal equivalent of each group of 4-bit, we get the decimal number,

9961

B

The program description language

B.1 Overview

As the programs get more complex, it becomes necessary for the programmer to use some tools to help in the writing and testing of the developed code. There are several graphical or text-based tools that can be used to simplify the tasks of program development and testing. In this chapter, we are looking at the program description language (PDL, or sometimes called the Pseudocode) that can be used to show the flow of control in a program before the program is written.

B.2 Program development tools

Simple programs consisting of no more than 10 lines of code can easily be developed by writing the code without any prior preparation. The development of large and complex programs is easier if an algorithm is first derived and the program are broken down into smaller modules. The actual coding becomes an easy task after the algorithm is available. An algorithm describes the operational steps of a program, and it can be in the form of graphical or text-based, such as flowcharts, data flow diagrams, structure charts, PDLs, and unified modeling languages (UMLs). Flowcharts can be very useful tools to describe the flow of control in small programs where there are no more than a few pages of diagrams. The problem with graphical tools is that it can be time-consuming to draw or to modify them, especially if there is more than one diagram extending over several pages. PDL is not a programming language. It is a collection of text-based keywords and actions that help the programmer to describe the flow of control and data in a program in a stepwise and logical manner. The main advantage of the PDL is that it is very easy to modify a given PDL since it only consists of text.

In this book, we are using PDL wherever possible, but flowcharts will also be given where it is felt to be useful. In the next sections of this Appendix, we shall be looking at the basic constructs of PDL and at the same time show the equivalent flowchart of each PDL construct.

Note: There are many free of charge programs available on the Internet that can be used to help draw flowchart easily. Some of these programs are Microsoft Visio, Dia, yEd Graph Editor, ThinkComposer, Pencil Project, LibreOffice, Diagram Designer, LucidChart, and so on.

ARM-Based Microcontroller Multitasking Projects. http://dx.doi.org/10.1016/B978-0-12-821227-1.00024-4

FIGURE B.1   BEGIN-END statement and its equivalent flowchart.

B.2.1 BEGIN – END

Every PDL description must start with a BEGIN and terminate with an END. The key-words should be in bold and the statements inside these keywords should be indented to make the reading easier. An example is shown in Fig. B.1.

B.2.2 Sequencing

In normal program flow, statements are executed in sequence one after another one. The operations to be performed in each step are written in plain text. An example sequencing is shown in Fig. B.2 together with its flowchart equivalent.

B.2.3 IF – THEN – ELSE – ENDIF

The IF-THEN-ELSE-ENDIF statements are used to create conditional statements and thus to change the flow of control in a program. Every IF statement must be terminated with an ENDIF statement. The ELSE statement is optional, and if used, it must be terminated with an ENDIF statement. It is also permissible to use ELSE IF statements in programs where multiple decisions are to be made. Figure B.3 to Figure B.5 show various examples of using the IF-THEN-ELSE-ENDIF statements.

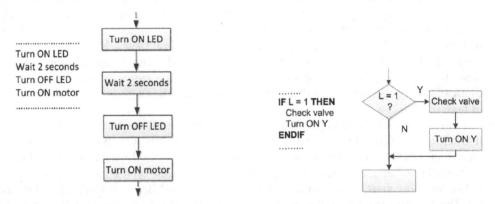

FIGURE B.2   Sequencing and its equivalent flowchart.   FIGURE B.3   Using IF-THEN-ENDIF.

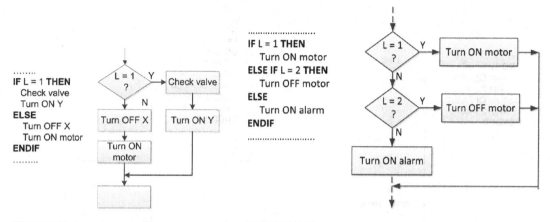

FIGURE B.4   Using IF-THEN-ELSE-ENDIF.   FIGURE B.5   Using IF-THEN-ELSE IF-ENDIF.

B.2.4 DO – FOREVER – ENDDO

The DO-FOREVER-ENDDO statement is used to repeat a loop forever. This kind of loop is commonly used in microcontroller applications where an operation or a number of operations are executed continuously. Fig. B.6 shows an example use of the DO-FOREVER-END-DO statement.

B.2.5 DO – ENDDO

The DO-ENDDO statement is used to create loops (or iterations) in programs. Every DO statement must be terminated with an ENDDO statement. It is permissible to use conditions after the DO statement to create conditional loops. An example DO-ENDDO loop is shown in Fig. B.7 where the LED is flashed 10 times with 2 seconds delay between each output. Another example DO-ENDDO loop is shown in Fig. B.8.

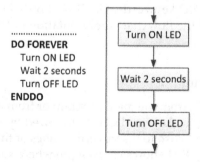

FIGURE B.6   Using DO-FOREVER-ENDDO statement.

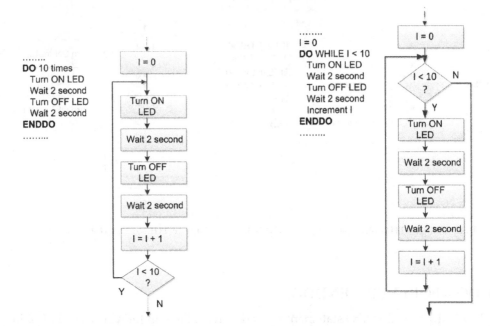

FIGURE B.7   **Using DO-ENDDO statement.**   FIGURE B.8   **Another example of DO-ENDDO statement.**

B.2.6 REPEAT – UNTIL

The REPEAT-UNTIL statement is similar to DO-ENDDO statement, but here the condition to terminate the loop is checked at the end and therefore the loop is executed at least once. Fig. B.9 shows an example REPEAT-UNTIL loop.

B.2.7 Subprograms

There are many ways that subprograms can be represented in PDLs and flowcharts. Since subprograms are independent program modules, they must start and finish with the BEGIN and END statements, respectively. We should also include the name of the subprogram after the BEGIN and END keywords. Fig. B.10 shows an example subprogram called DISPLAY. Both the PDL and the flowchart representation of the subprogram are shown in this figure.

B.2.8 Calling a subprogram

A subprogram can be called from the main program or from another subprogram. In PDL, a subprogram is called using the keyword CALL, followed by the name of the subprogram. In flowcharts, it is common practise to insert vertical lines at the two sides of the box where the subprogram is called. Fig. B.11 shows an example where subprogram DISPLAY is called from a program.

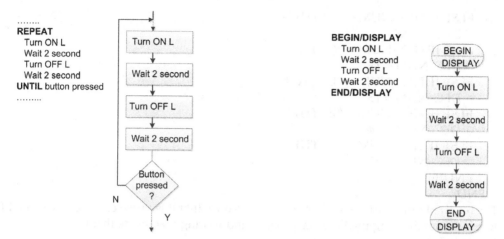

FIGURE B.9   Using REPEAT-UNTIL statement.

FIGURE B.10   Subprogram DISPLAY.

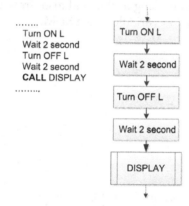

FIGURE B.11   Calling subprogram DISPLAY.

B.3 Examples

Some simple examples are given in this section to show how the PDLs and their equivalent flowcharts can be used in program development.

Example B.1

It is required to write a program to convert hexadecimal numbers "A" to "F" into decimal. Show the algorithm using a PDL and also draw the equivalent flowchart. Assume that the hexadecimal number to be converted is called HEX_NUM, and the output decimal number is called DEC_NUM.

Solution B.1

The required PDL is:

BEGIN
IF HEX_NUM = "A" **THEN**
    DEC_NUM = 10

```
   ELSE IF HEX_NUM = "B" THEN
      DEC_NUM = 11
   ELSE IF HEX_NUM = "C" THEN
      DEC_NUM = 12
   ELSE IF HEX_NUM = "D" THEN
      DEC_NUM = 13
   ELSE IF HEX_NUM = "E" THEN
      DEC_NUM = 14
   ELSE IF HEX_NUM = "F" THEN
      DEC_NUM = 15
   ENDIF
END
```

The required flowchart is shown in Fig. B.12. Notice that it is much easier to write the PDL statements than drawing the flowchart shapes and writing text inside them.

Example B.2

It is required to write a program to calculate the sum of integer numbers between 1 and 100. Show the required algorithm using a PDL and also draw the equivalent flowchart. Assume that the sum will be stored in variable called SUM.

Solution B.2

The required PDL is:

```
BEGIN
   SUM = 0
   I = 1
   DO 100 TIMES
      SUM = SUM + I
      Increment I
   ENDDO
END
```

The required flowchart is shown in Fig. B.13.

Example B.3

An LED is connected to a microcontroller output port. Additionally, a button is connected to one of the input ports. It is required to turn ON the LED when the button is pressed, and otherwise to turn OFF the LED. Show the required algorithm using a PDL and also draw the equivalent flowchart.

Solution B.3

The required PDL is:

```
BEGIN
   DO FOREVER
      IF Button is pressed THEN
         Turn ON LED
      ELSE
         Turn OFF LED
      ENDIF
   ENDDO
END
```

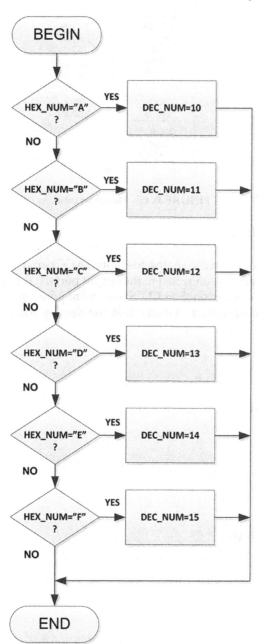

FIGURE B.12   Flowchart solution.

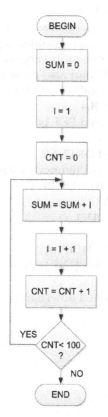

FIGURE B.13   Flowchart solution.

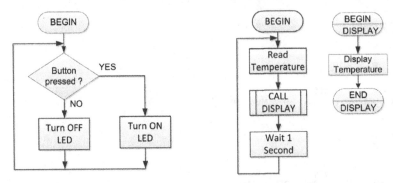

FIGURE B.14 Flowchart solution.   FIGURE B.15 Flowchart solution.

The required flowchart is shown in Fig. B.14.

Example B.4

An analog pressure sensor is connected to one of the analog-to-digital (ADC) input ports of a microcontroller. Additionally, an LCD display is connected to the output ports. It is required to read the pressure every second and then display on the LCD. Show the required algorithm using a PDL and also draw the equivalent flowchart. Assume that the display routine is a subprogram called DISPLAY.

Solution B.4

The required PDL is:

BEGIN

    DO FOREVER

        Read Temperature from ADC port

        CALL DISPLAY

        Wait 1 second

    ENDDO

END

BEGIN/DISPLAY

    Display temperature on LCD

END/DISPLAY

The required flowchart is shown in Fig. B.15.

Index

Note: Page numbers followed by "f" indicate figures, "t" indicate tables.

A

Aborting delay of FreeRTOS, 148
Absolute maximum ratings, 31t
Access individual bits, in MikroC Pro, 69
Acorn RISC Machine (ARM), 15
ADCs. *See* analog-to-digital converters (ADCs)
Analog comparator modules, 9
Analog-to-digital converters (ADCs), 9, 30
ARM. *See* Acorn RISC Machine (ARM)
ARM Cortex microcontroller development boards
  Clicker 2 for MSP432, 41
  Clicker 2 for STM32, 44
  EasyMX Pro V7 For STM32, 35
  EasyMx Pro V7 for Tiva, 39
  fusion for ARM V8, 43
  LPC1768, 33
  mbed application board, 38
  MINI-M4 for STM32, 40
  STM32F4DISCOVERY board, 36
  STM32 Nucleo family, 34
  Tiva EK-TM4C123GXL LaunchPad, 42
ARM microcontrollers, architecture of. *See also*
      Programming ARM-based microcontrollers
analog-to-digital converters, 30
built-in temperature sensor, 30
Cortex-A, 17
Cortex-M series
  compatibility, 18
  M0, 16
  M0+, 16
  M3, 16
  M4, 16
  M7, 16
  processor comparison, 17
Cortex-R, 16
digital-to-analog converter, 31
electrical characteristics, 31
external interrupt controller, 30
general purpose inputs and outputs, 27
nested vectored interrupt controller, 30
processor performance measurement, 18

reset, 31
STM32F407VGT6 microcontroller
  basic features of, 19
  clock circuit of, 23
  internal block diagram of, 21
  low power modes, 23
  power supply, 23
  timers, 30
ASCII chart, 84
Assembly listing, in MikroC Pro, 89
Auto reload register (TIMx_ARR), 362
Auto-reload timers, 255

B

Backup domain reset, 31
BaseType_t, 118
Battery-operated portable applications, 15
Binary semaphore, 225
Bit data type, in MikroC Pro, 70
Blocked state, 119
Bluetooth interface, 11
Bootloader program, 44, 52
Brown-out detectors, 8
Buggy, 423
Built-in temperature sensor, 30
Bus fault, 70

C

CAN interface, 11
Car park control, 397
Car park management system
  project 55: car park control, 397
Ccm, memory type specifiers, 69
Central processing unit (CPU), 5
Change timer period, 258
Changing LED flashing rate, 176
  from PC keyboard, 189, 206
Choosing scheduling algorithm, 108
CISC. *See* complex instruction computer
    (CISC)
Clicker 2 for MSP432, 41

Clicker 2 for STM32 development board
    input-output pins, 51
    On-board LEDs, 48
    On-board mikroBUS sockets, 50
    On-board push-button switches, 48
    oscillators, 52
    power supply, 49
    programming on-board microcontroller, 52
    reset switch, 49
Clock, 7
    circuit of STM32F407VGT6 microcontroller
        configuring clock, 24
        external clock sources, 23
        internal clock sources, 24
    generator circuit, 26f
    security system enable, 74
    selection, 76f
Code, memory type specifiers, 69
Communicating with Arduino, 315
Compiler case sensitivity, 114
Compiling template program, 115
Complex instruction computer (CISC), 8, 12
Complex real-time systems, 97
Configurable exceptions, 70
Configuring clock, 24
Contact bouncing problem, 357
Controlling Buggy
    lights, 431
    motors, 432
    remotely, 451
Controlling flashing of LED, 242
Co-operative scheduling, 99
Cortex-A, 17
Cortex-M4 based microcontrollers, interrupts in
    general, 347
    internal interrupts (timer interrupts), 361
    project 44-External interrupt based event counter, 354
    project 45-Multiple external interrupts, 358
    project 46-Generating waveform using timer
        interrupt, 363
    project 47-External interrupt with timer interrupt,
        365
    STM32F407 interrupts
        external interrupts, 349
Cortex-M series
    compatibility, 18
    M0, 16
    M0+, 16
    M3, 16
    M4, 16
    M7, 16
    processor comparison, 17
Cortex-R, 16
Counter register (TIMx_CNT), 362

CPU. See central processing unit (CPU)
Creating new task, FreeRTOS task-related functions,
    121
Critical sections
    project 42: critical sections-sharing UART, 339
    project 43: suspending scheduler, 345
    sharing UART, 339
    suspending scheduler, 344
Crystal oscillator connection, 26f
Current sink/source capability, 10

D
Daemon task, 255
Data memory, 5
    type specifiers, 69
Data types of FreeRTOS, 118
DEBUG functions, 67
Debugging, 83
Deferred interrupt processing, 372, 377
Digital signal processing applications, 2
Digital-to-analog converter, 31
Displaying task
    info on PC screen, 195
    list on PC screen, 192
    state on PC screen, 198
Display the free processor time, 324
Dynamic priority scheduling, 108

E
EAction, 334
EasyMX Pro V7
    for STM32, 35
    for Tiva, 39
Electrical characteristics, 31
Electrically erasable programmable read only memory
    (EEPROM), 6
Embedded controller, 1
EPROM. See erasable programmable read only memory
    (EPROM)
Erasable programmable read only memory
    (EPROM), 6
Ethernet interface, 11
Event bit, 235
Event counter, 266
Event groups
    creating and deleting, 236
    event flags and, 235
    project 25-sending internal and external temperature
        data to PC, 238
    project 26-controlling flashing of an LED, 242
    project 27-GPS based project, 246
    related functions, from interrupt service routine, 382
    setting, clearing, waiting For event group bits, and
        getting event group bits, 236

EWARM, 56

Example projects
  project 31-square wave generation with adjustable frequency, 271
  project 32: frequency sweep waveform generator, 275
  project 33: RGB light controller, 279
  project 34: home alarm system with keyboard, 281
  project 35: ultrasonic car parking with buzzer, 292
  project 36: stepper motor project, 302
  project 37: communicating with Arduino, 315

External clock
  pulse, 7
  sources, 23

External high-speed clock
  bypass, 74
  enable, 74

External interrupt, 348, 349
  based event counter, 354
  with timer interrupt, 365

External interrupt controller (EXTI), 30

External Li-polymer battery, 50f

External resistor-capacitor timing components, 7

EXTI. *See* external interrupt controller (EXTI)

F

Falling trigger selection register (EXTI_FTSR), 352

FIFO (First In First Out), 203

Finite-state machine (FSM), 99

First come first served, 107

Flash electrically erasable programmable read only memory, 7

Flashing at different rates after receiving notifications, 335

Flip-flop circuits, 357

For ARM, 61

FreeRTOS
  aborting delay, 148
  API function calls from ISR
    deferred interrupt processing, 372
    event group related functions from ISR, 382
    project 48-using function xTaskResumeFromISR(), 374
    project 49-deferred interrupt processing, 377
    project 50-using function xTaskNotifyFromISR(), 377
    project 51-using function xEventGroupSetBitsFromISR(), 383
    project 52-using functions xTimerStartFromISR() and xTimerChangePeriodFromISR(), 387
    project 53-using functions xSemaphoreTakeFromISR() and xSemaphoreGive(), 391
    project 54-using functions xQueueSendFromISR() and xQueueReceive(), 393

    queue related functions, 391
    semaphore related functions, 390
    task related functions, 373
    timer related functions, 386
    xHigherPriorityTaskWoken parameter, 372
  compiler case sensitivity, 114
  compiling template program, 115
  data types, 118
  developing project files, 112
  distribution, 110
  function names, 118
  headers files path and source files path, 114
  installing from MikroElektronika web site, 111
  macro definitions, 118
  project 9-displaying a task name, number of tasks, and tick count on the LCD, 148
  project 10-7-segment 2-digit multiplexed LED display counter, 151
  project 11-7-segment 4-digit multiplexed LED display counter, 159
  project 12-7-segment 4-digit multiplexed LED display event counter, 163
  project 13-traffic lights controller, 167
  project 14-changing LED flashing rate, 176
  project 15-sending data to a PC over USB serial link, 181
  project 16-changing LED flashing rate from the PC keyboard, 189
  project 17-displaying the task list on PC screen, 192
  project 19-displaying the task info on the PC screen, 195
  project 20-displaying the task state on the PC screen, 198
  task info, 195
  task list, 189
  task parameters, 200
  task-related functions
    creating new task, 121
    delaying task, 122
    deleting task, 130
    getting task handle, 131
    priorites, 136
    project 1-flashing an LED every second, 122
    project 2-flashing two LEDs, one every second, other one every 200 ms, 125
    Project 2-flashing two LEDs, one every second, other one every 200 ms ?, 122
    project 3-suspending and resuming task, 128
    project 4-flashing LEDs and deleting task, 130
    project 5-flashing an LED using function vTaskDelayUntil(), 134
    project 6-flashing LED and push-button switch at different priorities, 136
    project 7-getting/setting task priorities, 137

FreeRTOS (*cont.*)
  resuming suspended task, 128
  running at fixed intervals, 134
  suspending task, 127
  tick count, 134
  task state, 198
  task states, 118
  using LCD
    connecting LCD to Clicker 2 for STM32
      development board, 142
    functions, 143
    HD44780 LCD module, 141
    project 8-displaying text on LCD, 144
    task name, number of tasks, and tick count, 147
  variable names, 118
  yield to another task of equal priority, 148
Frequency sweep waveform generator, 275
FSM. *See* finite-state machine (FSM)
Function names, 118
Fusion for ARM V8, 43

G
Games-based applications, 14
General purpose inputs and outputs (GPIO), 27
  GPIO_Alternate_Function_Enable, 68
  GPIO_Analog_Input, 68
  GPIO_Clk_Config, 64
  GPIO_Clk_Disable, 64
  GPIO_Clk_Enable, 64
  GPIO_Digital_Input, 68
  GPIO_Digital_Output, 68
  GPIO_Set_Pin_Mode, 67
Generate square waveform, 263
Generating waveform using timer interrupt, 363
Get timer period, 258
GLCD bitmap editor, 85
Global variables, 203
GPIO. *See* general purpose inputs and outputs (GPIO)
GPS based project, 246

H
Hard Fault, 70
Harvard architecture, 11
H-bridge motor direction control, 428f
HD44780 LCD module, 141
Header files, 57
Headers files path, for FreeRTOS, 114
HID terminal, 85
High-level languages, 2
High-speed external (HSE), 23
High-speed internal (HIS), 24
HIS. *See* High-speed internal (HIS)
Home alarm system, with keyboard, 281
HSE. *See* High-speed external (HSE)

I
I²C. *See* integrated inter connect (I²C)
Idle task and idle task hook
  project 39: display the free processor time, 324
Input-output pins, 51
Installing from MikroElektronika web site, 111
Instruction cycle, 7
Integrated development environments support
  EWARM, 56
  Mbed, 56
  MDK, 56
  MikroC Pro, 58
  System Workbench for STM32 by AC6, 57
  TrueStudio for STM32, 57
Integrated inter connect (I²C), 9
Internal clock
  registers, 24
  sources, 24
Internal high-speed clock enable, 74
Internal interrupts (timer interrupts), 361
Internal oscillator of microcontroller, 7
Internal resistor-capacitor timing components, 7
Interrupt Assistant, 71
Interrupt for button at port pin PA10 (on-board button), 359
Interrupt mask register (EXTI_IMR), 352
Interrupts, 8
  assistant, 85
  and exceptions
    exceptions, 70
    interrupt service routine, 71
  sources, 348
Interrupt service routine (ISR), 8, 71
Interrupt vector address, 8
ISR. *See* interrupt service routine (ISR)

K
Kernel advantages, 98

L
LCD custom character, 85
LCD drivers, 9
LCD, using (FreeRTOS)
  connecting LCD to Clicker 2 for STM32 development
    board, 142
  functions, 143
  HD44780 LCD module, 141
  project 8-displaying text on LCD, 144
  task name, number of tasks, and tick count,
    147
Library manager, 88
Libstock website, 59
Lights (LEDs), 431
Longest remaining time first, 107

Low power
   modes, 23
   operation, 10
Low speed external (LSE), 24
Low-speed internal (LSI), 24
LPC1768, 33
LSE. *See* Low speed external (LSE)
LSI. *See* Low-speed internal (LSI)

M

Macro definitions, FreeRTOS, 118
Mbed, 56
   application board, 38
MDK, 56
Memory, 5
   management, 70
   type specifiers, 69
Microcomputer systems
   microcontroller architectures. *See also* ARM
          microcontrollers
      complex instruction computer, 12
      reduced instruction set computer, 12
   microcontroller features
      analog comparator modules, 9
      analog-to-digital converter, 9
      bluetooth interface, 11
      Brown-out detectors, 8
      CAN interface, 11
      clock, 7
      current sink/source capability, 10
      ethernet interface, 11
      integrated inter connect, 9
      interrupts, 8
      LCD drivers, 9
      low power operation, 10
      power-on reset, 10
      real-time clock, 10
      reset input, 8
      serial input-output, 9
      serial peripheral interface, 9
      sleep mode, 10
      supply voltage, 7
      timers, 7
      USB interface, 10
      watchdog, 8
      Wi-Fi, 11
   microcontroller systems
      electrically erasable programmable read only
             memory, 6
      erasable programmable read only
             memory, 6
      flash electrically erasable programmable read only
             memory, 7
      programmable read only memory, 6

random access memory, 5
      read only memory, 6
Microcontroller development kit, 2
MikroBUS pin configurations, 51f
MikroC Pro, 58
   access individual bits, 69
   for ARM, 61
   ASCII chart, 84
   Assembly listing, 89
   bit data type, 70
   creating new project
      uploading executable code, 78
   debugging, 83
   general purpose input-output
      GPIO_Alternate_Function_Enable, 68
      GPIO_Analog_Input, 68
      GPIO_Clk_Config, 64
      GPIO_Clk_Disable, 64
      GPIO_Clk_Enable, 64
      GPIO_Digital_Input, 68
      GPIO_Digital_Output, 68
      GPIO_Set_Pin_Mode, 67
   GLCD bitmap editor, 85
   HID terminal, 85
   interrupt assistant, 85
   interrupts and exceptions
      exceptions, 70
      interrupt service routine, 71
   LCD custom character, 85
   library manager, 88
   memory type specifiers, 69
   options window, 93
   output files, 93
   PORT input-output, 69
   seven segment editor, 86
   simulation
      setting break points, 83
   statistics, 88
   UDP terminal, 86
   USART terminal, 86
   USB HID bootloader, 88
MINI-M4 for STM32, 40
Mobile robot project
   Buggy, 423
   lights (LEDs), 431
   project 57: controlling Buggy lights, 431
   project 58: controlling Buggy motors, 432
   project 59: obstacle avoiding Buggy, 438
   project 60: controlling Buggy remotely, 451
   wheel motors, 427
Multilevel queue scheduling, 108
Multiple external interrupts, 358
2-digit multiplexed LED display counter, 151
4-digit multiplexed LED display counter, 159

4-digit multiplexed LED display event counter, 163
Multiplexed LED applications, 152
Multitasking
    choosing scheduling algorithm, 108
    kernel advantages, 98
    real-time operating system, need for, 98
    task scheduling algorithms
        co-operative scheduling, 99
        other scheduling algorithms, 107
        preemptive and nonpreemptive scheduling
            difference, 107
        preemptive scheduling, 105
        round-robin scheduling, 104
        scheduling algorithm goals, 106
Mutexes. See Semapores

N
Nested vectored interrupt controller (NVIC), 30, 349
NMI. See Nonmaskable interrupt (NMI)
Nonmaskable interrupt (NMI), 70, 348
Nonpreemptive scheduling, 99
NVIC. See nested vectored interrupt controller
    (NVIC)

O
Obstacle avoiding Buggy, 438
On-board LEDs, 48
On-board mikroBUS sockets, 50
On-board mikroProg programmer, 39
On-board push-button switches, 48
One-shot timers, 255
ON-OFF temperature controller, 214
Open-drain output pin, 28f
Options window, 93
Oscillators, 7, 52
Output files, in MikroC Pro, 93
Oven temperature control system, microcontroller base,
    3f

P
PcNameToQuery, 131
Pending register (EXTI_PR), 352
PendSV, 71
Phase locked loop (PLL), 24
Pin configuration of HD44780 LCD module, 142t
PLL. See phase locked loop (PLL)
Port bit set/reset register, 29
Port configuration registers, 28
Port data registers, 29
PORT input-output, 69
Port locking register, 29
Port pins, 29
Power-on reset, 10
Power reset, 31

Power supply, 49
Preemptive scheduling, 105
    and nonpreemptive scheduling difference, 107
Prescaler register (TIMx_PSC), 362
Priority inheritance, 226
Processor performance measurement, 18
Programmable read only memory (PROM), 6
Program memory, 5
Programming ARM-based microcontrollers
    integrated development environments support
        EWARM, 56
        Mbed, 56
        MDK, 56
        MikroC Pro, 58
        System Workbench for STM32 by AC6, 57
        TrueStudio for STM32, 57
Programming on-board microcontroller, 52
Project
    car park management system
        55: car park control, 397
    Cortex-M4
        44-external interrupt based event counter, 354
        45-multiple external interrupts, 358
        46-generating waveform using timer interrupt, 363
        47-external interrupt with timer interrupt, 365
    critical sections
        42: critical sections-sharing UART, 339
        43: suspending scheduler, 345
    event groups
        25-sending internal and external temperature data
            to PC, 238
        26-controlling flashing of LED, 242
        27-GPS based project, 246
    examples
        31-square wave generation with adjustable
            frequency, 271
        32: frequency sweep waveform generator, 275
        33: RGB light controller, 279
        34: home alarm system with keyboard, 281
        35: ultrasonic car parking with buzzer, 292
        36: stepper motor project, 302
        37: communicating with Arduino, 315
    FreeRTOS
        9-displaying task name, number of tasks, and tick
            count on LCD, 148
        10-7-segment 2-digit multiplexed LED display
            counter, 151
        11-7-segment 4-digit multiplexed LED display
            counter, 159
        12-7-segment 4-digit multiplexed LED display
            event counter, 163
        13-traffic lights controller, 167
        14-changing LED flashing rate, 176
        15-sending data to a PC over USB serial link, 181

16-changing LED flashing rate from PC keyboard, 189
17-displaying task list on PC screen, 192
19-displaying task info on PC screen, 195
20-displaying task state on PC screen, 198
FreeRTOS (API function calls from ISR)
48-using function xTaskResumeFromISR(), 374
49-deferred interrupt processing, 377
50-using function xTaskNotifyFromISR(), 377
51-using function xEventGroupSetBitsFromISR(), 383
52-using functions xTimerStartFromISR() and xTimerChangePeriodFromISR(), 387
53-using functions xSemaphoreTakeFromISR() and xSemaphoreGive(), 391
54-using functions xQueueSendFromISR() and xQueueReceive(), 393
idle task and idle task hook
39: display the free processor time, 324
mobile robot project
57: controlling Buggy lights, 431
58: controlling Buggy motors, 432
59: obstacle avoiding Buggy, 438
60: controlling Buggy remotely, 451
queue management
21-changing LED flashing rate from the PC keyboard, 206
22-using various queue functions, 210
23-ON-OFF temperature controller, 214
semapores
24-sending internal and external temperature data to PC, 228
software timers
28-reaction timer, 259
29-generate square waveform, 263
30-event counter, 266
task notifications
40: start flashing an LED after receiving notification, 331
41: flashing at different rates after receiving notifications, 335
time in different cities
56: time project, 413
Pull-down pin, 29f
Pull-up and pull-down resistors, 28
Pull-up pin, 29f
PulNotificationValue, 334
Pulse width modulated (PWM) signals, 428
Push-pull output pin, 28f
Push-pull output port, structure of, 28
Push-pull transistors, 28
PvParameters, 121
PvTaskCode, 121
PWM signals. *See* pulse width modulated (PWM) signals

PxCreatedTask, 121
PxPreviousWakeTime, 133
PxTask, 128, 134
PxTaskToResume, 127
PxTaskToSuspend, 125

Q
Queue functions, 210
Queue management
creating queue, sending and receiving data using, 204
deleting queue, name of queue, resetting queue, 209
functions, 213
global variables, 203
project 21-changing LED flashing rate from the PC keyboard, 206
project 22-using various queue functions, 210
project 23-ON-OFF temperature controller, 214
Queue related functions, 391
Queues, 203

R
Radio Frequency IDentification (RFID), 397
RAM. *See* random access memory (RAM)
Random access memory (RAM), 5
Raspberry Pi single-board computer, 15
RDM6300 RFID reader, 399f
Reaction timer, 259
Read only memory (ROM), 6
Ready state, 119
Real-time clock (RTC), 10
Real-time operating system, need for, 98
Reduced instruction set computer (RISC), 12, 15
Reset, 31
Reset input, 8
Reset switch, 49
RFID. *See* Radio Frequency IDentification (RFID)
RGB light controller, 279
RISC. *See* reduced instruction set computer (RISC)
Rising trigger selection register (EXTI_RTSR), 352
ROM. *See* read only memory (ROM)
Round-robin scheduling, 104
RS232 communication, 9
RTC. *See* real-time clock (RTC)
Running state, 119

S
Scheduling algorithm
goals, 106
others
dynamic priority scheduling, 108
first come first served, 107
longest remaining time first, 107
multilevel queue scheduling, 108
shortest remaining time first, 107

Schmitt trigger circuits, 357
Semapores
    creating binary, 226
    creating counting, 227
    deleting semaphore, getting semaphore count, 227
    giving and taking, 227
    Project 24: sending internal and external temperature
        data to PC, 228
    related functions, 390
Sending data to PC over USB serial link, 181
Sending internal and external temperature data to PC,
    228, 238
Serial input-output, 9
Serial peripheral interface (SPI), 9
Setting break points, 83
Seven segment editor, 86
Sfr, memory type specifiers, 69
Shortest remaining time first, 107
Simple resistor capacitor circuits, 357
Simulation, setting break points in MikroC Pro, 83
Sleep mode, 10, 23
Software timers
    change timer period, get timer period, 258
    creating, deleting, starting, stopping, and resetting a
        timer, 256
    project 28-reaction timer, 259
    project 29-generate square waveform, 263
    project 30-event counter, 266
    timer name and ID, 259
Sophisticated temperature controller, 4f
Source files path, for FreeRTOS, 114
SPI. See serial peripheral interface (SPI)
Square wave generation with adjustable frequency, 271
Standby mode, 23
Start flashing an LED after receiving notification, 331
State machines, 99
Statistics, in MikroC Pro, 88
Stepper motor project, 302
ST-LINK V2 programmer, 53f
STM32 development board, connecting LCD to Clicker
    2 for, 142
STM32F4DISCOVERY board, 36
STM32F407 interrupts
    external interrupts, 349
STM32F407VGT6 microcontroller
    basic features of, 19
    clock circuit of
        configuring clock, 24
        external clock sources, 23
        internal clock sources, 24
    internal block diagram of, 21
    low power modes, 23
    power supply, 23
STM32 Nucleo family, 34
Stop mode, 23

Supervisor Call (SVC), 71
Supply voltage, 7
Suspended state, 119
Suspending scheduler, 344, 345
SVC. See Supervisor Call (SVC)
SYSCFG_EXTICR1, 351t
SYSCFG_EXTICR2, 351t
SYSCFG_EXTICR3, 351t
SYSCFG_EXTICR4, 352t
System reset, 31
System Workbench for STM32 by AC6, 57
SysTick, 71

T
Task info of FreeRTOS, 195
Task list of FreeRTOS, 189
Task notifications
    project 40: start flashing an LED after receiving
        notification, 331
    project 41: flashing at different rates after receiving
        notifications, 335
    xTaskNotify() and xTaskNotifyWait(), 333
    xTaskNotifyGive() and ulTaskNotifyTake(), 330
    xTaskNotifyStateClear() and xTaskNotifyQuery(),
        338
Task parameters, 200
Task-related functions, 373
    FreeRTOS
        creating new task, 121
        delaying task, 122
        deleting task, 130
        getting task handle, 131
        priorites, 136
        project 1-flashing an LED every second, 122
        project 2-flashing two LEDs, one every second,
            other one every 200 ms, 122, 125
        project 3-suspending and resuming task, 128
        project 4-flashing LEDs and deleting task, 130
        project 5-flashing an LED using function
            vTaskDelayUntil(), 134
        project 6-flashing LED and push-button switch at
            different priorities, 136
        project 7-getting/setting task priorities, 137
        resuming suspended task, 128
        running at fixed intervals, 134
        suspending task, 127
        tick count, 134
Task scheduling algorithms
    co-operative scheduling, 99
    other scheduling algorithms, 107
    preemptive and nonpreemptive scheduling
        difference, 107
    preemptive scheduling, 105
    round-robin scheduling, 104
    scheduling algorithm goals, 106

Task state of FreeRTOS, 118, 198
Temperature control system, with Wi-Fi capability, 5f
Template program, 113f
TickType_t, 117
Time project, 413
Timer, 7, 30
   interrupts, 361
   related functions, 386
Tiva EK-TM4C123GXL LaunchPad, 42
Traffic lights controller, 167
TrueStudio, for STM32, 57

U
UDP terminal, 86
UlBitsToClearOnEntry, 334
UlBitsToClearOnExit, 334
Ultrasonic car parking with buzzer, 292
UlValue, 334
Universal synchronous-asynchronous receiver-
      transmitter (USART), 9
Uploading executable code, in MikroC Pro, 78
Usage fault, 71
USART. *See* universal synchronous-asynchronous
      receiver-transmitter (USART)
USART terminal, 86
USB HID bootloader, 88
USB interface, 10
UsStackDepth, 121
UxNewPriority, 134
UxPriority, 121
UxTaskPriorityGet(), 134

V
Variable names of FreeRTOS, 118
Voltage regulator circuit, 7
Von Neumann architecture, 11

W
Watchdog, 8
Waveform displayed on screen, 367f
Wheel motors, 427
Wi-Fi, 11
   capability, temperature control system with, 5f

X
XClearCountOnExit, 331
XEventGroupSetBitsFromISR(), 383
XQueueSendFromISR() and xQueueReceive(), 393
XSemaphoreTakeFromISR() and xSemaphoreGive(),
      391
XTaskNotifyFromISR(), 377
XTaskResumeFromISR(), 374
XTaskToNotify, 334
XTicksToDelay, 122
XTicksToWait, 331, 335
XTimeIncrement, 133
XTimerStartFromISR() and
      xTimerChangePeriodFromISR(), 387

Y
Yield to another task of equal priority,
      FreeRTOS, 148

Printed in the United States
By Bookmasters